Labour, Love and Prayer
Female Piety in Ulster Religious Literature, 1850–1914

By examining the central role played by Protestant and Catholic women in establishing the religious faith of their children and, by extension, the future of their respective communities, *Labour, Love, and Prayer* explores the construction of female stereotypes during a period of mounting religious tension in Ireland. Andrea Ebel Brożyna compares ideas of faith and family in both cultures, highlighting the remarkable similarities in their views and each group's stubborn refusal to acknowledge them.

Brożyna argues that Catholics and Protestants shared very similar views of Christian womanhood. Both lauded the influence of the virtuous Christian woman, used the same female role models from the Bible, and saw the home as the locus of the construction of female piety. Yet each group castigated the other for having antifemale values. Protestants developed the slovenly, drunken "Biddy" as a stereotype of Catholic women and Catholics portrayed Protestant devotional and family life as cold and arid. Observers of present-day Northern Ireland will find these historical contrasts of immediate relevance.

An interesting new look at the Irish problem, *Labour, Love, and Prayer* makes a valuable contribution to the histories of women, Ireland, and religion.

ANDREA EBEL BROŻYNA is an independent scholar who lives and works in Toronto. She is currently writing a biography of the Nun of Kenmare.

McGill-Queen's Studies in the History of Religion

Volumes in this series have been supported by the Jackman Foundation of Toronto.

SERIES ONE

G.A. Rawlyk, Editor

Labour, Love, and Prayer

*Female Piety in Ulster Religious
Literature, 1850-1914*

ANDREA EBEL BROŻYNA

The Institute of Irish Studies
The Queen's University of Belfast

McGill-Queen's University Press
Montreal & Kingston · Ithaca

© McGill-Queen's University Press 1999
ISBN 0-7735-1757-X

Legal deposit first quarter 1999
Bibliothèque nationale du Québec

Printed in Canada on acid-free paper

Published simultaneously in the UK, Eire,
and Europe by The Institute of Irish Studies,
The Queen's University of Belfast,
8 Fitzwilliam Street, Belfast,
Northern Ireland, BT9 6AW
ISBN 0 85389 722 0

British Library Cataloguing in Publication Data
A catalogue record for this book is available from the
British Library

This book has been published with the help of a grant
from the Humanities and Social Sciences Federation of
Canada, using funds provided by the Social Sciences
and Humanities Research Council of Canada.

McGill-Queen's University Press acknowledges the
financial support of the Government of Canada
through the Book Publishing Industry Development
Program for its activities. We also acknowledge the
support of the Canada Council for the Arts for our
publishing program.

Canadian Cataloguing in Publication Data

Brożyna, Andrea Ebel, 1965–
  Labour, love and prayer: female piety in Ulster religious
  literature, 1850–1914
  (McGill-Queen's studies in the history of religion)
  Co-published by Institute of Irish Studies, Queen's
  University of Belfast
  Includes bibliographical references and index.
  ISBN 0-7735-1757-X (McGill-Queen's University Press)
  ISBN 0-85389-722-0 (Institute of Irish Studies, Queen's
  University of Belfast)
  1. Religious literature, English—Irish authors—History
  and criticism. 2. Women in literature. 3. Piety in
  literature. 4. Women—Religious life—Northern
  Ireland. 5. Ulster (Northern Ireland and Ireland)—
  Religious life and customs. I. Queen's University of
  Belfast. Institute of Irish Studies. II. Title. III. Series.

PR8722.R4B76 1999   820.9'382   C98-901021-X

Typeset in 10/12 Baskerville by True to Type

For my mother, Wilma Andrus Ebel

Contents

Tables and Figures

Preface

The focus of this study is the ideal of Christian womanhood constructed in Ulster religious literature during the period 1850–1914. The creators of this construction were, for the most part, members of the middling ranks of Ulster society who had the leisure time to express their opinions on this subject. For bourgeois Ulster men and women, both Protestant and Catholic, the essential piety of women was a crucial tenet of their belief structures. Middle-class Protestants and Catholics – the latter being, of course, a small group – emphasized the central role of women in securing the religious faith of their families and, by extension, the future of their respective communities.

While "woman's sphere" was gradually accepted to include church and charitable activities, the locus of this construction of female piety was the home; female piety was seen as essentially domestic. Paradoxically, while both Catholics and Protestants lauded the influence of the virtuous Christian woman within her home, each group castigated the other as being anti-woman and anti-family.

Protestant and Catholic writers found models for the ideal Christian woman in the lives of female biblical figures and early saints. That the Virgin Mary was presented as a model of female behaviour and spirituality for Catholic women is not surprising, but that she was also used, albeit with great caution, in the Protestant literature, was one of the many seeming contradictions that was discovered in this comparative study.

The sense of mission that was presented to middle-class Ulster girls, their potential for Christian service at home and in their communities, was a theme common in both the Catholic and Protestant literature. The nature of this service differed between Catholic and Protestants only insofar as the relative wealth and degree of lay activity were higher earlier among Ulster Protestants than among Ulster Catholics.

The last third of this study examines the role of women in Protestant churches, the ideals (and anti-ideals) presented in temperance periodicals, and the image Protestant women created for themselves in missionary literature. Because lay Catholic women became active in these areas at a later date for economic and organizational reasons, this project shifts from a comparative structure to one in which the focus is primarily on Protestant materials. Catholic women are the subject of negative stereotyping in this literature; the "Biddy" persona typified all that good Protestants thought their own women were not.

Despite the perception of contemporaries that there was no common ground between Catholic and Protestant in Ulster, more similarities than differences emerge in this study of the creation of the ideal Christian woman in Ulster religious literature from 1850 to 1914.

Acknowledgments

In the course of researching and writing this book I have incurred many a debt of thanks. First of all, I must thank Donald Harman Akenson for his insight, encouragement, and wit. I benefitted immeasurably from his vast experience in the process of historical writing. While Dr Akenson was my supervisor at Queen's University, Kingston, three members of the faculty of the Queen's University of Belfast supervised my progress and assisted my work while I was in Northern Ireland. David Hempton, Professor of the School of Modern History, generously gave many hours of his valuable time in order to discuss my research. His thoughtful suggestions and kind encouragement rallied my spirits when I was unsure of the direction my work was taking. Ronald Buchanan and Brian Walker, Directors of the Institute for Irish Studies, were always willing to assist me in making contacts and finding sources during my time in Belfast. The cooperation and support of all the staff and fellows at the Institute were very encouraging.

The following individuals and organizations in Ireland assisted me during the critical stage of gathering material: Father Ambrose Macaulay, Raymond Refaussee, archivist of the Representative Church Body Library, Dublin, Marion Kelly, archivist of the Wesleyan Historical Society, Irish Branch, Belfast, Mr Bonar, archivist of the Irish Presbyterian Historical Society, the staff of the Presbyterian Women's Association, Church House, Belfast, the staff of the Public Record Office of Northern Ireland, the Linenhall Library, Belfast Public Library, The National Library, Dublin, the Periodical Branch of the British Library at Colindale, Douglas Library, Kingston, and Robarts Library, Toronto.

Two kind and patient friends, Joan Harcourt and Bob Scott, asked important questions at crucial junctures. Their intellectual and moral support were invaluable. I would also like to thank the many friends and family members who gave me their unfailing encouragement when I was researching and writing in Belfast, Pigotts, Gananoque, and Toronto. Joan McGilvray and Harvey Blackman provided excellent advice and expert editing; for this I am most grateful.

Social Sciences and Humanities Research Council of Canada Doctoral Fellowships, Ontario Graduate Scholarships, and funding from Queen's University, Kingston, and the Queen's University of Belfast provided the financial support for this work. For this I am very grateful.

Finally, I would like to thank my husband, Robert, for uprooting himself from his life in Canada to accompany me on the adventure of a lifetime.

Labour, Love, and Prayer

1 Setting the Scene

This study is located at the confluence of three streams of historical inquiry: Irish history, religious history, and women's history. To establish clear baselines, this chapter focuses on gender theory, sources, social and economic class, religion, and the location of the project in time and space.

GENDER

This examination of the ideal models of Christian womanhood presented in Ulster religious literature from 1850–1914 will focus primarily on the way gender difference has been constructed in the past. With regard to piety, virtue, and religiosity, women were said to be different from men. This does not make Ulster unique in Western culture; rather, this ideology was informed by trans-Atlantic religious notions that asserted the different spirituality of women. Ulster's evangelical Protestants borrowed material from, and contributed to, a discourse that had its origins in the United States in the late eighteenth century. Rosemary Radford Ruether and Rosemary Skinner Keller traced a growing emphasis on "woman's moral superiority, her greater religiosity, and her role as domestic evangelist"[1] in America during this period. This construction was refined and widely disseminated throughout the English-speaking world in the nineteenth century, and the language in which it was couched became more hyperbolic, sentimental, and dramatic.

As this study will show, Roman Catholic views about women were also informed by this type of representation. The religious literature read by the English-speaking classes among Ulster Catholics had its origins chiefly in Continental and American Catholicism, and later in Irish Catholic nationalism. That all of these diverse strands of religious thought should reveal, fundamentally, very similar attitudes towards the nature of female spirituality and the role of women within their various Christian communities speaks volumes about the pervasiveness of patriarchy in Western Christian life.

Yet the picture that emerges of attitudes towards the spirituality of women in Ulster is complex. The development of these attitudes occurred in different denominational groups at different times, and advanced at different times through different mediums. This complexity, however, does not alter the reality of a substratum of similarity amongst the Christian denominations in Ulster. The differences in the medium and in the timing of the evolution of this construction can be more readily and convincingly explained by differences in socio-economic status than by any religious differentiation.

Primarily, then, this study focuses on how the Christian woman was constructed in Ulster during the period under discussion. No attempt is made to establish the creation of historical reality – the "actual" religious experience of Ulster women – by this representation. That the language of this image of women informed or shaped to some degree the way in which these women experienced their spirituality and practised their religion is not being disputed. But that these words, this ideology, actually *created* the historical religious experience of Ulster women and men is an absurd notion. Aside from what it says about agency, this kind of linguistic determinism obscures the very thing that social historians are trying to seek: the complex and rich texture of life in the past. Assuming a priori that language and the constructions that arise from it automatically determine historical reality puts intellectual blinkers on any type of inquiry.

Nonetheless, representation is a very useful concept. If this analytical tool is used sensitively and rigorously, it can yield much fruit. Frequently though, those who use discourse theory, postmodern deconstruction, and semiotics use representation as a way of avoiding engaging with, or in denigrating the reality of, the material world of the past.[2] In speaking of gendered constructions of piety in Ulster, it is not my intention in any way to deny or impugn the fact that lived experience – historical reality – produced beliefs, ideas, words, and representations that in turn made their impression on how people in Ulster lived their religious lives.

The construction of Christian womanhood examined in this study exhibits several major features in common with the influential trans-

Atlantic[3] discourse on women's spirituality. A central concern was the proper, right, holy, or godly relation of women to the men of their religious group and of woman[4] to her Creator. This informed the creation of a separate-spheres ideology[5] circumscribing women's lives, in theory, to an area where their spiritual gifts could best be utilized and their delicate spiritual purity protected.

Another clear theme that emerges in the literature is the dual nature of female piety. While moral superiority, purity, and pious feeling were given predominance, an important, somewhat subterranean, anti-ideal emerged. It was thought that although women were (on balance) pure and spiritual creatures, they could also be spiritually degenerate. And if they were better than men when they were holy, they were far worse than men when unholy. The hue and cry against the tragic sight of a woman, that most refined and pure of God's creation, fallen from her lofty place, was a frequent refrain in Ulster religious literature, as it was in much of the prescriptive religious literature in trans-Atlantic discourse.

This paradoxical Mary/Eve or virgin/whore duality experienced some interesting transmutations in the Ulster context. Occasionally, evangelical Protestant literature used a stereotype of Irish Catholics – the Biddy persona – as the dark Eve, a sort of negative reference point all the better to provide a foil for the dazzling purity of the righteous Protestant female construct. In fiction written by Irish Catholic women, the dark woman is not given an archetypal construction; she is the woman (usually young) who either did not have or has abandoned a Catholic upbringing and who has been lured to destruction by worldly, modern, amoral Protestant/English temptations. In misrepresentations of the other group's religion and culture (across the Protestant/Catholic divide in Ulster the other group was depicted as "Other") these authors sought to prescribe adherence to the religious code of their own endogamous group. What supreme irony, then, that both groups were using patriarchal constructs in similar ways.

In both its separate spheres and its paradoxical virgin/whore manifestations, the issue of what constituted this perceived unique and different "feminine" spirituality lay at the heart of this construction. The data examined in this study clearly show that bourgeois Ulster Christians, the chief agents in the construction of this ideal, thought that women truly possessed an essentially different piety from that of men. Moreover, it was thought that women, for the most part, possessed a superior piety.

This leads to the following questions: 1) Was this construction of female piety a limiting one for women? and, if it was, 2) Why were many women intimately involved in its creation and diffusion? The first question is more readily answered than the second. An enormous potential for psychological dissonance was created by this construction of female piety. If women were equal spiritual members of the Christian laity, and if their natures actually surpassed those of men in their holiness and religious feeling, whence their subordination in the affairs of the church? Yet, women actively participated in this contradictory patriarchal discourse of women's spirituality, their voices closely echoing those of male clergy and lay writers in advocating the uniqueness of female piety and the "special place" of women. On the level of lived experience as well, these women devoted countless hours and many skills to the promotion of the churches that promulgated this limiting construction. Conservative or traditional women have frequently received short shrift from feminist analysis. Their very presence seems to be disquieting to many feminist scholars.

Delving into the onion skin-like layers of meaning in the religious Ulster literature under discussion, I hope to arrive at some understanding of how this construction could be palatable, if not empowering, for these Ulster women.

Another interesting facet of this construction is female resistance. Both Catholic and Protestant women writers, and, wittingly or unwittingly, their male editors, added a current of dissent while remaining within the boundaries of this construction. A powerful potential for broadening women's arena of action lay at the core of Christian thought. Female writers repeatedly cited the passage from Galatians 3:28, that in Christ "there is neither male nor female." These voices of dissent used notions that were integral both to Christian thought and to this construction of female piety in order to allow women greater latitude. As well, they used the logical inferences drawn from the assumption of female moral superiority to criticize perceived male impiety, carnality, and the sexual double standard. Granted, these voices of resistance were not dominant ones; indeed, they were frequently muffled. But they were there, and surfaced in the religious literature of Roman Catholics and Protestants alike.

Paradoxically, discussions of female spirituality among present-day radical feminist theologians seem to bear an uncanny resemblance to the prescriptive literature of Victorian and Edwardian Ulster. The current celebration of women's difference in the realm of spirituality echoes the thought of these most conservative Christians of the last century. Admittedly, women's "spirit" now is described as being both earthy and cosmic rather than as solely other-worldly, but nonetheless feminine spirituality is posited in both cases as being superior to its masculine counterpart. The works of the radical feminist theologian Mary Daly, among others, in exulting over female difference and

"womanspirit" seem to harken back to elements of Victorian patriarchal constructions of female piety.[6] Evidently this is not their purpose,
but still it is difficult not to see the similarities – and, perhaps, the
dangers.

Even in the more measured writings of feminist religious historians,
this emphasis on essential difference is taking centre stage. In the
introduction to *That Gentle Strength: Historical Perspectives on Women in
Christianity*, the editors state: "The question of female uniqueness in
some ways is the crux of the current research. The fact that research
indicates that female piety possesses an autonomous form, enables
(and encourages) scholarly exploration of this subject to bridge both
time and place."[7] One cannot help but wonder if "to bridge both time
and place" can be deconstructed to mean "to ignore both time and
place." We must keep in mind that the essentialist versus constructivist
debate in feminist thought is an ongoing one.

A nuanced gender analysis can provide us with a better understanding of the varied and complex literatures and lives of those who lived
in other places at other times. Balance is required in assessing the
influences of gender and of place, class, race, and other factors that
shape our perceptions.

By bringing to light and analysing the many substantial similarities
between Roman Catholic and Protestant constructions of female piety,
I would not like to give the impression that I am arguing in favour of
an "essentialist" feminist view of the lived experiences of these women.
Essentialist ideology has made Northern Ireland a *terra incognita* for
gender analysis. This is particularly true of the late twentieth century,
but nevertheless I believe this perspective could hinder the progress of
historical research into the nineteenth century and in earlier periods
as well. Because of seemingly overwhelming differences between
Roman Catholic and Protestant women, both real and perceived, it
has been impossible to speak, as the essentialists persist in doing, of
women as an ahistorical, cross-cultural group with fundamental or
"essential" similarities. Thus a barrier to using gender as a tool of
analysis has been erected. In a society that insists on maintaining a
cognitive/cultural chasm between two groups that neither class nor
gender is allowed to bridge, Protestant/Catholic barriers have had a
deadening effect on the development of feminism in Ireland.[8]

While seeking to cross this artificial gulf and demonstrate fundamental similarities between the representations and lived experiences
of Catholic and Protestant women as they manifested themselves in
Ulster religious literature, I am chary of introducing problematic
notions of gender determinism into the Irish historiography. To apply
this kind of ideologically based determinism in the Ulster context

would be to ride roughshod over the past.

In positing the substantive similarities of the images of female piety that evolved at this discursive level, I am not saying that the religious life of a wealthy Catholic convent-educated young woman and that of a Protestant mill girl were identical because of their shared status as women oppressed by Christian patriarchy, or that the lives of an Irish-speaking Donegal fisherwoman and a leisured, committee-organizing Belfast Presbyterian "lady" were essentially determined by their sex. That these women had more in common with men of their own social class and religious denomination I have little doubt.

American Marxist-feminist historian Elizabeth Fox-Genovese confronts this problem with force and clarity. She asserts that

Women's history, in part as a natural attempt to establish its own claims, has tended to emphasize what women shared across class and racial lines. It has, in short, tended toward an essentialist interpretation of women's experience ... By "essentialist," I mean a transhistorical view of women that emphasizes the core biological aspects of women's identity, independent of time and place, class, nation, and race. From the perspective of many women's historians, to emphasize the class and racial determinants of women's experience and, especially, women's consciousness is to compromise the integrity of women's perception and to mute the pervasiveness of sexism and male dominance.[9]

Fox-Genovese's belief that women, like men, are shaped by the social relations of their communities is particularly relevant in the context of this study. The extreme reluctance of Irish scholars to see anything other than difference between Catholics and Protestants might push women's history, after an initial breakthrough point not yet reached, in the direction of essentialism. Ironically, the need to get beyond the entrenched ideologies of Nationalism and Unionism could result in a kind of historical writing about women that ignores anything other than their "essential" being as women. "If we try to work with a general, not to mention an essentialist, view of women's nature," Fox-Genovese cautions, "we must end in banality."[10] I hope this study contributes to a carefully woven tapestry of women's historical experience in Ulster that is as subtle and nuanced as their lives were varied and complex.

SOURCES

Perhaps the most frustrating aspect of historical inquiry into religious matters is the interior nature of spirituality and piety – these intangibles that are the crux of religious experience itself. I have not attempted to describe or analyse the interior religious experience of Ulster women. Very rarely can we, as historians, obtain glimpses of this inner life. Even the ability of such intimate documents as diaries to reveal the workings of the soul have been questioned. Thus we can only view personal piety at several removes. Filters of conformity, propriety, and distance allow us to see the inner spirituality of these women only through a glass darkly. That being said, these documents can provide a rich source of information about gender relations and the particular religious cosmology of Ulster women.

The primary source materials used in this study require careful examination and sensitive handling. One must not coerce them, or try to massage the data so that they appear to answer questions which they are incapable of answering. Although we might feel that certain questions are urgently in need of answers, if the material cannot provide the required insight, we do both the questions and the source material a disservice by forcing their alliance. I have endeavoured to avoid the intellectual and methodological snares of asking my primary sources questions which they cannot address, even indirectly.

The data used in this study chiefly consist of material published in denominational periodicals[11] and under the aegis of religious societies: articles, sermons, columns, poems, and stories. These types of materials were widely disseminated in middle-class homes throughout the province. As the eighteenth century progressed, both periodical literature and popular novels became cheaper, and thus an unprecedented deluge of printed material flooded Ulster, as it did the rest of the United Kingdom.[12] With increasing literacy and the free distribution of tracts and copies of religious periodicals, these materials were even more widely read.

This literature had a clear didactic function. Sometimes subtly, sometimes not, it provided prescriptions for the orthodox conduct of the "gentle sex." Obviously, men were exhorted to proper Christian behaviour as well, but here I focus specifically on models for females. To those who wrote this literature, the correct "feminine" Christian conduct of the women of their religious group was very significant. They went to great lengths to single out what they considered to be specifically feminine characteristics and roles. Thus, this literature contains specific prescriptions for women and constructs an ideal type of Christian womanhood. These prescriptions presented Ulster women with an ideal of pious thought and action and also with the antithesis of this ideal, the fallen, corrupted woman. Lest this sounds as if the women were presented with a didactic *fait accompli*, let me hasten to reiterate that women contributed to this construction and also, through their writing, voiced their dissent from some of its central tenets.

The eclectic sources used in this study vary in the degree to which they reflected women's lived religious experience. Spiritual advice columns, providing a dialogue between their editor and her female readers, provide more insight into the actual spiritual burdens and concerns of these women than, say, a sermon pontificating on the duties of the Christian wife. This latter type of document, though, tells a great deal about the values of the male religious elites of this society and of their feelings toward, and perhaps ambivalence about the nature and power of the women in their midst. Prescriptive literature written by members of the male religious elite on women's piety can act as a projective test – an inkblot, if you will – whereby we can determine what values and mores were important and sometimes troubling to those who held the actual reins of power in this society.[13] This prescriptive literature will also provide a window into what mattered or was, to use one of their own phrases, "dear to the hearts" of these conservative, loyal[14] women who through exhaustive efforts contributed their writings, their time, and their money to the support of the substructures on which this construction was raised.

While analysing the contents of this ideal of female piety for meaning, I have also attempted to assess, where possible, the potential impact of this model on women's lives. Necessarily, this connection will, at times, be tenuous, for the gendered construction embedded in these sources was not a timeless, transhistorical phenomenon. Rather, a close reading of these texts detects discernable changes over time, especially during political crises. When Protestant and Catholic groups were engaged in controversies, the tenor of the discussion of female piety became heightened and decidedly more shrill.

The didactic nature of sermons and articles based on biblical exegesis is readily apparent. Religious fiction, however, can be somewhat more elusive, but this is not an insurmountable difficulty. The fiction discussed here had a clear purpose, and that purpose was not literary. It was written first, to instruct, second, to edify, and third, to entertain. Thus, despite its almost surreal hyperbole and cloying sentimentalism – these were certainly not photographically accurate vignettes of Ulster life – religious fiction is a useful source in the task of examining the gendered construction of piety and in assessing the connections between this world of high drama and that of lived experience. For if it were to instruct its female readership properly, it had to be recognizable to them. These readers had to see something of themselves or their neighbours in the heroines of these tales. But because these novels and stories are not great literature – they do not try to transcend time and place – they make for valuable social history documents. Despite the melodrama and gushing emotionalism, these tales still speak to the religious, cultural, and social values of the class that spawned them. If we listen carefully, they can tell us what the people of these bourgeois religious cultures – both evangelical Protestant and Roman Catholic – said they valued.

ECONOMIC AND SOCIAL CLASS

In undertaking this study one might wish for the rigorous method of the laboratory in order to understand clearly the causality at work in perceived Catholic/Protestant differences, but this is not a luxury afforded to social historians: in matters of culture, causal variables cannot be isolated with clinical precision. Yet we can approximate this rigour by scrupulously examining the manner in which our collection of sources may be skewed. The materials examined herein are drawn from an overwhelmingly English-speaking, literate, and resolutely bourgeois culture. Social class, then, can be held constant in this study, as far as the producers of the literature are concerned. And when we deal exclusively with historical data left by the literate, modernising, middle-class in Ulster, be it in the various Protestant or small Roman Catholic communities, startling similarities emerge in the discourse on female piety.

The persistence of sectarian divisions in Ulster has hampered the development of serious discussions of social class. When the people see their province divided along a religious/cultural fault-line called Protestant versus Catholic, it has been difficult to raise awareness among members of either group that they might share some interests or oppressions or advantages with members of the other religious group.

Yet, for more than a century, it has been frequently put forward by those who study Ireland that the differences between Irish Protestants and Irish Catholics were not caused by religion as such, but by economic discrimination and cultural differences. Unfortunately, as D.H. Akenson has pointed out, attempts to get a broader perspective on Irish religious differences "frequently have exchanged the shackles of an overly narrow definition of religion for the gyves of an unconscious racism."[15] Akenson's chronicle of this persistent stereotyping of the Irish is melancholy reading indeed. In his attempt to locate real differences in nineteenth- and early twentieth-century Ireland one of the tests he applies is that of occupational stratigraphy. Using A.C. Hepburn's groundbreaking study titled "Work, Class and Religion in Belfast 1871–1911," Akenson comes to the conclusion that "the

Table 1
Religious Distribution of Female Commercial Clerks in
Belfast, 1891–1911 (100=Equality)

Years	As % of all occupied females	Roman Catholic	Church of Ireland	Presbyterian
1891	0.4	32	90	163
1901	1.8	37	97	145
1911	3.9	44	99	138

Source: A.C. Hepburn, "Work, Class and Religion in Belfast,
1871–1911," Irish Economic and Social History 10 (1983): 38.

degree of anti-Catholic discrimination in the northeast of Ireland in
the early twentieth century was so great that one cannot conduct
controlled observations of Protestant and Catholic socioeconomic
behaviour under equal conditions."[16]

Information about the socioeconomic status of the different denominational groups in Ulster can, however, help us see to what extent
members of the various denominations had the wealth and leisure
time to add their voices to the literature on women and religion. Thus
we shall return to Hepburn's generative article.[17] From 1871 to 1911,
Hepburn informs us, the economic position of the Roman Catholics
of Belfast worsened. They did not have a skilled male worker elite, as
the Protestants[18] did, and their absolute numbers, even in the
unskilled categories, dwindled over the course of this period.[19] Moreover, in the rapidly growing and increasingly fluid category of lower-
middle-class employment (e.g., civil servants, clerks, teachers, bank
workers) Catholics males, though making considerable gains, still held
a relatively low proportion of these positions.[20] Particularly notable for
our purposes is the occupational distribution of Belfast females.
Catholic females performed similarly to males in the lower-middle-
class category of commercial clerks.

Extremely rapid growth took place in this sector of employment and
Catholics, despite signs of progress, were severely underrepresented in
this lower-middle-class occupation. However, Catholic women were
over-represented in the most difficult and least well-paid work sectors
in Belfast. Because of the low remuneration of domestic work, city girls
with opportunities for higher-paying mill work avoided this occupation. Thus the phenomenon of importing predominantly Catholic
country girls as domestics for service in the thriving middle-class
homes of all denominations became an established practice.[21]

The last section of Hepburn's work that needs to be mentioned here
is that concerning general religious proportions in the workplace. As

Table 2
Religion and the Workforce, 1901 (% of population with stated occupation)

	Roman Catholic	Church of Ireland	Presbyterian	Number in Sample
Males (12 and over)	89	88	89	8,374
Females (12 and over)	56	45	43	10,615
Females (16–49)	62	50	49	7,848

Source: A.C. Hepburn, "Work, Class and Religion in Belfast, 1871–1911" *Irish Economic and Social History* 10 (1983): 43.

Table 2 indicates, there is no difference among males of the three denominations shown. The differences for females, however, are notable. Whether all females above school age or all women in the child-bearing age group are considered, more than three in five Roman Catholic women worked, while only one in two Protestant women were in the workforce.[22] Hepburn does not comment further on this data, yet they bear closer examination.

The bourgeois religious literature circulating in Ulster, both Catholic and Protestant, abhorred the presence of women in the industrial workplace. There was no place for independent female economic activity in Christian bourgeois domestic ideology. Mill girls, with their loose morals and lighthearted ways, and modern girls, with their typewriting machines[23] and attendant maladies of body and soul, almost invariably met unfortunate ends in this didactic literature. Their only salvation lay in mending their ways, marrying, and becoming "keepers at home." These were concerns that touched at the heart of the patriarchal middle-class family nexus. Respectability could not be maintained if the women of the family worked outside of the home.

In the period under discussion, Ulster Catholics had not yet made major inroads into the middle ranks of society.[24] The Catholic contribution to the "genteel" construction of female piety, while frequently written by men and women with their origins in the province, was mostly published in Dublin. It was there that a sufficiently large bourgeois Catholic base existed. A prerequisite for this type of literary production by the Christian laity was a comfortable degree of wealth and its accompanying leisure time (for women this meant having domestic servants) in which to pursue writing.

I have attempted not to use the words "bourgeois" and "middle class" loosely. Yet, because I do not subscribe to the orthodox Marxist concept that classes are self-conscious historical entities, the issues of social classes and socioeconomic rank are problematic. Many attempts have been made by social historians to arrive at a precise definition of who is being referred to under the rubric "bourgeois." The authors of the sizable literature on bourgeois religion in the United States have struggled valiantly, yet ultimately unsatisfactorily, with this very question.[25] The term middle class seems to suffer from the same sort of terminological confusion that has plagued "peasant" and "worker." All of this does not render the terms bourgeois and middle class devoid of meaning. Precision may be lacking, yet it is also lacking in contemporary usage as well. Thousands of minute details of life – the style of one's dress, the refinement of one's speech, proper deportment, etc. – indicated one's status as a respectable member of the bourgeoisie. Income levels and property ownership were only part of the cultural phenomenon that was called the bourgeoisie. Thus, in this study of gendered constructions, a keen awareness of the class base and complex class assumptions of the participants is crucial.

RELIGIOUS CONTEXT: PROTESTANTS, CATHOLICS, AND EVANGELICALISM

What makes all of Ireland, and Ulster in particular, so fascinating in the period under study is the divergence from the alleged secularizing trends of the Western world. Granted, some secularisation did occur in Ireland, but it met more resistance there than in most other Western societies. Religious adhesion and practice increased in Ireland while practically everywhere else in Western Europe they were waning.[26] It is against this backdrop of increasing religious participation that this gendered construction of female piety developed in Ulster.

In Emmet Larkin's groundbreaking article titled "The Devotional Revolution in Ireland" and in his subsequent work on the Irish Catholic Church in the nineteenth century, we are offered a picture of a national church and its laity in transition. According to Larkin, the Famine's devastation of the poorest classes of Irish peasant society left the Church with a "stronger devotional nucleus relative to absolute numbers in 1850 than 1840."[27] It was among these members of the middle ranks of Irish society, with their aspirations for greater respectability, that a "first wave" of a devotional religion was to be found. Moreover, during this post-Famine period their influence was growing. Larkin also suggests that the "modernizing" forces in the Church – those who sought to discourage the quasi-pagan elements in the practice of Irish folk religion[28] – benefitted from the "psychological impact that the famine had on those who remained in Ireland."[29] He puts forward the idea that an acute sense of sin and of God's wrath were defining characteristics of the Irish Catholic mentality after the

Famine. Thus, the people were psychologically and socially ready for a devotional revolution and the Church was marshalling the economic and organizational resources to provide it.[30] This consolidation of Church power, led by Cardinal Paul Cullen, was brought about by the introduction of a range of devotional exercises that not only encouraged a more regular religious practice but that also instilled a greater sense of veneration through an increased appreciation of the "ritual beauty and intrinsic mystery" of the sacraments.[31]

In her work, Irish historian Caitríona Clear develops the theme of the significance of the Catholic devotional revolution for women who were contemplating a religious vocation: "Becoming a nun offered the comfort of the familiar and the challenge of a new way of life, and in an evangelical age, it apparently ensured salvation."[32] Clear characterizes the religious orientation of the clergy of the Roman Catholic Church as evangelical during the period under study. Clear states that the "evangelical Catholicism of the era appears to have given nuns a sense of shared purpose and a definite feeling of being part of a movement."[33] The middle-class[34] subjects of Clear's study of nuns in nineteenth-century Ireland were attracted to a social and religious ethos that was found in Protestant circles as well: that of gentility, respectability, and activism.

I suggest that a gendered construction of female piety was a corollary of this revolution. For within the prescriptive literature of Catholic nationalism a highly sentimental image of the pious Irish[35] woman emerged. That this resolutely genteel portrait of Catholic womanhood bore a notable similarity to the construct of an ideal woman presented in the Protestant denominational literature is all the more surprising, given the growing cleavage between Catholics and Protestants.

Increasingly throughout the period under study, sectarian strife affected the symbolic importance of an ideal of Christian womanhood. With the antagonism between the Protestant and the Catholic communities rising to a fever pitch during the three Home Rule campaigns (1886, 1893, 1913–14) and the signing of the Ulster Covenant (1912), descriptions of the pure and pious nature of their respective womenfolk acquired greater urgency.

The evangelical nature of Protestantism in Ulster is the subject of David Hempton's and Myrtle Hill's book titled *Evangelical Protestantism in Ulster Society, 1740–1890*. Their study examines the many unique religious developments in Ulster Protestant society from the origins of Ulster evangelicalism in the 1740s to the Home Rule controversy of the 1880s. They hasten to add, however, that despite the perception of Ulster as a peculiar place populated by a peculiar people, this did not preclude its participation in broader religious and cultural phenomena. Rather, Ulster's religious life converged with many of the era's characteristic developments in Britain, Europe, and North America, and it shared the various problems that confronted evangelical movements in other countries. In the shared trans-Atlantic evangelical religious literature, Ulster Protestants participated in the construction of female piety.

I have already mentioned that various scholars of Roman Catholicism and Protestantism in Ireland have explored the evangelical nature of those at the cutting edge of these groups in the latter half of the nineteenth century. David Bebbington's assertion that "conversionism, activism, biblicism and crucicentrism"[36] form the cornerstones of evangelicalism is generally accepted by historians of religion as a definition that reflects the reality of the evangelical experience. Clearly, the Methodist literature examined in this study is unequivocally evangelical. Both Ulster Presbyterianism and Anglicanism gradually became more evangelical in their outlooks as the nineteenth century progressed. David Hempton has noted that even as early as the 1830s evangelicalism had "made substantial headway within the Church of Ireland and within the self-regulating Presbyterian community of the north."[37] While Hempton notes that denominational conflict still existed, not to mention intradenominational conflict, he also asserts that "the foundations had nevertheless been laid for a pan-evangelical and interdenominational" spirit among Ulster Protestants, particularly when it came to anti-Catholicism.[38] The very use of the word Presbyterian and evangelicalism in the same sentence might strike some scholars of Calvinism as somewhat odd, but historians of religion now contend that evangelicalism and Calvinism are not mutually exclusive. George Rawlyk explained that Presbyterians and Anglicans in British North America played down conversionism and activism, "replacing it with a largely intellectual acceptance of the New Birth."[39] Rawlyk also observed that by the twentieth century biblicism had replaced conversionism at the centre of evangelical Calvinism.[40] His observations are in keeping with what I found in Belfast-based publications such as *The Irish Presbyterian, The Evangelical Churchman and Presbyterian Review*, and *The Church of Ireland Parochial Magazine*. The zeal of the Catholic church in its ultramontane and evangelical form and the anti-Catholic cohesiveness of evangelical Ulster Protestants contributed to sectarian tensions. Ironically, those who participated fully in all of these evangelical movements, both Protestant and Catholic, shared middle-class cultural values that cherished respectability and an essentialist understanding of gender roles.

Roman Catholicism was at its weakest, numerically, in Ulster relative to its position in the other three provinces of Ireland. The reverse was true for Protestantism. By the middle of the nineteenth century the geographic concentration of Protestantism in Ulster was an accomplished fact.[41] By this period, evangelical attempts at proselytism in the south and west of Ireland had largely failed. Desultory attempts to convert Catholics continued, but for the most part, among Ulster Protestants, conversionist activism was replaced with a garrison mentality. The centrality of the conversion experience to evangelical Protestants left a legacy of bitterness between Catholics and Protestants long after most Protestant efforts at proselytism had ceased.[42] All of this informed religious antagonisms that were latent within both groups' ideal view of the religiosity of their female members.

The Ulster Revival of 1859 – commonly referred to as the Year of Grace – has been described as having a unique place in the religious history of Ulster. Hempton and Hill note that the Revival has a two-fold value for historians. First, it demonstrates the depth of evangelical Protestant influence in Ulster's religious culture by the late 1850s, and second, it is a pivot within popular Protestantism. Before it occurred, the Revival was prayerfully anticipated; after it was gone, it was recollected with great nostalgia. Thereafter, memories of the Revival performed the function of a spiritual litmus test of the current vigour of evangelical life in the province.[43] Thus the rest of the late Victorian and Edwardian period in Ulster Protestantism has popularly been looked at as a sort of long postscript to the great outpouring of religious feeling that was the Revival. Yet, the denominational literature on women does not reflect this supposed preoccupation. This could be explained, in part, by the class bias of my sources. As Janice Holmes observes in her study of the Revival, the majority of the women involved in this experiential religious phenomenon were from the lower classes.[44] Conservative critics found the hysterical religious ecstasies of these women to be a particularly disturbing aspect of a movement derailed. The "public displays" of these women did not accord with the bourgeois sensibilities of the critics. Those who approved of the Revival saw in the conversion and elevation to virtue of some of the most uncouth members of the female sex – illiterate mill girls, domestics, and prostitutes – the miraculous workings of God's grace.[45] Either way, a feminine ideal of purity and submission was maintained, even if for a brief period during the Revival some Ulster women exercised more than the usual degree of spiritual authority.

Ulster evangelical Protestants looked to the appearance of another Revival to invigorate and expand their ranks, and in this regard they were in keeping with other evangelical movements. In the evangelical construction of female piety, the role of wife and mother was crucial in assuring preparedness for such an event.

TIME AND PLACE

The time frame of this study, 1850 to 1914, provides a fruitful setting, in part because of the enormous social and demographic changes that took place in Ulster.[46] Whether the Irish Famine (1845–1850) was the watershed of Irish history that much nationalist scholarship and popular wisdom would lead us to believe it was[47] is outside the scope of this inquiry; however, the decades after the Famine do show a pronounced divergence between Ulster and the rest of Ireland with regard to population growth and urbanization.

L.A. Clarkson notes that in the thirty-year period before the Famine, population developments in Ulster were "broadly similar" to those in the other three provinces.[48] After the Famine, however, demographic trends in Ulster deviated considerably from those of the rest of Ireland. During the Famine decade (1841–51), Ulster lost less than 16 percent of its population, compared with a 20 percent decline throughout Ireland. Population decline during the Famine decade varied considerably among different Ulster counties, with Antrim losing 10 percent and Cavan and Monaghan each losing almost 30 percent. Throughout the whole period examined by Clarkson (1841–1911) the three southwestern counties of Cavan, Fermanagh, and Monaghan experienced the greatest decline in population, approaching 60 percent.[49] The severe population loss of these Catholic-majority areas was part of the broader picture of a declining Catholic presence in the province. Figure 1 illustrates this trend throughout the period of this study.

The phenomenon of rapid urbanization in Ulster has been well documented.[51] The most significant development in this population shift from country to town was the phenomenal growth of Belfast. The city grew from a population of 75,000 in 1841 to 387,000 in 1911: a remarkable rate of growth by both Irish and United Kingdom standards. A.C. Hepburn observes that of the ten largest cities in the United Kingdom in the period 1841–1911, none grew more rapidly than Belfast.[52] All other urban growth in Ulster was dwarfed by the mushrooming of Belfast. While the proportion of towns over the size of 2,000 persons grew in all nine counties between 1841–1911, frequently this meant that the towns, particularly west of the River Bann, were just bleeding population at a slower rate than the surrounding countryside. It was the phenomenal growth of Belfast that provides the explanation for two of the dominant trends in Ulster's population history in this period: the province's increasing proportion of Ireland's total population and second, the increasing urbanization of the

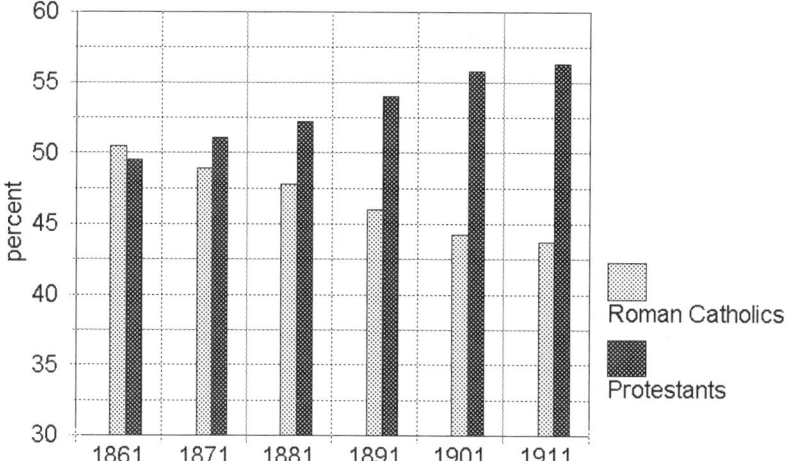

Figure 1   Ulster Religious Distributions, 1861–1911

Sources: Census of Ireland for the year 1861, report on religion and education, 10–11, [3204–III], H.C. 1863, LIX; *Census of Ireland for the year 1871, religious professions and education of the people*, 1046–7, [C.964], H.C. 1874, LXXIV; *Census of Ireland for the year 1881, religious profession of the people*, 993, [C.3204], H.C. 1882, LXXVIII; *Census of Ireland for the year 1891, religions professions of the people*, 995, [C.6626], H.C. 1892, XCII; *Census of Ireland for the year 1901, religious profession and education of the people*, 36–7, [Cd.1123], H.C. 1902, CXXVI; and *Census returns for Ireland 1911, religious professions of the people*, 1383, [Cd.6051], H.C. 1912, CXVI.[50]

people of Ulster.[53] The political, financial, and industrial dominance of Belfast within Ulster in the late nineteenth and early twentieth centuries is uncontested, but it may also be posited that this bustling "line-nopolis" was the cultural heart of the province.

The emergence of Belfast as the centre of Ulster in economic and demographic contexts led logically to its predominance in the arts, publishing and religious activity. The epithet "provincial" applied to their proud city has raised the ire of Belfastians during the past two centuries. But provincial has two meanings, one of these being a local capital. Belfast flourished as a provincial capital during this period; goods, services, and information flowed to this staunchly Victorian city on the Lagan. The periodicals read in the villages, hamlets, and farmsteads of Ulster were, if not published in Belfast, at least distributed through networks that were based in the city. Information flowed from this metropole into the hinterland. While its importance in the British Isles was not that of London or even Dublin, Belfast was ranked among those other grimy wonders of the Industrial Revolution: the equally provincial Liverpool, Birmingham, and Manchester. But within the boundaries of the nine counties of Ulster, Belfast held sway.

The variables discussed in this introductory chapter combine to make an investigation of ideals of female piety in Ulster religious literature a challenging one. The present-day reader finds in this literature a foment of ideas and aspirations, prescriptions, and challenges. The meanings this religious literature had for its original readers in their individual social, economic, and religious spheres of life has to be carefully examined and assessed by the researcher. That is my goal in this study.

2 "The Right to Labour, Love, and Pray": The Cult of Domesticity in Ulster Religious Literature

I came to this study of lay female piety in Ulster with preconceived assumptions about the differences between Catholics and Protestants. Surely two communities with such cataclysmic cleavages in theology, politics, social class, and myriad other areas of life would view and represent Christian womanhood in radically different ways. They would follow different models and embrace different gender constructions. Yet the religious literature that I have examined does not bear out these assumptions. Both Roman Catholics and Protestants in Victorian and Edwardian Ulster presented in their publications an idealized portrait of Christian womanhood that was fundamentally the same. The key elements of the construction of female piety varied little, whether the source was Methodist, Presbyterian, Irish Episcopal, or Roman Catholic. These traditional Christian groups presented the same ideal Christian Woman as a model for the women of their respective congregations.

During my discussion of this prescriptive ideology of female piety, I will examine the shades of difference that existed among the three main Protestant groups. However, because of the common spine of reflexes and cultural beliefs that these main Protestant groups shared – frequently in an unspoken and non-theological way – it is possible to treat them as a single entity. In their religious publications these groups frequently discussed events and developments in each other's churches, borrowed (frequently without attributing their source) articles and poems, and shared to a large degree evangelical ideas. This cohesiveness within Ulster evangelical Protestantism helped forge these theologically dissimilar groups and allowed pan-evangelical cooperation while at the same time accentuating the gulf between Protestantism and "Popery." Ulster society was divided along a Protestant/Catholic fault line, and from this ensued fundamental mutually held misconceptions.

Thus Ulster Protestants and Catholics did not choose to emphasize or even acknowledge any fundamental similarities. When Presbyterians wrote of how Christianity "elevated women" or when Roman Catholics described the awesome power of a Christian mother's faith, their refusal to see the other group as being "truly Christian"[1] prevented any understanding or appreciation of their shared values.[2] Moreover, despite the fact that Catholics and Protestants both subscribed to the middle-class nineteenth-century idea of "true womanhood" and the concomitant "cult of domesticity,"[3] each portrayed the other as being anti-family and anti-female.

The Protestant charge that Roman Catholicism was antagonistic to females and to their sacred duties in the home revolved around two aspects of Catholic practice. First, Protestants charged that the priest's role in the confessional was "unnatural" because through it he entered the "sacred" and private realm of the family, thus coming between family members and breaking precious familial ties. Much of the Protestant literature on this topic has a puerile or titillating tone; fear of sexual taint on the purity of domestic bonds is thinly veiled. Second, celibate orders, especially enclosed convents, were reviled for their "monkish" and, again, "unnatural" thwarting of female domesticity. The home was the "natural" habitat of Christian women, and thus nuns, "thwarted" and "stunted" by cruel separation from their proper sphere, were written of in pitying tones. Harsh criticism was aimed at a religion that had such little regard for a woman's God-given role.

Roman Catholics presented Protestantism as cold, harsh, and secular, all qualities that stood in contrast to the warm, loving, pious, hearth-side faith of the ideal Irish Catholic woman. In serial stories and other works of religious fiction, the happy and warm home life of the pious Celts was contrasted with the crass materialism and irreligion of "Anglo-Saxonist" Protestant homes. Roman Catholic writers singled out what they saw as Protestant disrespect for Mary, the Mother of God, as being indicative of the low regard in which Protestants held "the daughters of Mary," as good Roman Catholic women were designated.

Both groups focused on differences and failed to see how fundamentally similar were their beliefs regarding female piety and domesticity. There existed, especially in the latter part of the period under discussion, political reasons for this mutual misconception. The defensive posture of both Protestant Unionists and Catholic Nationalists made the home and the family crucially significant. When fulminating on the sacred duty of Christian mothers, neither side was engaging in a trivial exercise. The pervasiveness of the cult of domesticity in Ulster religious literature and the increasingly hostile tone of the attacks on "the other side" for being anti-family indicate that, far from being a side issue, the construction of a virtuous ideal Christian woman was of great importance to Ulster's main religious groups. Their understanding of female piety lay at the core of how they saw themselves as a people.

"THE RIGHTS OF WOMEN"

While it is not the purpose of the present study to examine the actual roles that women played in Ulster society, the debate concerning women's proper "sphere" informed and influenced the developing ideal of Christian womanhood. Ulster religious literature, particularly in the latter half of the period under discussion, is replete with references to the rights of women and the emergence of the "New Woman" and with sometimes acrimonious debates over the propriety of an extended sphere of activity for Christian women. The expanding role of Ulster women in evangelical Protestant churches and their entry into the "public" sphere of politics and business have not been closely examined. It has been suggested that the increased prominence of women in Protestant evangelical churches was of greater significance than feminism in carving out a larger and more powerful niche for women in Ulster life.[4]

Yet the portrait of Christian womanhood that emerges from Ulster religious literature is an overwhelmingly traditional one. Voices of dissent do emerge, and some do chafe at the double standards and limitations that are a part of this patriarchal creation.[5] For the most part, however, the male and female authors of this gender ideology concur in their support for an essentially different female piety whose areas of operation are the home and the church. In the Victorian period, religious writers clearly castigated as "unnatural" the "mannish woman" who, they said, usurped male authority and debased her own womanly nature. By the Edwardian period, however, many female writers in Ulster were, in very moderate language, suggesting the practicality and reasonableness of an extension of women's sphere and of female suffrage. In doing so, they did not repudiate the ideal of Christian female piety that had emerged in the literature; rather, they built upon it. Even those who argued for suffrage and a decent wage for single working women did not call into question the domestic ideology that designated the duties of Christian women as being first and foremost service and sacrifice for those in their home circle.[6]

The idea of "the rights of women" was used as a foil by religious writers to present their own argument against any alteration of the gender status quo within the Christian household. The appropriation of the phrase "the rights of women" conjured up images of "blue-stockings" and shrill, radical women. Thus the reader could be surprised and his or her fears assuaged when they read the following assessment of women's "rights."

The Rights of Women

The rights of woman! What are they?
The right to labour, love and pray,
The right to weep with those who weep,
The right to wake when others sleep.

The right to dry the falling tear,
The right to quell the rising fear,
The right to smooth the brow of care,
And whisper comfort in despair.

The right to watch the parting breath,
To soothe and cheer the bed of death.
The right when earthly hopes all fail,
To point to that within the vale.

The right the wand'rer to reclaim,
And win the lost from paths of shame.
The right to comfort and to bless
The widow and the fatherless.

The right the little ones to guide
In simple faith to Him who died,
With earnest love and gentle praise
To bless and cheer their youthful days.

The right the intellect to train,
And guide the soul to noble aim,
Teach it to rise above earth's toys,
And wing its flight for heavenly joys.

The right to live for those we love,
The right to die that love to prove,
The right to brighten earthly homes
With pleasant smiles and gentle tones.

Are these thy rights? Then use them well,
Thy silent influence none can tell;
If these are thine, why ask for more? –
Thou hast enough to answer for.

Are these thy rights? Then murmur not
That woman's mission is thy lot.
Improve the talents God has given –
Life's duty done, thy rest is Heaven.[7]

This poem encapsulates the core values that informed the construction of female piety as it emerged in Ulster religious literature
from 1850–1914. The ideas and values found in this poem were
highly durable. At the turn of the century a modified version of this
poem was published in the Methodist weekly, *The Christian Advocate*,[8]
in an article taken from an address given at the "adult Bible Class for
Girls," Grosvenor Hall, Belfast. The speaker noted that this poem was
"old-fashioned, but how beautiful, that we women to-day have such a
rich legacy of rights."[9] The poem was "old-fashioned" perhaps, yet was
still in keeping with the patriarchal ideology that dominated the
discourse on female piety.

These "women's rights" poems prescribed what women should do
fully to claim their rights as Christian women, but they also proscribed
forbidden things that "true" Christian women should not do. A selected article from the London *Christian Times* was reprinted in the *Irish
Presbyterian* with the following rider: "It contains much good sense;
and, without indorsing [sic] it as perfect, we may commend it to the
notice of the sex, and of the gentlemen also."[10] The female author
asserts her belief that it is

woman's right to keep silence in public assemblies, and to leave the task of
public instruction to those better fitted by nature and circumstances to
fulfil that important duty. I believe that most women, if they listen reverent-
ly for the voice of God and nature in their own souls, will find themselves
drawn rather to acts of love and mercy in private and domestic life, than to
grand public schemes for ameliorating the condition of the race. I believe
that woman's natural and appropriate position is that of companion and
assistant to man. I believe in woman's right to submit unreservedly to her

husband in everything, save in matters of conscience between God and her own soul.[11]

Rather than interpreting these concessions as restrictions on women's freedoms, they are seen as a part of women's God-given "rights." Female authors, such as this one, found these "rights" empowering; strengthening their faith and their relationships within their families.

While this gender ideology had its own unique manifestations in Ulster, its primary source for Protestants, and to a lesser extent for Catholics, was American evangelicalism. The writings of the popular American preacher and moralist the Reverend T. DeWitt Talmage on the topic of women and Christianity appeared frequently in the Presbyterian publication *The Witness* and in the Irish Methodist *Christian Advocate*, both published in Belfast. Talmage's views on the rights of women accord with those expressed in the anonymous "rights of women" poems that were a mainstay of the religious discourse on female piety. *The Witness* published an address by Talmage titled "Woman's Rights," in which he argues that women need not look outside their Christian homes in order to possess their highest rights. He does not believe that the Christian Woman should concern herself with gaining "other rights" but rather that with God's help she should "rise up to the appreciation of the glorious rights she already possesses."[12] He asserts that all women have "one grand and all-absorbing right" which "is *to make home happy* ... O woman! thank God you have a home, and that you may be queen in it."[13] American evangelicals advocated the single-minded dedication of Christian women to their domestic "rights" as part of their attempt to shore up the "separate spheres" ideology that was unravelling by the turn of the century.[14]

This conservative, Christian "declaration of women's rights," the language of which was largely imported from America, was seized upon with alacrity by Ulster evangelicals. How and why the "right" to be a virtuous, self-sacrificing "keeper at home" developed in the Ulster religious literature will be addressed in this chapter.

The Protestants were not alone in their assertion of women's "rights" in this manner. Roman Catholic authors wrote of the role of Christian women in very similar terms. The popular and controversial Nun of Kenmare averred, "There is no woman who has not influence ... There are, thank God, women who do use all their influence, not in noisily demanding their "rights," but in using their right – the truest and best right – the right to exercise a most happy influence over all with whom they associate."[15] The similarity between this passage and the "rights of women" poems which circulated among evangelical Protestants indicates that the same view of the place and influence of Christian women found an audience among Catholic readers. An excerpt from the poem "Women's Best Vote," which appeared in the pages of the Catholic *Irish Monthly* in 1912, provides another example of this shared emphasis on women's "right" to service and influence within the home first and foremost

> Heroes and saints proclaim in grateful choir
> The mother-heart the glory of the race, –
> The cradle-song the clearest voice of grace, –
> The filial tie chief motive to aspire.[16]

The author of the poem added a footnote which explained that while he was "in favour of women being allowed to exercise their privilege, or rather do their duty as citizens," he did not "consider the mere political vote so overwhelmingly important as to justify violence or to obscure higher duties and privileges."[17] Thus Catholic women's "best vote" lay with their "higher" calling as Christian wives, mothers, sisters, and daughters.

Why was this description of "women's rights" so enduring and widespread in Ulster's popular religious literature? The right to "labour, love and pray" was not the prerogative being sought by those who were agitating for women's political, economic, and legal rights. The "right" being demanded for women in this conservative religious discourse was to remain eternally the same. While the modern world all around them was irrevocably changing gender roles, Ulster Christians sought to stem the tide of change. The gender ideology of the "virtuous woman" and the "cult of domesticity" was largely imported from America, England, and the Continent. It was homeostatic and readily adapted to meet the needs of a conservative, middle-class social order that was threatened by change. Maintaining the gender status quo was important for conservative middle-class Irish Christians because it shored up their own defensive structures when both Roman Catholics and Protestants felt their communities increasingly threatened: the Protestants by rising Irish nationalism and modern irreligion, the Catholics by English cultural imperialism and godless modernism.

In both Catholic and Protestant religious literature the "old-fashioned" "womanly woman" was highly praised. Concern that the established "natural" ideal of the Christian woman within her home and church was being eroded by radical suffragism, "loose entertainments," and all of the other concomitant evils of modern society was clearly expressed in this literature. The serial story "A Medieval

Modern," published in *The Catholic Bulletin and Book Review*, exhibits throughout this fear of what a modern, secular world will do to gender relations. The heroine of the story, Desiree, and her mother possess all of the virtues of a Christian woman that the "cult of true womanhood" required: "piety, purity, submissiveness and domesticity."[18] Desiree and her avowedly medieval mother share the same romantic and refined view of the world. Mother and daughter, as befits "true women," are very close.[19] Desiree has two cousins who turn their backs on their mother, their Celtic faith, and their own womanliness. Needless to say, they both come to tragic ends. One of the cousins, Gladys, is a suffragette. Gladys's description of her activities prompted the following exchange between Desiree and her mother. " 'Desiree, promise me that you will never be like these wretched women who trample their self-respect in the mud, who live like pagans, and who die like animals.' I was amazed at mother's vehemence, for she was usually reserved and self-controlled. 'Indeed I can easily promise what you ask. I am as much out of touch with the spirit of the times as you are,' I returned, adding with a smile, 'Muriel calls me an anachronism.'"[20] The woman who rejects the rights of the "New Woman" in favour of the traditional rights of women to "labour, love and pray" is singled out for praise. She is presented as a role model in both Protestant and Roman Catholic popular literature.

This delineation of the "rights" of the Christian woman clarified the role of women within church and home and provided a guide for proper conduct and a bulwark against change. But in order for the notion of a Christian wife and mother's proper domestic sphere to be entertained, the very nature of the female inhabitant of this sphere must first be ascertained. In a regular column in the *Irish Presbyterian*, "Woman's Sphere: Domestic and Social", the rhetorical question "What is a True Home?" was the title of a selected article. The author lauds the woman who seeks above all other honours the right to rule in her home as a queen. "To preside there with such skill that husband and children will rise up and call her blessed, is nobler than to rule an empire. 'Woman's rights!' Has man any that surpass this?"[21] Clearly he does not.

This brings us to an important pre-condition of domestic piety. Men had clear privileges and prerogatives in this patriarchal society. Yet in this "cult of domesticity" it was allowed that women were superior to men in their piety and in their potential for good. According to this gender rhetoric, man had no rights which approached the importance of woman's "right" to use her holy influence and sacrifice herself for the salvation of her family and the state. This belief that women alone were suited for this important task was tenable only if their very natures declared them fit. Ulster religious literature describes women as morally superior to men and naturally more pious than men. This elevation of female piety had significant implications for the importance attached to the "cult of domesticity" in Ulster.

"VIRTUOUS WOMEN" – AN ESSENTIALIST VIEW OF WOMEN'S "NATURE"

"There is that in true womanliness before which every true man bows."[22] So wrote a contributor, M.D.A., to the "King's Daughters in Council" column in the *Christian Advocate*. Members of the "Council," which was conducted by a Belfast Methodist minister's wife, Mrs William L. Coade, under the pseudonym of "Charity Hope," were encouraged to write in with their views on topics ranging from full sanctification to the morality of wearing stuffed birds on millinery. This column treats at length the many themes in this essentialist view of the "virtuous woman" that one finds scattered throughout the literature. The author goes on to say that modern men may admire a clever or attractive young woman, but that if these qualities are "not united with that most essential of all her attributes, womanliness, in their hearts they despise her."[23] Not only was "womanliness" something without which a Christian woman was thought to be less than a woman, but this "pure, high ideal of womanhood"[24] caused men to show "spontaneous reverence"[25] for a "true" woman. Men would bow before and revere womanliness because it contains within it something that is morally superior to manliness. Of course M.D.A. does not baldly express such a sentiment. Instead she expresses the conventional notion that God never intended women to enter into rivalry with men; women were created to help men. It is precisely in this role of "help-meet" that her superiority may be located. M.D.A. elaborates on the "power that is crushed into that word womanliness" by observing that after he had created everything but woman, "God saw that the world with all its beauties was incomplete, and He added this last best gift."[26] Another contributor to the Council, Joan,[27] asserts that God did not intend women to be inferior to men: "If man is the head, she is the crown – a crown to her husband, the crown of visible creation."[28] The rhetoric of female moral superiority raised women to dizzying heights. Men suffered by comparison.

Woman

Not she with trait'rous kiss her Saviour stung,
Not she denied Him with unholy tongue;
She, while Apostles shrunk, could danger brave,
Last at His cross, and earliest at His grave.[29]

Just as Christ's female follower in Browning's poem displayed a piety that outshone that of the male disciples, nineteenth-century Christian women were said to possess a greater loyalty to their faith than their male counterparts. As the Reverend J. Kennedy Elliott of Magherafelt noted, "Woman furnishes the brightest specimens of pure and unde-filed religion."[30] The very nature of women, then, was thought to be inherently more pious and refined than that of men.

The way in which this gender ideology of female moral superiority was presented in the literature ranged from the very romantic,

> ... Religion seems most fair,
> When woman wins the heart to thought of peace,
> 'Twas woman shed on it its noblest light,
> When heav'n through her stoop'd down to kiss the world.[31]

to the pragmatic: "Woman is ... no sentimental abstraction, no impos-sible deity ... [yet] in moral power she is the superior of man."[32]

It may appear paradoxical that this essentialist glorification of the superior morality of women occurred within patriarchal[33] Christian groups. Did this approach to gender and religion result in the erosion of male spiritual authority within the homes and churches of Ulster? As has been mentioned above, a chief source for this idea of female moral superiority was American religious literature. A survey of the central works of this literature by American researchers indicates that the "feminization" of American Protestantism occurred in the nine-teenth century.[34] Barbara Welter has asserted that the newly developing middle-class masculinity[35] – based on merciless economic competitive-ness – had no room for traditional Christian morals. Victorian ministers proclaimed women the moral superiors of men and declared domestic-ity and religion to be women's special sphere.[36] Ann Douglas has argued that an alliance developed between a marginalized clergy which no longer had the influence in the community that Puritan divines had maintained during the colonial period, and economically marginalized and newly leisured middle-class women who now played no role in production and were instead consumers and reproducers. A mutual dependence developed between the Protestant clergy and its female parishioners. Women depended on the churches and their various orga-nizations for a meaningful role and the clergy depended on women to fill their churches and run, as volunteers, the various church min-istries.[37] As Christian morality became irrelevant to the lives of modern American men, Christian ministers preached a new, more "feminine," sentimental theology that emphasized the "feminine" nature of Jesus – his meekness and his obedience – to their "flounce filled pews."[38]

The chief motor of this social and religious change in America was economic change. With rapid urbanization, gender roles were unstable and the creation of the timeless, pious, virtuous woman was seen as an attempt to retain some degree of stability from the rural past. Rapid industrialization, urbanization, and the creation of a burgeoning Protestant middle class were all themes in the economic history of Ulster during the period under study here.[39] I would be wary, however, of importing this American model wholesale. For example, Barbara Harris has argued that the middle-class cult of "true womanhood" with its concomitant emphasis on the moral superiority of women was, by mid-century, firmly entrenched as the dominant set of values for the large American middle class and for the many that aspired to middle-class respectability.[40] In contrast, in Ulster rapid industrialization occurred later and was less sweeping in its influence. Within short distances of Belfast, Ulster's industrial centre, there existed communities in which traditional economic patterns and familial relations remained intact. Therefore, despite the apparent absorption by the Ulster religious press of American ideas about gender ideology, I would argue for Ulster's distinctiveness. The same English words can have very different connotations, depending on the social context within which they are used. Ulster was a very different context indeed.

To return to our discussion of the essentialist view of female piety in Ulster, it should be noted that the espousal of the view that females outshone males in the realms of morality and spirituality occurred both frequently and, significantly, obliquely in Ulster religious literature. Rarely was it the subject of feature editorials or major published sermons; rather this portrait of female superiority was frequently to be found in the Methodists' "King's Daughters in Council" column, in the Presbyterians' "Woman's Sphere" sections, and in fiction written by women of all denominations, including Roman Catholics, for a primarily female audience. It seemed that this ideology was a secret shared by middle-class women, clergymen and a few knowing male laymen. Would this overtly nonorthodox ideology of the superior piety of women have been acceptable to Ulster laymen if it had been presented as forcefully as it had been in America?

How much power and influence, within the domestic realm, did this gender ideology afford women? It portrayed the essentially pious woman as a spiritual guide to her husband, brothers, and other men in her family circle, a woman who held fast to her faith while her menfolk doubted and prevaricated. Sometimes seriously and sometimes through humour, the spiritual predominance of women within the home was championed.

"Woman, according to creation and history, is a means to an end ... The end is that she may grandly lift up man"[41] wrote the author of an article that appeared in a "Woman's Sphere" column of *The Irish Presbyterian*. The author relates an anecdote of how the great evangelist, Charles H. Spurgeon, dealt with a young woman who said that she refused to "come into the church" because she could not accept the teaching "that man is the head of woman." Spurgeon replied "with truth and wit" that she should not let this matter trouble her for she could let man be the head "and she could become the neck on which the head was set, and turn the man hither and thither, round and about, whichever way she wished ... that is the way women have been doing from the beginning."[42] While this passage gently mocks men as being puppets controlled by the women in their lives, the author does assert that when Christian women act according to their "true" natures men always benefit: For "when woman is what she ought to be, pure, wise, spirit-filled, a mighty love power, that is what is best for men."[43]

In the poems and stories of popular religious literature we see the spiritual influence of women over the men in their lives. The idea of women as the "neck" that moves the "head"[44] may have been presented in a tongue-in-cheek fashion, but nonetheless it is in agreement with frequently expressed sentiments concerning the relative spiritual influence of women and men. Christian husbands, fathers, and sons were described as being at a loss without the solid faith of their womenfolk.

In the poem "Woman's Trust," the husband, a farmer, worries that his family will meet with economic disaster. His wife tells him, "There is a Heart, there is a Hand, we feel, we cannot see,/We've always been provided for, and we shall always be!"[45] The gloomy, doubting husband criticizes his wife's simple faith. Cuttingly he declares "'That's like a woman's reasoning – we must because we must,' She softly [says]: 'I reason not; I only work and trust.'"[46] The male is presented as sceptical and unfaithful, a "doubting Thomas," while the essentially emotional, not rational, and pious wife remains steadfast in her faith.

It is not difficult to discern who is the true Christian here. It is the woman who takes the spiritual lead, rescuing her husband from his disbelief. Her faith gives him strength to go on: "He kissed the calm and trustful face; gone was his restless pain, She heard him, with a cheerful step, go whistling down the lane." The scriptural role of the "headship" of the husband is not overtly challenged. Yet if this gender ideology of the moral superiority of women was actually believed by the authors and the readers of this literature, how significant could the theology of male "headship" still be?

Female moral superiority was rarely stated overtly in Ulster religious literature. It ran as a subtext through stories in which a woman's simple faith was stronger than her husband's. Maude Lutton, a popular Belfast Methodist writer of short religious fiction, unequivocally presents this gender ideology of female moral superiority in the thoughts of a Christian mother contemplating her prospective daughter-in-law. The mother is distressed that her Arthur, "who had carried into his bright young manhood the unsullied soul of a boy", "desired to marry, a little girl with fluffy golden hair, and an inane giggle."[47] The woman knew what she must do: "She must probe for the womanhood in that little fluffy-haired girl, she must inspire her to an ideal, and lift her towards it – aye, even urge her *higher than Arthur in soul stature* – for the man must reverence the woman, and the woman must respect the man."[48] The mother in the story was successful in communicating to her new daughter-in-law the sacred trust of being a true wife. She impressed upon the girl her holy responsibility in influencing Arthur for good. Arthur is not presented as a dull or plodding lad. He does not need intellectual guidance. It is in "soul stature" that his wife must lead him. Arthur was being passed on from the moral guardianship of his Christian mother to that of his Christian wife.

A corollary of the superiority of female piety was the emphasis on women's irrationality. This view that women were fundamentally irrational beings was implied in the hearty praise of their piety and spiritual insight. In "The Worth of a True Wife" the anonymous author urges male readers to rely on the good counsel of their wives. The author says of a "true wife" that "Her impressive nature, which renders her indisposed slowly to reason, is furnished with an instinctive perception of the right which is better than logic."[49] In matters of morality, the wife's intuitive piety surpasses in importance her husband's logic.

Throughout this strand of the discourse on female piety it is women's intuitive piety rather than her intellect that is praised. For if in matters of piety women were regarded as superior to men, in many other areas the "weaker" sex was deemed to be wanting. Paradoxically, the view of women as "naturally" irrational, foolish, spiteful, cunning, and possessing myriad other negative traits existed in the literature alongside the gender ideology of the "virtuous woman." Women were urged to make an effort to overcome these defects in their "nature:" "Women's nature is finer than that of men; it is more sensitive, yielding, more flowery and gay, and more capable of attending to littleness, minuteness, and patient painstaking than that of men. The moral extremes of women differ very much from those of men. They are more superficial than men; they are apt to err in their estimate of mere outside, of gay trifles, of vain display and unreal pleasures, and are ready to bid for these more than their value. It is the wisdom of individuals to study their extremes and to direct the efforts of moral discipline to remedy these as far as possible."[50] Thus this essentialist view of women did not always redound to women's advantage. Women may have been made of finer, purer moral stuff, but the vessel in which it was contained was described as being very weak. In the late nineteenth and early twentieth centuries, female writers argued that women could retain all that was best in their "natures" – especially their piety and domesticity – while ridding themselves of their weaknesses. In a "Woman's Sphere" column on the subject of the New Woman, the author maintains that woman "longs to lose her own feminine weaknesses – jealousy, petty spite, and love of gossip ... while retaining her own gentleness."[51] Proponents of the New Woman argued that it was in man's favour for women, through education, to discipline the weaker side of their "natures" that they might "raise themselves up" and be of even greater assistance to men.[52]

CATHOLIC GENDER ESSENTIALISM

Thus far we have looked at how Ulster Protestant religious literature presented an ideal, essentially virtuous Christian womanhood. Middle-class Catholic readers found a very similar gender ideology in their popular religious literature. Catholic writers of this genre also held that women's nature was an essentially pious one, and that their faith was instinctively truer and stronger than that of men.

As in the Protestant literature, Catholic women are viewed as moral guides and "helpmeets" to their husbands, fathers, and brothers. In a short story in the popular *The Catholic Monthly*, the characters Dorthea and her husband, Theodore, are described as being "'God's gift' to one another; he temporally to her, she spiritually to him."[53] The wife's contribution to the marriage is her inherent piety; the husband makes no such contribution. In the serial story "A Valiant Woman," published in *The Catholic Bulletin and Book Review*, the young daughter, Anne Sheridan, must remain at home to look after her father and younger siblings, and tend not only to their physical needs, but their spiritual needs as well. The irreligious father is incapable of this duty. Young Anne pours her heart out to an old priest who is her confidante: "'My father is a careless Catholic, he does not even go to the Masses of obligation. The Canon says that the boys and Alice may follow his example if I leave them. Who is to see that they attend Mass, instructions and religious duties?'"[54] Through Anne's holy influence, her father and the rest of her family are brought back to their faith. The heroines of

Catholic religious fiction are essentially pious; in every way their faith outshines that of the laymen in their circle.

Sister Mary Francis Cusack, in her 1874 publication titled *Woman's Work in Modern Society*, asserted that "woman is essentially, I had almost said constitutionally, religious."[55] Cusack added that if woman's essentially religious character should change, "and she becomes indifferent or sceptical, men may look out for 130 evils which they will find themselves very powerless to avert."[56] "It was women, too, who had the courage of their opinions, which men very frequently had not,"[57] Cusack wrote of the penal times. She is particularly damning in her indictment of male intellectuals and sceptics, whom she believes consider religion appropriate only for weak and foolish women.

As a general rule men like women to be religious, that is, provided their religion does not obtrude itself too much. It must be respectable, and by no means interfere with masculine comforts or prejudice. Men have a sort of dim "misgiving" that women want religion, that it is necessary for them, a necessity which they attribute with miserable self-complacency to the mental weakness of the sex. They look on it as a sort of luxury, to be tolerated with even a partial approbation, much as you give babies toys to keep them out of harm, by providing innocent recreation for their infantile minds.[58]

It is difficult to say if Cusack's appraisal of men's view of women and religion is at all accurate. Clearly she is not speaking of men who were faithful, practising Catholics or clergymen. Rather, the men she is attacking are sceptics, atheists, and intellectuals. Nevertheless, we still see the juxtaposition of woman/spiritual/emotional against man/secular/rational – the same essentialist gender ideology that existed in Protestant religious literature.

As in the Protestant literature, the view that women, while "naturally" pious were also "naturally" unintellectual is put forward, if slightly less frequently, in Catholic periodicals. In an article in *The Irish Monthly*, Charlotte O'Conor Eccles took issue with an essentialist view expressed by an unnamed writer in another Catholic publication. Eccles quotes the offending passage, noting that "The writer says: – '*When I hear a woman use intellectual arguments, I am dismayed.* Her best reason, as it is the world's best reason, is the inspiration of a pure and believing heart.' Is, then, a pure and believing heart incompatible with intellectuality?"[59] Interestingly, that unnamed author who thought that women's innate piety was incompatible with rationalism and intellect was writing on the subject of the Blessed Virgin Mary. Eccles sees a discrepancy in the author's argument and asks, "Does, then, the writer seriously contend that intellectuality was not one of those gifts of Her whom the Church invokes daily as 'Seat of Wisdom,' 'Queen of Prophets,' and 'Mother of Good Counsel'?"[60] Eccles may be technically correct in her assertion that the Church considered Mary all of these things, yet Catholic religious literature does not hold up the Virgin Mary as a model of intellectual acuity; rather it is for her unprecedented piety and holiness that she who was "most blessed among women" was revered. This brings us to an important point about Catholic gender ideology: belief about the nature of the Mother of God informs every aspect of the Irish Catholic understanding of women and piety. As the Virgin Mary and ideals of female piety are the subject of a subsequent chapter, suffice it to say here that Catholic writers saw in "true" wives, mothers, sisters, and daughters – all with the legacy of being daughters of Mary as well as daughters of Eve – the essential piety that was central to their understanding of the Virgin's nature.

Eccles uses the same argument for female moral superiority used by the various Protestant editors who cited Elizabeth Barrett Browning's poem, "Woman." In her argument for the intellectual ability of pious women she discusses Christ's rapport with his female followers. Eccles asks rhetorically: "In return, who loved Him as women did, followed Him as women did, when His disciples fled?"[61] Echoes of "last at his cross, earliest at His grave" can clearly be heard in this question.

For Protestant and Roman Catholic writers alike, women were essentially pious. For some writers this precluded intellectual depth and rationality in women; for others, such as Cusack and Eccles, piety was but one facet of women's "nature." This construction of "natural" female piety was crucial to the development of the domestic ideology that came to dominate the middle-class discourse on gender and religion.

LIFE WITHIN THE DOMESTIC SPHERE

Where could the "virtuous woman" best exercise her holy influence? The clear consensus on this question, for both Catholics and Protestants, was in the home. The domestic sphere was lauded as woman's kingdom[62] in which she would exert her blessed influence through her "right" to "labour, love, and pray." In her labours she was to be, above all, self-sacrificing, giving all of herself for her family, even to the point of death. A woman's love was described in superlative terms as being more powerful and redemptive than the love of any other save Christ. The ideal of the faithful, constant, and true woman praying when all hope seemed past permeates the religious literature. The common strand running through all of this is the power, the privilege, the influence, even from beyond the grave, of the life of a "virtuous woman" within her domestic circle.

While home life always was primary, women's sphere gradually expanded in this period to include church activities. This was not seen as a break with but rather as a continuation of the existing domestic ideology. The virtues that women exercised in their extended sphere – the church – were the same as those they exercised at home. The extent of the participation of lay Catholic women in church organizations was not as great as it was in Protestant circles, yet the ideology that informed any move from the hearth to a wider sphere was similar. Christian women did not seek power in the church; they sought service.

The piety of Christian women within the home was ideally to be expressed through their Christ-like selflessness. Women's labour within their homes was in itself an act of piety, their service a gift from God. In the poem "Granted Wishes," two girls who were just leaving school asked each other what they wished to be. One girl wanted to "be a queen and rule" and the other said "the world I'd see."[63] When they met years later, we find that the girl who wanted to be a queen had her wish granted:

> "A poor man's wife am I, and yet,"
> Said [she], "I am a queen."
> "My realm a happy household is,
> My king a husband true;
> I rule by loving service;
> How has it been with you?"[64]

Her friend who had desired to see the world replied:

> ... "Still the great world lies
> Beyond me as it laid;
> O'er love's and duty's boundaries
> My feet have never strayed.
> Faint murmurs of the wide world come
> Unheeded to my ear;
> My widowed mother's sick bed-room
> Sufficeth for my sphere."[65]

These ideal women do not view their lives of selfless labour as a sacrifice; rather they see their dutiful lives of service for others as a gift from God.

They clasped each other's hands; with tears
Of solemn joy they cried,
"God gave the wish of our young years,
And we are satisfied."[66]

This brief poem captures the ideal of female sacrifice central to Protestant domestic ideology.[67] As wives, mothers, sisters, and daughters, the Christian women portrayed in religious literature placed their families' needs before their own. Yet "bearing the cross" of sacrifice and service does not bring misery; it is the source of true happiness, because when a woman devotes herself to others she "fulfils the law of her being."[68] Thus women's self-sacrificing domestic labour is a "right" or a "privilege" which men do not have the honour of possessing.

Roman Catholic popular periodicals glorified the "right" of women to sacrifice and be blessed for it with greater feeling and frequency than did their Protestant counterparts. The ideal of the self-sacrificing Christian woman is fundamentally identical in both literatures.

The prescriptive article titled "Some Practical Hints on the Education of Children" urges Catholic women to live their lives in such a way that their children see the "beauty of holiness" in their mother's example. The author wonders if her readers might find it extreme that a mother should revolutionize her life in order to provide a good example. Nevertheless she asserts that just such a revolution is required, "for real motherhood (and we don't care for the imitation), means *just this*, an utter self-abnegation, and a concentration of every thought and feeling on the work before you, of training souls for the kingdom of heaven."[69] These sacrifices are viewed as acts of piety because they are done for holy purposes. The ideal Catholic mother is willing to sacrifice all in order to influence her loved ones for good: "The true mother has no thought of self: all her life, all her love, are given to her husband and children."[70]

Mothers and wives are not the only Catholic women who were expected to make sacrifices according to this ideal of domestic piety. The faithful Irish daughter is described as nobly sacrificing her own interests for those of her family. The poem "In a Mud Cabin" describes the light which a daughter's devotion to her sick mother brings to a poor hovel. "Yet 'mid the gloom there shines a sacred light ... it is a daughter's love."[71] For her mother's sake, the daughter "Goes hungry, sleepless, cold, /Nor deems her cross a sorrow, wears the while,/ A patient, pleasant smile."[72] The daughter's sacrifice is considered an act of piety; it pleases her God. The recording angel "Takes every daily loving sacrifice /To gladden heavenly eyes."[73] Finally, the daughter's impoverished life of sacrifice in the mud cabin is described as being far more rewarding than a life of selfish indulgence.

> And oh! I know on many a downy bed
> Where bitter tears are shed,
> An aching heart would barter earth's bright gold,
> To feel the loving fold
> Of mother-arms, to lay upon her breast
> A throbbing head to rest.[74]

The Catholic mother's love and sacrifice for her daughter have taught and inspired the daughter to be a pious and self-sacrificing woman as well.

A similar tale of an Irish Catholic daughter's sacrifice is told in "A Jewel Unknown." Margaret immigrated to America and had been getting on well when she received news that her aged parents were very ill. She returned to nurse them and lost her youth and beauty as "a household drudge." The narrator of Margaret's story tells his friend that "During the years that have gone by since she came back no one has ever heard her say a word of complaint. It is God's will, she will tell you, and it sums up her faith in Him ... Can you not see the heroism of the soul that takes up such a burden without ever a thought of reward? ... It is those jewels unknown, unthought of, uncared for, that shine through the gloom of uncertainty, and show us the way to make life beautiful."[75] In this portrait of ideal female piety and filial love, Margaret's life of sacrifice and drudgery is not wasted; it serves as a beautiful Christian example to others. The theme of female domestic sacrifice that we saw in the Protestant literature, typified by the Presbyterian poem "Granted Wishes," is also central to the Catholic construction of the ideal woman, be she mother, wife, daughter, or sister.

The proverbial capacity of a mother to love is an integral part of her piety. Her love is described as constant and unfaltering, excelled only by the love of God. Even women who do not have children but who have a true "mother-heart" can exercise a similar influence in the lives of others through their capacity to love.[76] An unnamed author in an early number of *The Irish Presbyterian* says that a mother's love "is certainly the gift of God, infixed in the female heart for wise purposes, the development and manifestation of which are seen in every domestic circle."[77] This mother love was said to have awesome redemptive powers: "Its redeeming and reclaiming power has been felt when all other means, save the Gospel, have proved ineffectual."[78] It was depicted as never being harsh or judgemental; a mother's love was constant even if the object of that love, a wayward child or a sinful husband, was not deserving: "Her language is – 'I but know that I love thee, whatever thou art.'"[79]

A mother's love is presented as analogous to God's love. In one tale a young woman had suffered many sorrows and could not understand God's love or that he was "the Great Comforter." While she is having a discussion about this with an elderly clergymen at a seaside resort a sudden storm blew up and the woman began frantically searching for her boy; she was worried that he would be frightened without her. After she found and comforted the child, the clergyman whispered to her, "*As one whom his mother comforteth so will I comfort you.*" The woman replied, "I understand it now ... I did not trust Him as my boy trusts me, but now I will throw myself into His arms as a little child, and remember His promise, 'As one whom his mother comforteth so will I comfort you.' I never felt the depth of Divine love as shown in that promise before."[80] A mother's love and power to comfort come second only to God's love; moreover, through a mother's love we can begin to apprehend the love of God.

The depiction of a "true" mother's love in the Catholic literature is very similar to that found in the Protestant literature. Evidence of this view of the power of a mother's love is found more in fiction than it is in prescriptive articles. Sentimental poetry was a favoured mode of expression for eulogizing a mother's love. The description of the Catholic mother's love includes her desire for her children to be spared any pain or the stain of sin. Her love manifests itself in care for their physical needs and prayer for their spiritual condition. In "A Mother's Reverie" the loving mother has this wish for her sleeping child: "God guard you, little daughter, and in all life's thorny way/Keep your heart as pure and painless as it beats, my Elsie now."[81] The mother's love that is described in the Catholic literature is also one which renders the mother sympathetic and nonjudgemental. Like the ideal Protestant mother who says "I but know that I love thee, whatever thou art," the ideal Catholic mother's love causes her to overlook failings and sins and regard the wanderer "with maternal piety and tender forbearance."[82] This portrait of the ideal Christian mother's love remained constant over time and across denominations.

The final key component of an ideal woman's domestic piety to be examined is her faithfulness in prayer. This emphasis on a woman's prayer life is in keeping with essentialist notions about her innate spirituality and with her domestic role. Prayer did not take women out of the domestic sphere; on the contrary, it was from within their home circle that they exercised this "right," this privilege, this awesome power. While the following passage ludicrously underestimates the

material concerns and workload of even middle-class women with servants, it does give us some insight into attitudes towards domestic
piety. The unnamed author asserts that "the wife remains at home
[and] as in a school of wisdom collects her thoughts, and can occupy
herself with prayer and reading Scripture ... she is disturbed by no one;
she can enjoy perpetual quiet."[83] Despite the unlikeliness of this
portrait of a woman's domestic solitude, it does help to explain the
phenomenon, present in both the Protestant and Roman Catholic
literature, of women being the sole "keepers of the flame" in the area
of prayer. With very few exceptions[84] it was a praying mother, grandmother, wife, sister, or other female member of the household who was
described.

Why were praying men so rarely mentioned? The "cult of domesticity" theories examined by American researchers could partially
explain this. Middle-class men, buffeted by the evils of the world of
commerce and harried by the long hours spent in the service of Mam-
mon, relied on their "angels in the house" to create a restful, pure,
and spiritual atmosphere upon their return home. Personal prayer was
a domestic function. Men spent the vast majority of their waking hours
outside of this "blessed realm"; thus the role of "prayer warrior" fell to
their womenfolk, who were, as fortune would have it, essentially pious
and constant in their faith despite the turmoil of the modern world.[85]

In one anecdote, recycled many times in the Protestant evangelical
press, the members of a theological seminary[86] are asked how many of
them have praying mothers, or sometimes, in more dramatic versions
of this story, those who had praying mothers were asked to rise. Of
course the overwhelming majority of young men "preparing for the
sacred ministry ... were the offspring of *praying mothers*."[87] The question was never put to them if they had praying fathers. Again we see
prayer as an exclusively female domestic activity.[88]

The praying woman, especially the praying mother, was an emotional touchstone in the religious literature. Memories of a praying
mother were said to sustain and renew the faith of those for whom she
prayed. A man who once saw his mother kneeling and praying for him
wrote about it in a poem titled "My Mother's Prayers," published in *The
Monthly Messenger* in 1879. This poem became a popular gospel song
entitled "My Name in Mother's Prayer." This man, a busy banker, said
he "never ceased to hear and be moved by the echo of his own name
in the prayer of his mother." While male authors tended to write about
the praying mother in very sentimental tones, in women's columns the
power for good of praying women was emphasized. A contributor to
the "King's Daughters in Council" urges her sisters on to greater effort
in their prayer life, for "If all the mothers in our Methodist families

would seek this above all else, and pray for it night and day – the conversion of every child in the family – what an ingathering of souls there would be into the fold of Christ!"[89] The praying woman in this construction of female piety is a spiritual force, a partner with Christ in the work of salvation.

The centrality of prayer to female piety is no less crucial in the Catholic context. Fundamentally, the pious Catholic mother is depicted as being a praying mother. As in the Protestant literature, the subject of praying fathers is passed over in silence. It is the mother's prayer that demonstrates the love she has for her children and for her faith. Of the many poems dedicated to the theme of praying mothers, the following verses by Ulster poet "Magdalen Rock" are particularly apt for our discussion because they show the fundamental similarities between Catholic and Protestant views of the power of domestic prayer. But this poem also shows the uniquely Catholic use of the Virgin Mary as not only an example of a praying mother[90] but also as an agent of grace, adding her own prayers to those of earthly mothers.

> God only knows the power and might
>   Of all the prayers that mothers say
> For those they love, at dead of night
>   Or in the gladsome light of day.
> . . . .
> For myriad angels fair and bright
>   Their prayers to Heaven bear straightway,
> There God's own Mother will unite
>   Her prayers with those that mothers pray.
> God only knows the power and might
>   Of all the prayers that mothers say.[91]

The faithful Catholic mother at prayer is said to exert an enormous influence by her example. Reflecting on the image of the mother at prayer with her children was an emotional experience for adult Catholics. In "To an Irish Mother" an expatriate Irish priest asks:

> O, will you, dear, on bended knee
> With blessing words remember me
> To help my priesthood day?
> . . . .
> So when the little children
> Are near you with the beads
> O, whisper them a stranger's name
> And tell them of my needs

. . . .
And all your prayers that now are mine
I'll thank in Mass at Mary's shrine.[92]

The responsibility of women to provide an example through their
domestic prayer[93] and the power of that prayer to effect good were
clearly presented in this construction of female piety.

THE FAR-REACHING INFLUENCE OF WOMEN

A Christian woman's influence was the chief source of her power to
effect good in her family and in the world. In the literature on female
piety the word "influence" appears time and time again. In exercising
her self-sacrificing right to "labour, love and pray" the ideal Christian
woman was said to wield a far-reaching influence. Though this paragon
of Christian virtue operated within the confines of home and church,
women's influence was thought to be felt throughout the nation.

The Protestant view of a mother's influence is effectively captured in
the following passage "What is to be the destiny of children, both in
this world and the next, will depend upon the piety, and prayers, and
the fidelity of mothers."[94] The influence for good of the Christian
mother over her children is commented on at length, but the influence of the wife over the husband is seen as significant as well. In "A
Model for Mothers" the pious life of a young wife and mother is
described. Her husband honours her for her perfect attention to the
spiritual needs of the household and for the regenerating effect that
her holy influence has over him. "Here is a picture of a sacred family,
a Christian household. Here is 'the husband sanctified by the wife.'
And will not God rain down abundant blessings on that little circle?"[95]
Indubitably the intended answer to this rhetorical question is, yes, he
will. A holy wife and mother's influence is not limited to this temporal
realm; the life of a pious mother has influence for good even from
beyond the grave, for remembrances of her sanctified life can bring
sinners back to the fold.[96]

It is important to note, however, that if awesome influence, power,
and privilege came with the role of Christian wife and mother, the
responsibility of this role was also great and the result of failure disastrous. Charity Hope warned her readers that "no influence is so powerful as yours for moulding the young life ... would you care to think
that some inconsistency of yours was just the one thing that led them
to take a false step?"[97]

Condemnation for failure came in no uncertain terms: "how many
mothers at home destroy their children's souls by not bringing them

to Jesus!"[98] Failure to "labour, love and pray" made a woman odious according to writers of Ulster religious literature. "A prayerless woman in every rank of life is a pest wherever her influence reaches"[99] intoned Ada Whitla, herself a great promoter of prayer and an unfailing critic of women who did not measure up to her high standard of Christian womanhood. A woman who refused to make sacrifices, particularly a working-class woman who had no time for domestic virtues, was castigated by Whitla as being "a bag full of holes – an abomination."[100] If the glory of being a Protestant mother was great, the ignominy of failure was greater.

Irish historian of religion Patrick Corish remarked that it is indeed odd that the piety of the Irish mother has been so entirely overlooked by historians "in view of the position of power so widely attributed to her, responsible, it would often be claimed, for all of both the good and evil in her children."[101] Catholic women too were seen as having an enormous influence for both "weal and woe." As we have already seen, when a Catholic woman "laboured, loved and prayed" her influence for good was enormous. "'A mother,' says a holy writer, 'is a child's first idea of God.' To the little ones she is omnipotent … In all God's Church there is no work so far-reaching as hers; she is at 'The beginning' for good or ill."[102] If a Catholic woman uses her influence for good, the benefits for her family and for society are incalculable. If mothers live up to this "sacred obligation" they are deemed deserving of "the traditional halo of motherhood."[103] As in the Protestant religious literature, a virtuous Christian mother exerts a holy influence even from beyond the grave "The memory of a holy and devoted mother is a strengthener of faith and of many other virtues."[104]

The double-edged sword of the cult of domesticity operates in the Catholic literature as it does in the Protestant. While on the one hand Christian women are praised for their innate piety and for the positive influence they have on their home circle, on the other they are castigated for any deviation from the ideals of this gender ideology. It is interesting to note that in this middle-class literature those who fail to meet the standard of domestic piety are "idle" working-class women and "flighty" upper-class society women; both groups were criticized for neglecting their homes. Mrs Frank Pentrill, writing in *The Irish Monthly*, scolds "Biddy" for her domestic failings. "She is, it is true, the kindest of mothers and the most faithful of wives, but she sadly neglects her home, and wastes in idleness the time she should devote to the comfort of her household."[105] While Pentrill does not call poor Irish women who fail to meet her standards of domestic virtue "bags with holes," she does nonetheless blame Irish peasant women for their husbands' greatest moral failing: drink. "The Irish woman is the hearth-queen of her peasant home, its absolute mistress, except when her husband is tipsy; and if he be tipsy so often, the fault is greatly hers."[106] According to Pentrill, most Irish women needed to be educated as to their power and influence over their sons and husbands for "if they but knew it, they would thus prove themselves true guardian angels, and would rescue many a soul from the grasp of the tempting demon."[107]

Sister Mary Francis Cusack presents a grim portrait of failed motherhood in chic social circles "The drunken mother in the lowest strata of society, who beats her child to death, is surely not more cruel than the fashionable mother who starves her child's soul."[108] As a Catholic educator Cusack was concerned with what she saw as the negative impact made upon their children by irreligious mothers:

And what shall we say of the moral education which Christian mothers give their offspring? Sometimes, indeed, they quote the precepts of Christianity with their lips; but what Gospel do they show in their lives? What grotesque contrasts are brought before the young and susceptible mind! The Catholic mother, perhaps, attends daily mass and nightly balls with equal assiduity ... How can such a mother teach her children Christian morality? Does she, indeed, love her neighbours as herself? And if she does not do so, is she likely to teach her children to do so? How the lessons which are taught in the cloister are untaught in the ballroom and the boudoir![109]

The influence of Christian women, especially mothers, was a cause for concern in both Protestant and Catholic circles. So much depended on their being virtuous and true to the ideals of Christian womanhood. Just what was at stake in this discourse on female piety? The authors of religious literature felt that the very existence of their respective religious cultures and societies hung in the balance.

MUTUAL MISPERCEPTIONS

The influence of the Christian woman, both Catholic and Protestant, was presented as having an awesome power for good. Next to Christ and his church, she was the instrument most used of God to effect salvation in the world. This construction of female piety was not exclusive to Ireland. As has been noted, the feminization of religion in America and, to a lesser extent, in England in the nineteenth century, is a well-documented phenomenon. The peculiar confluence of religious and ethnic antagonisms in Ulster during this period gave this ideology of female moral superiority and domestic salvation a certain significance and urgency that it did not possess, in this exact formulation, elsewhere. In Ulster, questions of hearth, home, women, purity, and religion were a formidable mix.

Both Catholics and Protestants saw a Christian mother's influence as a bulwark against irreligion, false religion, and national decay. This is a theme in the Protestant literature from the beginning of the period under study and one which developed in the Catholic literature as Irish Catholic nationalism became a more potent force in Irish life. The decay of home life was a threat to the nation, in whatever form it happened to take. The Reverend Mr Andrews of Portadown wrote with foreboding of the sorry fate of the Israelites after they abandoned the law of God within their homes. "Religion crept out and heathenism crept in. The household hearth was dishonoured – the nation was gradually poisoned at its core ... The fortress of Home was first desolated, and then every *other* fortress was speedily seized by the Canaanite."[110] For Ulster-Scots Protestants with their siege mentality and their fear of "popery," the protection of religion within the home was of the utmost importance.[111] The story in Joshua of the destruction of God's chosen people through their neglect of domestic piety provided a sobering lesson for those Ulster Protestants who also considered themselves chosen of God: "The same law of spiritual life prevails in our own land to-day. Destruction may come to us as it came to Israel. Therefore our Church is alarmed at hearing there is much neglect of family religion throughout our congregations; for that means the destruction of all religion, of all prosperity, of everything good – if this plague of indifference be not stayed."[112] Episcopalians, Presbyterians, and Methodists alike decried the decay of domestic piety as posing a threat to the nation. An article in the Methodist *Irish Christian Advocate* reports a sermon given by Canon Rawnsley on the subject of home influence. Referring to the home life of Christ, Rawnsley states that "the nursery of the salvation of the world was home and home life."[113] He goes on to laud the domestic vitality of the ancient Hebrews "The foundations of national glory are set in the homes of the people, and they will only remain unshaken while the family life of our nation is strong, simple, and pure."[114] Given women's ascribed role in influencing family life, female piety was central to the defence and development of the religious and civil polity "For the success of pure and undefiled religion there need be no fears, while the mothers of the Church keep presenting their offspring to the Lord, in love, in faith, in hope, and prayer."[115]

Domestic ideology is no less central to an understanding of Irish Catholic nationalism and its aspirations than it is to uncovering the crucial touchstones in the Ulster Protestant worldview. For Catholic writers in the late nineteenth century the role of Irish women in preserving the "true faith" during the penal days provided a model for "modern" Irish women "In Irish households, high and low, the women throughout those troubled times kept well up to the Christian standard, cherishing the domestic virtues, accepting with patience their own share of suffering, defying the temptations held out by the enemies of the faith, refusing to barter the souls of the young, in the midst of calamity keeping the eternal reward in view, and daily exercising works of charity and zeal."[116] Female piety, exercising its holy influence within the domestic sphere, determined the progress and strength of "the faith." It is not surprising, then, that mutually antagonistic Catholics and Protestants should attack each other on matters of such fundamental importance: female piety and female domesticity. Yet it is ironic that through mutual miscomprehension these two groups viewed each other as being so fundamentally different in areas in which they constructed very similar ideals of behaviour. It is to these perceived differences to which we now turn.

Ulster Protestants presented a portrait of Catholic family values that was unrecognizable to Ulster Catholics. Protestant polemicists presented Catholicism as being, first and foremost, anti-family. "Romanism has interfered with the family institute. It has entered it with a rude and violent hand, or it has entirely destroyed it. It has sought to contravene the law of nature and of God in this instance,"[117] opined the Reverend James Morgan in his fiery anti-Catholic tract, *Rome and the Gospel.* Morgan points to the convent and the confessional as two "device[s] of Rome" which break sacred family ties and degrade women. Roman Catholic convents were described by polemicists such as Morgan as being unnatural and ungodly. Convents were painted as traps into which the Church lured unsuspecting innocents. "It is [the Roman Catholic Church's] desire to drag away the young and unsuspecting from the hearth of happy homes, and immure them in the gloomy cells of the convent ... They are made the slaves of Rome, and must do her bidding. They have fled from God's wise and gracious institute of the family, and have cast themselves at the feet of a tyrannical and oppressive brotherhood or sisterhood."[118] Another Protestant author depicts the "moral martyrdom" of giving up the "tenderest ties" of the domestic realm to "enter upon a joyless wretched life of self-inflicted penances and suffering ... till the whole nature is changed and they are converted, if one may say so, into icicles – moral icicles."[119] According to this representation of convent life, nuns are un-women because "the finest feelings of ... woman's heart" are crushed by the "tyranny" of the convent and because convent life forces women to "quit their own proper sphere in society."[120] Ulster Protestants who wrote on this subject were not in the least reticent in voicing their opinions. With searing vituperation they castigated Catholicism for its supposed violation of the "natural," domestic life of women.

The Reverend John Bryson, an Ulster Presbyterian minister, in a book supposedly on the topic of the historical Marys of the Gospels, but which was in fact an egregious attack on Catholicism,[121] puts forward his belief that "Nunism is *unnatural.* It formed woman into the most unnatural of beings, namely – woman without mind, woman without heart, woman without home."[122] He also attacks convent life – though he calls it "nunism" – because he feels it "denuded females of their natural rights and liberties."[123] And what are the natural "rights of women" in this discourse? To "labour, love, and pray" – to exert her Christian influence at her own hearth. Accordingly, Bryson contrasts the debasing nature of "nunism" with what he sees as an exclusively Protestant domestic ideology: "the religion of the Bible has also elevated her [woman] as a moral agent, to whose influence the flame of domestic piety burns most brightly. The worth of a Christian mother is inestimable."[124] The very existence of the celibate, cloistered life as an option for Catholic women made Catholicism anti-domestic and unnatural in the eyes of its Protestant critics.

Many other aspects of Roman Catholicism were seized on as being unnatural and "pagan"[125] by Ulster Protestant writers, but the convent and the confessional were the two which were singled out for their deleterious effects on the sacred institution of the family. While "nunism" was attacked for tearing helpless women from the bosom of their families and turning them into pathetic un-women, the confessional was reviled as the serpent in the garden, insidiously wending its way into the sacred realm of the family and destroying family ties. "But the worst of all remains – the confessional. The family is allowed to remain together, but its secrets must all be known. Hence the constant morning and evening prayer. Hence the ever-open chapel. It is to give opportunity to the confessor. A stranger come between husband and wife, son and father, mother and daughter ... There is an authority without it that is far above any that is within it."[126] The possible existence of an authority outside of the family – the priest – which could undercut the God-given authority of the "head" of the family – the husband and father – sent male Protestant writers into paroxysms of anxiety. Such a system was dangerous because it might spread to "infect" their own homes.[127] Women, though naturally pious, were also portrayed as naturally weak – they were the most susceptible to the "blandishments" of the "agents of Rome." Priests, like the serpent in the Garden, took advantage of this weakness. Satan "perceived that the constitution of her mind was more plastic, her nature more susceptible of good or evil influences than that of the man"[128] and in like manner priests "strive to bring chiefly the female mind beneath their mysterious deadly control. Well do these crafty agents of "The Wicked One" calculate, that if, as of old, they can thus secure the "weaker vessel" – through her influence again they will have but little difficulty in securing her husband, children, friends."[129] Fear of the vulnerable nature of the cult of domesticity is clearly revealed in this passage. If a woman's influence was so crucial to the moral and spiritual welfare of her family and, by extension, to the welfare of the state, and yet if women were weak and susceptible to evil,[130] the protection of the "virtuous woman" and her ideal domestic realm was of the highest priority.

The charges laid against Catholicism that it was, because of the existence of convents and the confessional, a supporter of "unnatural" roles for women and that it was anti-domestic are unfounded. We have seen in the preceding discussion that popular Catholic literature heartily subscribed to the gender ideology of the "virtuous woman" and the cult of domesticity.

While the option of the celibate religious life existed for Catholic women, a life that was praised in superlative romantic language, Catholic writers did not denigrate the ideal of women as wives and mothers. Rather, they spoke of the two vocations open to Catholic women: that of the nun or that of the mother.[131] Both vocations were "natural" for women and both were ordained by God: "It was their [Irish women's] vocation to be either the guardians and example of the faith in the household ... or in religious life the light of the ignorant, the comfort of the sorrowing, the support of the poor."[132]

This topic of "dual vocations" will be treated at length in a subsequent chapter; suffice it to say for now that the existence of the religious life as a possibility for Catholic women did not dampen the enthusiasm with which Catholic writers glorified the domestic destiny of women. Clearly, Catholic writers elevated the sanctifying role of holy motherhood to the same heights as their Protestant counterparts did. Nora Tynan O'Mahoney was unstinting in her praise of Catholic motherhood when she wrote, "A mother's influence, a mother's dignity, is very sacred and holy; hardly less so, one might say without irreverence, than that of the priesthood itself. I know one poor old mother ... possessed of every womanly virtue, seasoned and leavened by a mother's love and suffering, to whose words I would listen and for whose blessing I would kneel with almost the same reverence and humility."[133] As to Protestant concerns regarding the negative influence of the confessional on family life, there is no reason to conclude that there is any merit to these criticisms. The domestic realm, and the idealized mother within it, were praised as being at least as significant as that of the Church. As in the Protestant literature, God's work was frequently described as being done by the clergy and women; this subtle undercutting of lay male authority was common to both of these somewhat "feminized" religious groups.[134]

Of course, the misperceptions concerning domestic piety were not unique to Protestants. Catholics portrayed Protestant culture as being irreligious, anti-family, and denigrating to women. It should be noted that Catholic writers were not addressing their criticisms so much to actual Protestant belief and practice (with the exception of their criticisms of Protestantism as being anti-Marian) as they were assailing what they saw as a bigoted, secular, and English culture that was a threat to the "true faith."

The popular Catholic literature that I have examined is unabashedly nationalist. The domestic vocation of Catholic women and their pious influence on their homes were presented as a necessary prerequisite for a successful regeneration of "Catholic Ireland." In her column "For Mothers and Daughters," *Bean A'Tighe* (young mother) tells her readers: "We Irishwomen need only determine to make our homes and our immediate surroundings happier and brighter, our influence more helpful and uplifting in the New Year. If each one of us did this "for the glory of God and the honour of Erin," the "nation" that we long for would surely benefit – one of the best assets of a country being the happy homes in which the coming race are being educated in faith, patriotism, and noble aims."[135] Thus the sanctity of the home and the concomitant cult of domesticity were no less critical for Irish Catholics than they were for Ulster Protestants. At the end of the serial story "A Medieval Modern," the beloved family friend Father Mahon, praises the devotion to their faith, country, and to each other of the young heroine, Desiree, and her mother. The priest declares that he wishes everyone "would learn the three M's, ... that is to say, love of Mother Church, Motherland, and their own mother. Religion, Patriotism, family affection – these are the foundations on which our National edifice must be reared."[136] While Catholic writers asserted that these "three M's" were shared by all good Catholics, they held that Protestants were sadly lacking in their respect for her who was the Mother of all Christians, the Virgin Mary. Thus Protestants could not truly respect and value Christian womanhood. Catholic writers also held that Protestant laws had tried to break apart Catholic families during the penal days and were still separating children from the faith of their parents; such a people could have no respect for domestic ties. Lastly, British Protestant culture was regarded as arid, secular, and immoral.

Catholic authors presented Marian devotion as an indication of the high regard Catholicism had for women "The Church, which alone assigns to the Blessed Virgin her proper place in the hearts of men, and in the heart of her Son and her God, has done most of all to elevate with Mary all the daughters of Mary."[137] Protestantism, by contrast, was made to seem less understanding of the "true nature" of Mary and her earthly daughters. A young, motherless Irish girl who was being raised as a Protestant by her father was quoted as saying, "I shall become a Catholic, for I want to belong to that Church which makes me honour the Blessed Virgin and pray for the soul of my own mother who is dead."[138] Catholicism is presented as the religion that values true feeling, the Virgin Mary, and earthly mothers "I should not embrace Protestantism whose harshness dries up the soul, the heart, and the conscience ... I would return and throw myself on my knees before the Holy Virgin."[139]

The evangelical Protestant literature I have examined is hardly harsh and unemotional when it comes to the subject of women. Rather it embarked on many romantic flights of fancy in its description of a mother's love. The domestic realm was held to be sacred in both the Catholic and Protestant literatures. Protestants condemned Catholicism because Catholic institutions such as the convent and the confessional were said to sever the "tenderest ties" between Catholic family members. Ulster evangelical Protestants wrote with dread of the spread of "Romanism"[140] and its "unnatural" doctrines concerning women and the family, yet their writings were primarily a criticism of what they believed Catholicism did to its own members, how it supposedly denigrated domesticity amongst its own. Catholic censure of Protestant anti-family activities was, however, based on criticism of what Protestants were accused of doing to Catholics. Catholics did not charge Protestant practice with tearing apart family ties within Protestant congregations; rather, they assailed Protestantism as having no family feeling because of the way it allegedly treated Catholic families.

The penal laws were presented as evidence of this Protestant tendency to be anti-family because they "sought to make the fourth commandment a dead letter by encouraging disobedience to parental authority, and rewarding rebellion with privilege and wealth. The code supplemented this attempt to set children against their parents, by endeavouring to disturb the relations between husband and wife ... Disruption of the strong and tender bond that held the Irish household as a Christian family was not to be affected by royal proclamation or parliamentary decree."[141] The unspoken question in this passage is whether a people whose legislators so callously tried to disrupt the "strong and tender bond" of a Christian family could have any real appreciation of domestic ties. The prospect of Irish Catholic children losing "the faith of their fathers" in state-run workhouses and orphanages featured prominently in the Catholic literature. In "The Workhouse Children: A True Tale," the author cites the dying words of a widowed mother to her concerned priest. She fears that her children will be forced to be Protestants by the guardians of the workhouse, as the child of a friend of hers had. " ... the poor little boy, he cried so! and said they beat him if he made the sign of the cross or said his own prayers."[142] At that, her own son exclaimed, "I would be beaten to death sooner than give up being a Catholic, mother!"[143]

The Protestantism that would thus come between the shared faith of mother and child is presented as a monstrous thing. In an article on St Brigid's Orphanage in Dublin, written by Father Matthew Russell, S.J., editor of *The Irish Monthly*, the issue of Catholic orphans being "lost" to the Church through public institutions of the state was again raised. The vehemence of Russell's polemic against Protestant institutions is captured in the following passage. "And what of the fledglings that the vultures have torn from the mother's nest? ... How dare they try to rob the poor Irish children of their only treasure, the Faith? What religion do they pretend to offer in exchange? ... can they have the cruelty, the cowardly wickedness, to steal these innocent babes from the embrace of that one only Church which bears the marks and tokens of God's Church?"[144] According to Russell the Protestant "vultures" were doubly cruel, for they tried to break the sacred bond of faith between deceased parents and orphan children and because they tried to take Irish Catholic children away from "this Mother of souls [who] clasps these orphans to her heart."[145]

Finally, Catholic writers decried what they saw as the pernicious influence of modern, English Protestant ideas on Irish Catholic families. Be it through the penny press, theatres, picture palaces, or other avenues of amusement, "Anglo-Saxonisms" were insidiously creeping in to erode the "hearth-side values" of the Catholic Celt.[146] Ironically, evangelical Protestant periodicals of the period were replete with articles and stories about the dangers of all modern "godless" amusements. Protestant women were urged to make their homes cheery and bright in order to keep their children and menfolk from straying into sin via these modern entertainments.[147] Although both groups cherished traditional domestic values, Catholic authors saw the source of the "poisonous tide"[148] as being a godless, secularizing, Protestant England.

Mary Butler's "A Medieval Modern" relates the tragic fate of a Catholic home broken up by the influence of "modern" and "fashionable" non-Catholic influences. By the end of the story, the contrast between the happy life of the traditional and pious Desiree, and the tragic fates of her two "modern" cousins forms a cogent critique of what Catholic writers saw as the anti-family nature of English Protestant culture.[149] One cousin, the suffragette Gladys, is in jail and the other cousin, Muriel, has met an even worse fate. She has gone into debt through gambling and agreed to marry her Protestant bookie at a registry office in order to clear her debt. Aunt Caroline bitterly tells Desiree and her mother that Muriel is now "... beyond the pale – not only a social but a moral outcast." She shuddered – 'Married at a Registry office: the descendant of one of the oldest Catholic families in the country! And now the poorest Catholic woman in the land will pull her skirts aside as she passes – the woman who has disowned her God, deserted her Church, disgraced her family.'"[150] Again we see the description of an immoral, anti-family, English Protestantism perverting the sacred domestic realm.

Despite the various charges lodged against them by their sectarian opponents, Roman Catholics and Protestants held very similar ideals of Christian womanhood and domestic piety. Moreover, both groups presented women's influence within the home as being of crucial significance to the defence and progress of their respective communities. Perhaps it was the very emotional heat surrounding the issues of female virtue and domesticity and their great significance to the ideologies of both groups that caused each to project a warped image of their perceived enemy. Despite a similar understanding of the value of the Blessed Virgin Mary as a model for Christian women, she too was the focus of Protestant and Catholic controversy.

3 The Virgin Mary: Model of Christian Female Spirituality

The Virgin Mary was held up as the ideal woman in both the Roman Catholic and various Protestant traditions. That this should be the case for the former is a matter of no great surprise, but that she should have been so honoured by the latter might perhaps be seen as at odds with stated Ulster Protestant beliefs.

The way in which the Virgin Mary was presented as a model for Christian womanhood differed between Protestants and Catholics. Catholic women, particularly those who attended convent schools, were exposed to images of the Blessed Virgin Mary and to rituals centred on her cult. In keeping with the traditions of the Roman Catholic Church, the Virgin Mary was presented in Catholic devotional literature and in Catholic periodicals as the venerable "Queen of Heaven" and as the humble "maid of Nazareth." Although the former description, which sent Protestant polemicists into paroxysms of indignation, was central to Mariology,[1] its role in the construction of Catholic lay female piety is negligible. While Catholic writers averred that the honour the Church paid to the Blessed Virgin Mary resulted in Catholics having a greater respect for womankind than non-Catholics, the actual prescriptive role that Mary played in the Catholic literature was based on her humble motherliness, not on her awesome power as Queen of the Universe. In the latter role she was "alone of all her sex" in her elevation to the status of divine co-redemptress and mediatrix of grace. These quasi-divine aspects of Mary – particularly her sinlessness – could not have any prescriptive value among the "fallen daughters of Eve." Thus it was in her persona as the humble maid-servant that Mary provided a paradigm for female virtue. She was presented as the ideal woman: loving, obedient, selfless, and kind. Female Catholic writers celebrated the beauty of her life in poems, dramas, and prayers. Moreover, they sounded a clarion call to Catholic women to imitate her holy life. As part of their personal piety, Catholic women were urged to seek Mary's guidance and intercession.

Protestant women were not urged to do likewise. "Mariolatry" was denigrated in no uncertain terms by Irish evangelical Protestants. They thought that Catholic titles such as "Mother of God" were blasphemous. To give a mere human woman such a lofty title was to displace the Trinity from the centre of Christian worship. But Protestants did not restrict their involvement with Mary to the debunking of her Catholic cult. Rather, they carefully, almost reluctantly, "reclaimed" her as an important role model – and nothing more – for Protestant women.

Clearly, Mary figured much more prominently in Catholic literature than in Protestant. Among those few articles in Ulster Protestant periodicals which took the Virgin Mary as their subject, most castigated what the authors saw as Mariolatry, while a few stressed her importance as a role model for Christian women. Those Protestant authors who did praise the Virgin Mary for her humble and obedient "womanliness" had to navigate the minefield of sectarian controversy. They took great pains to point out that their praise of Mary in no way meant that they condoned the Catholic cult of Mary. Other biblical women, especially Mary and Martha, the sisters of Lazarus, received far more attention in the Protestant literature than the Virgin Mary did, probably because they were less controversial figures.

What I think is most important here is not these seemingly incontrovertible differences between Protestant and Catholic methods of presenting Mary as a model of female spirituality. The core message sent to Ulster women, Catholic and Protestant, is fundamentally the same. The model Mary provides in both her Protestant and Catholic incarnations is one of submission and sacrifice. Thus this paradigm fits seamlessly into the existing discourse on domestic ideology, on both sides of the religious divide.

MARY THE QUEEN, AND MARY THE MOTHER

In the Catholic Church in Ireland and elsewhere the nineteenth century was the century of Mary. The dogma of the Virgin Mary's Immaculate Conception[2] was promulgated by Pope Pius IX in 1854.[3] The Popes of the nineteenth century were devout Marians, especially Leo XIII (1878–1903), who was known as the "Pope of the Rosary."

The Marian temper of Catholicism in the late nineteenth century is clearly made manifest in the Irish Catholic literature of the period. Peter O'Dwyer's *Mary: A History of Devotion in Ireland* describes the particular devotion of Irish Catholics to the Marian cult and the popularity of the doctrine of the Immaculate Conception among them.[4] O'Dwyer also discusses the profound impact on the spread of Marian devotion in Ireland of the apparition of the Virigin Mary at Knock, Co. Mayo on 21 August 1879.[5] The founder and editor from 1873–1912 of the popular Catholic periodical *The Irish Monthly*, Father Matthew Russell, S.J. was an enthusiastic Marian. His devotion to the Blessed Virgin Mary is reflected in his own poems in *The Irish Monthly* and in the books of devotional poetry that he published. In "Maria Sine Labe Concepta" Russell outlines the basis for the doctrine of the Immaculate Conception. In this poem the dual nature of Mary as sinless Queen of Heaven and as loving mother is presented.

> Immaculate! Immaculate!
> All sinless, spotless, pure and fair!
> And yet these sinful hearts of ours
> To love that sinless Heart must dare.
> For God, who kept that Heart all pure,
> And filled it with each richest grace,
> Has filled it, too, with mother's love
> For every child of Adam's race.
>
> O Mother, canst thou love ev'n *me?*
> Thou canst! From heaven thy smile doth fall
> On all for whom thy Jesus died —
> And Jesus died for me, for all.
> Sweet Mother, bless me through the days
> That I on earth must work and wait,
> Until in heaven I greet heaven's Queen,
> Immaculate! Immaculate![6]

All of her titles[7] and graces do not make Mary a remote figure in this poem. In no way does her role as "heaven's Queen" impede her role as mother to "every child of Adam's race." Her awesome ability to command the hosts of heaven might make Mary seem like a daunting figure –

> Lo! where wave the countless wings
> Circling Mary's throne in heaven

> Forth an angel darts, and kneels
> To the mandate by her given:[8]

were it not for her motherliness –

> Have pity on my sinful state,
> O Virgin Queen Immaculate!
> From thy celestial Throne above
> Smile down with mother's yearning love;
> And, bidding guilt and fear depart,
> Take me, O Mary, to thy heart.[9]

Thus magisterial authority and motherly love are combined in this Roman Catholic view of the Blessed Virgin Mary. As was discussed in the previous chapter, the ideal of motherhood and the concomitant emphasis on a mother's influence and power resonated deeply in Ulster religious literature. There is a potent combination in Mary's dual role as Queen of Heaven and as Mother to each individual devotee. The Queen without the Mother would offer little comfort to the Catholic faithful, for why would one whose life was perfect and blameless – "O sinless heart! O Stainless heart!"[10] – wish to consort with wretched humanity? Yet Mary as Mother without her queenship would not command the influence with her son and over creation that was integral to the Marian cult. Thus, in concert, the facets of Mary as the Queen and as the Mother comfort and provide assistance for her devout followers. In *The Two Mothers: A Contrast*,[11] this duality is vividly captured. Mary's cooperation in the Divine plan – "that light of our salvation, purchased for us by her generous sacrifice of her Son" – gives her a very special status. "She is no longer a mere gladsome mother rejoicing over her first-born, nor even the mother of our God dazzling us with her dignity; she is the mother of our Redeemer, she is our own Mother, loving us so 'as to give for us her only begotten Son,' after the example and with a charity like that of our Heavenly Father."[12] Mary the Queen and the Mother chooses sacrifice, the loss of her beloved son Jesus Christ, because of her love for her human "children."

Mary the "Queen of Heaven" was frequently praised by Catholic authors for her role as the second, better, Eve. An anonymous author in *The Irish Rosary* honoured the Virgin Mary with the following tribute: "Greater than Eve – the mother of our nature – our spiritual mother has vindicated our race in her immaculate person, and we hail her as the glory of the human family, as 'our tainted nature's solitary boast.'"[13] According to Marian doctrine, Mary's own work as co-redemptress with Christ afforded her access to heaven's highest realms. It is interesting to note that Protestant criticism of Mariology was inconsistent on this matter of the "second Eve." In his polemical anti-Catholic work *Rome and the Gospel*, the Reverend James Morgan attacks the queenship of Mary, stating that "the crowning idolatry is the reverence and direct worship addressed to Mary. She is styled, 'Mother of God, queen of seraphim, refuge of sinners, gate of heaven, morning star, queen of heaven, most faithful, most merciful.' The attributes and works of the Most High are directly ascribed to her."[14] Moreover, he complains that Roman Catholic "divines were now teaching that as a woman brought in death, so a woman was to bring in life; that as a woman brought in sin, so a woman was to bring in holiness; that as Eve brought in damnation, so Mary was to bring in salvation; and that the effect of this opinion was largely to increase the reverence and worship given to the Virgin Mary."[15] Ordinarily, Protestant polemics against Marian doctrine contained this type of criticism, decrying a major role for Mary in the drama of salvation. Oddly enough, however, in *The Three Marys of the Four Gospels*, an anti-Catholic attack throughout, the idea of Mary as the "new Eve" receives hearty approval. The author, the Reverend John Bryson, notes that a woman's role in the redemption of the world reveals "a peculiar meetness in this pleasing arrangement of a gracious Providence."[16] For Bryson, there was a "meet" element of "moral restitution" in Mary as the "new Eve," for if woman was "At first the instrument of the ruin of the human race, she is afterwards selected as the instrument of human redemption. At one time, the medium of the temptation of Satan; at another time, the medium of the mission of the Saviour; now, the channel of the enmity of hell; anon, the exalted and chosen receptacle of the grace of heaven; in the beginning of the first dispensation, the occasion to our species of death; at the commencement of the second the occasion of life even life everlasting."[17] While it appears curious that such a staunch anti-Catholic writer as Bryson could commend so highly Mary's role in salvation, the rest of his book provides an explanation for his attitude here. He spends most of *The Three Marys of the Four Gospels* attacking Catholic theology and practice, so if he has glorified Mary at all in the above-quoted passage it was entirely unintentional. Rather his focus seems to be on the "fitting" nature of Providence choosing a woman to rectify what another woman had ruined. At work here is misogyny, not "Mariolatry." While he was certainly no Mariologist this degree of concord between Bryson's view and those of Catholic writers on the subject of the "new Eve" indicates that common ground existed on the matter of women as agents of redemption. As was mentioned in the previous chapter, both Catholics and Protestants held that godly women had a redemptive influence. Thus we see a poet in a Methodist journal praising the "true wife" by declaring "If woman lost us Eden, such/As she alone can restore it."[18] Clearly, Ulster evangelical Protestants were aghast at what they considered the "excesses" of the Marian cult, such as the Queenship of Mary, yet this did not mean that even with regard to the Virgin Mary they could not share the view with their Catholic brethren that women were agents of redemption.

While I do not wish to underplay the significance placed by Catholic writers on Mary's role as "Queen of Heaven," it is the motherliness of Mary that provides the greatest insight into female devotion to Mary. Her motherhood, divine and human, is the aspect of her personality which predominates in the religious literature. Her compassion and pity, her inability to refuse the pleadings of her "children," make her a compelling subject of love and veneration. Great comfort was to be found in her mother love.

In Catholic short stories, the characters looked upon Mary as their true mother who cared for them and helped them withstand hardship. In one such tale, Ailie, a poor Scottish orphan of Irish parentage, was persecuted by her Protestant caretakers and peers for her staunch Catholicism. When some Catholic laywomen inquired of the child what she knew of her faith they determined that Ailie was aware that "she was a Catholic, her faith different from the faith of those around her, her lot apart from theirs, that somewhere she had a mother, the 'Mother of God,' who cared for and protected her, these things she knew."[19] It was not as the awesome Queen of Heaven that simple folk characters knew Mary; they knew her as a loving mother, modelled along similar lines to the ideal earthly mother. It was to Mary as the loving mother that these characters addressed their petitions and concerns. "The Month of Mary" tells the story of a young Catholic girl who, against her parents' wishes, married a Protestant and ran away to a distant village. Her vile husband drank and beat her and the only good to come of their short union – happily he died soon after the marriage – was the birth of their daughter, Marie. Marie was dressed in white and dedicated "to the purity of the Mother of God." The author informs the reader that "Our good Mother in heaven is so ready to hear all who earnestly implore her assistance, that it is no wonder that little Marie, at the age of six was more like an angel than a mortal child."[20] The Virgin Mary has power to assist her devotees, yet it is her motherly love that impels her to do so.

> Mother of pity and grace thou art,
> So let the pity of thy heart

Go out for one who suffered much,
And show thyself the Mother. ...[21]

In devotional poems and prayers, it is the motherly side of Mary's personality that is appealed to by her weak and struggling daughters.

O my Mother, fair exceeding,
With the lovely smile august,
And the true lips, ever pleading
For the holy things and just,
To thy little one's great needing
Thou hast bent thy gracious heeding ...[22]

As the perfect mother Mary comforts the distressed and heeds the call of her own. While this representation of the Blessed Virgin Mary was no doubt very attractive to her male followers such as Father Russell, her motherliness made her highly appealing to women, for it was thought that she empathised with the pain and suffering of earthly women, particularly mothers.

In "A Mother's Lament" the author, a mother grieving after the death of her son, urges other grieving mothers to seek comfort in their mother, Mary. To those mothers who feel they should have done more for their children, the author reassuringly says that while God gave children human and imperfect mothers, he gave everyone the gift of the perfect mother, Mary. "Go to Our Lady. She / Has been, and is, a perfect mother. She / Alone can fully understand your grief."[23] Female Catholic writers focused on this unique bond of understanding between Mary and human mothers. Mary alone, not the remote God the Father or even the Holy Ghost the comforter, could understand a bereaved mother's grief. Magdalen Rock writes, "The Mother of Sorrows is the Consoler of the Afflicted; and among all the afflicted surely poor human mothers have a special claim to be comforted by Her who stood beside the Cross of her Son."[24] Thus Mary's own suffering as a mother makes her sympathetic to the sorrows of other earthly mothers.

And that Mother-Queen in Heaven
In her bliss remembers still
Fear and dread and dolours seven,
Calvary's steep and blood-stained hill.
Grief, through her, is changed to gladness,
Joy, through her, succeeds to woe:
She whose heart knew bitter sadness
Comforts all who to her go.[25]

Though she is still the "Queen of Heaven," Mary is an approachable figure because of her own sacrifice and sorrow. While Mary was presented as the spiritual mother of all the faithful, Catholic writers paid particular attention to the bond between Mary and her female devotees. In her *Miracle Plays*, popular Irish author Katherine Tynan includes a prayer in which the Virgin Mary is exhorted to assist her earthly daughters: "*Maid and mother, turn with speed/ To all women in their need.*"[26] Throughout the *Miracle Plays*, Mary is shown kindly aiding the women she encounters. Her tenderness and her devotion to suffering women[27] in these plays highlight Mary's special relationship with women and the significance of her own motherhood.[28]

Much has been written in the late twentieth century on the subject of Mary as the feminine aspect of the divine.[29] While those who wrote for Irish Catholic periodicals did not explicitly state that Mary was the feminine side of God – this would have given far too much fuel to their Protestant critics who already accused them of treating Mary as a goddess – she was presented as an approachable, motherly, heavenly persona, one to whom women in particular were encouraged to appeal. The following poem aptly illustrates the connection that women felt to the "Blessed Virgin."

> More than mortal help I need,
> More than mortal pity;
> Yet I fear to pray to God
> In His starry city.
>
> I would have a woman's help,
> Know a woman's pity.
> Is there none to hear my prayer
> In God's starry city?
> Women would to women pray
> In the hour of pity.[30]

Mary was a woman whom Catholic women petitioned for assistance. This powerful "Queen of Heaven" interceded with Christ on behalf of her supplicants whom she was thought to love in a motherly way. During our examination of domestic ideology we found that in Ulster religious literature, a mother's love was considered second only to the love of God in its enduring strength and in its redemptive power. For Roman Catholics, Mary was the quintessential mother. Her motherly love and compassion were celebrated in poetry and prose. Yet did Mary's vaunted status as "Queen of Heaven" in her Catholic cult cause the Roman Catholic ideal of Christian womanhood to diverge

significantly from its Protestant counterpart? In other words, did the
fact of "Mary the Mother of God" also provide a model of female
power and authority for Ulster Catholic women? To what prescriptive
use was Mary put in both Catholic and Protestant religious literature?

THE VIRGIN MARY AS THE IDEAL
CHRISTIAN WOMAN

Although, in her Catholic version, Mary the mother of Jesus was both
the "Immaculate Queen" and the humble "Maid of Nazareth," it is
only the latter aspect of her personality that has prescriptive value. For,
Mary's status as "Queen of Heaven" derived from her perfect sinlessness. Given that she was truly "alone of all her sex," her earthly daughters, who were also daughters of the sinful, first mother Eve, could not
aspire to Mary's lofty position.[31] Accordingly, it was only from the humble, loving, self-sacrificing, motherly aspect of Mary's nature that an
example for Christian womanhood could be taken. This portrait of
Mary as the ideal woman and mother was very similar in both Protestant and Catholic religious literature. Here was common ground
where both Catholics and Protestants could find ideal qualities to
inform their construction of the ideal Christian woman. As the theologian Stephen Benko has observed, "... it is a common homiletic
device, even among Protestants, to refer to Mary as the paragon of wife
and mother."[32]

In her biography of Mary Xaveria Fallon, the Foundress of the Institute of the Blessed Virgin in Ireland, Katherine Tynan describes the
importance of Mary as a model of Catholic womanhood. "Mary,
Mother of God, is the ideal set before all Catholic women. From their
childhood they are taught to weigh their actions by her modesty and
humility and patience. She pleased God so perfectly as to be chosen
for the highest office He ever conferred upon a human creature.
Being human, though dowered with unspeakable graces, she is not so
out of sight that one may not, as a pool mirrors a star, try to imitate her.
So it is that some of her loveliness descends upon her copyists."[33]
Catholic women were directed to imitate Mary's humbleness and
selflessness; these pools could only mirror the quintessentially
feminine and submissive aspects of the Divine Mother. Tynan notes
that the young Irish girls who were Children of Mary[34] were presented
each day in their May devotions with "a new virtue of the ideal woman,
the Mother of God, to be reflected upon."[35] The Virgin Mary's virtues
were those of the ideal Christian woman already discussed in the
previous chapter, with perhaps added emphasis on humility and
obedience. In "The Virgin Mother," Mary is depicted as a "young active

and industrious housewife"[36] who exercises the ideal woman's right to "labour, love, and pray." Despite the time-consuming labour involved in lovingly looking to her household affairs, Mary also "could find time for prayer, time for the reading of the sacred books."[37] She was a model Christian wife indeed, for her "whole conversation was in heaven" and to her "might be applied these beautiful and sage words of the Psalmist: 'All the glory of the king's daughter is within the interior of her house.'"[38] Mary of Nazareth was presented as a veritable paragon of domestic womanhood, notwithstanding her eschatological part in the redemption of humankind. Although Catholics hailed her as the immaculate Mother of God, they also painted portraits of Mary as an ideal wife and mother.[39]

But it was Mary's unique role in human salvation, her humility and obedience to God's plan, that makes her the perfect role model of femininity. In her play "*The Annunciation*," Katherine Tynan portrays Mary as the "spotless lily" going about her duties at home, praying for the coming of the Messiah, and daydreaming about somehow assisting the mother of the Christ: "I would I might be hand-maiden / Unto His mother. Blessed then / To sweep and cleanse of soil and stain / The house for that fair Boy."[40] The humble Mary in Tynan's play could not even imagine that she could be worthy to be the mother of the Messiah; rather her greatest hope was to be a helper: "Perchance, His mother would Him lay / Once in mine arms, on some sweet day / When she was sudden called away. / Then should I die of joy."[41] Such humility was chief among Mary's virtues according to the writers of Catholic religious literature. In the Marian poem "Her Darling Virtue," the poet asserts that "to Mary's heart" her humility was even more important than her virginity.

> Yet was there still a virtue that had place
> In her blest thoughts, before virginity –
> The safeguard of all virtues and their base,
> Best-lov'd of God and heav'n – HUMILITY![42]

The poet continues in this vein by adding that even when Joseph doubted Mary's purity she did not tell him of the "mystery divine that in her dwelt" for "The Maid was mute: too humble to explain" and thus "Silent, she hid her glory from his ken; Sinless, she bore the stigma scorned of men."[43] Mary's persistent humility, despite her great glory as the immaculate Mother of God, makes her an ideal woman. She did not clamour for acknowledgement or acclaim. She was content to do her part, to use her influence in a supporting, background role. The emphasis of the cult of domesticity on the powerful "silent influence" of Christian women for good makes the humble Mary the most worthy of women. The accolade "Blessed above all women, unblessed, unprized, unknown;/Obscurity and silence far more than royal throne,"[44] encapsulates the praiseworthiness of Mary's truly "feminine" humility.

The Virgin Mary's obedience is another of her defining characteristics and one which Catholic women were urged to emulate. Praise of Mary's total obedience tends to focus, naturally, on the Annunciation and her ready agreement to participate in God's plan of redemption. Attie O'Brien's "A Rosary of Sonnets" describes Mary's obedience at the Annunciation.

> The Angel speaks. The maiden trembling hears
> Of her great part in the eternal scheme,
> And, when allayed are virginal faint fears,
> Her aid she gives the lost earth to redeem.
> 'Behold his handmaid!' In the Virgin's breast
> God is incarnate – and the world is blest.[45]

Mary overcomes her weakness and her fear and obediently acquiesces to God's will for her. In somewhat more fanciful language, Katherine Tynan also described the fateful moment when Mary gives her assent to the angel.

> GABRIEL
> His Power and Kingdom shall not end.
> Power of the Highest shall descend,
> The holy Ghost shall hover and bend
>   Above thee, blessed maid.
>
> MARY
> Behold the handmaid of the Lord!
> Be it according to His Word.
> Now come, Thou great and golden Bird!
>   No more am I afraid.[46]

In Tynan's prose Mary's obedience is joyfully given; Mary embarks on this unknown path with simple faith and trust in her God. Later on in her life, after much sorrow and hardship, Mary's obedience and patient acceptance of God's will are described as constant and true. In O'Brien's sonnet "The Resurrection," the bereaved Virgin Mary remains obedient to God's will even though it means the loss of her son. "The childless Mother kneels within her room / Serene and patient, though she ever sees / The dear dead face that lay upon her knees."[47] As the perfect example of female obedience, Mary does not rail against the plan of her creator; with serenity and patience she forbears. Her earthly daughters were urged to imitate her holy example and do likewise. For Catholics, Mary was the personification of the feminine ideal.

But this "feminine face of the divine," though exercising enormous power in heaven, was not a model for female empowerment. The Virgin Mary's attraction for Catholic women lay in her tender sympathy and her understanding of their earthly condition. By following her example of obedience and humility, they could become ideal Christian women and look forward to the world to come; but this interpretation of Mary's life did not provide a model for empowerment in this world. Marina Warner observes that Mary's virtues should not be scorned in themselves, yet "the type of virtues decreed feminine degenerate easily: obedience becomes docility; gentleness, irresolution; humility, cringing; forbearance, long-suffering."[48] The Irish Catholic use of Mary as a prescriptive model of feminine virtue is clear, then, but what of the Protestants?

THE VIRGIN MARY IN
ULSTER PROTESTANT DISCOURSE

Protestant homiletics in which Mary the mother of Jesus was depicted as the ideal Christian woman had to maintain a delicate balance lest praise of the Virgin Mary might "smack of Popery." Mary's virtues and honours were always carefully qualified whenever she was mentioned. The life of the Virgin Mary as depicted in the New Testament,[49] her domesticity and perfectly feminine submission and humility made her a logical member of the pantheon of ideal Christian women who were used as models of domestic piety.

The problematic nature of discussing the Virgin Mary in evangelical Protestant circles was commented upon by the Reverend Arthur Mursell, an Ulster Presbyterian minister. In his sermon "Mary, the Mother of Jesus," Mursell suggests that "We have such a wholesome horror of falling into the great error of rendering worship to Mary, that we fall into the lesser mistake of withholding from her any honour or notice at all."[50] Reading through Protestant publications such as *The Irish Presbyterian*, *The Christian Advocate*, and *The Church of Ireland Parochial Magazine* bears out this assertion. Scant direct attention was paid to the Virgin Mary while other biblical women, some of them remarkably obscure, were put to prescriptive use. Mursell decided to proceed in these roiled waters, all the while keenly aware of the invisible line of "Mariolatry" that must not be approached, let alone breached. Given that no less than "angelic lips" declared to Mary, "Blessed art thou among women,"[51] Mursell assures his audience that "surely it becomes us to regard Mary, as she is represented to us, as specially 'blessed'; ... But while this deference is claimed from us, we must not violate the claims of truth in recognising the claims of Mary."[52] Thus even while arguing in favour of regarding Mary as specially blessed of God and worthy of our affection, Mursell again retreats and carefully establishes his evangelical Protestant orthodoxy. In broaching the subject of the Virgin Mary, Mursell expresses his concern over the paucity of biblical information on her life and the pitfall of excessive use of the powers of imagination. In his lengthy and creative description of the life of the "blushing peasant girl" from Nazareth, Mursell admits that "It is hard to refrain from letting fancy fill up the outline"[53] given the lack of detail in the biblical texts. This troublesome matter did not prevent Mursell from embellishing the dry summary of Mary's life that is provided in holy writ.

It was, however, a sticking point for other Ulster Protestant writers. Bryson's *The Three Marys of the Four Gospels* takes a decidedly terse, biblicist approach to the life of the mother of Jesus. In fact, in his chapter on the Virgin Mary, titled "The Blessed Among Women," Bryson almost entirely managed to avoid mentioning Mary per se. After briefly praising the Virgin Mary for meriting divine favour, he proceeds to spend the larger part of the chapter fulminating against the Roman Catholic doctrine of the Immaculate Conception and its perpetuation of "idolatry."[54] Mary's own life and actions do not figure largely in the discussion.[55] To Bryson, this is as it should be, for "Very brief is the Scripture history of the mother of Jesus. Imagination, being fostered by superstition, has largely supplied the supposed deficiency of the sacred narrative ... No doubt, in this limitation of the revealed history of the virgin, the foreknowledge of the Spirit had in view the diminution of every vestige of material which folly or wickedness might possibly work up into the idol Maryolatry."[56] Thus a reason is supplied for the scantiness of the biblical record with regard to the Virgin Mary's life: the desire of God to thwart idolatrous tendencies. Nevertheless a few Protestant writers, such as Mursell, were willing, in this period of romantic and melodramatic Victorian prose, to embellish somewhat for the sake of edification.

Like Catholic writers, Protestants chose to highlight Mary's obedience and humility. She was also portrayed as a paragon of domesticity and womanliness – she was the archetype of the woman who "laboured, loved and prayed."

Just as Katherine Tynan and Attie O'Brien described Mary's obedience at the Annunciation as evidence of her great virtue, Mursell writes glowingly of Mary's willingness to be used of God. "She has just the presence of mind to falter out the question 'How shall this thing be?' But immediately she feels that submission becomes her better than enquiry, and she meekly acquiesces in the communication 'Behold the handmaid of the Lord; be it unto me according to Thy word.'"[57] Submission and acquiescence are considered no less "becoming" womanly virtues by this Protestant writer than they were by Catholics. The Anglican Reverend. T.A. Gurney, praised the mother of Jesus for her obedient service at the wedding of Cana "where *a woman's readiness unlocked the fulness* [sic] *of Christ.*"[58] During this crisis, "obedient, ready faith was wanted, and this Mary, the Mother of Jesus, supplied 'Whatsoever He saith unto you, do it.'"[59] Gurney urges the readers of *India's Women*, a Church of England women's missionary magazine, to, like Mary, be "ready whatsoever the Lord, our King, doth appoint. As the eyes of a handmaiden are toward the hand of her mistress (Psalm 123:2), so our eyes are to wait upon the will of Him in Whom all fullness dwells."[60] The Virgin Mary's obedience to her Lord was something that could be endorsed as eminently worthy of imitation by Protestant women.

The Virgin Mary's humility was also applauded in Protestant publications. Again, praise of Mary was carefully measured and restricted to literal interpretations of the biblical texts concerning her. The author of a series on "The Women Workers of the Bible," the Reverend J.E. Sampson, tentatively declares that "Mary, though more blessed than any woman, – no, I will not say so, for the Lord rebukes the saying, for He has declared that 'rather blessed are they that hear the word of God, and do it' – Mary did not come to be in the front. Is not such humility an important element in real work for God? I think so."[61] In case the prescriptive message aimed at female lay workers was unclear, Sampson says, "I think [Mary] is a fair type of many quiet workers even now. The work of women for the Lord must necessarily be quiet. It is more the *influence* than the *effort* of their lives."[62] Mary's quiet humility and circumspection are presented to the female readers of *India's Women* as being worthy of imitation. The author suggests that "if we had known what she knew, I am afraid we should have proclaimed it upon the house-tops – *she* 'kept all these things and pondered them in her heart.'"[63] Mary's humble acceptance of God's will for her life and her willingness to remain quietly in the background of events made her an ideal model for Christian behaviour within this conservative discourse of middle-class female propriety.

Finally, in a more general sense, the Virgin Mary was portrayed as a model of domestic virtue. The message of the cult of domesticity comes through with considerable forcefulness in Protestant descriptions of the maid of Nazareth. In speaking of "women workers," among whose number the Virgin Mary was included, Sampson notes that "Home is their sphere, or rather their centre, the point from which there radiate many holy, powerful influences for God."[64] Protestant women are advised, like the "mother of our Lord," to work for God in a quiet and unassuming manner for "the mightiest work of God is the still, unseen, untraceable operation of the Holy Spirit ... It is therefore no disparagement of work when we speak of it as still, quiet, unrecorded often."[65] Sampson paints a tender, homely, and decidedly idealized portrait of the social intercourse between the "venerable Elisabeth" who was "righteous before God" and her gentle, young cousin, Mary. These women did not indulge in idle chatter; rather their talk at the hearthside was of the glory of God as Mary "so quietly and meekly, said, 'My soul doth magnify the Lord, and my spirit hath rejoiced in God my Saviour.'"[66] The home where Mary and her kinswoman dwelt was a sanctified, holy place. Clearly, this little vignette of domestic piety was held up as an example for the female readers of this Anglican magazine.

The Virgin Mary was described by Mursell in his sermon "Mary, the Mother of Jesus" as that most cherished of creatures in Victorian religious literature: the "true woman."[67] Mursell's enthusiasm is palpable in his description of Mary's womanliness "Every reference that is made to her, all the details given of her life, concur to write this fair word, woman, in its fairest syllables across her memory. There is no coarse, broad, masculine line drawn on her character. Not a speechifying woman; not a woman who would want a vote or a seat in Parliament."[68] Mary is a truly domestic, feminine woman. Mursell seems eager to reclaim her, to use this most feminine of biblical women in the task of constructing the ideal contemporary Christian woman. From brief biblical passages, he derives this almost breathless interpretation of Mary's actions. "How feminine and womanly was the way she talked with the angel and with Christ, and how beautifully coy was the manner in which she received the first annunciation of the honour which was to be put upon her. Feminine simplicity, strength of mind, and gentle submission, breathe through the entire narrative."[69] While disappointed with the lack of detail in scripture concerning Mary, Mursell still believes that there is sufficient material from which to render the following glowing assessment of Christ's mother: "the portrait, or rather the outline sketch, which we have of Mary, on the page of the gospels, presents to us a woman."[70] For such an enthusiastic member of the cult of true womanhood as Mursell evidently was, this is no mean accolade. As if fearing he had gone too far in his praise, the minister continues: "It (the biblical portrait of Mary) paints no halo of ethereal glory round the brow; it tints the nature with nothing *super*-natural. It only gives it as much of the colouring of divinity as God has flung into the one word, *woman*."[71] Mursell ends his sermon with a call to the female members of his congregation to imitate Mary's prayerful faith in her God: "Of the woman whose trust is thus filled and made secure, it may be said, indeed, 'God shall help her, and that right early.'"[72] This is a promise, then, from holy scripture, that a woman who is faithful in like manner as Mary will receive her maker's help.

MUTUAL INCOMPREHENSION

Mursell's sermon "Mary, the Mother of Jesus" was not typical of writings concerning Mary in Ulster evangelical Protestant literature. Rather, when Mary was mentioned at all it tended to be in connection with Protestant diatribes against the "latest extravagances of Romanism."[73] Yet Mursell's descriptions, though too fanciful for sterner divines, did not fall outside of evangelical Protestant gender orthodoxy. He sums up what was, in his eyes, the crucial difference "In the Church of Rome Mary appears as a goddess; in the Church of Christ she is merely hailed as a godly woman."[74] Without disputing the quasi-divine status the Blessed Virgin Mary attained during the reigns of the Marian popes of the late nineteenth century, I would venture to assert that the "goddess" features of her cult during this period in no way detracted from her prescriptive value as "a godly woman" in Irish Catholic discourse. Rather, because of her ready acceptance in Roman Catholic circles, the homiletic use of Mary as a paragon of female virtue was more tenable than it was among Ulster Protestants, to whom the very name "the Virgin Mary" brought uncomfortable associations with Catholic practice. Because of Mariology, Ulster Protestants could scarcely mention the name of the Virgin Mary without qualifications and riders.

While Protestants found Catholic Marian devotion unfathomable, Catholics found Protestant disdain for Mary equally perplexing. Without entering into the doctrinal fine points of this debate, suffice it to say that when Irish Protestants and Catholics referred to Mary of Nazareth they thought their own religious group was the only one to represent this "godly woman" accurately. For example, Catholics complained that Protestants did not understand the distinction Catholicism made between the *latria* (adoration) owed to God and the *hyperdulia* (special veneration) owed to Mary, while Protestants could not

see how Catholics could say that the infinite God the Father who had
always existed could have a mother.[75] Roman Catholics felt confused
and slighted at the lack of understanding of those outside their rite.
Note the puzzled and annoyed tone in the following passage from
The Irish Rosary "It is a singular phenomenon to find those who profess
to love our Lord, and who would have us believe in the sincerity of
their zeal for His honour, speaking slightingly, or grudgingly, or at
least without due reverence, of her whom He honoured above all
others, none excepted;"[76] Irish Catholics felt that Protestants understood neither Mary's rightful role nor Catholic doctrine concerning
her merits. The following excerpt from one of Father Matthew
Russell's poems on this subject gives a clear indication of the Marian
position.

> Nor let the impious slanderer say
> That Mary's clients turn away
> The worship due to God alone,
> And lift a creature to his throne.
> Was e'er the vilest fanatic
> Duped by this hideous, lying trick?
> The simplest crone that tells her beads –
> Her cross the only book she reads –
>
> Knows well that She, upon whose breast
> The Babe divine doth sweetly rest,
> Is still a woman, meek and mild,
> Though Jesus, Jesus, is her Child!
> They, too, who raise this parrot-cry
> Of a besotted bigotry,
>
> Know well, themselves – for o'er and o'er
> We've stooped to tell them – we adore
> One only God, of lords the Lord,
> Eternal Trinity, whose word
> Made all created things to be,
> And, foremost of mere creatures, Thee;
> Thee, Mary, whom God raised so high
> That saint and angel come not nigh.[77]

Neither Protestants nor Catholics saw the other's view of Mary in a
way that the other group thought fair. Morgan encapsulates the Ulster
Protestant understanding in the following manner "The present Pope
seems desirous to immortalise himself and his reign by elevating the

honour of Mary to a height which it never reached before. He has invented a new doctrine ... It is styled the 'immaculate conception of the Virgin Mary.' She who said, 'My spirit hath rejoiced in God my Saviour,' is now declared to have been ever perfectly sinless, and never to have needed a Saviour."[78]

Both Irish Protestants and Catholics accused each other of distorting their understanding of the Virgin Mary, and, by extension, of failing to give true womanhood, which was modelled on her standard, its due. Neither recognized that the virtues of this ideal "godly woman" were an exact match with the gender ideology of their religious antagonists. All that the Catholics could see was that Protestants disdained Mary and all that Protestants would admit was that Catholics worshipped Mary. Mutual misunderstanding resulted.

The Virgin Mary was not the only biblical woman whose life was put to didactic and prescriptive purposes. The description of the lives of various mortal sinners and model saints affords us a further view of this discourse of ideal Christian womanhood.

4 Women of the Bible and the Early Church: Mortal Sinners and Model Saints

The lives of biblical women, famous and obscure, sinners and saints, provided Ulster Protestant religious writers with authoritative examples of both commendable and unwomanly behavior. The former was to be emulated; the latter was to be shunned. For Irish Catholics, women of the New Testament[1] who were also well known saints – the Virgin Mary, Mary Magdalen, and Martha of Bethany – and major female saints of the early Christian period, the most popular of whom was St Monica – comprised the pantheon of female worthies from whom the writers of devotional poetry and prose drew their inspiration. Regardless of the source of their inspiration, both Protestant and Roman Catholic writers used the stories of these women's lives to press their own particular view of female piety. Though the odd voice emerged which criticized the dominant construction of "virtuous womanhood" in its essentially domestic and submissive form, in the main the articles, stories, sonnets, and verse that make up this literature extolled the cardinal virtues of the cult of domesticity by highlighting them in the lives of these women of scripture and legend. Even those Protestants who were avowed biblical literalists frequently rode roughshod over their biblical texts in order to pursue an agenda which insisted on the self-denial, subservience, obedience, and domesticity of biblical women.

Occasionally Catholic authors used biblical sources in a manner similar to their Protestant counterparts – using specific passages from holy writ on which to base their compositions – but this was not a common practice. Protestants, of course, usually provided chapter and verse.[2]

Sometimes they used remarkably obscure or brief references as the starting point for lengthy sermons or treatises on the virtues of some particular woman of the Bible. Roman Catholics rarely used the Old Testament and infrequently used the New Testament except for passages relating to major female saints. Unaided use of the Bible by the laity was not a part of the Roman Catholic tradition; moreover, particularly in Ireland, there seems to have been an air of suspicion of biblicism on the part of Roman Catholics. Katherine Tynan, a popular Irish Catholic novelist, caught this mood in the following passage from the second volume of her memoirs: "we never knew anyone who talked about the Bible who was not a hypocrite. In those days [1890s] – perhaps to-day – the Irish Protestants looked upon the Bible as a Protestant book and the Irish Catholic peasants had no doubts about it being an exclusively sectarian production. It had been used against them so often in the hands of their enemies."[3] The Protestant and Roman Catholic literatures that will be discussed in this chapter take as their inspiration disparate sources, yet the prescriptive message that was brought home to its reading audience time and time again was very similar. Regardless of the ostensible subject of a poem or sermon, the actual historical woman in question mattered less than the message about the true "nature" of holy women that could be derived from her story; the message was very similar.

MARY MAGDALEN

Mary Magdalen, the archetype of the whore with the heart of gold, was, next to the Virgin Mary, the most important woman in Irish Catholic religious literature. The lives of sinful women, such as the Magdalen, demarcated the parameters of acceptable womanly behaviour; their errors were signposts, warning of the dangers of stepping outside the boundary of the feminine ideal. The Magdalen is a much beloved figure in Catholic literature; her human frailty and sinfulness make her an approachable figure, one with whom penitents could identify. Her passionate and faithful love for Christ was also a key aspect of her attractiveness. Her loving nature, a decidedly womanly attribute, was praised above all her other qualities. Still, it was her sexual misconduct, her fallen state before redemption, that was her defining characteristic.[4] Mary Magdalen's sinfulness provided a stark contrast to the spotless purity of the Virgin Mary. In the poem "The Two Marys," this contrast is shown in bold relief.

> They stand beneath the Cross: the one so good
> That angels bow her innocence before;

The other sorely stained and smirchëd o'er;
Sin-blasted, wrecked, her fair sweet womanhood.

Yet both, in love, embrace the blood-stained wood
Whereon He hangs, the Lord whom both adore;
Their mingled tears as in one torrent pour,
Magdalen's hand clasps Mary's 'neath the rood.[5]

Marina Warner posits the theory that "together the Virgin and the Magdalen form a diptych of Christian patriarchy's idea of woman."[6] Christian society's paradoxical view of women – they are either angels or demons, virgins or whores – informed the development of the Magdalen's cult as a foil to that of the Virgin Mary.[7]

When examining Protestant and Catholic literature about Mary Magdalen, it is often unclear as to who is actually being discussed. The confusion arises from differing Protestant and Catholic interpretations of the New Testament. The authors of the gospels were frequently ambiguous when describing women. They often did not give female characters names, and when these women possessed the common name of Mary the writers frequently failed to clearly explain which Mary was being referred to. Thus Catholic and Protestants came to a different understanding of who Mary Magdalen was.[8]

In the Roman Catholic Church[9] Mary of Bethany, the sister of Lazarus and Martha; Mary of Magdala, disciple of Christ and witness to the resurrection; and the "sinner" who "loved much" have been combined to make up the persona of St Mary of Magdala. The Ulster Protestant sources I have investigated generally identify Mary of Magdala as the unnamed "sinner" of Luke: 7, but they did not view Mary of Magdala and Mary of Bethany as the same person.[10]

MARY MAGDALEN AS A MODEL FOR WOMEN

Mary Magdalen's loving nature was that aspect of her personality which was the most strongly emphasized by Irish Catholic writers; her sinfulness was not mentioned as frequently, despite its being her defining characteristic. Rather, discussions of sin and redemption centred on those earthly fallen daughters who were called Magdalens.

Attie O'Brien's dramatic and vivid poem "Magdalen" presents a picture of this saint, which, while admiring of her loving nature and heartfelt penance after her conversion, clearly portrays this "sinner" as unwomanly.[11] The opening lines of the poem describe a beautiful, wealthy young woman arrayed in costly garments "Her waving hair, as golden as the light, / In soft abundance wreathes her haughty head."[12]

The physical description of the Magdalen reinforces the notion of "the ruined temple of her soul": "Her breast is bare and jewelled to the throat, / Her naked arms are gleaming in the sun."[13] Despite her beauty and wealth, her life of sin – publicly flaunted, "brazen" sin – made her the antithesis of the true, domestic woman as constructed in late Victorian Irish religious literature.

> A woman gone from woman's hidden life
> Of holy influence, unselfish aims,
> And quiet ministration to pure ends
> That leaves the hot world with a cleaner heart
> Than elsewise were its doom.[14]

Her sexual sin, which, of course, casts her from beyond the pale of true womanhood, is compounded by its brazen, public nature. She and her "gay companions" are selfish pleasure seekers, always looking for something "to stimulate exhausted appetite."[15] This empty life of self-indulgence is the polar opposite of the domestic ideal of female self-sacrifice and obedience.

The reaction the Magdalen creates when she enters the house where Jesus was a guest heightens the contrast that O'Brien draws between the "brazen" Magdalen and modest women. As the Magdalen seats herself at the wedding feast "the gentle women shrink, / And hide their heads beneath their modest veils."[16] For all the "unwomanliness" of her life of open sin, this saint was still described by O'Brien as possessing a "woman's heart." When the Magdalen's eyes first meet Christ's, "The woman's heart gives one convulsive throb, / She sees the face of Jesus – and herself."[17] Through Christ her sinfulness is revealed to her and she immediately repents and renounces her former life.

The unwomanliness of "Magdalens" was described in language similar to that used to portray their namesake. In a poem addressed to a "Magdalen" the poet Sir Wilfred Meynell states:

> Thou art a woman, of thy glory shorn, —
> A woman, in whom woman's self is dead.
> Ere this of thee or any should be said,
> 'Twere best that thou and they had ne'er been born.[18]

Yet in the second verse of the poem, he moderates his tone. He speaks of fallen sisters who are like lost lambs: "Yea, and I love thee for *her* [Mary Magdalen's] sake so sweet / Who washed with her warm tears the Saviour's feet."[19] In and of themselves there was nothing left that was lovable about "Magdalens," but the example of St Mary Magdalen's beautiful life of penitence inspires tolerance and compassion for the "fallen."

In a series in *The Irish Rosary* on the subject of "Our Dublin Charities," an article appeared called "The Magdalenes of High Park." The "fallen girl" was said to be "a disgrace to her sex, a blot on society, one that must be avoided as the leper of old, because she is 'unclean.'"[20] The author gives the individual case history of a "fallen girl" who sought refuge at High Park Convent. A young nun greeted the girl at the door. "A greater contrast is scarcely possible. Innocence and guilt face to face! The bright cheerfulness of unsullied virtue so near to the most abject wretchedness of multiplied sinfulness! The spotless lily side by side with the rank, noxious, foul-smelling weed that grew up in the dark shadows of the tomb! The consecrated nun speaking to the polluted outcast!"[21] There are clear similarities here to the above-cited poem, "The Two Marys"; female virtue and female sin are in sharp contrast.

Protestant writers also highlighted the contrast between sinner and saint, virgin and whore, in the story of Mary Magdalen. In the poem "Magdalene," the following warning is presented to the female readers of the temperance magazine, *The Irish Templar*:

> She had fallen so deep in her fearful sin;
> When a woman does fall from her high purity,
> Her fall is so great, and she falls so low,
> We can scarce follow the depth of woe.[22]

Because the poet spends the rest of the poem chastising Christian women for their lack of effort on behalf of "fallen women" – "Rouse up! ye careless, who dwell at ease, / living for naught but yourselves to please" – and urging them into action – "Living in hopelessness, wretchedness, sin, Our sisters – sisters, though fallen so low; / Can we not in God's name with helping hand go"[23]– we can discern that she is writing for a female audience whom she presumes does not include any "Magdalens." Rather the author assumes that they share with her a belief in their own lofty status as virtuous women. They are urged to work and pray in order to win the accolade given by Jesus to Mary of Bethany: "'She hath done what she could,' / Is the word we can gain if only we would."[24] Nevertheless, even for Protestant women who were temperance activists, it bore keeping in mind that women's high position was a precarious one. Given their "frail" nature[25] coupled with the disastrous results of a "fall" from true womanhood, it behooved women to be vigilant against any stirring of their "passions." Protestant writers would concur with their Catholic counterparts that "Once she has made the dreadful plunge into crime her downward progress is quick and short. Strong passions and temptations find now a willing victim."[26] A dedicated life of labour, love, and prayer was a safeguard against such a dreadful occurrence.[27]

It was the Magdalen's great love and generosity that seemed to capture the imagination of those Irish Catholic writers who were devoted to her cult. Of course, this stems from Christ's words to the unnamed sinner of Luke's gospel: "Her sins, which are many are forgiven; for she loved much." (Luke 7:47). If the word "Magdalen" primarily meant female sexual sin, it also conjured up strong associations of female love.

The Magdalen's loving "heart" or nature was frequently the focus in Catholic literature. The sonnet "Magdalen's Tears" begins:

> Tears, Tears – the ceaseless language of her heart,
> That passionate poor heart the Saviour breaks,
> And, filling with his blessed sorrow, takes
> All that is evil from, with tender art.[28]

Mary Magdalen's loving heart was described as the reason for her forgiveness. "She loved the Christ, she wept beside his grave, / And He for that love's sake all else forgave."[29] This superlative praise of the Magdalen's loving nature by her devotees is perhaps captured best in a sonnet entitled "Nec Virgo Nec Martyr." In this work the anonymous poet asserts that even though Mary Magdalen is neither a virgin[30] nor a martyr, she should be a much beloved saint. Mary Magdalen has no halo, yet her very unadorned hair was the instrument of her glory.

> Oh! more than virgin in thy penitent love,
> And more than martyr in thy passionate woe!
> How should thy sisters equal thee above
> Who knelt not with thee on the gory sod?
> Or where the crown our worship could bestow
> Like that long gold which wiped the feet of God?[31]

Her loving act of wiping Christ's feet with her hair, symbolic of her great love, and her great sorrow at the death of her Lord[32] were, for followers of her cult, enough to redeem her, to put her above the virgins and martyrs of the liturgy.[33] Mary Magdalen was a comforting figure for her frail human devotees. Virgins and martyrs could seem somewhat remote, but the woman whose sins were forgiven because she loved much was a figure with whom the penitent could identify.

This affiliation of sinners with Mary Magdalen was not confined to her Catholic cult. Her penitent and loving nature provided an appropriate prescription for Protestants as well. The sonnet by Hartley Coleridge[34] titled "She hath loved Much" was printed in *The Irish Monthly*'s "Magdalen Sonnets" feature and in the Ulster Presbyterian periodical, *The Witness*.

> And He wiped off the soiling of despair
> From her sweet soul because she loved so much.
> I am a sinner, full of doubts and fears:
> Make me a humble thing of love and tears.[35]

Without adhering to the Catholic cult of St Mary Magdalen, Protestant writers still felt a kinship with Mary's sinfulness and sought to emulate her humble contrition. It was only in her supposed sexual impropriety that Mary Magdalen violated the Christian cult of true womanhood; most writers allowed that her love and her faithfulness after her repentance made her an appropriate model of Christian penitence.

In a lengthy article in *The Evangelical Witness and Presbyterian Review*, an anonymous Ulster Presbyterian writer sought to "redeem" Mary of Magdala from her "infamy." The author's biblical literalism is coupled with romantic flights of fancy which were not common in Protestant writing on biblical subjects. Perhaps, as with the Virgin Mary, so little is said of the person's background that the temptation to embroider the bare fabric of the narrative was irresistible. Nonetheless, of this woman whom the author says "embodied all that is pure, and tender, holy and beautiful in woman, and in saint,"[36] no taint of impurity could be imagined. This author holds to Origen's exegesis of three separate Marys and therefore only takes the woman in question to be Mary of Magdala when she is specifically named as such. Thus for this author, Mary of Magdala is the woman from whom Christ cast seven devils, who accompanied him during his ministry, and who was at the crucifixion and resurrection. This Presbyterian author is adamant that Mary of Magdala was not the "sinner" of Luke: 7. The reasons for this insistence on the Magdalen's sexual innocence are quite illuminating. Of course the author begins by giving biblical reasons for disossociating Mary of Magdala with the "sinner." On very slim biblical evidence – that Mary was an associate of the wife of Herod's steward and that she could buy costly spices – he creates a pious and comfortable home for Mary. "Growing up within that moral and reputable home she must have been safe from temptations to gross sins."[37] The author contends that it is "not hard to picture" the youthful Mary of Magdala "She was ardent, eager, full of energy and enthusiasm, yet gentle and timid as a fawn. Capable of the purest, most impassioned love, she possessed the nervous sensitiveness that is always allied with it."[38] Clearly, this description of the Magdalen's character is not based on any reasonable interpretation of scripture; it is pure fancy. Yet the direction taken by the flight of the imagination is worth noting. The author could not possibly have known, based on the biblical record, that this "womanly" saint was pure, gentle, timid, and sensitive. Rather if the Magdalen was a "true woman" and this construction of female piety was said to be constant through time or "natural," then it would not be difficult for this author to assume, leaving aside biblicist scruples, that a "womanly" woman in the New Testament such as Mary of Magdala, would possess the same virtues as the ideal Christian woman of the Victorian period.

Mary of Magdala's supposed demonic possession is then discussed at length in this article. In her Roman Catholic cult, almost all mention of Mary having seven devils cast out of her was expunged.[39] But this author focuses on the topic of demonic possession which, he mentions, was particularly virulent in Galilee during Christ's ministry. More importantly for the author's purpose of reclaiming Mary Magdalen from those who had stained her pure name with "infamy," he asserts that those afflicted with demons should be considered unfortunate victims who did nothing to bring this plague upon themselves. The author becomes rather heated in Mary's defence at this point. "She had been guilty of no profligacy. No immorality had stained her life. In the world's eyes her conduct and character were irreproachable. Her name was not the synonym of infamy. She never was "a Magdalene." There is not a shadow of proof for the calumny which eighteen centuries have uttered and believed against her. It is time that it should cease. Too long has she worn the foul and flaunting garments of the courtezan [sic] in which foul-minded monks arrayed her. That Mary was demoniac, was her misfortune, not her fault."[40]

The author continues his effort to restore Mary of Magdala's good name by asserting that the identification of her with the sinful woman of Luke: 7 is "utterly proofless." He argues that Mary of Magdala is introduced by name in Luke: 8, as if for the first time. Leaving all this aside, however, the author makes a more striking argument. The most compelling reason, he claims, for believing that Mary of Magdala was a woman of virtue and innocence was her relationship with Jesus Christ. Her status as the woman closest to Christ was, for this writer, proof of her purity, for "the Lord never admitted into the inner circle of His brethren those who had been profligate in conduct or scandalous in character. He might eat with sinners, but He did not live with them."[41] The author clearly believes that there was a limit to Christ's tolerance of past female sexual indiscretion. "Women that were sinners He forgave freely, spoke tenderly to; but He always said – 'Go in peace,' never, 'Follow me.' For all such there is a place in Christ's Church, but it is not where He placed Mary Magdalene."[42] The author has found justification in Christ's ministry of his own reluctance to allow "all such" redeemed fallen women any visible place in the church. He states, "The Lord's example might be followed with advantage in these days, and much of hurt and scandal be thereby avoided."[43] This entirely ignores the fact that the Gospels indicate that Christ seemed to care little about the scandal his association with sinners caused to the righteous. Clearly the author of this article, probably an Ulster clergyman, had his own agenda for defending Mary of Magdala's "good name" by dissociating her from female sinners, even redeemed ones, who would never be entirely acceptable true Christian women. Mary Magdalen's story, confusing though it might have been in the biblical record, served as a screen on which religious authors could project their own understanding of the acceptable limits of womanly behavior.

SENSUAL SINNERS

The "woman at the well" and the "woman taken in adultery" are two nameless women of St John's gospel with whom Jesus spoke and ministered. For the most part, the religious literature focuses on how these women had ruined their "true womanhood" through their sexual transgressions. In their biblical stories the sinful state of these women was stated simply and without embellishment. To the Samaritan woman whom he met at Jacob's Well Jesus demonstrated the fact that he was aware that she was an adulteress and then he went on to reveal, for the first time, his Messiahship, after which the woman went to the town and brought back men to hear Jesus' message (John 4:5–42). In Protestant literature, though, the story of the "woman at the well" revolves more around the woman's fallen state and her redemption than simply around Christ's message of "everlasting life" (John 4:14). In the poem "The Woman of Sychar" the "erring daughter" finds in Christ's message an avenue by which to return to her "sin-stricken soul" her lost "purity."[44] While allowing the Samaritan woman a place among the ranks of the "women workers of the Bible" because of her role as Christ's messenger to the men of her town, the Reverend J.E. Sampson, in his series of prescriptive articles about biblical women, does not hold her up as a model for the "women workers" of his Anglican reading audience. Though he commends her zeal in a back-handed fashion – "this woman, who had not learnt to subdue her evil passions, could not now control her holy zeal"[45] – he disapprovingly notes that she went to speak only to "'the men.' Her sin had been with the men. The folly and shame of her past life had been among men. She had lost, I suspect, the modesty which is the charm of woman-hood."[46] Thus Sampson's view of the "woman at the well" is decidedly mixed. She may have been used by Christ to spread his message, but her lack of "modesty" meant that Sampson would not "hold her up for imitation."[47] The sinful woman who had lost her purity, who had abro-gated the conventions of the cult of true womanhood through her selfish indulgence of her own "evil passions," could find salvation, according to this reading of the biblical text, but she could not find true acceptance. This was a clear warning to female readers; salvation was always available for the fallen, but once the sexual conventions of this construction of female piety were broken, they could never be entirely repaired.

In looking through the periodical literature, published sermons, tracts, and other writings of the major Ulster religious denominations, I found a fascinating poem about the "woman taken in adultery" of St John's Gospel. It first appeared in its lengthy entirety entitled "Stone the Woman – Let the Man Go Free" in *The Irish Monthly*, and then it appeared in an abbreviated version, with no mention of its having first been published in a Catholic journal, in *The Irish Presbyterian*, with the title shortened to "Stone the Woman" and with the name of the author omitted. In the longer version of the poem, the writer, Attie O'Brien, paints a vivid picture of Jerusalem at the time of Christ, contrasting the beauty of the surroundings – "an azure sky/ Bends o'er the lovely land" – with the misery of the woman: "in their midst a wretched woman moves, / A blot upon the beauty of the day."[48] This adulteress is, for O'Brien, a creature entirely bereft of her pure "womanhood"; she is un-woman.

> Shame clothes her as a garment, while her soul
> Shudders within its desecrated shrine,
> Stained and unutterably dishonoured,
> So sad a sight, so loathsomely deformed
> That angels weep and tremble as they gaze.[49]

In describing what this "woman taken in adultery" has lost, O'Brien provides a checklist of all the benefits of true womanhood and the cult of domesticity. She can never

> taste again the simple joys of home,
> The tender sweetness of modest ways,

> A husband's love, the touch of infant lips,
> The trust of friends, the happy firelit hearth,
> The little tendrils of joys that softly cling,
> And give their perfume to a clean sweet life.[50]

Perhaps most revealing of the attraction of this construction of female identity are the lines "Oh, never, more through the long waste of years / Can she walk upright in the ways of men, / And look the wide world bravely in the face, / Strong in the untouched whiteness of her life."[51] Strict adherence to the principles of sexual chastity was supposed to bring women strength; their purity was a personal citadel.

O'Brien may have been an enthusiastic supporter of the "cult of true womanhood," yet her creative interpretation of this biblical text in her prose includes a stinging critique of the sexual double standard that was its corollary. Sexual chastity may have defined women, and, conversely, sexual sin was their undoing, yet "what of men?" O'Brien's poem asks. At the dramatic peak of this scene O'Brien has Christ make the following statement: "'Let him,' He says, 'who knows that he is pure / Cast first the stone at her.'"[52] Notably, she uses "pure" – with its sexual connotation – rather than "without sin" (the biblical phrase) in this scene. The woman's accusers then "slink abashed away" leaving Jesus and the woman alone. After she receives his injunction to "Go sin no more" she goes forth "To mend the ruined beauty of her life, / To wash her soul in penitential tears / And ever after with undying love / To follow Christ, lamenting."[53] So a penitent she will remain for the rest of her days. Once the delicate fabric of the conventions of true womanhood is rent, it cannot entirely be mended.

The "woman taken in adultery" will always be denied the happiness of the ideal domestic life that O'Brien depicted, but "where is he, the sharer in her guilt? / The man whom God appointed as the head, / The shield of woman in her weaknesses."[54] Is he not racked by guilt like the woman, is he not surrounded by an accusing mob "That look on him with loathing, holding up / His shamèd manhood, his insulted God"?[55] The answer is no, as O'Brien next describes the sumptuous scene at the seducer's wedding feast. He is still a respected member of the community and about to marry an unsuspecting maiden.[56] The last two verses are a warning to young women and a call for justice. O'Brien highlights the folly of only judging women for sexual transgressions by showing how high-minded young maidens spurn "fallen" women but unwittingly marry unchaste men.

> Pass her, O maiden, with a pure, proud face,
> If she puts out a poor, polluted palm;

But lay thy hand on his on bridal days
And swear to cling to him with wifely love
And tender reverence. Trust him who led
A sister woman to a fearful fate.[57]

O'Brien's contempt for the sexual double standard is clearly demonstrated in the lines "Yes, stone the woman – let the man go free! / Let one soul suffer for the guilt of two."[58] Here she condemns the flawed judgement of her own society and proclaims that a higher authority will see things differently. Of the final judgement day, O'Brien asks, "Shall sex make *then* a difference in sin? / Shall He, the searcher of the hidden heart, / In His eternal and divine decree, / Condemn the woman and forgive the man?"[59] In criticizing the sexual double standard of her day, O'Brien did not attack the cult of true womanhood itself or its uncompromising standards of sexual purity for women. Instead she was calling for, in effect, a cult of true manhood to hold men accountable to the same high standard of behaviour. Purity was a cogent, if muffled, critique of impious men in both Catholic and Protestant discourse. O'Brien's "Stone the Woman" could appear in *The Irish Presbyterian*, without any reference to the author's religious affiliation, because the sentiments contained therein were in keeping with those made within Protestant circles.[60] The sanctity of the domestic sphere and woman's holy mission within it were threatened by the impiety and impurity of the very men who were supposed to be "the shield of woman." In this gendered discourse, the imperative for domestic purity was something upon which Protestants and Catholics could agree.

MARY AND MARTHA, THE SISTERS OF LAZARUS

Mary and Martha, the sisters of Lazarus, were presented in Ulster religious literature as archetypes of two very different kinds of female virtue: the contemplative and the domestic. While both sisters were praised for their service to Christ, it was made clear that neither woman in and of herself was completely ideal. Rather it was frequently stated that a combination of Mary's piety and Martha's work was necessary for the ideal Christian woman.

Martha, "the perfect Christian type of the domestic woman,"[61] did not appear in Roman Catholic literature with the frequency of her more famous sister.[62] Those who performed their household duties well, without consideration of self, were praised for having acquired "the virtue of Martha."[63] Attitudes towards Martha were more

ambivalent in Protestant literature. While several writers[64] enthusiastically praised Martha's self-sacrifice and service, holding them up as an
example of "home work" to be emulated by female readers, others
interpreted Christ's rebuke of Martha as an indication that her
bustling work stifled spirituality. The latter interpretation made the
phrase "a Martha" a term of criticism rather than one of praise for
Christian women.

Perhaps the nastiest, though the most clever, critique of overzealous
"Martha-like" female charitable activity may be found in a serial story
about the trials of an Anglican parish clergyman. An overworked
curate, Mr Brant, received an ostentatiously decorated prospectus for
a new parish organization called the "Female Benevolent Society for
Teaching the Hottentots the Art of Paper-Flower Making." The orga-
nizer of the proposed society was described as follows: "Mrs Cooper
was truly a Martha. It would have been difficult to name any Society,
from the oldest and best of our religious societies to the latest inven-
tion of idle minds to raise funds for some *novelty* wherewith to amuse
themselves, and relieve the ennui of fashionable life, which she did
not patronize."[65] In this case, being "a Martha" was no badge of
honour. Instead, women's benevolent activities were determined to be
silly, frivolous, and devoid of any spiritual significance. Generally,
criticism of the "busyness" of "Marthas" was less damning in tone. In
an article in *The Christian Advocate*, Dr Alex Whyte reflects on how
Christians can harm their spiritual lives by being too much like
Martha "And we, too many of us, are like Martha in her cumbered
kitchen that night; and we are, too few of us, and [sic] too seldom
like Mary."[66] Dr Whyte urges his readers to put aside the encum-
brances of being "Marthas" and try to gain some of the spiritual
insights of Mary.

Martha was not without her staunch defenders in Ulster Protestant
literature, however. Ada Whitla, a very active woman in Belfast
Methodist circles, wrote a book titled *The Sisters, A.D. 33. You Sisters,
A.D. 1902*, and dedicated it to the members of her Young Womens'
Bible Class who had studied Mary and Martha at their meetings. While
Whitla presents both Mary and Martha as models for Christian
women, it is undoubtedly Martha to whom she relates the most readily. "There is nothing in the story of Martha we can fail to understand;
she was a woman with a generous heart, who did her best; she had no
thought of reward, the joy she had in doing her duty was enough. It is
her failings that give us strength; she was only one of ourselves; we are
thankful she is handed down to us as she really was, and not represented as someone past our standard."[67] Whitla takes issue with the
custom of considering Martha as inferior to Mary. She tends to over-

look Christ's rebuke of Martha and chooses instead to laud Martha's service. Despite the biblical account of Christ rebuking Martha for "being troubled about many things" when her sister Mary had chosen the "better part" of listening to Christ's teaching (Luke 10:38–42), Whitla sees Martha's efforts as "the very essence of discipleship."[68] While this assessment of Martha may accord with Whitla's own understanding of female piety, and it certainly agrees with the construction of domestic piety as it emerged in Ulster Evangelical literature, it does not fit the biblical story of Christ's reprimand of Martha. Clearly, in Luke: 10, Martha's behaviour was not considered "the very essence of discipleship" by Christ. Nevertheless, Whitla cautions her female readers against "throwing mental stones" at Martha, for "It is easier to blame her than to answer the question, what would life be without our bustling, busy Marthas?"[69] It matters not to Whitla that Martha's was not the "better part," for she is among those "who love the memory of Martha, and desire to follow in her footsteps."[70] It appears as if Ada Whitla is defending Martha's actions as a way of justifying the sanctity of her own work and of spreading the ethos of the cult of domesticity.

Despite the fact that Martha's labours were not overtly praised by Christ, the combination of her service and her sister Mary's piety was considered the ideal one for Ulster Protestant women. Together, Mary and Martha form the ideal of Christian womanhood "Martha represents to us labour, and Mary prayer. This combination is needed to make up the sort of home sister who would sanctify her daily work."[71] Martha's home at Bethany is spoken of by Whitla in awe-hushed tones. For Whitla, the home at Bethany – Christ's haven from the difficulties of his ministry – was an ideal of domestic piety: women serving and men being refreshed and restored. Whitla does not ignore Mary; indeed she urges her readers to develop the spiritual sides of their natures and find "the calm that Mary sought and found."[72] But unquestionably she feels that busy Ulster Protestant women who were striving to meet the ideal of domestic piety felt more akin to Martha "We know God has only imperfect women such as we are and Martha was to do His work. It rests with ourselves to grow into fire-side saints, proving ourselves not useless, superior sort of persons, but serving as Martha did, to the best of our ability."[73] Oddly enough, this evangelical writer, who considered herself a biblical literalist,[74] repeatedly praised Martha for the very thing which Christ criticized.[75] Christ's insistence on the spiritual over the material – "Consider the lilies of the field; they toil not, neither do they spin" (Matthew 6:28) – is entirely absent from Whitla's account.[76] It was almost as if writers like Whitla felt compelled to defend Martha's service because their own lives were so entirely devoted to service in their homes and in their churches. Articles on the subjects of "consecrated tea-tables" and "fire-side saints" demonstrate that it was important for evangelical women to see their domestic labours regarded as work for God.[77] Martha was the "patron saint" of domesticity, and thus it was important that her work be validated. Thus it would be comforting for women who subscribed to the cult of domesticity to hear that Jesus knew the motives of each sister, and that "he loved each for her own sake."[78]

Martha's sister, Mary of Bethany, was also considered an important role model for Christian women. Despite the impatience evinced by busy "Marthas" like Whitla with Mary's contemplative nature, Mary's spirituality was viewed as ideal. In Roman Catholic literature, Martha's sister – thought to be the Magdalen – was praised for taking the "better part." A writer in *The Irish Rosary* examined how Christ's promise that Mary's "better part"[79] would never be taken from her was fulfilled. The writer notes that in the medieval *Golden Legend*, we find the tale of Mary Magdalen and her siblings, Martha and Lazarus, being set adrift on the sea by enemies of the church. When they landed in the South of France, Mary "withdrew from her companions, and retired to the mountain cave at St Baume, or, as another tradition has it, was transported thither by angels ... There could scarcely be found on earth another spot so meet for contemplation."[80] Like other great hermitesses, many miracles were attributed to Mary when she lived her life of solitary contemplation.[81]

In the Protestant tradition, praise of Martha's sister, Mary, is not quite so vaunting, nor is it chiefly her love of quiet reflection that is praised. While the "spirit of Mary" which was "rarer than that of Martha"[82] was presented as exemplary, her actions were also the focus of attention. Her act of anointing Christ's feet with costly ointment and wiping them with her hair was deemed highly worthy. The Reverend John Bryson, in his *Three Marys of the Four Gospels*, applauds Mary's act by asking his readers to "recall, then, to mind the features of the love whose appellation is, 'She hath done what she could.' It is UNSELFISH, SELF-SACRIFICING, and CHRIST HONOURING."[83] Though contemplative by nature, Mary of Bethany also fulfils the ideal of domestic womanhood by her active sacrifice and selflessness. This emphasis on "doing" is echoed again when Bryson observes that "*She hath done what she could*, is our Lord's legacy to all who be good and do good."[84] "She hath done what she could" became the ultimate accolade for Protestant women. Together, Mary and her sister, Martha, fulfilled the prescription for Christian "women's rights," for they demonstrated the virtues of labour, love, and prayer.

WOMEN OF THE EARLY CHURCH

A common theme running through the poems, sermons, and articles which took the Christian women of the fledgling Christian church as their subject was the devotion of these women to serving those in their "circle," be it their family or household members, or the apostles themselves. Of course, their spiritual faith was mentioned as well – their steadfastness in the new faith and their trust in God – but it was their domestic work, their "Martha" service for the new church that was emphasized in Ulster Protestant literature. The work of women in the early church as leaders, missionaries, and teachers was not the focus of this literature; instead, the reading of New Testament texts was tailored to fit the construction of the ideal Christian domestic woman.

The poem "Lost Names" refers to "those women which laboured with me [Paul] in the Gospel," whose "names are in the book of life" (Philippians 4:3). The poet praises these unnamed women workers for "they lived and they were useful; this we know / And nought beside."[85] Again, all that is known is that these women laboured faithfully in the gospel: "One only thing is known of them, they were / Faithful and true / Disciples of the Lord, and strong through prayer / To save and do."[86] The unspecified tasks of these unnamed women could have been any number of roles within the teaching and missionary branches of the early church. Yet in prescriptive articles and sermons, the actions of these women were presented as essentially "women's work" of domestic service and devotion.

The word "Dorcas" conjures up images of busy female charitable work in Victorian Christian discourse. "Dorcas societies," groups of women who performed charitable work for the poor, proliferated during this period. Dorcas[87] was presented in the literature as a model of female Christian service. In Acts of the Apostles 9:36–42, Dorcas's work, death, and resurrection are briefly narrated. The author of the "Bible Lesson" section of *The Christian Advocate* notes in a lesson on the subject of Dorcas's miraculous resurrection that when she is called "a certain disciple" in verse 36 it was a unique occurrence: "She is the only female disciple known by this name in the Bible. She is the elect lady, in whom we see the graces peculiar to womanhood finding their perfect expression in Christ's service."[88] The author pointedly observes that "it was reserved for the gospel, while thus preserving the natural distinctiveness of woman, to place her, in her own sphere, side by side with man."[89] This reading of the scriptural account of Dorcas's life demonstrates the pervasive nature of notions of gender essentialism – "graces peculiar to womanhood" – and of "separate spheres."

There is nothing in the brief account of Dorcas's work in Acts of the Apostles to indicate that she operated exclusively within what Victorians considered women's "separate sphere." Her "good works and almsdeeds" could have given this female disciple a very important leadership role in the Church at Joppa. But within a religious culture that was struggling with definitions of gender roles and the "woman question," such an interpretation of Dorcas's role would not have been satisfactory. Rather, she is the ultimate domestic woman, "usefulness" being her crowning virtue.[90]

In the Revereld J.E. Sampson's series on "The Women Workers of the Bible" Dorcas, the female disciple, is portrayed in uncompromisingly domestic terms. Sampson interprets Dorcas's "good works" as necessarily being needlework: "She was a worker indeed, and her work was womanly. Work is the term among women when the use of the needle is in question."[91] Sampson then goes on at length to sing the praises of the nimble female hand plying the needle, averring that it is a gift of God. It is important to remember that he was writing for women who belonged to the Church of England Zenana Missionary Society and its Hibernian Auxiliary. The main fundraising activity of these societies was their annual "sale of work"; a bazaar at which needlework and baked goods were sold to raise funds for mission work. Whether Dorcas did petitpoint is a moot question; what was important in this series on "women workers" was that its female audience have its own work affirmed and sanctified through the use of Dorcas as a holy example.

Sampson sees Dorcas as a woman whose "silent influence none can tell." Despite the fact that she was alone among women in the New Testament in being accorded the title of disciple, he assumes that she did not preach the Gospel. Instead, Sampson makes this observation: "I do not read that she *said* much. Not one word she had spoken is recorded. She was a worker, not a talker."[92] For Sampson, that is as it should be for a woman worker: needlework, not preaching. We see, then, that the biblical text that says Dorcas was "full of good works and almsdeeds which she did" (Acts 10:36) was interpreted to fit the prevailing gender orthodoxy of female domesticity.

Lydia, the seller of purple of Acts of the Apostles, chapter sixteen, was a woman in charge of her own business and household who also met to pray with other women. When he came to Philippi, the apostle Paul sought out Lydia; clearly she was an established leader of those seeking spiritual truth. Lydia was baptised, and her whole household with her, and afterwards she asked Paul and Silas to stay in her home (Acts 16:12–15). In the first of his "women workers" articles, the Reverend J.E. Sampson describes Lydia's "lowly service."[93] Focusing on the baptism of the members of Lydia's household rather than on her meeting to pray with the women of the city, Sampson again highlights domestic piety: "See where her love for souls is first shown – *at home.*"[94] Sampson cautions his female readers against letting their efforts for Zenana Mission Societies and other charitable works be the cause of their neglecting to provide a good example at home. "Sometimes a zealous 'worker' is said to be unkind, and ill-natured, and selfish at home. Irritated when interrupted in work for the sale, peevish and fretful before home annoyances, believe me, you work for God to little purpose. Be very watchful of this. If you would honour your Lord anywhere, you must 'learn first to show piety at home.'"[95]

Sampson provided this example of a biblical woman who as a "mother in Israel" served the lord at home in order to reassure those Christian women who have "almost despairingly asked this question. 'I cannot go forth to India, to China; I have home duties and family ties preventing me; what can I do?'"[96] Lydia was used as a model of female "piety at home." Lydia's work outside of her home, her work in the marketplace, and her role as the leader of a group of women in the city who were seeking God, were entirely ignored; the lesson to be taken from Lydia's story is that "the work of the house goes on ... she is a keeper at home, because home is her sphere. She has clear duties there, and no call to go elsewhere."[97] Thus Lydia, the independent woman of Acts of the Apostles chapter sixteen, is made to accord with the prevailing construction of domestic piety.[98]

Along with Dorcas and Lydia, many other women of the early church were praised as models of domestic female piety. Phœbe, the "succourer of many" of Romans 16:1, for instance, is presented as doing work "which only a woman's hand can bestow,"[99] the work of nurturing and caring for others. This type of work includes "motherly work," and the influence of mothers is another important theme which Protestant writers drew out of the brief references in scripture to women in the early church.

A parallel may be found in the explication by Catholic writers of the life of an influential female saint, Monica, the mother of St Augustine. Among the many women workers mentioned by Paul in Romans, chapter sixteen, the mother of Rufus, "so touchingly saluted by the Apostle, as 'his mother and mine'" attracts interest because of her "mothering" of the Apostle.[100] Sampson says he can see Paul "mothered also, cared for in his needs and infirmities by a godly matron. I love to think of that 'mother's' work, though I know so little of it."[101] But he says that it will suffice to "learn a lesson from this loving word – *mother,* 'his mother and mine.'"[102] Despite being a strict biblical literalist, Sampson asks his readers to "Think how the eyes of the

Christian mother of Rufus would dim with grateful tears when she read those two interjected words, and saw how her little, perhaps her forgotten, acts or words had been remembered."[103] Motherly nurture is, according to Sampson, the key to understanding what is meant by "labour" when the women of this passage are described. The work done by all of the Christian women workers at Rome – Priscilla, who is Paul's "helper in Christ Jesus," and Tryphena and Tryphosa, "who labour in the Lord" – was seen by Sampson as exclusively "motherly," nurturing, and domestic. Given the adherence of Sampson and of other clergy and lay writers to an understanding of female piety and the role of women within the church that they thought was based on an essentialist understanding of women's "nature," the women of the early church had to demonstrate the characteristics of the ideal, domestic, "virtuous" woman.

In a published sermon by the Reverend R.J. Arnold, a Presbyterian minister from Dunmurry, entitled "Lois and Eunice. A Sermon For the Times," the writer presents the mother and grandmother of Timothy as perfect models for the women of his congregation.[104] He begins by trotting out the hackneyed notion (discussed in the previous chapter) that motherhood played an important part in the redemption of women: "by *woman's sin* we and all more were overwhelmed by woe; but through her the Saviour appeared on earth ... His unfathomable mercy and matchless grace and love has lifted her up out of the mire into which *her* sin had plunged her, and elevated her to her true and lofty place!"[105] Arnold observes that Lois and Eunice are worthy models for the women of his congregation because of their "unfeigned faith" (I Timothy 1:2), but they are remembered in holy writ primarily for "*their relationship to a notable man.*"[106] Arnold enthusiastically admonishes his female audience to "Think much and deeply of *Lois* and *Eunice* ye mothers of the flock: emulate their example, that you may share their glory!"[107] Not surprisingly, this leads into a discussion of the great power of mothers. "Who shall estimate aright the value of a pious mother's influence, example, and prayers?" asks Arnold, who then continues by adding that God "has conferred the greatest, most enduring power on earth, upon a mother's tender heart. Nothing in all the universe [is] to be compared to the love of God save the love of a godly mother."[108] Arnold allows that this "enduring power" might not be recognized during the mother's lifetime. However, at the Judgement Day "a countless line of Female Worthies 'unknown to fame' on earth" will be acknowledged, and then all people will see what they owe to the "holy heroism and devoted zeal, and unflinching faith, and devoutest piety of the holy women of the olden and the latter time, who lived, and laboured, and wept, and prayed for the spread of Christ's religion in the souls of men."[109] Biblical mothers such as Lois and Eunice whose fame lay solely in their relationship to a "notable man" were put to prescriptive use in order to reinforce a key concept of the cult of domesticity: the power and influence of the devoted Christian mother who was willing to live a life of self-sacrifice, a life given over to labour, love, and prayer.

Irish Catholic religious writers found an exemplary model of Christian motherhood in St Monica, the mother of St Augustine. Using Augustine's *Confessions* as their main source of inspiration, Catholic authors wrote poems and articles praising her patience, her long-suffering, and her devotion to her son.[110] While Ulster Protestant writers tended to refer to Catholic saints only when they were ridiculing the "excesses" of Catholic cults,[111] The Irish Presbyterian carried a brief series on the life of Monica. The message for female readers was identical, whether the source was Roman Catholic or Presbyterian: all women should strive to be as dedicated a Christian mother as Monica.

How did these writers describe this "model of Christian mothers"? The situation in her household is described as a difficult one, yet she won over her alienated mother-in-law through "kind offices, forbearance, and meekness." Her pagan husband, Patrick, was described as "hot-tempered and impulsive," yet they never quarrelled, as "she had the priceless gift of knowing when to hold her tongue and when to speak."[112] Monica's prudence and persistence with regard to her husband were rewarded when Patrick converted to Christianity near the end of his life. St Monica was an ideal wife and daughter-in-law under adverse circumstances and her example, as presented in the pages of *The Irish Monthly*, encouraged women to do likewise and live lives of patient self-denial. But it is her relationship with her son, her role as the mother of the great St Augustine, for which St Monica was most highly regarded and remembered.

The author of an article about Monica in *The Irish Presbyterian* quotes a phrase frequently used by Augustine: "Ab utero matris maeae," since Augustine believed that "even from [his] mother's womb"[113] he was consecrated to God. Monica's great sorrow lay in her son's long period of apostasy. Yet she never utterly despaired of her son's salvation. For this she is applauded in glowing terms "This is Monica's supreme praise – that she so saturated her son's life with the influences of Christ – with his mother's milk, he confesses, he drew in Christ's name and love, in such measure that he could not forget, could not find rest away from Christ – she so built up herself, her life, her tears, her prayers between him and death, that he could not pass over, could not be lost; and so she has become in her conquering faith a messenger of hope to all mothers."[114] Monica's example, it was thought, would provide some encouragement to mothers with "wandering" children, but a note of caution was also sounded here; the author stated that the story of Monica's life might also "warn some careless one lest she come to that deepest place of torment – to be the mother of a lost soul."[115]

Poems from Irish Catholic sources expressed the same sentiments as this Presbyterian article did. Father Matthew Russell, the long-time editor of *The Irish Monthly* and the author of many books of religious verse, was particularly devoted to St Monica.[116] Her patient endurance was thought to be both example and inspiration for Catholic mothers.

> St Monica, still many a mother shares
> Thy strong maternal faith,
> Still sheds such bitter tears, still breathes such prayers,
> To save from death
> Some soul perchance from all hearts else exiled
> As vile or wicked, yet *her* child, her child!
>
> Be *Monicas*, oh, mothers! pray and weep,
> Send ceaseless sighs to heaven,
> That ye for heaven and God secure may keep
> Whom God has given.
> Love them, but save their souls at any cost-
> "The child of holy tears cannot be lost."[117]

St Monica, then, was a model for Christian women because of her relationship to a "notable" Christian man. Her story was used to reinforce the widely held belief that a Christian mother's influence for good was incalculable, or as Russell rhetorically asked in his poem "St Monica," "How large a mother's part in hero's glory?"[118] Both Catholic and Protestant authors lauded St Monica for her exemplary Christian motherhood. As these portraits of Monica demonstrate, the model of the Christian mother who "laboured, loved, and prayed" knew no denominational boundary.

WOMEN OF THE OLD TESTAMENT

The Old Testament presents special problems because of the violence and drama contained in its pages, yet Ulster religious writers continued to read their own construction of female piety onto the women of scripture. When women were in positions of leadership, their role was viewed as an aberration from women's natural sphere. The actions of such female leaders of Israel as Esther were praised for their obedience to God's plan, but there was always some concern that such a role would be damaging for a woman unless she somehow carefully maintained her "womanliness." When a woman committed bloodshed, her act, even though ordained by God, made her unwomanly, left her "unsexed." The passages from the Old Testament that were most frequently selected for their prescriptive value were those dealing with the virtues of domesticity. References to "the virtuous woman" of Proverbs, chapter thirty-one, were scattered throughout the Ulster literature. Sometimes it was only a brief reference to a "woman whose price was above rubies," or one "whose children praised her in the gates." The story of this woman from Proverbs was common cultural currency among Ulster Protestants.[119] Even prophetesses and queens were praised, not so much for their strength, courage, and faithfulness, as for their ability to maintain the proper balance in their lives: to be modest, virtuous, "womanly" women despite their unusual positions. "The *conduct of holy women is recorded in Scripture as an example to others of their sex*," opined Joseph Beaumont in the *Primitive Wesleyan Methodist Magazine* in 1852.[120] According to this writer, then, the very reason for the inclusion of women in the pages of holy writ was that they should provide a model for other women. Given their belief in the purpose of the appearance of women in scripture, it is understandable that authors who wrote about biblical women might regard every passage that mentioned a woman's actions as potential material for female instruction.

Ulster Protestant religious writers demonstrated considerable discomfort in dealing with the lives of powerful and independent women in the Old Testament. The public lives of these women could not readily be made to fit the confines of the prevailing cult of domesticity.[121] Their solution to this vexing problem was to minimize the public role of biblical women or to explain it away as aberrant and to return repeatedly to their theme of the fundamentally domestic nature of the women of ancient Israel. While granting that one of the most notable facts concerning the women of the Old Testament was that they were not "debarred from the prophetic office," the author of "Hebrew Women" goes on to remark that a "peculiarity of the women of the Bible is that neither prophetesses, teachers, nor heroines were severed from the ordinary ties of domestic life."[122] The author's reading of biblical texts was evidently coloured by the sentimental view of the home as an oasis of peace. "Numberless are the traits of tender domestic affection to be found, like wild flowers in the wilderness, inexpressibly cheering in the midst of those sandy wastes."[123]

A host of Old Testament women were praised for their ideal domesticity in Ulster Protestant literature, but as was mentioned above, "the virtuous woman" of Proverbs, chapter thirty-one, was the ideal type of this genre. In the lead article of the March 1864 number of *The Evangelical Witness and Presbyterian Review*, a study of Proverbs 31:10–31 was presented. In his or her examination of this passage of scripture, the author found the opportunity to assert the virtues of essentially domestic Protestant female piety against the anti-domestic nature of Roman Catholicism. "The truth is, this chapter is sorely controversial and decided against Romanism. Its 'virtuous woman,' whose price is above rubies, is not a lady abbess, nor a Sister of Mercy, nor a recluse of any kind whatever, but a good, true wife, a prudent mistress in her own house, and the mother of boys and girls who will rise up and call her blessed. Romanism has no place here."[124]

The "virtuous woman" demonstrates "this type of womanly worth among the common duties of daily life. Sensible, judicious, and painstaking, she fills her place adequately."[125] Not only does she go about her work efficiently, but she also tenderly shows to others God's mercy and love. "Is this a strong-minded, bustling woman, merely doing well for her family? No. Feminine energy without feminine softness is not lovely. But the virtuous woman has a breast to pity and a hand to help."[126] She is the ideal woman who labours, loves, and prays. Finally, the author of this article proclaims that the "virtuous woman" of Proverbs, chapter thirty-one, is a "looking-glass for ladies, which they are desired to open and dress themselves by; and if they do so, their adorning shall be found unto praise and honour and glory at the appearing of Jesus Christ."[127] The "virtuous woman" was an ideal for Ulster Protestant women. It was not only living women who were to "dress themselves" in accordance with her example; other biblical women were made to conform to her perfect, domestic image as well.

The story of Ruth and Naomi was a favourite one in Protestant popular literature. In an article for *The Irish Presbyterian* which focused on the domesticity of Ruth's story, L.A.M. Priestley notes, with relief, that after the "clang and clash of arms" of Judges, with Ruth the sacred narrative looks inward at the "poetry and pathos" of everyday family life: "... there is a sense of rest and idyllic beauty in the domestic drama here unfolded."[128] The author clearly admires Ruth's many virtues, her kind treatment and loyalty towards her mother-in-law, Naomi, and her obedience in the course of all her actions. "And who can follow her history without feeling glad at the happy ending of the little romance of the harvest field?"[129] enthuses the author. Edifying short stories and novels written for women by Christian authors, both Catholic and Protestant, frequently reinforced the notion of reward – a happy home and husband – for women who followed the ideal of the "virtuous woman"; if, like Ruth, they put their duty to others before their own interests, they would be rewarded. The sheer romance of

Ruth's tale of domestic triumph – poor girl in straitened circumstances acting in noble selfless fashion, attracts the attention of a chivalrous, wealthy hero and marries him – clearly appealed to the female author of this article. Ruth was deemed a model for Christian women "Ruth, because of her unselfish devotion and faith, stands out pre-eminently among the women of the Bible as a singularly attractive and noble character."[130]

In a paper read at a meeting of the Cliftonville Guild, Belfast, and subsequently published in *The Irish Presbyterian*, the author, under the pseudonym "Lyncaeus," extolled the virtues of three women of the Old Testament: Vashti, Esther, and Jephthah's daughter, who is unnamed. After briefly referring to the modesty of Vashti[131] and the courage of Esther, the author spent the balance of the paper discussing the rather obscure[132] story of Jephthah's daughter. Jephthah had been cast out of his father's house by his brothers because he did not have the same mother and Lyncaeus imagines him living the life of a "banditti" who, like the bandits of romantic literature, had a particular attachment to his family life. Thus Lyncaeus paints a tender scene of the outcast Jephthah's domestic life and the attachment between father and daughter. The unnamed daughter is described as winning and beautiful; a lovely maiden charming her lonely father. (Lyncaeus assumes that because no mother was mentioned, Jephthah was a widower.) Lyncaeus tells how Jephthah promised God that if he gave his assistance in battle, "whatsoever cometh forth of the doors of my house to meet me when I return in peace ... I will offer it up for a burnt-offering" (Judges 11:31). Jephthah was victorious and upon returning home, to his horror, "who is this that comes first to meet him? It is his daughter. With songs of victory on her lips, still warm with her father's parting kisses, she comes to hear from his pale lips the terrible sentence of death."[133] When she listens to her father tell her of his vow to God, "we can almost see the transformation of the merry maiden into the sublime heroine. We watch her look of agony melt into one of unearthly calmness."[134] To this author, Jephthah's daughter's act of ultimate self-sacrifice showed she possessed "the great characteristics of true womanhood."[135] In her "sublime submission" this "heroine" embodied the best of a loving, womanly nature, for "How rare is such love that perishes, if needs be, for the good of a beloved one!"[136]

While I do not think that Lyncaeus in his or her romantic enthusiasm for the drama of this passage of scripture was actually suggesting Ulster women sacrifice their lives if their fathers demanded it, the author clearly thought the story of Jephthah's daughter contained a valuable lesson in the virtues of obedience and loving sacrifice. The example of the "true-hearted women" discussed in Lyncaeus's paper was to provide a counterweight against the "New Woman." "In these days [1898] of clamour for Woman's Rights, she will do well to reflect that there is one right which has not and cannot be taken from her, and that is the right to be virtuous and lovable, and by means of the love of fathers and brothers, husbands and sons, to rule mankind."[137]

Even such a singular biblical woman as Jephthah's daughter was used to reinforce the construction of the ideal woman who claimed her right to "labour, love and pray" and sacrifice to the very last.

Powerful Old Testament women such as Queen Esther and Deborah the Prophetess were described as being torn between their womanly "natures" and what God demanded they do. In an article urging Ulster Protestant women to "rise up" and fight against Home Rule, the example of Esther was used "Esther did what is always the hardest thing for a conscientious woman to do. She set aside conventional rules, defied customary restrictions, and struck out for herself a course of action, entirely without precedent."[138] Yet as a rule women such as Esther were not used as models for average women. Dr DeWitt Talmage, whose sermons were frequently printed in the Presbyterian periodical *The Witness*, granted that occasionally God called "a Miriam to strike the timbrel at the front of a host" but, "generally, Dorcas would rather make a garment for the poor boy; Rebecca would rather fill the trough for the camels; Hannah would rather make a coat for Samuel."[139] The participation of biblical women in the religious and political affairs of Israel puzzled Irish writers: "She (Deborah) was an anachronism, a phenomenon. How is she to be accounted for?"[140] The author partially explained Deborah's exceptional position by stating that Deborah was a widow with "no home ties." This "mother in Israel" was assumed to be an elderly widow.[141] Regardless, she was not of the aggressive type of "New Woman;" rather, she was supposed to be first and foremost a lady. The author of this paper presents Deborah as an archetype of a better more truly womanly "New Woman," not one who "clamours for votes and a seat in Parliament," but a more refined version. "Had Deborah lived to-day she would have been on the School Board and the Board of Guardians, and would have been the foremost in the work of her Church."[142] In other words, she would have been doing what the author of this paper and her other influential female friends were doing in their communities. But they were not prophetesses or leaders of their nation in war. Authors of this kind tended to bring biblical heroines to their own level of activity or "sphere of influence," to use their own words, in order to validate their own commitment to ideals of true womanhood.

Finally, women of the Old Testament who engaged in bloodshed were condemned as being unwomanly. In a lengthy poem for *The Irish Monthly*, the Reverend Joseph Farrell describes the story of Judith, the Israelite woman of the Apocrypha who brought victory over the enemy by murdering their leader, as told by Judith herself. Judith is an old and lonely woman in Farrell's poem. She says that she is proud to have "won a people's thanks" and "Proud to have snatched a name – a woman's name – / From out the nameless host that pass obscure / From birth, thro' happy motherhood, to death, / And leave no record save in children's hearts."[143] The childless Judith admits that "proud thoughts are these, but ah, not happy thoughts,"[144] for she has violated her own feminine "nature" in accomplishing the deed that made her famous and brought her people victory. Of the actual deed, killing Holofernes, the general of the Assyrian army,[145] Judith says:

> That my hand slew him I have no regret;
> But what a load to lay on woman's heart!
> At too great price a woman buys renown;
> And, when her name goes forth from her own doors,
> A host of troubles sit about her hearth.[146]

In Farrell's poem Judith speaks of her longing for children and for the comforts of a peaceful domestic life that could never be hers. She regrets that all anyone will know of her is her "man-like deed" rather than her love for her dead husband, Manasses, and her hope that she kept within her "woman's heart" for children and grandchildren. Instead, because she stepped over the boundaries of true womanhood, Farrell portrays her as being filled with sorrow and regret.

> But mothers who, me childless, shall proclaim
> Mother of Israel, yet shall shrink to lay
> Their innocent children on my widowed lap;
> And innocent maids shall shudder secretly,
> And deem that blood, though justly shed, leaves stain
> Upon the hand that shed it, and deem too
> The deed that made me great left me unsexed.[147]

In the tragic and morbid conclusion to "Judith," Farrell describes with great pathos the consequences of Judith's deviation from the natural, domestic place of women: "But never child of mine shall stroke my face, / Nor touch those chords within my lonely heart / That only baby fingers skill to touch. / Thro' time to be, my child shall be my deed."[148] Her murderous deed was to provide her cold comfort indeed in Farrell's interpretation of her story. The story of Judith in the Apo-

crypha, however, has a decidedly more celebratory and less regretful tone. In Judith she is called "the joy of Israel" and the "honour of our people" (Judith 15:10, Douay). Her chastity was described as a source of her strength and virtue. Oddly enough, given the common view that Roman Catholics valued the celibate over the domestic life, Judith's celibate widowhood is not celebrated in Farrell's poem; rather her childlessness, the coldness and loneliness of her old age, reinforce notions of the joys of the domestic hearth.[149]

Mary Magdalene, "the woman at the well," Mary and Martha, Lydia, Ruth, Monica, Judith, and the other female "sinners and saints" mentioned in this chapter lived their lives in periods and places far removed from Ulster in the late Victorian and early Edwardian eras. Yet their stories provided the vehicle for a didactic discourse that was to touch on matters of fundamental importance to the authors and audiences of Ulster relgious literature. Whether their authors claimed strict adhesion to principles of biblical literalism or not, these sermons, articles, and stories tell us far more about these Irish authors and the religious culture in which they participated than they did about the lives of the "women of old."

The lives of biblical women were used to reinforce religious and cultural norms for women that were deemed crucial to the survival and continued success of the projects of Ulster's main religious denominations. The "saints" among these women – the Monicas, Marthas, and Lydias – were lauded chiefly for their domestic virtues. Self-sacrificing and virtuous, these mothers, daughters, wives, and sisters were presented by male and female writers in this discourse as the foundation on which a godly society was built. The "sinners'" ruin provided a warning against any deviation from the norms of virtuous womanhood; no brazen, selfish, or sensual behavior would be tolerated.

The lessons to be taken from the lives of the women of sacred history were not just for grown women; these examples were also impressed upon middle-class Ulster girls. The moulding of the Christian character of these girls is discussed in the next chapter.

5 "A Future of Blessing and Service": The Moral Education of Ulster Girls

The experiences of middle-class Ulster girls as they passed through the rigours of young womanhood were as individual and varied as were the girls themselves. Yet there were clear prescriptions and guideposts provided by the clerical and lay leaders of their respective religious denominations. Increasingly, towards the end of the nineteenth century and into the early decades of the twentieth, ever more material was made available to aid these girls in their development into Christian women. The authors of both Roman Catholic and Protestant literature for girls sought to reinforce the ideals of true womanhood (the woman who "laboured, loved, and prayed") and the concomitant appropriate gendered behaviour.

The "enfant de Marie" of the Loreto convent school at Newry and the "Girls in Council" correspondent who attended "Methody" in Belfast each lived in very different worlds, surrounded by rituals and regulations that the other girl would not recognize or even find comprehensible. The content of their religious educations was markedly different: a steady diet of catechism, saints' lives, Church history, and devotion to the Virgin Mary for the former, and scripture study, "improving" literature, and the development of a personal relationship with God for the latter. These substantial differences in the content of girls' religious education do not obviate the significant similarities in the goals and ideals behind the pious curriculum. Both girls would have been imbued with ideals of purity, holiness, service, and self-sacrifice. Their religious education – at home, at school, and within their churches – groomed the majority of them for the role of Christian wife and mother.

In this chapter, I intend to look at the ideals of female piety presented to girls within their schools, the opinions of the supporters and the critics of religious education, and the stated goals of character formation of those concerned with the development of female piety. Protestant criticism of Roman Catholic female education and vice versa will also be discussed. Religious fiction written for girls, which increased in popularity towards the end of the period under study, provided an important source of pious prescription. The heroines of these tales embody the ideals for which Christian girls were expected to strive. Throughout this literature I found that Roman Catholic and evangelical Protestant girls alike were being prepared for a life of Christian service for others, be it in the home as sisters, wives, and mothers or through church organizations as lay activists or as nuns. This literature impressed upon girls that their contribution to their homes, schools, churches, and to their broader communities was a valid one. Ulster girls were told that their obedience, cheerfulness, helpfulness, and other ideal "girl qualities" made a positive contribution to the lives of those around them. The increasing focus on the "usefulness" of girls' pious efforts coincided with their participation in a proliferation of organizations aimed at developing their characters and providing the Christian community with female workers.

CONVENT BACKGROUND

The phenomenal growth of female religious congregations in Ireland in the nineteenth century – in 1800 there were 120 nuns, in 1851, 1500, and in 1901 over 8,000 – made a significant impact on the lives of all Irish Roman Catholic women. Most of the new congregations founded in the eighteenth and nineteenth centuries were not enclosed. Their sisters were active in teaching, hospital work, and other philanthropic activities. The first of these new active congregations was the Presentation order, which was founded in Ireland in the 1770s under the leadership of Honora Nagle, a Catholic gentlewoman of independent means from County Cork. After several decades of struggle the Presentation order flourished, and following in the train of its success the rest of the important Irish foundations appeared in the first half of the nineteenth century.[1]

What type of educators were these women? Teaching congregations of Irish nuns saw their pedagogical duties in religious terms.[2] As will be discussed, moral training took precedence over academic endeavours, and this moral training had a clearly bourgeois tone. Tony Fahey, in his examination of the reports of the national school inspectorate of 1864, came to the conclusion that "the public perception of the sisters went far beyond an appreciation of their piety. They were also seen as paragons of educated bourgeois femininity."[3] The nuns of the Mercy convent in Armagh were remarked upon by the inspector as having "received the education of ladies," and of the Poor Clares in Belfast it was said that "their acquirements are ladylike and such as would be expected of persons in their position."[4] Fahey notes that unlike the overtly nationalist Christian Brothers, the nuns' educational message was not political; rather its focus on "moral instruction" inculcated a respect for religious and civil authority. Rather than showing any particular interest in the Gaelic past or the Irish language, the nuns, Fahey asserts, demonstrated a "provincial fondness for French literary polish."[5] Based on his review of the 1864 school inspectorate, Fahey purports that the teaching congregations "pursued the embourgeoisement of Irish culture with missionary conviction."[6] The emphasis on ladylike modesty and refinement and other tenets of bourgeois respectability and on French cultural models found in the literature for convent schoolgirls bears out Fahey's claim. These nuns shared with Ulster evangelical Protestant teachers and social reformers a keen commitment to inculcating middle-class values of female propriety in the young girls in their charge.

For Irish Roman Catholics the religious training of girls was a topic that bore close examination. Pioneering teaching nuns such as Honora Nagle were honoured by Catholic writers because these women were considered important carriers of Catholic culture during its "darkest days." In *Irish Homes and Irish Hearts* Fanny Taylor describes the key role played by the sisters. "A vast number of young ladies were trained to become good Christians by the Ursuline nuns; and by their means the faith was preserved and revived in many and many a home."[7] In her biography of Mother Mary Xaveria Fallon of the Institute of the Blessed Virgin, Katharine Tynan is effusive in her praise of the role of teaching nuns in Irish life. After the "long rust of penal days," Tynan says, the education of well-to-do Irish Catholic girls begins to run smoothly thanks, chiefly, to the efforts of teaching congregations such as the Institute of the Blessed Virgin. What was the attraction of convent education? According to Tynan, "Irish fathers and mothers love to give their little girls to the nuns for training ... The nuns make the girls ladies, if that is at all possible; for every nun is a lady, and the standard of refinement in convent and convent school-life is, if anything, excessive ... and who shall say that the fine and delicate purity of Irish women is not kept to its standard as much by this rarefied atmosphere, in which the most susceptible years are lived, as by inherited disposition?"[8] This is no trifling matter. Belief in the "fine and delicate purity of Irish [Catholic] women" was an important part of Irish Catholic cultural identity. The conviction that Irish Catholic women were more chaste and pure than were Protestant women in Ireland and other women in the rest of the British Isles was deeply cherished and widely held by Irish Catholic Nationalists. That convent education was thought to make a positive impact on this important aspect of the Irish Catholic self-image – sexual purity – indicates the importance of the role of teaching orders to, as Fahey terms it, the "embourgeoisement" of Irish Catholic life. While romantic Nationalist myth holds high rates of sexual chastity and low illegitimacy to be a constant feature of Irish peasant life[9] in the nineteenth century, this can only be said to hold true for the latter half of this period when the Catholic devotional revolution, with its legions of priests and nuns, instilled a new set of highly ascetic sexual mores and rigid middle-class notions of propriety into the Catholic population.

For Katharine Tynan, convent life contained within it everything that stimulated her romantic imagination. "Much of the poetry of the world seems to me to conserve itself in the convents. There is a high ascetic poetry in the resigned wills, the cheerful abnegation, the patient service, the hardship to delicate bodies, which is a rule in all religious orders."[10] Such an idealized picture of convent school life would hold that this rarefied atmosphere was the optimum one for the moulding of the characters of Irish Catholic girls. As we shall see below, critics of convent education, both Catholic and Protestant, were not so sure. Others who argued in favour of Catholic religious education for girls during the same period, took a more practical approach than Tynan's.

In *Woman's Work in Modern Society*, Mary Francis Cusack, popularly known by her nom de plume, "The Nun of Kenmare," downplays the genteel side of convent education and stresses the practical benefits of sound religious training for girls. Cusack's chief argument for the religious education of girls is one that was examined in chapter 2. "Women have the early education of men and if women have not a complete and definite religious education, it is not likely that they will confer it to their children."[11] While this was the traditional argument for female education from the time of Mary Wollstonecraft's *A Vindication of the Rights of Woman* (1792), Cusack sees the systematic development of female morality as a crucial check against a tide of male irreligion. Throughout the chapters of her book that deal with female education, Cusack lashes out at male sceptics and intellectuals who she feels are responsible for the moral decline in modern society. "The fashionable teaching about religion in certain circles of modern society is, that it is a convenient method of governing the vulgar ... Women and the mob must have some kind of religion; it is necessary for them because we [the intellectuals] wish to keep them in subjection ... but as for us others – we are quite above such superstitions."[12] While these men may scorn religion, Cusack says, even they recognize the primary importance of religious education of girls. For even while their own irreligious writings may be leading others to perdition, "they do not care to see their sister or their wives infidels, because they know that the next step will be that they shall see them immoral."[13] Given what she sees as the hypocrisy and apostasy of fashionable intellectual trends, Cusack feels that female piety is more crucial than ever before; women can be "the salvation of the country." Cusack argues that "If men, by their infidel teaching, are pouring in a broadside of destruction on all ranks of society, let women take their own place, in their own sphere, and let them do the noblest mission that women has [*sic*] ever done."[14] Cusack and Tynan presented two very different views of why Irish Catholics should support the kind of moral training for girls provided by convent school education, but both would agree that moulding the characters of Irish girls along lines that accorded with Catholic ideals of female piety was of the utmost importance.

IDEALS OF CONVENT SCHOOL LIFE

If one based one's knowledge of Irish convent schoolgirls on poems published in Roman Catholic periodicals, one would be left with the strong impression that most of the girls' moral training was somehow concerned with horticulture. Rare is the poem on convent life that does not mention girls picking roses, gathering daisies, seeking quiet in the convent school garden, or strewing flower petals on holy days. The argument could be made that this concern with flowers, perhaps culminating in the frequent reference to the girls themselves as "lilies," is a symbolic reinforcement of notions of purity and innocence.[15]

The girls, together with their teachers, the nuns, were considered to be, ideally, like flowers in their innocent beauty, fragility, and purity. Father Matthew Russell, editor of *The Irish Monthly* and author of many books of devotional poems, expressed a deep fondness for convent children and an enduring interest in their education and development. Yet his prose presents an idealized portrait of convent girls and their blossoming piety. In "The Little Flower Strewers,"[16] Russell tells the "dear children" to see their hearts as flowers, lovingly and obediently given to God. "Yes, let your flowers be emblems of holy thoughts and prayers / That from your hearts are springing – for hearts alone *He* cares. / Oh! may your hearts before Him with loving worship glow, / While thus you throw your flowers and kiss them as you throw."[17]

The innocent girls, "With lips unstained and rosy, kiss all the roses fair," yet they must be warned of the dangers and hardships of life and urged to accept God's will. "But thorns lurk 'mid the roses, and life is full of care. / Accept its thorns and roses – *both* come from God, you know: / So bear your crosses gaily, and kiss them as you go."[18] In this poem we see Russell's ideal of the convent child with her heart aglow with love for God, innocent and "unstained." Even these "innocent flowers" must be warned about the hardships of life – the "crosses" – which they must bear. "To Mercedes On the Day of her First Communion" contains similar themes.

> Thy childlike innocence to-day finds echoes all around,
> And watchful hands will guard the seed which springs from fruit-ful ground;
> But shouldst thou feel, in days to come, the scathing breath of sin,
> O Lily, fold thy little leaves, for Jesus is within![19]

The beauty of these ideal little flower-like children possessed a great charm for adults harried by the busy round of modern life. "Spared!" is the story of a "modern" Catholic mother whose child became seriously ill while away at a convent school. Initially the mother had misgivings about sending her child away to a convent school, but on her first visit, when she heard "the sweet voices of the children as they played on the green terraces" and saw "Rosary Walk" where "the roses grew in wild profusion," she was won over. Her little girl, the mother reports, loved her school and loved the nuns: 'I love them *all*, mother; they are *all* good to me.' Under such conditions her child blossomed until struck down with a severe case of the measles. A Protestant friend suggested she take the child away from the convent to nurse her, for nuns were not to be trusted in such grave matters. But, instead, the mother went to stay at the convent during the child's illness and found her own faith renewed in the hallowed atmosphere within the convent walls. One day in the chapel, she found her daughter's little classmates praying for her recovery. "One little girl I noticed especially; she seemed about seven years of age, and as I looked at the rapt flower-like face, I could see the baby lips moving in the intensity of her fervour."[20] The piety of the children and the holiness of the convent brought the mother back to God. After her daughter's recovery the mother went to the convent cemetery – "ablaze with sweet spring flowers" – on the last day of her visit. She was told by "the bright-faced nun" at her side that the flowers had suddenly blossomed with the late sunshine. "As I turned away," the narrator says, "I felt that something else had blossomed in my heart, in the love and sympathy of the last few days – something that I would never quite lose again."[21] The author draws a portrait of an exemplary convent school, one that had a positive spiritual impact on all those who came in contact with it. The piety of its "flower-like" students had the power to touch the souls of the lapsed and unbelieving. Catholic writers who lauded convent education only presented to their readers extraordinarily holy and benign descriptions of convent school life. Whether this ideal had much basis in the realities of day-to-day convent school living is not important for our purposes here. Rather, what is significant is the evident belief that these high ideals of piety and holy purity were to be found within Irish Catholic convent schools.

ENFANT DE MARIE

A further aspect of the moral and religious development of Irish Catholic girls that bears investigation is the construction of Catholic female piety that may be found in the material concerning the sodality of the "*Enfant de Marie.*" "May and Mary's Children" is an enthusiastic account by an Irish nun of the origins of the sodality and what it means to be a member. Sister Delores notes that while all Roman Catholics are Mary's children, those "who can claim as our own the sweet title of 'Child of Mary'"[22] are specially consecrated to the love and service of the Blessed Virgin Mary. After giving a brief history of the sodality, Sister Delores proudly adds that although "Mary's Children" are found throughout the world, "nowhere are they more numerous or more fervent than in our own green isle, where love for the Mother of God has always been deep in the people's hearts, even in their darkest hours."[23] According to Sister Delores, attendance at the sodality's meetings, where members would practice various Marian devotions such as saying the Rosary, was edifying for all who participated.[24] It brought the "Children of Mary" closer to the Virgin and to each other. Some "Children of Mary" met in mixed groups, but all-female associations were more common and the "*Enfant de Marie*" was most popular in girls' convent schools. [25] Sister Delores declares that upon her "Children" the Blessed Virgin bestows "choice blessings," both spiritual and temporal. But what does Mary ask in return? She asks imitation. "Mary expects her children to imitate her as far as they can, and this is the surest proof of love – imitation; for will not a child who loves its mother do all it can to be like her?"[26] As our discussion of the Virgin Mary in chapter 3 revealed, her life provided a model for perfect female piety. "If we study the life of Mary on earth ... we shall see that her days went by in the perfect performance of the ordinary duties of her state, duties not unlike our own; so she does not require anything extraordinary from us, only that we try to be like her in her charity, humility, and entire submission to the Divine will in every detail of our lives, as she was; and this she will help us to be if we only ask her."[27] The phrase "duties not unlike our own" subtly excludes men from association with this model and reinforces Mary's connection with women. Catholic women and girls who were "Children of Mary" were urged to pattern all aspects of their everyday existence after the Blessed Virgin. Sister Delores's assertion that "[the Virgin Mary] does not require anything extraordinary from us" seems to fly in the face of Mary's perfection; surely perfection is not readily attained. The possible frustration in this model is mitigated by the votary's personal relationship with the Virgin Mary and the willing assistance which the Virgin Mary lovingly bestows on her "children." Despite her perfection, the Virgin Mary was not a remote or unapproachable figure to her followers; rather sodalities such as the Congregation of the Children of Mary fostered a deeply personal and emotional affection between Mary and her devotees.

As Sister Delores points out, the "Child of Mary" phenomenon was an international one, and the influences that were most noticeable in Ulster convent schools were continental. Irish organizations, such as the Dublin-based Catholic Truth Society, made frequent use of European pious stories for their publications. "The Month of Mary" is one of a number of stories about continental Catholic piety found in the book *Tales of the Festivals*.

"The Month of Mary" is the tale of a disobedient, French-speaking Swiss girl named Minnette, who left her devout Roman Catholic parents to marry a Protestant in a distant village. Not surprisingly, he was a drunken and abusive husband who, fortunately for Minnette, the author informs us, died quite suddenly. Shortly thereafter, Minnette gave birth to a little girl. She called the child Marie, and resolved that the girl would be dressed in white for her first fourteen years "to honour the purity of the Mother of God." The author does not say whether Marie or her mother formally belonged to the sodality of the Children of Mary, yet the child is constantly referred to as being an "*Enfant de Marie.*" Minnette begged the Virgin to help her rear her child and her petition was answered. As the author informs the reader, "Our good Mother in heaven is so ready to hear all who earnestly implore her assistance, that it is no wonder the little Marie, at the age of six was more like an angel than a mortal child."[28] Madeleine, a local girl and *Enfant de Marie* who assisted Minnette when little Marie was battling a serious illness, has a discussion with the precociously pious Marie about what it means to be a child of Mary. "'Ah,' said Marie, seriously. 'But then you must be very good, and pure, and obedient, or you will not please Mary, even by that white dress, which you wear in honour of her purity.' 'What a dear little child you are,' said Madeleine, kissing her. 'Am I a dear little child?' asked Marie. 'But that is because I am the child of Mary. It is so sweet to be her child. I hardly know which I love the best, the Mother of Jesus in heaven, or my own mother upon earth.'"[29] Little Marie was the ideal child of Mary. Sweet, innocent, and pious, this little child-angel was almost "too good for this earth." "The Month of Mary" ends with Madeleine telling the desperately ill, though uncomplaining, Marie the history of the Feast of the Sacred Heart, the moral of which is that the people whom God loves the most must suffer.[30] While we might find "The Month of Mary" cloyingly sentimental in its description of holy little Marie, this story was in keeping with the sentimentality that was attached to children in this period and to matters of sacrifice and suffering in Roman Catholic literature.[31] In Marie we see the nascent form of the ideal adult Catholic woman. Self-sacrifice and obedience were her hallmarks.

"*Madonna: Verses on Our Lady and the Saints*"[32] contains several poems that give a glimpse of the ideals of Marian piety that were taught young *Enfants de Marie* in their convent schools.[33] In "Our Lady's Lamp," Father Russell writes that "a certain Irish *Enfant de Marie* informed her *chere Maman*, in a letter home from school"[34] that she rises at six in the morning to light the lamp in front of the Virgin Mary's shrine. Russell uses the devotion of this convent girl *Enfant de Marie* as an example and as a metaphor for the devotion of every member of the sodality. While this "pious maiden" literally lights a lamp before the Virgin's altar in the cold early morning hours, Russell urges all *Enfants de Marie*, especially those no longer within convent school walls, to keep their own flame of devotion to the Virgin alive.

> So in holy convents, where gay children cluster
> Round the childlike Angels that guard them well;
> So in holy convents, more tranquil, where *these* only
> Live their life of prayer in choir and cell;
> So in holy homesteads, *in* the world, not *of* it,
> Peaceful homes and pure, kind friend, like thine
> May we all, at least in heart, keep burning
> The lamp of love before Our lady's shrine.[35]

The pious lessons learned as a convent girl *Enfant de Marie* were supposed to prepare a Roman Catholic woman to create a "holy homestead" in which the Marian ideals of purity and obedience were inculcated in the next generation. From mother to daughter the ideal of domestic piety was passed, thus ensuring the continuted survival of "Catholic Ireland."

Father Russell's *Madonna* contains many other poems that provide an idealized portrait of young *Enfants de Marie* joyously doing their pious devotions, garbed in spotless white dresses, their silver Marian medals gleaming from their blue Child of Mary ribbons.[36] In "Enfant De Marie,"[37] he addresses the nature of Marian piety as expressed in this particular sodality. Russell's own pride in this organization of which he was a member and keen supporter is evident in the opening lines of the poem: "'Child of Mary.' Name of honour, / Prouder far than kingly crown." In this poem, he describes how Christ called his followers to consider the Virgin Mary as their mother; when dying on the cross he said to St John, "Lo, your Mother!"[38] Russell continues, noting that sinful humans are not worthy to call Mary "mother," yet she receives all her children. "Thou of Mercy's self art Mother, / And thy heart is meek and mild; / Open wide thy arms and take me / As a mother takes her child."[39] The final verse of the poem sums up the all-encompassing commitment to Mary of the ideal *Enfant de Marie*.

> "Child of Mary." May my feelings,
> Thoughts, words, deeds, and heart's desires,
> All befit a lowly creature
> Who to such high name aspires.
> Ne'er shall sin (for sin could only)
> From my sinless Mother sever –
> Mary's child till death shall call me,
> Child of Mary *then* forever.[40]

Schoolgirl *Enfants de Marie* were presented as having Marian ideals of femininity and pious practices that they were supposed to carry with them for life. It may readily be seen how such intense moral training within the *Enfant de Marie* milieu of convent schools[41] prepared young girls to become devout, obedient women, followers of the Marian cult who would train their own children to respect the Church's teachings and to love her saints.

"'GIGGLING' METHODS:" QUESTIONING THE ADEQUACY OF CONVENT TRAINING FOR GIRLS

Few voices critical of the nuns' methods of providing girls with a moral education were raised in Irish Roman Catholic circles. Rather, effusive praise of convent schools, like that given by Katharine Tynan or various other authors of poems and didactic articles in *The Catholic Bulletin* and *The Irish Monthly*, was the norm. But Charlotte O'Conor Eccles, in her article "The Girls of To-day and Their Education," provides a different point of view. She was concerned that traditional Catholic education did not prepare girls satisfactorily for their role as wife and mother. It is curious that Eccles's criticisms, which were occasionally reminiscent of typical Protestant attacks on the frivolity of convent education, were published in the very pro-convent journal, *The Irish Monthly*. By the turn of the century, however, when this article was published, Irish Catholics seemed to be more secure about their religious institutions and more ready to hear moderate lay criticism. Eccles's criticisms of the current training of girls were substantial. While not directly attacking the convent schools' emphasis on refined lady-like pursuits and sentimental piety, she does say that an education should fit a person for the life that they are going to lead and, moreover, that convent education does not sufficiently prepare girls to be wives and mothers in the world outside of convent walls.[42] She argues that within convent schools " ... girls are educated to live in a world of quite a different kind to that in which they find themselves. A sort of ideal world is built up before them, a place they picture vaguely. They are told they will meet with "temptations," which they must resist, but what the nature of these temptations may be, they have not the faintest idea."[43] Though Eccles says she would be the last person to want "premature knowledge of evil" to taint a young girl's mind, she does believe that the older girls need to be taught many things about the world. She uses the example of temperance education, saying that when she was at school, drunkenness was considered a vulgar subject and never mentioned, even though it is a "national vice," the evils of which she feels girls should be warned.

Throughout this article Eccles expresses her fear that Catholic girls are woefully unprepared by their teachers in many different areas, but that they were particularly ill-informed about the realities of the relationships between men and women. She supposes that only a few girls had mothers who could guide them in this area, for she believes most women are not competent to train their own daughters. What she feels is needed is "motherly counsel" from the girls' teachers on the subject of men and women. Eccles's frustration with convent school education is evident when she writes that "these [relationships between women and men] are the important things of life, – not keeping silence in the ranks, nor winning a prize, but how they are ignored!"[44] Eccles criticizes the inadequate way Catholic teachers handle serious matters."From the Teacher's studied reticence has arisen what I may call the 'giggling' method of discussing vital questions like love and marriage."[45] According to Eccles this "giggling" method left Catholic girls singularly unprepared for what was "for most women the supreme duty in life ... to be a good wife and mother."[46] While it cannot be denied that the ideal of Catholic moral training for girls was to create young women who were first and foremost devout Christians rather than girls who were prepared to tackle every exigency of the cruel world, a reading of the literature would suggest that most Catholics who were concerned with this subject thought that that the virtues learned in convent schools *did* prepare girls to be virtuous mothers, wives, sisters, and daughters.

A fictional convent girl who was more than ready to take on the rigors of managing both spiritually and temporally in the domestic sphere was Anne Sheridan, the young heroine of Nora Hanrahan's serial story, "A Valiant Woman." The story begins with Anne confiding in her elderly parish priest, Father Cussen – something she continues to do throughout the story – that she does not want to do her duty as eldest sister and look after her widowed father and his household; she wants to be a nun. Anne tells the priest that her poor, unhappy mother always felt that "she had missed her vocation, that she ought to have been a nun herself – and then she was so pleased and comforted when she knew that I was to be substitute for her."[47] Despite Anne's objections – like her mother, she detests the dull routine of farm life and longs for the peace and beauty of St Ursula's convent – the priest convinces her that it is God's will for her to stay at home. He tells Anne that her father is a "careless Catholic" who cannot be trusted to raise the younger children in the faith; their souls are in her keeping. "Make the sacrifice willingly," Father Cussen advises Anne "and His strength will sustain you."[48] As she settles into her routine at the farm, the sound of the church bells pealing from the distant town tempt Anne to "cast duty to the winds, and fly to where her heart was set," St Ursula's. Anne dreamily thinks of her beloved convent with its "spiritual comfort and calm ... the nuns so dear and kind, the bright-faced girls, the total absence of the sordidness and worldliness of life."[49]

At this point, it seems as if Anne's story bears out the criticism of those who accused convent education of leaving girls ill-prepared for the "real world." Anne's reluctance to stay at home and work for her family makes her seem selfish and otherworldly. Yet her convent training in self-abnegation stands her in good stead in her new duties. Despite her yearnings for the convent, the self-disciplined, pious, and obedient Anne puts all of her energies into the task at hand. She transforms her father's home into a model of order and beauty; two attributes she learned to cherish at St Ursula's. It is interesting to note that in her difficult task – the place had suffered under her mother's poor management – Anne had the assistance of a sort of "female support network". Nanna, who had been a friend of her grandmother and who had nursed the whole family, is described as a "faithful henchwoman," and Mrs Carberry, the "wise, gentle" invalid next door also gave her counsel and, moreover, "spiritual refreshment."[50] Thus, outside of the convent, young Anne finds Catholic laywomen from whom she receives guidance on matters both mundane and sublime. Without criticizing religious life, the story is turning into a celebration of the glories of domestic life and the benefits of convent education as a preparation for domesticity.

The next instalment finds the family and the poor of the community flourishing under Anne's gentle care. Anne, who has "advanced views," visits the cottagers, and her advice and suggestions had all the more weight, the narrator tells us, because her words and actions were totally devoid of patronage. "'Miss Anne is that understanding about the poor,' old Nanna was wont to say, 'she never makes a mistake, and never hurts their feelings. 'Tis she has the great heart and head.'"[51] At the same time, her father, Pat, is acting like a new man. Because Anne had practically worshipped her mother and was blind to her faults, she had assumed that the fault for her parents' unhappy marriage lay with her father, but it was her mother's own thwarted desire for convent life that poisoned their home. "Embittered and disappointed," the narrator tells us, "she lived her own selfish existence, a martyr to nerves, moods, and extreme depressions."[52] Father and daughter become very close, spending cosy evenings together discussing their various interests, and gradually Anne comes to revise her previous judgement of him as a cold and harsh man. Pat Sheridan no longer goes out in the evenings; he stays by his own hearth in the company of Anne and the children. "'Remember that talents and accomplishment are powerful weapons in the hands of a good woman,' Mrs Carberry had said to Anne during one of their many intimate talks, 'and ones to which our men folk are specially susceptible. You will be your father's chief companion, Anne, and you will use all your arts and gifts to soothe and alleviate his weariness.'"[53] Anne takes the advice of this godly Catholic woman, and these were the happiest years of Pat Sheridan's life "when this gentle-voiced elder daughter ministered to his comfort and saw so well to the ways of his household."[54] Anne has become a sort of substitute wife for her father, clearly superior to the original. Father and daughter are described as true companions and soulmates, sharing the joys and sorrows of daily life. Without openly disparaging the dead, Anne wonders how her mother could have been unhappy with a man so tender, thoughtful, and generous as her father.[55] Although just a young girl, not a wife and mother, Anne is becoming a model of domestic piety as she "labours, loves, and prays" in her domestic sphere.

By dutifully attending to her domestic duties Anne has made an enormous spiritual impact on her family; her father is again a devout Catholic, her brother Jack intends to become a priest, and her sister, Alice, wants to enter St Ursula's as a novice. From the time that Anne took over running her father's household, it had been assumed by the family that once the children were raised, Anne would take "the rose-strewn path that led to St Ursula's." Alice's decision did not cause any conflict, though, because now Anne realizes that her vocation was the domestic sphere, not the religious life. Anne is concerned that her "changeable" nature is a character flaw, but her old friend, Father Cussen, assures her that that is not the case. He wonders if perhaps it was her mother's desire that she should be a nun and her own love of her school life at St Ursula's that made her mistakenly think that she had a vocation. Father Cussen tells Anne that in her domestic role she has garnered "a rich harvest" of souls. The story ends with Anne's marriage to Mrs Carberry's nephew, an owner of considerable property in the district, who, most importantly, promises not to come between father and daughter. As the young couple drive away after their wedding, Pat Sheridan calls out, "God bless her! ... she has been the angel of our home." Father Cussen then lays his hand on Pat's shoulder and says, "Who shall find me a valiant woman? From afar, and the utmost bounds is her price ... the woman that feareth the Lord she shall be praised!"[56] Pious, loving, and capable, Anne Sheridan is an ideal type of Catholic laywoman. In "A Valiant Woman" Anne's success in the domestic realm is directly related to the important lessons in obedience and self-sacrifice which she learned at St Ursula's.

While Eccles was one of few Catholic laypersons who expressed concern about the adequacy of convent schools for the moral training of girls, the verdict of most authors, such as Nora Hanrahan, was that they were havens of piety and refinement which prepared the majority of their young pupils to take their place in society as pious Catholic wives and mothers.

PROTESTANT GIRLS' EDUCATION

The discussion on female education that emerged in Protestant religious literature, chiefly in the latter part of the nineteenth and in the early twentieth centuries, was not concerned as much with moral training and piety. There seemed to be an almost unspoken assumption that everything that Protestant girls participated in should prepare them to be the mothers of future generations of Christians. This is implicit throughout Protestant debates about the cult of domesticity and the role of women. As will be discussed, many girls themselves were keen participants in discussions about their character formation and their proper pious behaviour. Yet as far as the debate on the formal education of females was concerned, the crux of the matter was the gradual introduction of more academic subjects, examinations, and entry into higher education.

The conventional wisdom concerning women and intellectual activity was that academic pursuits were injurious to their health. Even at the very end of the period under study some educators and physicians were protesting against the ill-effects of "grinding" for examinations on the constitutions of delicate young ladies. A pamphlet advertising The Lodge, Fortwilliam Park, Belfast, a ladies' school run by a Miss Rentoul, proudly proclaims that since the establishment of the school, no pupil has been prepared for or sent to any type of public examination because it is "the belief of the Principal that severe Competitive Examinations ... are detrimental to true education, and entirely valueless to all girls except those intending to become teachers."[57] The pamphlet goes further, adding that the principal "is also convinced that the strain which preparation for examinations must of necessity involve is injurious to health in very many cases, and in some leads to permanent injury."[58] The author of the pamphlet backs up the principal's statement with a quotation by Dr Joseph Nelson of Belfast. "One can often diagnose an Intermediate student by observing the rounded shoulders, the peculiar gait, the wearied and anxious expression, before examining the eyes at all. I think the system is for the nation a vicious one."[59]

The well-known Ulster temperance activist, suffragist, Unionist, and founder of the Belfast Ladies' Institute, Isabella Tod, was at the forefront of those who thought the views of Dr Nelson and those of his ilk were ludicrous and who called for higher education for girls.[60] One of her early pamphlets arguing for more rigorous academic training for girls is titled *Advanced Education for Girls of the Upper and Middle Class*. In her pamphlet Tod boldly contradicts this prevailing belief by stating that a certain unnamed "medical gentleman" – who had great experience with the treatment of the insane – said that "in a fearfully large proportion of the cases of insanity among ladies that he had met, it had been caused simply by emptiness of mind, by having nothing interesting to do."[61] Eventually the opinions of Tod and other education reformers won out, and attitudes toward women and higher education changed.[62]

Tod presents arguments that are similar to those put forward by the "Nun of Kenmare," Mary Francis Cusack. A woman's pervasive influence as wife and mother requires that she be properly educated for her duties. According to Tod, "If a woman's tone of mind be low, or even striving unsuccessfully after better things, her influence upon others cannot be either very good or very happy. The higher and finer her mind, the better for all about her; the more her sources of interest and satisfaction ... the brighter is the light she will shed on other hearts."[63] In contending that "a highly literary and scientific education is as well adapted to prepare for the performance of feminine duties as masculine," Tod makes some interesting arguments. For example, she asserts that if a knowledge of the classics is considered a good preparation for a young man who intends to practice law, then it is no less important "for the management of the thousand forms of charity which lie in the hands of ladies."[64] Likewise, if "mental science" is necessary for a young landowner, it is also required by his young wife in order that she perform well her duty of training her children, her servants, and the poor on their estate. In case these specific examples were not sufficiently persuasive, Tod concludes this part of her argument by stating that the advantage of ensuring that a young woman possesses a "well-trained mind" is that such a trained intellect can "do any duty in the best manner practicable."[65] The justification that education would help a Christian woman perform her sacred duty of influencing for good those within her "sphere" was a logical one for education activists like Tod to use.

Finally, we will leave aside the unresolved question of the medical effects upon girls of either too much or too little study and return to the question of moral training and character formation. Protestant women, girls, and clergymen earnestly discussed this matter of a girl's proper Christian development – her "true education" – in the pages of Ulster Protestant periodicals outside the context of formal questions concerning educational methods, exams, and curricula. Perhaps the forum in which this discussion was conducted with the greatest diligence and enthusiasm was in "Charity Hope's" column in *The Christian Advocate.*

PREPARING FOR A LIFE OF CHRISTIAN SERVICE: "GIRLS IN COUNCIL"

"Girls in Council" columns began in the Methodist weekly The Christian Advocate in 1898, and transmuted into "Kings' Daughters in Council" when older women were invited to join the discussion in 1900. When reading these columns one is struck by the rapport that developed between the council's moderator, Charity Hope,[66] and her girl, and later women, correspondents. As her pseudonym indicated,

Charity Hope was a women who valued the potential of young women and urged them to live their lives, especially their spiritual lives, to their fullest potential. There is a confiding, chatty tone to her columns; one almost feels as if one is eavesdropping on private conversations. Topics ran the gamut from the mundane to the intensely spiritual. At all times Charity Hope took her girl correspondents' concerns very seriously and consciously tried to avoid, in her own words, being "preachy" when dispensing advice. The warmth that she felt for "her girls" and the optimism that she had for their futures may be found in all of her writing.[67] In one of Charity Hope's first columns after she opened her "Girls in Council" to women, she printed a letter from a correspondent who expressed her concern at the direction that the education of the modern girl was taking. "Girls are taught every 'ic and 'ology, but how much they need to be taught the infinitely more important subject, the growing of character, and what a girl's highest ambition should be."[68] As we have seen, by the turn of the century "'ics" and "'ologys" were fairly well established as part of the education of most middle-class Protestant girls. Nonetheless, adults who were active in the plethora of religious organizations in which girls participated – the Girls' Auxiliary, the Band of Hope, the Christian Endeavourers, the Girls' Brigade, the Girls' Bible Reading Band, and various Sabbath Schools, among others – were still very much concerned with the moral development of young girls.

Charity Hope and her correspondents discussed both the pitfalls facing girls – their weaknesses and faults – and the important strengths that girls possessed, which included their vitality and enthusiasm in doing "their Master's work." The chief fault that Charity Hope thought needed to be corrected in young girls was their tendency to nervousness and hysteria.[69] Writing at the turn of the century, she noted that thanks to better discipline and hygiene, the "hysterical woman" was almost a thing of the past, yet girls needed to be watched carefully for signs of highly strung nerves and they needed to discipline themselves to combat this tendency.[70]

What did this discipline consist of? It involved learning to give onself entirely to God. Charity Hope provides the example of two bereaved women; the first lost her child, the second her husband. The first woman was not trained as a girl to have "a disciplined heart" and she sank into utter misery, rebelling against God and spiritually poisoning all around her. The second woman was smitten by the loss of her husband, yet she bore her loss because she knew it was the will of God. "Her strong, brave nature asserted itself in the face of calamity."[71] A "disciplined heart" was one which helps a girl or woman overcome her weakness and calmly, bravely accept God's will. A woman who gives in to her "nerves" and despairs, as the bereaved mother in this example did, was deemed undisciplined and selfish. In the Roman Catholic religious literature as well, girls were told to prepare themselves to accept God's will obediently in all things; to accept the "thorns" among the "roses." In both Roman Catholic and evangelical Protestant religious cultures, young women had to be steeled against the trials that they would face – especially that of bereavement, a frequently discussed subject in literature for girls and women – and taught to assuage the pain of their "crosses" through perfect acceptance of the divine plan and trust in God's love for them.

In another of Charity Hope's columns, we can see how hysterical female behaviour was regarded as unGodly and, above all, selfish. Charity Hope cautions her "Girls in Council" readers against succumbing to their own wilful inclinations in all areas, especially that of Christian service. Charity Hope tells her readers of a girl at school whose "spiritual mind was suddenly captured by the idea of a selfless, Christlike life, or what she interprets that to be." In a religious fervour, ignoring the wishes of her parents who had been educating her at considerable expense, and the counsel of her teachers and pastor, she leaves school to try to pursue some sort of missionary work, but she is utterly unqualified for any sort of service. Family dissension results and any potential good that the girl might have done at home or elsewhere is ruined by her wilful impetuosity. Charity Hope urges her girls to beware of "hysterical religion" and adds, "Let us ask God for the gift of 'sanctified common sense.'"[72] Clearly, it was thought that a young girl's moral development could be fraught with snares, given their "natural" weaknesses, however, for the most part, authors like Charity Hope had a great deal of praise and enthusiasm for the potential of "their girls."

Charity Hope was a woman who obviously enjoyed "seeking counsel together" with her young correspondents, and, in general, she had a very high opinion of the worth and potential of young Ulster Methodist women. In one of her columns she writes glowingly of having a friendly chat with "... girls who are beginning to take serious views of life, and whose God-given instincts are reaching out after the highest and best in it. I do like to meet a girl like that. It seems to me that everything is possible to her, with her high hopes, and noble aims, and brave, determined front presented ever to the world."[73] In this particular column she articulates ideas that permeate her "chats" with the girls and her responses to their questions. She repeatedly validates the contribution that young girls made in their homes and churches and urges them on in their spiritual and moral development. She does not belittle their activities and queries;[74] although she occasionally apologizes for being "preachy," she obviously was very concerned about "her girls" and their development into "true women."

What did Charity Hope want for "her girls"? She spells out her ambition for them in the following manner. "The mission of girls is to perfect themselves in everything that will fit them for a future of blessing and service to others, which will be their mission – their God-given mission – as women."[75] Women's role of service to others may appear humble, she notes, but it is "really a very important one." As will be discussed in the next chapter, Charity Hope was a vocal champion of the gradual expansion of the role of Methodist women so that they could be of service to the wider sphere of their churches and communities. She sought to instill in "her girls" a sense of the greatness of the mission that they had received from God and of the great importance of the work that they could piously and obediently do now, as girls, which would prepare them for their duties when they were grown women. She ends this column with the following message. "God help you all, dear girls, to be ministering angels in the home and the world around you. So will you fulfil the noblest mission that ever human being could be called. – Your sincere friend, Charity Hope."[76]

Whether "her girls" were "bachelor girls" making a living as typists in the unfamiliar surroundings of commercial Belfast or whether they were still schoolgirls or "co-eds" at Queen's University, Charity Hope praised their every effort and urged them on to further Christian service. In a "Girls in Council" column in which she talks about the particular niche that God has for every one of his workers, young and old, Charity Hope exhorts her "dear girl-workers for God" not to be timid or afraid in doing God's work. She beseeches them not to listen to discouraging voices who say that they are being too pushy or presumptuous. "Try to get rid of this enervating self-consciousness and vanity and lack of moral courage, for all such fears spring from just these hateful sources. Be bold to obey your Master and carry out His directions on the lines He has laid down for you."[77] Many other "Girls in Council" and "King's Daughters in Council" columns deal with this subject of girls training themselves – developing the necessary moral stamina and selflessness – to be of service within their homes, churches, and communities.[78]

Charity Hope tells her readers that she considers uncomplaining service to others to be the mark of true heroism. She informs them of one such girl who was tried by this test of duty and "found to be true gold." The girl had aspired to a "noble career of usefulness" in the world outside of her home, but her hopes were dashed when her parents called on her to return home and help them. She uncomplainingly worked as the household drudge, receiving no recognition or praise from her family for her sacrifice. Charity Hope calls attention to the girl's "brave patience, her cheerful courage, her unflinching devotion to most distasteful duty. It is all done for Jesus' sake; that is the secret of her heroic life."[79] The idea that even the smallest, most thankless task, if done for Christ, had value, impressed on these girls a sense of their own value and worth. Through their service for others they could become holy heroines. The ideal Roman Catholic convent-trained girl – as exemplified by Anne Sheridan of "A Valiant Woman" – was likewise trained to believe that her obedient service in her home and community redounded to God's glory.

Those who wrote about and for evangelical Protestant girls sought to make them aware of the power for good inherent in what they did in their daily round. The themes expressed in the story "The Service of Margaret"[80] encapsulate this idea of validating girls' contributions. Young Margaret Wilson set out one lovely afternoon from her comfortable bourgeois home with a list of frivolous personal items to purchase in town. On her way to do her shopping she returned a lost child to its mother, assisted an elderly gentleman to his home, stopped some children from fighting, visited with a little crippled girl who was one of her Sabbath school pupils, read to an old woman a letter from her emigrant son, fetched some medicine for her washer-woman's sick child, and helped an anxious country woman find a city address. All of this Margaret did cheerfully and willingly, all the while realizing that if she did not hurry, she would miss the last tram into the city. Of course, she missed her tram and went home empty-handed, only to be teased by her brother who said it was just like a girl to take an entire afternoon not to buy a dress. When her parents inquired as to what she had been doing with her time, Margaret bemoaned the fact that she had "wasted the whole beautiful after-noon." Margaret was surprised when her parents showed deep inter-est in her recitation of the tasks that she had accomplished, since to her they had seemed mundane and trivial. Her parents earnestly assured her that her afternoon had not been wasted: " 'You may not have realized it, Margaret,' said her father, looking into her sweet face, 'but you have been serving the Master Himself, for He said, 'Inasmuch as you have done it unto one of the least of these, you have done it unto Me.'"[81] "The Service of Margaret" presents an idealized portrait of the cheerful, giving, middle-class Christian girl who puts service for others ahead of her own wishes and plans. It is a light-hearted story, yet it sets out the goal of service to which young Protes-tant girls were to aspire. These goals of service for family and com-munity were presented to Catholic girls as well, as we have seem from "A Valiant Woman" and "Kathleen O'Mara's Petition."

SABBATH SCHOOL TEACHING AS A
TRAINING GROUND[82]

"Laurie," a "Girl in Council" and young Sunday school teacher, had
these earnest words to say about making the best use of the weekly
hour that Sunday school teachers spent with their young charges:
"There should be no useless talking, that every word almost ought to
be full of power."[83] Charity Hope told "Laurie" that she was glad to
hear that she took her Sunday school work so seriously, for "the young
souls of the scholars are committed to them [the teachers] as a sacred
charge to be accounted for some day ... May God give you the joy of
seeing them, every one, saved."[84] Sunday school teaching was a training ground for the young women who figured largely in the ranks of
its workers.[85] Of course, young girls usually were Sunday school pupils
before they became teachers. But the tendency to have girls begin
teaching Sunday school in their early teens meant that they ceased to
be instructed at an early age. In the October 1868 number of *The Irish
Presbyterian Sabbath School Teacher*, a lesson for a senior class of girls is
provided. The subject is "the virtuous woman" of Proverbs, chapter
thirty-one. All of the virtues of female domestic piety are present here.
The text of Ada Whitla's "Girl's Bible Reading Class" at the Grosvenor
Hall were printed in *The Christian Advocate* (August and September
1900). The texts afford an interesting perspective on what the instruc-
tor thought were the flaws and foibles of girls were – gossip, pettiness,
spitefulness – and their remedies. Through Sunday school teaching
they were to develop habits of discipline, selflessness, and nurture.
Sunday school teaching was to prepare them for their roles as wives
and mothers and as active Protestant laywomen, while at the same time
their involvement was supposed to make an important contribution to
the ministry of their churches. A paradoxical relationship existed
between the importance accorded to this branch of the churches'
work and the lack of prestige given to the actual teaching of Sabbath
school classes.

A Church of Ireland clergyman, the Reverend Samuel Hutchison,
wrote in *The Irish Church Quarterly* that "it will be readily conceded that
there is no more important branch of parochial organization than the
Sunday school. It is the Church's nursery. It contains the men and
women of the future."[86] Charity Hope makes a similar statement,
observing that "next to preaching, Sunday-school teaching is the most
important part of the Church's ministry," but she wonders if this "most
important" work has become "a despised form of Christian service,
and, if so, why?"[87] Charity Hope surmises that the primary reason for
Methodist Sunday-school teaching's lowly status is that "it so often

happens that unqualified teachers undertake the task, perhaps very young ladies who ought to be imbibing knowledge themselves."[88] In an article providing advice for Sunday school teachers, Miss Nixon of Castlebalfour, Lisnaskea,[89] lamented the fact that all too frequently when a young person became converted they were seized upon by well-meaning superintendents as potential Sunday school teachers "without considering if there be any aptitude for imparting knowledge or impressing Gospel truths on a child's receptive mind, or pausing to ascertain if there has been a Divine call to the work."[90] Inexperienced and inefficient Sunday schoolteachers were considered a problem[91] in this female-dominated field of Christian endeavour.[92]

Those responsible for organizing Sabbath schools seemed to be aware of the particular difficulties of the work of young female teachers. Apparently, only women taught the youngest children – "the infant class." In an article on the subject of "the infant class" in a Sabbath school report, the author, Miss Higginson, describes the trials of a young Presbyterian teacher as she tries to instruct her squirming and talkative class of "wee" scholars. "Finally, just as she has determined to give up altogether, the bell tinkles, and with a sigh of relief she sees her small flock troop out of the room. 'Well! that's over for another week,' she mentally remarks as she follows them."[93] This was not an ideal situation. However, the author acknowledges that "it requires effort and patience – endless patience – and much preparation; but if one knows how to work and how to gain and keep the children's interest, the reward is sweet beyond words."[94] "Besides," Miss Higginson assures them, "there is no class so important, so full of infinite possibilities, so rich in precious opportunities, as that class of 'wee' restless, talkative mortals."[95] As was the case in the discourse on women's influence within the domestic sphere, Sabbath school literature was replete with references to the possibilities and power inherent in this "most important work" of influencing the young.

But as we have seen, this work was neither easy nor sufficiently appreciated. By way of encouragement to "self-denying, faithful young teachers," Charity Hope related her own struggle as a young woman with her Sunday school duties. At first she found "this Sunday teaching irksome and uninteresting, the hour with my class to be sped through as easily as possible, and with a minimum of beforehand preparation."[96] But she had a change of heart when she felt a personal call from God: "my work was suddenly glorified. Here was a ministry for me, all my very own."[97] Though Charity Hope adds that she hopes the story of her own Sunday school work as a young woman does not sound "egotistic and selfpraiseful," clearly she thinks that here was something that young women could feel was their own; something valuable that they could contribute. Charity Hope ends this column on Sunday school teaching with these words: "It is a high duty and privilege to be allowed so to fit and fashion lives that hereafter may bless and uplift the world."[98] Because the "natural" maternal role of women in this discourse was to nurture young souls and to bring them to God, Sunday school teaching was an appropriate extension of the domestic sphere.

If they did not receive sufficient praise for their work in life, in death young female Sunday school teachers were depicted as paragons of female Christian virtue. The obituary of a Miss Curry, late of Belfast, presents a typical portrait of an active, involved evangelical laywoman. From her youth (she died at the age of twenty-eight) she was a Sabbath school teacher, church organist, and active member of the Christian Endeavour. She is described as having been a faithful and diligent Sabbath school teacher for many years; "both loved and looked up to" by the girls in her class who "greatly miss her and mourn her loss."[99] Her extraordinary piety and devotion to her class of girls are brought out in the following testimonial. "She longed during her illness to get back to her loved work in the Sabbath school. She felt she could be of much more use to her class in consequence of the lessons she had learned during her illness, and the deeper insight she had got into the meaning of Scripture, as the result of the rich spiritual blessing she had received at the Lord's hand."[100] After describing the powerful influence that her illness and death had on all who knew Miss Curry, the author of the obituary concludes, "thus lived, and thus died, this humble, thankful, gentle, unselfish soul."[101] This was the greatest commendation that could be given a "true woman" in Victorian Belfast.

The redemptive power in the work of a girl Sunday school teacher is sentimentally presented in a Methodist short story, "The Little White Teacher." Flossie Hunter was visiting her elder sister, a minister's wife, before she left Ireland to live with her parents who were missionaries in Japan. Her sister taught a Sunday school class, and Flossie accompanied her sister to the Sunday school on her last day in Ireland. Due to a shortage of teachers, Flossie was asked to take a class and she unselfishly gave up her last few hours with her sister in order to do so. Flossie's exact age is not given, but she is described in great detail as being a tiny woman of pale complexion all dressed in white. No doubt this was symbolic of her purity and innocence. To Flossie's great discomfort, the class that she was assigned to teach was comprised of great, unruly "boys" all of whom were larger than she and some were older. Upon seeing their dainty teacher, the young men "giggled, sniggered, and whispered together in a tantalising fashion that brought the rich colour to her cheeks."[102] Flossie faced her task bravely, but the ringleader, Theo Harcourt, set them to creating bedlam. Before she dismissed her class Flossie reproached the "boys," saying "I will never be with you again. Tell me, if the Lord Jesus Himself had come to teach you this afternoon, what would He have thought of your conduct?" Flossie's words haunted Theo and he deeply regretted being unkind to the "little, white-faced girl" whom he would never see again. More importantly, because of her reproach, Theo began to think about his errant ways; that night he made things right with God and when he told his overjoyed mother of his salvation, he added that "'it was all through the little white teacher.'"[103] Several months later Flossie received a letter from Mrs Harcourt telling the girl of her role in Theo's conversion. As Flossie read the letter she felt "the gratitude of a mother's heart" being poured out before her; "'It was so little,' murmured Flossie, 'so little, and yet God used it.'"[104] Again and again, girl readers of evangelical Protestant literature had it impressed upon them that their "little all" could make an enormous spiritual impact. At the same time that this literature reinforced ideals of submission and obedience, it also empowered girls through its promotion of the idea that what they did in their service for others, and thus for God, mattered.

COMMON CONCERNS

Those who were engaged in the discourse on the moral training of girls, both Protestant and Catholic, had shared concerns regarding the "pernicious" influences that could thwart the proper development to pious womanhood of these young women. In fiction, the influence of bad companions invariably started the hitherto pious girl on the path to ruin. A brief comparison of two stories, "Ellen Dalton" (1853 – Church of Ireland) and "Lillie's Lapse" (1907 – Roman Catholic) shows that despite their chronological and cultural disparity, concerns about evil influences on impressionable young Christian women were expressed in a variety of Irish religious periodicals.

Ellen Dalton was the prize senior pupil in a rural Church of Ireland Sunday school, organized by philanthropic ladies, the Misses De Bohun. Much to the dismay of the ladies, Ellen had become inattentive and had let her lesson preparation slip. The source of this unfamiliar conduct in their favourite pupil was her consorting and competing with Mary Brown, a girl with an excessive "love of dress." Ellen had begun to emulate Mary, seeking to create fancy garments which she was told were inappropriate "to her station."[105] Despite her teachers' warning that her newfound "love of dress"[106] would ruin her,

Ellen continued on the downward slope. She was pert and disobedient to her parents and began walking out at "indecent" hours with Mary Brown. Ellen begins to meet secretly with her "lover," a Roman Catholic, who convinces her to run off with him to be married. He assures her that her family will forgive them once the deed is done. The couple remove to Dublin where, of course, they live a miserable existence. Ellen's husband begins to drink heavily and then he absconds to Australia, leaving Ellen alone with their newborn baby. When by chance the Misses De Bohun find Ellen in Dublin they give aid to their former pupil and try to bring about a reconciliation with her parents. Ellen, the former star Sunday school pupil, is penitent, but her life is ruined.

The heroine of "Lillie's Lapse" does not meet with utter disaster as Ellen Dalton did, but her "lapse" was due to the same "pernicious" influences of bad companions and love of frivolity. Lillie was an orphan who had an idyllic life at the convent school in a small town where she was raised by loving nuns. When she was of age, Lillie left that small town and the convent to live with her mother's sister in Dublin, where she was to learn how to make her living as a typist. At first, under her aunt's watchful care, Lillie flourished in her new life and kept up her regular religious devotions as she had done at the convent. But after the sudden death of her aunt, Lillie began to keep "fast company" with girls from her office who prized fancy clothes and theatre-going. Lillie began missing daily mass and neglecting her other devotions. The same evil influences that fifty years earlier ruined the Protestant fictional character Ellen Dalton almost brought about the the downfall of pious, Catholic Lillie. There is one important difference between the two stories. Lillie did not marry outside of her faith;[107] she was "going about with" an irreligious Catholic man, but he was not a barrier to her spiritual restoration. It was her "*Enfant de Marie*" training that proved to be Lillie's salvation. During the month of May – the month of Mary – Lillie saw some white-clad girls entering a church and she followed them inside where

A host of children in snowy raiment, carrying tiny banners, and singing the praises of the Virgin Mother, walked round the church. As Faber's beautiful hymn, "Sweet Star of the Sea," fell from the childish lips, a crowd of memories came to Lillie. The May evenings long ago, Our Lady's altar fragrant with wild flowers, primroses and the sweet wild hyacinths, the lovely spoils of the wood-land, the procession round the convent garden and she, Lillie Gray, a tiny child, running to darling Sister Paula, to beg her to adjust the veil which would keep falling off her curly hair.[108]

The May procession and its memories of the beauty and holiness of the convent brought Lillie back to the faith. The following Sunday, when her swain asks what form of amusement they should take in, Lillie firmly replies, "*I am going to Vespers.*"[109] "Dear me, what an emphatic *I!*" responds Charles, "And pray, may I not accompany your ladyship?"[110] Charles is readily led back to the regular practice of his faith by the winsome and newly pious Lillie. They marry, and Charles's verdict on his convent-raised spouse was that she makes "the best little wife in the world."[111] Lillie's "lapse" was not a fatal one; the lessons inculcated in her as an *Enfant de Marie* ensured that she did not stray too far from the faith; she did not break the irreparable taboo of marrying outside the faith. Yet the causes of her "lapse" were of grave concern to Catholic and Protestant moralists alike. Bad companions and a love of worldly frivolity, especially in dress, were the things that might take away from their respective churches the pious wives and mothers of the future.

Another matter that was discussed in Catholic and Protestant circles with great urgency, especially towards the end of the nineteenth century, was the problem of suitable reading material for young girls. In the early decades of the period under study, the reading of novels was reviled for the poor habits it encouraged in young girls. "A constant dissipation of mind and idle waste of time"[112] was how one critic described the ill effects of novel-reading on the characters of young females. Katharine Tynan describes her own running wars with her mother and with the nuns at her convent school over her love of novel-reading. Her tolerant father brought her books by Maria Edgeworth and the Brontës, but the women in her life thought she should only read the saints' lives and the *Imitation of Christ.* Facetiously, Tynan notes that in becoming a famous Irish Catholic novelist, she had not really broken her pledge with the nuns, for she had only promised that she "would not read novels. They did not ask a pledge against writing them."[113] By the latter decades of the nineteenth century, educators and parents were more concerned with the content of the girls' reading, rather than with the form. Now that the novel was an established part of a girl's reading, the concern was that it be wholesome fiction.

Writing in 1911, Nora Tynan O'Mahoney happily noted that "the modern Irish young girl" may find in the works of such Irish authors as Rosa Mulholland and Katharine Tynan "pure and wholesome literature – stories which, as someone said, 'leave a clean taste in the mouth' – they will find plenty to amuse and enthral, and at the same time, ennoble and uplift."[114] As long as the contents were edifying, novels and stories were now considered suitable for Catholic girls.

While they approved of the novels of Catholic writers such as Tynan and Mulholland, Catholic moralists were gravely concerned about "unhealthy and pernicious literature with which the country is flooded, the penny dreadful, the novelette, which depends for its attractiveness upon its power of describing sensuous passion and of inciting the same feelings in the mind of its reader."[115] The source of much of this "insidious poison," according to the Irish Nationalist *Catholic Bulletin*, was the "English Press."[116] It was felt that wholesome and edifying tales by Irish authors, grounded in Catholic morality, could act as an "antidote" to this "flood" of evil literature.[117] Catholic educators were also concerned with a lack of uniquely Irish Catholic books for children. The author of an article on domestic libraries warns parents to be careful when purchasing picture-books, "for often under the pretty petals of the English rose, the proselytising thorn lies hidden."[118]

"What shall we read?" was a question Charity Hope asked "her girls" in a series of columns. Their own responses indicate that while they enjoyed reading frivolous stories, they knew they should devote more of their time to "serious" literature, religious biography, devotional works, and, of course, scripture study. Charity Hope outlined the problem thusly: "We have been considering lately another of the deadly drifts, the pernicious habit which is growing upon us of reading cheap, foolish, scrappy literature."[119] One of the girls, "Sartor," writes: "I say unhesitatingly that sensational stories have a demoralising effect on young girls. They enervate, and if persisted in the mind becomes unfit to grasp or to concentrate on work of any depth."[120] Clearly, reading was such an important subject because it was thought to make a major impact on a girl's character formation. Charity Hope exhorts her readers to revolt against the low, "trashy" standards of literature that secular magazines offered to young women. "Are you going to perpetuate the mistakes of the past, or are you resolved that the mental, moral, and spiritual state of women shall be on a higher, nobler level?" she challenges her readers.[121] In the pages of all the denominational magazines aimed at a family audience, reviews and advertisements for "uplifting" religious fiction were printed. Thus even "novel-reading," in moderation, became accepted as long as the works themselves contained the approved ideals of female piety that were to mould the characters of young women.

While both Protestant and Catholic educators, parents and writers had similar concerns about the snares that might entrap pious young women – bad companions, love of frivolity, and pernicious literature – they believed the pious values that they imparted to their own girls were markedly different than those imbibed by "the other" girls. For the most part, Catholic writers presented Protestant female education as being irreligious and excessively academic.[122] Father Matthew Russell opined that Catholic education for girls should, first and foremost, develop their characters. He disparages the training of Catholic young women by governesses that leaves them with a few "accomplishments" and little else; such an ill-trained girl may "chatter as gracefully, or at least as incessantly as Protestant young ladies of the same standing."[123] Yet according to Father Russell, this is a travesty, for "she enters life almost as a great child as if she had never been educated at all; and though she may perhaps succeed in passing through it innocently, she is not at all likely to pass through it usefully."[124] Catholic writers presented the ideals of convent education, with its holy refinement, development of pious practices, and lessons of self-discipline, as being fundamentally different from the moral training received by Protestant girls.

Evangelical Protestant writers' criticism of Catholic schooling usually came within the same compass as general anti-Catholic literature. Convents were considered vile and unhealthy places for women, and injurious to girls. Ulster Protestant writers told with horror of unthinking Protestant parents who sent their girls to Continental convent schools because of the status accorded a European education. Stories were told of Protestant girls being carried away by the "romantic" atmosphere of the convent and converting to Catholicism.[125] Many Protestant writers criticized what they saw as the "superstitious" and "pagan" elements of Catholicism. Moreover, they believed that "smells and bells" rituals were used by the nuns to sway impressionable, refractory pupils.[126] Yet Charity Hope had words of praise for the nuns and some criticism of Protestant schools after she interviewed a woman whose daughters had converted to Catholicism after their stay at a Continental convent school. The mother reported that: "The girls told me of the saintly lives the nuns lived, of the atmosphere of peace that surrounded them, and in particular dwelt upon their habit of praying about everything they did. 'We were taught to put God and religion first,' they said ... We were in two Protestant boarding schools and we saw very little importance given to religion. The real business of the day was study, study, study, grind for exams., &c. Oh, there is no doubt of it God was not put first."[127] While she acknowledges that some Protestant schools have principals and teachers who emphasize "the injunction of Matt. vi., 33" – "seek ye first the Kingdom of God" – they are not the majority. Charity Hope also praises the lives of the teaching nuns. "There is no doubt these nuns practise what they preach. They lead humble, self-denying lives."[128]

Spiritually and morally, what both Catholics and Protestants most valued for girls and women was the development of well-disciplined character that enabled them to carry out their roles in a spirit of humility and self-denial.

The focus of this study now shifts from a direct comparison of Protestant and Catholic religious literature to an examination of Protestant literature in the areas of roles for women, and women's temperance and missionary work. The reason for this shift is twofold: First, Catholic literature is sparse in these areas during the period 1850–1914, and second, the literature that did emerge provides significant opportunities for examining the development of ideals of Protestant womanhood which were often constructed in opposition to a stereotype of Catholic women who were defined as "un-women," "other," or "heathen." While the focus of the next three chapters will be on Protestant literature, Catholic ideals and counter-ideals will also be presented.

Substantially, as has been demonstrated in the preceding chapters, the differences that existed between Protestant and Catholic constructions of ideal female piety were not truly meaningful. They created the same Christian woman. What can account for the superficial differences between Protestants and Catholics? The economic and institutional divergence of the Protestant and Catholic communities in Ulster provides the key to understanding why the Catholic laity was not involved in the reform and outreach activities of their church to the same high degree that evangelical Protestants were. For institutional reasons, the discussion of an expanding role for laywomen in the church came later in Catholic circles than it did among Protestants, and thus chapter 6 deals, chiefly, with Protestant arguments and viewpoints. Again, because of the later date at which the Catholic laity became significantly involved as organizers and activists in temperance and missionary endeavours, Protestants are also the focus of chapters 7 and 8.

This is not to say that matters such as the role of women in the church, temperance, and missions were not of interest to some Catholics. The growing Catholic urban professional bourgeoisie in Dublin was beginning to take an interest in these subjects by the end of the period under study. The Catholic lay community in Ulster, however, did not have sufficient hierarchical support, wealth, and leisure time to allow for activism in these areas.

6 "The Wind in Women's Wings": Defining Roles for Women in Ulster Protestant Churches

During the last two decades of the nineteenth century and the opening years of the twentieth, the intensity of the debate surrounding the issue of the expanding sphere of activity for Protestant women increased. In subsequent chapters I will examine how women's participation in particular areas, such as temperance societies and missionary work, influenced the developing discourse on female piety; here I intend to assess how the gradual increase in lay female involvement in the activities of the various Protestant churches was perceived.

This discussion of the expansion of women's sphere from the domestic realm to include church work was always informed by essentialist views of the nature of women. Developments that were broadly approved of, such as greater female participation in charitable works, received approval largely because they did not cause a break with traditional views of women's nature. While evangelical women in particular spent more and more of their time engaged in a dizzying round of church activities and far less of it within the prescribed domestic sphere, the importance of the cult of domesticity was not diminished. In the discussion of women's proper sphere it was frequently reiterated that woman's place, because of her very nature and the needs of society, was first and foremost at her own hearth. Church work that was viewed as a natural extension of women's nurturing role within their own homes could be added as a corollary to domestic ideology. Dissonance occurred only when matters such as female preaching raised the spectre of "unwomanly" women who forgot their naturally supportive, subordinate, and nurturing role.

Although Ulster evangelicals presented the domestic destiny of women as an eternal phenomenon even in the recent past, evangelical women played a larger part in the public aspects of the churches' ministry. David Hempton has observed that in England and Ireland in the late eighteenth and early nineteenth centuries "evangelical religion offered new windows of opportunity for women in preaching, teaching, and philanthropy before the hardening of denominational structures reestablished more conventional gender relations in the second half of the nineteenth century."[1] While evangelicals had not entirely forgotten their recent history, they tended to view it as an aberration from prevailing norms. In the period 1850–1914 tensions existed between those who argued for a more public role for Protestant women and those who felt that female piety was best exercised within circumscribed areas of home and church. Both groups used conventional arguments and called upon tradition to establish the orthodoxy of their viewpoint.

This chapter is in three sections: first, an examination of the debate concerning appropriate roles for laywomen within the Protestant churches, including a discussion of the ideal minister's wife; second, an analysis of the insistence on the primacy of the home for female Christian workers and the perils of neglecting their most important obligation; and third, an examination of the handling of contentious issues such as female preaching and the acceptable response of Christian women to the model of the "New Woman."

WOMEN'S ROLE: SERVICE AND SUPPORT

Plotting with any degree of precision the exact growth and expansion of the role of women within Ulster's Protestant churches is beyond the scope of this study. That information requires a detailed institutional study of the plethora of religious organizations led, staffed, and financed by women during this period. However, even an exploratory reading of the literature gives the impression of an explosion of activity among laywomen in the late Victorian era. Women had always made contributions to the work of their churches, yet in the late nineteenth century their level of activity was unprecedented.

The "feminization" of Protestantism,[2] which Ann Douglas and other historians have suggested took place in America, may also be detected in Ulster, although starting at a later date. An alliance of interests between male clergy and female laity similiar to that which has been traced in America also is in evidence in the North of Ireland during this period. This phenomenon did not occur on a unified front in America or in Ulster. Various denominations placed their own limits

on the appropriate sphere of action of the women within their churches. It should be remembered that all of these Christian churches were
patriarchal in the organization of their hierarchies, even though their
message and method was increasingly "feminized."

Yet some denominations allowed women an increasingly public role.
In Ulster it was generally conceded that the Methodists were the most
"advanced" in their views in allowing women greater "scope" in the
church and society. A report in *The Irish Presbyterian* noted that at the
opening of the new Methodist Church House at Westminster a speaker "made the boast that theirs is a Church admitting women to their
councils to a fuller extent than most other communions."[3] In
response, the Presbyterian reporter noted that, "Whilst there may be
some amount of truth in this, it can hardly be said of us Presbyterians
that we have not taken advantage of the services of women."[4] It was in
the Methodist and Presbyterian churches of Ulster that the participation of women was given the most encouragement. Accordingly, it was
in their periodicals that a lively discussion of the proper nature of
women's role in the church was undertaken.

As we have seen in chapter 2 on domestic ideology, the locus of
female piety, for Irish Protestants and Roman Catholics was the home.
How, then, could women's work outside of their homes and in their
churches be viewed as nonthreatening to this crucial domestic ideology? This was accomplished in evangelical discourse by viewing the
church, metaphorically, as a large family. Without oversimplifying
matters, it can be asserted that Methodists and Presbyterians viewed
the church, ideally, as the family writ large. A former student of
Victoria College, Belfast, a woman whose education would have been
steeped in prescriptive teachings about domestic piety, argues that
woman's work for the church begins in the home, where she raises her
children to a knowledge of Christ and an understanding of the importance of Christian service; her daughter, then, going out from a
Christian home and "into the larger sphere of service, is most
efficiently equipped for her appointed place in the Church, which
should be, for the members of the family of Christ, the *ideal* home."[5]
There is no break in continuity here. Home and church came to be
viewed as a practically seamless entity, united in purpose and plan.

If the church was seen as a family, or as an extension of individual
families, then this view would have dictated the form taken by the
discussion of the role of women within the church. Necessarily, in this
larger "family" women would have responsibilities and limitations
similar to those that operated in the domestic sphere, and they would
make use of the same "natural" feminine virtues that they employed in
their domestic duties. All of this meant that the discussion of women's

work in the church was informed by the same essentialist language that dominated the literature on women's domestic mission.

Articles addressing this topic of women's role in the church tried to define or set out the appropriate, "natural" range of women's church activities. Overwhelmingly, religious periodicals praised the enormous work that women were taking on in Ulster congregations. Only activities on the margins of acceptability, such as female preaching, received serious criticism. For the most part, women's work in evangelical churches accorded with accepted norms of womanly behaviour – modest and humble, not drawing attention to itself. Thus there was no need (except for instances when it was thought that church work interfered with domestic life) for a critical reappraisal of women's activities. Rather, most writers were concerned with spurring their female readers on to greater service in their churches, all in keeping with the accepted gender norms set out in the cult of domesticity, of course.

What church work was most suitable for Protestant women? Charity Hope addressed this question in a column titled, "Sisterliness." She admonishes her fellow "King's Daughters" to leave off their selfish total preoccupation with their own families and help the needy. The "tender care of the destitute and needy" was, according to Charity Hope, consummately women's work. Their very "natures" were suited to this kind of Christian service. Such "womanly" work should not be left to men and to a few single women for "It is mother's work, pre-eminently, and married women who have comfortable homes of their own, and some leisure should be doing the motherly work of the Church."[6] The phrase "motherly work of the Church" could be applied to every field of church endeavour which was officially sanctioned for women's participation. The motherly ideal of female behaviour prescribed for women roles that were loving, giving, and self-sacrificing.

The following passage printed in *The Witness* bears citing at length because its language is representative of the tone of much of the literature. "There is a sphere in which woman has moved with ever-increasing usefulness, and with none to dispute her right to be there. In the Church of God she has found a field for all her powers. There her best culture and her finest laurels have been secured ... The chief working force in our churches and Sabbath-school are women, as the main body of teachers everywhere, in schools and seminaries, are women who have been called of God to this high vocation of teaching. The nature and value of their service in the divine kingdom can neither be defined nor estimated."[7] Although this piece was reprinted from an American periodical, *Christians at Work*, it does capture the sense of the *significance* of women's work that pervaded the Ulster literature on this topic. In a column in which she argues for the inclusion of women at the annual Methodist Conference, Charity Hope enumerates some of the details of women's role in Irish Methodism. "Church membership numbers more women than men. There are the Sunday-school, the Band of Hope [a temperance organization for children], the Junior Christian Endeavour – all important parts of Church organization, and all peculiarly part of woman's sphere of influence."[8] Note that the organizations Charity Hope mentioned all involve women working with children. Women rarely instructed mixed groups of males and females when the children were into their teens. Women could instruct female-only classes when the students were of any age. This work with children and other women was considered to be the "motherly work of the church" and an entirely appropriate extension of women's "natural" domestic sphere.

While the importance of women's contribution was increasingly commented upon and lauded in superlative terms, it was not work that brought with it great prestige or public attention. But this was seen, by women as well as by men, to be as it should. Participation in church activities blurred the boundaries between "private" and "public," yet the use of the metaphor of the church as a family meant that the same gendered hierarchy presided within church departments as existed within the evangelical home. Woman was a "helpmeet" to man as his spouse, and she was a "helpmeet" to man in the church.[9] Her role was to serve. It was seen as only fitting that the divinely ordained gender orthodoxy prevailed to no less an extent in the church than it did in the home.

This ideal of "lowly" service was described by female Christian workers as forging a unique link between women and Christ. Frequent mention was made of Christ's choice to use the weakest and most unfit and to transform their paltry efforts into a powerful force to aid the coming of his kingdom. This type of argument validated women's auxiliary, supportive work and gave spiritual significance to their humble activities. "He who uses the weak things of the world" – Christ – was said to be calling women to engage in the work of the church.[10]

BALANCING DOMESTIC AND CHURCH DUTIES

In an essay read at a meeting of the Blackrock Methodist Literary Society, Mrs E.M. Bewley sketched the lives of such "Noble Women" as Elizabeth Fry, Florence Nightingale and Anne Askew (a Lollard martyr). After highlighting the achievements of these "notable women," Bewley hastened to add that "It is far from my desire to note only those women distinguished by their public virtues, nor do I believe the true nobility of womanhood shines brightest where many eyes can behold its lustre.[11] While she extols the virtues of these "Noble Women" who made an impact outside of the domestic sphere, Bewley shows herself to be a firm adherent of the cult of domesticity. She notes that "domestic" women such as Susanna Wesley "inspire us to noble living in our common social lives, and making home the fountain of our graces, we shall not fail to contribute to the dry and thirsty land around our dwellings streams of blessing and truth."[12] Bewley urges her audience never to forget that "while aspiring to a high standard of goodness and duty, that true happiness will always be within the home circle, where the nobility of a true woman's heart, and a noble woman's mind must be manifested ere it can reach the outer world."[13] Bewley by no means suggests that women's sphere should be entirely limited to the home. Rather, she states that "the sphere in which woman influences the world for good is much wider than society often supposes."[14] Yet this near omnipotent influence of women for good must begin in the home. According to this under-standing of women's nature and their God-given role, without this domestic foundation women would not truly be women and, thus, their influence would be for naught.

In a poem echoing the sentiments of "The Rights of Women" verses, Bewley provides her concluding thoughts on the proper sphere of women.

> Noble women are those whose lives
> Are spent for the souls they love,
> Whose highest joy is forever found
> In serving the needy and sad around
> In the strength of the One above.
>
> ....
>
> Noble women are those who love
> With a heart supremely true
> The kindred spirits who form a part
> Of the treasures of life, of home and heart
> Which ever are sweet and new.
>
> Noble women are those who die,
> At the close of a life well spent,

To leave behind them undying fame
Of grace and strength through a Saviour's name
By using the talents lent.[15]

Thus even though the balance of her paper was spent describing the lives of women who had earned fame through their activities outside of the home, Bewley insisted, particularly at the end of her poem, on the primacy of women's domestic role.

The question that seemed most pressing for evangelical women who were increasingly involved in religious activities outside of their homes was one of balance. While the ideal evangelical woman was a good Christian worker, there was the concern that involvement in church work might cause dereliction of home duties. The busy church woman with a dirty home and hungry family was a stock character held up for ridicule. "In these days of multitudinous claims of philanthropy," warned a Methodist layman in a paper given at the Dublin District Convention, "there have grown up in our homes too many Mrs Jellaby's [*sic*] – women who can instruct others, but fail to regulate their own homes."[16] In the concluding paragraphs of his paper, this layman addresses the widespread concern that female church activity, while important, could lead to neglected Christian homes. "The value of women's work in the Church cannot be estimated; but you may depend upon it that when it results in home neglect, the Divine order has been inverted."[17] Here we see an affirmation of women's domestic mission as divinely ordained. Women's "Christian service," while increasingly important to the church, was not women's primary sphere; it was considered a secondary, natural extension of her God-given domestic role. The equation for proper balance in the activities of the ideal Christian woman was not a quantifiable one, yet it was made clear to women where their primary responsibilities lay. "Let woman take her stand, side by side with man, in the work of the Church, ... but let her still be the angel of the house."[18] As long as she was still the "angel of the house," it was thought that a woman's church activities were properly balanced with her domestic ones.

In a column titled "A Devoted Life," Charity Hope presents to the "King's Daughters" the life of Isabella Macpherson as an example of someone who skillfully balanced the demands of home and church work. Charity Hope complains that most of the biographies of good women "written for our benefit, fail of their purposes, because the experience of ordinary women do not accord with those portrayed in them."[19] According to Charity Hope most women had little in common with the wealthy, leisured heroines of these works. Charity Hope thought that, like herself, her readers were almost entirely engrossed in looking after their daily round of home life, caring for children, and supervising servants. In Isabella Macpherson, though, Charity Hope thought she had found a Christian heroine to whom she and her readers could relate. Macpherson (1842–88) was a Scottish Presbyterian who devoted herself first to her brother's mission work and then to her clergyman husband's church. Charity Hope says she chose Isabella Macpherson's life as her text "because she is an answer to the oft-repeated assertion that a woman who is a devoted Church worker must needs neglect her home duties."[20] Macpherson was reputed to have "ministered the gospel" to upwards of twenty thousand souls on an individual basis, "all of which Christian work, 'with much more of the same kind, was simply a labour of love, and carried on side by side with laborious domestic duty.'"[21] Macpherson's priorities were clear. "Only when a hard day's domestic work had been gone through did she reckon herself free as one of Christ's volunteers."[22] Charity Hope considered Isabella Macpherson an exemplary model for her "King's Daughters" because she balanced perfectly the demands of the domestic sphere and those of Christian service. "To her the field was one and undivided. She served her Master as heartily on the one side of it as on the other."[23] With the proper balance, woman's sphere could be an "undivided" continuum between home and church. A "womanly woman" used the same virtues and graces in her peculiarly womanly work in the church as she did in her domestic work.

Despite this insistence on "home first" for evangelical women, some concern was expressed that too much emphasis was being placed on the role of women as Christian workers instead of on their role as wives and mothers. The centrality of the cult of domesticity to evangelical religious culture may be seen in this critique of women's extra-domestic mission. In a poem titled "In Error," Margaret E. Sangster[24] describes a Christian woman's longing to be given a special mission from God. Though she prays for "Some blessed station near thy [God's] side;" the woman could find no special work to do. Christ appears to the woman and she is convicted of her error.

> ... In shame I blushed,
> In shame my weak complaining hushed!
>
> For, lo! all day, the swift hours through,
> The work, Christ given, for me to do
>
> In mine own house had slighted been,
> And I, convicted so of sin,

Could only lift my look to His,
The grace of pardon as for this,

That I had yet to learn how sweet
The home tasks at the Master's feet.[25]

If a Christian woman was doing her "home tasks" thoroughly, then she was fulfilling Christ's mission for her. Extra work might be taken on, but for all women their work for Christ began at home.

We have seen in chapter 2 how a woman's care and nurturing of her family's spiritual and physical needs were viewed as a holy mission with great potential for good. Hospitality towards fellow church members, especially clergy, and towards strangers was viewed as a particularly womanly activity that could be an important Christian ministry. Thus hospitality within the home was regarded as work for the church. Again, the lines between home and church – the metaphorical home – are blurred in this undivided field. In a column printed on *The Irish Presbyterian's* "Woman's Sphere" page, the value of hospitality as an important work of the church is expounded upon. Pointing to the biblical precedent of Sarah's entertaining angels "unawares," the author notes that "the approval of God has rested on the womanly virtue of hospitality."[26] This aspect of Christian service was not without its drawbacks, however. The author expresses concern that the trivial worries of entertaining can result in a neglect of spiritual matters, rendering hostesses not unlike the "over-bustling" Martha of Bethany.[27] A belief in Christ's approval of the virtue of hospitality ameliorates the situation of the careworn hostess. "Sure of the Master's sanction and ... strengthened by His help" she finds "dignity add[ed] to the meanest bit of domestic drudgery."[28]

This view of hospitality as a God-given mission for women was the central theme of a tribute paid by a Methodist clergyman to the late Mrs R. Crawford Johnson. She was described as a woman full of kindness and womanly sympathy, always ready to extend her assistance to those in need. Her minister assessed her contribution in the following manner. "Mrs Johnson's ministry was pre-eminently a home ministry. Not a ministry confined to the home or the members of her family, but one in which the home was made the centre of a wide and holy activity. She had early learned ... few ministries can compare with that of a home which is the temple of Christ, dedicated to His service, and consecrated by much prayer and holy living ... Such a home Mrs Johnson created and maintained, its power and charm deepening and widening with the passing years. Here she was a queen in her own realm."[29]

A recurring theme in this tribute to an ideal evangelical woman was that of influence and power. The "home ministry" of Mrs R. Crawford Johnson and other women of her ilk was praised by evangelical clergy and laity for its "womanliness" and for its far-reaching, incalculable influence. That a woman could have such an important Christian ministry while remaining at home provided validation for those women who believed that it was, primarily, in their own homes that they could make the greatest spiritual impact. One need not venture much further afield if such power and influence could be wielded in the domestic realm.

This single-minded emphasis on the glories of home life for women resulted in an expression of palpable frustration with the "home first" ideology in Charity Hope's "King's Daughters in Council" column. A column which began with the words "We are getting so tired of the parrot-cry 'women should stay at home,' that we propose to have a little practical talk about it."[30] stirred up some very negative responses from her readers. While the Methodists were perhaps the most "advanced" of the Ulster Protestant denominations when it came to discussing "the woman question," Charity Hope's criticism, however mild, of conventional domestic ideology met with enough conservative opposition that she felt she had to clarify her position and seek common ground with her opponents – all older women whom Charity Hope thanked for their "motherly" chastisement – in a subsequent column.

Charity Hope's comments were not as radical as the opening sentence of her column might indicate. She bemoaned the constant repetition of the "keepers at home" refrain in middle-class[31] Protestant circles, yet she did not criticize its use because she did not believe woman's sphere was primarily domestic. Indeed, in other columns Charity Hope wrote glowingly of the domestic mission of women. Her frustration with the "keepers at home" advocates stemmed, primarily, from economic and social changes that were occurring in middle-class Ulster society in the early twentieth century. Angrily, Charity Hope asked, "What do men mean when they say, women should stay at home and mind the house? What women, and what houses? If every woman had a house to keep and plenty of money to keep it on, there might be some sense in adjuring her to look after it."[32] She upbraids "modern man" for saying he cannot afford to marry and for refusing to support maiden sisters or aunts, thus leaving women without homes. Aside from these economic questions, she also passes hard judgment on middle-class clergy and laymen for parroting the "keepers at home" cry, all the while depending on the extensive service of middle-class women within the churches. "We wonder," asks Charity

Hope, "how would the less congenial and more exacting duties of the Church be done if women refused to be so 'unwomanly' as to engage in outside work." She goes on to describe "an army of noble women, whom no man can number, who sacrifice home comfort and ease in their work for humanity." She thinks it passing strange that when countless women quietly and faithfully collect money for church work they "are not dubbed 'pushing' and 'unwomanly,'" yet if a woman agitates for legislative reform to ameliorate the condition of "her oppressed sisters" she is denounced by men as "one who neglects her home."[33] In the Ulster Presbyterian newspaper *The Witness*, a physician's views on women's natural sphere were cited. "The danger lies in attempting to compete with men in the strain of public life ... women cannot dispense with the physiological functions of their nature ... A man's work lies in the bustle and violent struggle of life; a woman's in the quietude and sanctity of home. There are plenty of men already in the world, and the addition to their ranks of a few weak feminine imitations would be a poor compensation for the loss of genuine women ... it is physically as well as morally impossible for women to do their duty to their children if they are to go rushing about as doctors, lawyers, or political agitators."[34] The work that women did within their churches, while not technically within the home, was not considered to be within the realm of "public life." For the most part, women's work within the church – "womanly," nurturing work – was viewed as a natural extension of their domestic lives. As Charity Hope points out though, this work could entail much time and sacrifice of home concerns, yet there was no major outcry against this work as "unwomanly" because it was so necessary for the churches.

Charity Hope's outspokenness resulted in letters to the "Council" that "rebuked" her for what her critics thought was an audacious attack on evangelical gender orthodoxy. Charity Hope vigorously[35] defended the orthodoxy of her position – she was still a believer in "home first," but not in "home only" – but at the same time maintained her critique. "My article was written to expose the fallacy that women's only proper sphere is the home, when the large majority of women are denied that sphere, and when another large proportion have God-given talents for wider freer service for humanity. Certainly if a woman has a home and husband and bairns, her sphere is her home, and she may find in it fullest opportunity for the cultivation of gifts that will be of use and blessing to the world, without neglect of one of her immediate claims and duties."[36] Again we see home and church work – a "blessing to the world" – presented as one unified field of endeavour for the Christian woman whose life possessed the desired balance.

A QUESTION OF BALANCE: THE DUTIES
OF "THE MISTRESS OF THE MANSE"

Perhaps the group of Protesant women who were expected to live up to the highest ideal of perfect balance between home and church work were ministers' wives. They had to balance their home duties and church responsibilities to the satisfaction of their husbands and of the people of his congregation. Charity Hope, herself a minister's wife, observed that it was expected that ministers' wives participate in, if not lead, a plethora of church and social activities. "Indeed," she wrote, "I have heard very hard things said about those who devoted themselves entirely to the care of their children and manses, and refused all other interests."[37] The Protestant literature on the role of ministers' wives fell into two broad categories: articles that prescribed the proper behaviour for ministers' wives, and pieces that described the difficulties of balancing the duties of their position and that urged women to support their ministers' wives. The latter type of material was usually written by ministers' wives themselves.

In a selected article in *The Witness*, a portrait of the ideal Presbyterian minister's wife was presented. While she must have all the qualities of a good wife, she should possess other "endowments" over and above those of the ordinary Christian wife. She must avoid embroiling herself in gossip or choosing favourites and she must not do anything that might cause her husband embarrassment. But, "above all, she should have sincere and consistent piety, that she may be the comforter of her husband and an example to his flock."[38] In keeping with Protestant domestic ideology, "her first duties, after those she owes to God, are to her husband and her children."[39] Yet the question of her role within the various departments of the church is also addressed. If she has the required "fitness" for the work, she should "preside in meetings of the female members of the church, and take the lead in prayer-meetings and benevolent enterprises."[40] Finally, the ideal minister's wife "should be a modest, earnest woman, equally ready to lead or to follow in every good work."[41]

A perfect balance between domestic and church work was required of the minister's wife. If she should neglect her husband or children because of her church duties, condemnation would be swift in coming and, conversely, as Charity Hope noted, if she devoted herself entirely to life at the manse and participated but little in the activities of the church, harsh words would be spoken against her. This near impossible standard was made all the more difficult by the excessive demands made by congregations upon their ministers' wives and by the decidedly uncharitable criticism of the less than ideal "mistress of the

manse." In a fictional account "founded on fact" of "A Day's Visiting"
by a Presbyterian minister's wife, the heroine of the tale recalls reading in the *Witness* the following lines describing the model clergyman's
wife.

> Wanted a Christian lady, active, gentle, refined,
> With every beauty of person, and every endowment of mind,
> Fitted by early culture to move in all grades of life,
> Consider the want – O reader –
>   Wanted, a minister's wife!
>
> A very domestic person – to callers she must not be out,
> It would have such a flighty appearance for her to be gadding
> about;
> Yet she must visit the parish every day of her life.
> Sympathising at births, deaths, and marriages.
>   Wanted, a minister's wife![42]

The gently mocking, comic tone of these verses on the ideal minister's
wife reveals an acknowledgment of the fact that theirs was a uniquely
difficult role.

Significantly, ministers' wives were the group of Protestant women
whose opinions were regularly voiced in Ulster's religious periodicals.
For those who were so inclined, "taking up their pens" to write articles
and stories on subjects ranging from the spiritual to the practical for
religious publications – both those aimed at a general church
audience and those written specifically for women – was a part of the
"mission" of many ministers' wives. These literate, usually moderately
well-educated[43] women with a little leisure time[44] took the opportunity to make the laity of their denominations aware of the difficulties
involved in their role and to point out some of the unreasonable
demands which congregations placed upon them. "Parson's or
Church's Wife" tells the story of a minister's wife who relates to her
husband the impossibility of her position as both his wife and the
congregation's wife.

> Which shall it be? Which shall it be?
> I said to John; I can't agree
> To be both church's wife and thine,
> For in two spheres I cannot shine;
> And yet the parish seems to think
> That, by some strange, mysterious link,
> I've truly bound myself to be

As good a wife to it as thee.

Yet, well I know, no wedlock band
It ever placed upon my hand;
No faithful pledge it gave to me,
And *why* I'm bound I cannot see;
If *ordination* vows were said,
I'd have it clearer in my head
What *duty* is – and what my work,
For John, you know, I am no shirk.

I cannot boil the pot at home,
And oft to other households roam;
You cannot do without your dinner
More, John, than any other sinner;
And then, you know, our children five
Demand my wits just to contrive
How best to clothe and feed and train,
And keep the lip and soul from stain.

John, I have pledged my love to you,
And I'd be faithful wife and true
Full well I know your calling high —
No higher is beneath the sky;
Most gladly I would do my part,
I'd seek for souls with prayerful heart;
But I've not fingers by the scores
To do the daily parish chores.[45]

Her husband agrees that his congregation has made too many demands on her – she has a fear of public speaking, yet she has been forced to "lead the women's meetings" – and he promises her that he will tell the parish that she can serve them better in "her own sweet way" by attending to her family and ministering on an individual basis to the poor and sick of the community. The second verse of the poem strikingly brings out the ambiguity inherent in the extra-official role of minister's wife. Ministers' wives were, technically, not church employees; they were neither hired nor paid for the church work they did.[46] Yet clearly a great deal was expected of them.

A young clergyman's wife describes in the following manner her weekly round in a city charge. "Through the week I ought to attend prayer meetings, missionary meetings, temperance meetings, soirees, lectures, and every other dissipation peculiar to the Church Presbyterian."[47] Her use of the word "dissipation" here – with its connotation of wastefulness and frivolity – is highly unusual. While allowing that their duties were often onerous and sometimes unnecessarily added to by unthinking laity, ministers' wives generally regarded women's work as essential to the ministry of their churches. This particular minister's wife, however, seems to have been frustrated with the unduly social aspect of church life: the neglect of the spiritual in favour of fashionable and time-consuming events such as soirees, recitals, and concerts. The endless round of activities in which she was expected to participate in her husband's city charge, coupled with the burden of performing her domestic duties on a small stipend, left this young woman with the impression that "To a woman of independent spirit the life [of a minister's wife] could not be anything but one of self-sacrifice, and can only be lived as she is enabled to lift the cross for sake of One who hath blessed all drudgery."[48] Despite this tale of woe, the young author of this article believed that the life of a minister's wife could be a happy and ideal one if only she could look after her home duties first without fearing criticism from the members of her husband's congregation. She adds that "the position of minister's wife brings many responsibilities in its train, but they are responsibilities entirely connected with her duties to her husband and her home, and thus indirectly with the congregation."[49] Most ministers' wives who wrote on this topic, including Charity Hope, agreed that their primary responsibility lay with succouring their husbands and children; they were their husbands' wives first and their congregations' "wives" only in a secondary sense.

Difficult though their role might have been – frequently in the public eye and subject to much criticism – the piety, courage, and influence for good of minister's wives were celebrated in fiction and in memorial tributes. In "The Minister's Missing Wife," C. Hope[50] sketches a portrait of Nellie, a young wife and mother, who, as "mistress of the manse," keeps everything at home and in her duties in the church running smoothly for her kind, yet hopelessly impractical, husband. When Nellie has to stay out in the country overnight nursing a sick woman and protecting her from her drunken[51] and murderous husband, she sends a message to her husband telling him of her whereabouts and asks him to take her place as leader of the women's prayer meeting that evening. Of course, the message does not get to the minister and he is faced with looking after his wife's domestic and church duties, all the while worried about her sudden absence. He is not up to the task. The good man could not handle the servant, Bridget, who "required constant management," nor even provide sustenance for his hungry, unruly young children. He was also inadequate as a class leader and the members of his wife's group duly informed him of his shortcomings. After a fruitless search for his wife in the poorer districts of the town where she often visited, he returned in the morning to his cold and comfortless house that "felt like a big, damp, soundless vault" without her.[52] Sitting by the cold, dirty grate praying that the children would not awaken and start crying for their mother, it occurred to the minister that he had been wrong to smile indulgently at his wife for her frequent prayers about what he called her "absurd little trifles."[53] He resolved that "the dear little woman" was right in taking all of her cares to God. The minister was greatly relieved when his wife arrived with her tale of the bungled message and of her work at the home of the sick country woman. Nellie had succeeded in rendering the woman's husband "utterly cowed" when she told him that his abuse was responsible for his wife's precarious condition and she managed to get him to sober up, get medicine for his wife, and sign "the pledge." Throughout, Nellie is portrayed as a highly capable, yet gentle[54] woman who has total mastery of her "undivided field" of domestic and church service. Her husband is not portrayed as a complete fool, yet it is from this incident that he comes to appreciate not only her amazing practical capabilities, but also the effectiveness of her simple piety. Stories such as "The Minister's Missing Wife" celebrated the piety, courage, and ingenuity of this unique "band of sisters."

Isabella Moffat Thompson (1848–1904), wife of the Reverend A.J. Wilson of Belfast, was hailed as the ideal minister's wife even though illness prevented her from carrying out many of the church activities which ministers' wives were expected to perform. In a lengthy two-part feature memorial article in *The Irish Presbyterian*, an ideal portrait of her life as "mistress of the manse" was described. While still making an important contribution to her husband's ministry before her illness, she was first and foremost a mother to her children. "God had called this woman to the high mission of motherhood, and her whole nature responded to the call."[55] The description given of her relationship with her children is reminiscent of the injunction to "labour, love and pray," for "she suffered for them, toiled for them, talked with them, prayed for them, brooded over them, whether present or absent, with a love that never slept and never wearied."[56] During the period 1870–85 she gave birth to eleven children, ruining her health in the process and making her remaining years ones of constant pain. Thompson's grown children frequently sought her counsel at her sickbed and thus "it came to pass that "mother's room" became the holy of holies of the whole household, and the worn sufferer high priestess there, her sacrifice always ready to be laid on the altar for her children and her husband, her intercession ascending unceasingly to the Eternal Pity and Eternal Love on their behalf."[57] Her loving self-sacrifice was held to have done incalculable good in influencing the hearts and minds of her large brood of children, many of whom were to become Irish Presbyterian ministers and missionaries. Because of her illnesses and large family, she could not actively participate in congregational life to the extent that she wished. The author of the memorial said that Thompson often dwelt with regret upon the fact that she could not help her husband more in his work. No doubt, those who did not know the extent of her illness or those who were simply uncharitable would have criticized her absence from the various organizations of the church normally led by the minister's wife.[58] Her eulogizer, however, saw her role in the church as a crucial one. Her constant intercessory prayer for the needs of her husband's congregation made her intimately aware of their difficulties and concerns. She also knew all of her husband's anxieties and in her own quiet way she soothed away his cares. This unseen domestic work of "restoring and refreshing" God's appointed ministers of the Gospel was considered to be of no small consequence. Indeed, the author goes so far as to compare the minister's wife to Mary of Bethany – and, by extension, he compares the minister to Christ – because she quietly soothes and ministers to the care-worn messenger of the gospel. The world, or even the church, opined the author of the memorial, does not bother to estimate this type of assistance rendered by ministers' wives such as Isabella Moffat Thompson, yet her quiet, domestic work did the church incalculable good.[59] The epigraph of her memorial is a succinct expression of the fact that even those most public and active of evangelical Protestant women, ministers' wives, could still fulfil their God-given mission if they gave their all within their domestic sphere. That alone was enough. Isabella Moffat Thompson's epigraph was "*Of flowers that prosper in the shade.*"[60]

Roles for women may have been changing, spheres may have been enlarging, but the traditional woman who "laboured, loved and prayed" in her own home, for whatever reason, and who considered all of this sacrifice done "as unto the Lord" saw fulfilment in the mission of motherhood. While ministers' wives, like all married Protestant women, were first of all "keepers at home," they were supposed to play very visible and vital roles in their husbands' churches. A perceived failure to balance this dual role as mother to their families and as first lady among those who performed the "motherly work" of the church led to stinging criticism by the members of their husbands' congregations.[61] For all of its difficulties, however, Ulster ministers' wives wrote of the spiritual rewards of their lives. They considered their home and church work to be a ministry in which they were the important "help-meets" of their husbands.

Ministers' wives such as Charity Hope advocated "home first" for Christian women, not "home only." Their own active roles within the churches provided a model for increasing female involvement in the ministries of the evangelical Protestant churches. They exhorted women to attend first to their "innermost circle," after which time it was acceptable for them to allow their sphere to "widen naturally and unobtrusively."[62] If women's role in the church was a "womanly," "motherly," subordinate one, the progression from home to church was deemed a "natural" one. It was only when some women began arguing in favour of the inclusion of women in leadership roles that serious discord arose.

STRETCHING THE LIMITS: HOW FAR COULD WOMEN'S SPHERE EXTEND?

Even those who chafed at the limits placed on women's role in the church still tended to use conservative, essentialist language when arguing their case. Several of the "King's Daughters in Council" correspondents argued in favour of such "advanced" innovations as women's suffrage, female preaching, and the representation of women in the councils of the church. Yet they did so without abandoning their belief in women's unique "nature." In one such column advocating, among other things, women's suffrage and an expanded role for women in the church, "Joan" maintained that "God's plan was that a woman should have equal rights with a man in telling the Gospel story, and working on behalf of souls, in all things consistent with her womanly position and domestic experience; but that did not mean that she should step out of her sphere and become a mannish woman."[63] Thus even those who argued for radical change couched their views in terms that were "consistent" with the ideal of the True Woman. I did not find any evidence to suggest that this was calculation on the part of those arguing for change of the gender status quo. Rather, for evangelical Protestant women, the notion of a woman stepping outside of her divinely appointed sphere – whatever its boundaries might have been – and consequently becoming a "mannish woman," was anathema. Expanding what the clergy and laity considered acceptable as women's role meant stretching the elastic membrane of this amorphous sphere.

Elastic though the boundaries of "woman's sphere" might have been, for most Ulster Protestants it had its limits. The question of whether a woman could take a leadership role, lead in prayer at a "mixed" (male and female) assembly, be a conference representative or a preacher, and still preserve her womanly nature was considered a significant one. On balance, though, this question of women in leadership roles only concerned a few activists and their opponents within the churches.[64] In this conservative religious culture, questions such as the orthodoxy of the use of instrumental music in Presbyterian services generated more printed material than the subject of women's role in the church. Nevertheless an examination of the debate concerning the role of women in the church illustrates how essentialist thinking dominated the logic used both by those in favour of and those against including women as representatives at Methodist Conference[65] and allowing women to preach.

In concluding this examination I will also look at reactions to and reinterpretations of the secular phenomenon of the New Woman and what impact it was hoped, or feared, this model would have on conceptions of the ideal evangelical Protestant woman.

The matter of whether or not to allow women to be admitted to the annual Irish Methodist Conference was discussed for some fifteen years before women were accepted. This issue makes an interesting case study of the debate about women's role in the church because it demonstrates the pervasiveness of essentialist thinking in evangelical Protestant religious culture. An editorial in *The Christian Advocate* in 1895 included the observation that while the question had generated some interest in America and England, where several failed attempts to have women admitted as conference representatives had taken place, the matter was of little importance in Ireland. It was "in no sense ... a burning question,"[66] according to the editorial. Arguing in favour of removing the bar to female representatives, the editorialist enumerated the important role of women in Irish Methodism. "Women constitute a majority of the members of the Church; they are at least as active as men in the work of the Church; they are not inferior to men in piety or influence."[67] No one would deny these facts of Methodist life, yet this did not mean that work in the legislative body of the Methodist church was commensurate with woman's "natural" abilities and inclinations. Did her sphere extend this far? The question was taken up occasionally in *The Advocate* over the next few years, but the inclusion of a "Ladies Meeting" – at which speakers on such subjects as women's temperance or mission work would address an all-female audience – at Conference seemed to satisfy female Irish Methodists, for a time, as an adequate platform for their interests in church work. During this period Irish Methodist women gradually took a larger role in the leadership of the church. They were admitted as leader of the circuits in the quarterly meetings of many Irish circuits.[68]

An analysis of the comments made for and against the passage of a resolution to admit women as Conference representatives in 1910 illuminates the views of clergy and laymen with regard to the question of women's role in their church. A layman, Mr Alexander M. Fullerton, moved a resolution for the admission of women as Conference representatives that made the standard references to the prominent and crucial role of women within the life of the various Methodist connections. He said that he did not make the resolution as "a spokesman of Irish Methodist women knocking at the door of the Conference for admission. Their Irish women were too modest to adopt tactics of that kind."[69] They were regarded as true "womanly" women, who would not stoop to show or spectacle. Rather, Fullerton informed Conference that he brought forward the resolution as a spokesman of Irish Methodist clergy and laymen who felt that it was time to remove the barrier to participation at Conference of these important, faithful, and loyal members of their church. The unspoken contrast between modest Methodist women and the caricature of the suffragette clamouring for the vote speaks volumes. The men who supported the resolution were asking that women's sphere be expanded; they thought that there was no danger of Methodist women stepping out of their appointed sphere and becoming what "Joan" called "mannish" women. Employing an argument similar to one frequently used in favour of women's suffrage, the Reverend W.B. Merrick said that the inclusion of women at Conference would add dignity to the proceedings and "their presence would have a softening influence on their debates."[70] The Reverend John Magill asked, in support of the motion, "what the world and the Church would do without the ladies?"[71] Throughout, it was argued that the presence of "consecrated womanhood"[72] would be a benefit to the proceedings of Conference and to the workings of the church. The comments of those opposed to the resolution, which are also very revealing of the state of the discourse on women's sphere, were recorded in *The Advocate* as well. Those who opposed uttered no overtly misogynist statements, nor did they in any way denigrate the work that the women of Methodism were doing. If anything, they outdid their opponents in their effusive praise of Methodist womanhood. The Reverend J.O. Park, an opponent of the resolution whose remarks were quoted at length, was described as justifying his opposition in the following manner: "Because of the high and unqualified conviction he had of the most noble and most beautiful mission of woman he opposed the motion."[73] First of all, he stated that the womanhood of the church did not want to be legislators. Park thought that "it was a great mistake to allow questions that began in public politics to influence the action of the Christian church."[74] Clearly, he was alluding to suffrage, a movement which he alleged was not "for the honour of womanhood."[75] The Reverend Park argued that, in her role as "helpmeet" in both the home and church, woman had great power. Moreover, this was a role with which she was, rightly, content. Making her a legislator, something that went against her nature, "would greatly weaken her power for good. They would do her a great wrong by forcing her into a position which she did not want."[76] Finally, the Reverend J.W. Johnston weighed in on the side of the "nays" with the comment that "woman's sphere was in the home," and that the members of Conference "were making a profound blunder in dragging women from their homes to take part in their business ... In his view they would do women no honour and no service by throwing open this door to them."[77] Opponents held that the legislative aspect of Conference membership made it outside of women's "natural" sphere. Supporters argued that "women's" natural piety and faithfulness in the work of the church, coupled with the positive influence it was thought their womanly demeanour would have on the tone of Conference sessions, made them ideally suited to this sphere of activity. Essentialist phrases such as "consecrated womanhood" and "the beautiful mission of womanhood" were accepted by both sides. In language they found common ground; their differences lay in diverging interpretations of the exact nature of woman's sphere.

The debate concerning whether women should be allowed to preach created some controversy among Ulster Presbyterians and Methodists. For the most part though, female preaching was perceived by the Ulster Protestant laity as something that occurred elsewhere. They were self-admittedly conservative on such matters. "Lady evangelists" from England and the United States who held meetings in Ulster were usually favourably reviewed in Ulster religious periodicals. But the enthusiasm of the writers for this type of female role was tempered by a great deal of caution.[78] Miss Wakefield, an English "womanpreacher" who held several missions in Ulster, was praised by the editor of the "Women's Causerie"[79] column in *The Christian Advocate* for her sensitivity to the call of the Holy Spirit.[80] Her position was considered to be unique, because: "for the most part the lives of women are made up of small events and narrow interests."[81] Miss Wakefield's willingness to listen to the call of the Holy Spirit and broaden her sphere to include public preaching was said to be, by this writer, a noble sacrifice: "let us give all honour to such; and let us, if the call comes to us (never before) arise and do likewise."[82] But given the static caused by the confusing biblicist arguments concerning female preaching and the deafening clamour caused by the adherents of the cult of domesticity, it was unlikely that Ulster women would have been able to hear such a call if it came.

Polemical articles either for or against female preaching usually took a biblicist approach by listing scripture verses that supported the author's position. Interestingly, the activities of women in the New Testament were used to support diametrically opposed points of view. Throughout these articles, the paramount concern was allowing women their proper influence and role in God's work without having them abrogate God's law by stepping beyond divinely ordained or "natural" boundaries.

In addressing the question "Should women preach?" the author of a piece published in *The Irish Presbyterian* acknowledges from the outset that "by most of our Presbyterian people the reply to this question would be emphatically in the negative."[83] The author uses biblical references and the great success of Ulster Presbyterian female missionaries in India in order to disprove the conventional wisdom on this subject. Evidence of women prophesying[84] in the Old Testament was used to support the legitimacy of female preaching and the author's somewhat radical[85] interpretation of the role of women in the New Testament was also used to support her argument. "These passages[86] show that in the early Church women did speak or prophesy, pray, and take part publicly in Gospel work, and were ordained by the Church for such work."[87] The reaction to the publication of this unorthodox view was swift. In the following two numbers, articles titled "Should Women Preach?" answered the question firmly in the negative. The articles were "extracts from 'Practical Christianity'" sent in for publication "by Mrs John McRobert, Crossgar." Using I Corinthians 14:33–35 and I Timothy 2:8–15 as texts, the author of these articles argues that women are to remain entirely silent in church. Women are informed that it is best for them that they should be in a state of "quietness ... with the ear ever open, and the heart ready to receive whatever God may communicate."[88] This verdict on the question of female preaching interpreted the role of women in the New Testament in a way that was consonant with the received wisdom on this subject in Ulster Protestantism.

In a similar vein, Salome (pseud.) contributed an article to *The Christian Banner*[89] in which she[90] argues that women should not preach for nine different reasons. Among her arguments was one which allowed that while women did prophesy in the Bible, the time of prophesy in the church had passed away with such other biblical phenomena as visions and miracles.[91] Salome interprets all of the examples of women's activities in the New Testament as being non-public or non-instructive ones. Finally, Salome cites the fact that the Apostle Paul "exhorts Christian women to 'shamefacedness' – that is, modesty."[92] The modesty argument was used as the clincher, with no further explanation, because it was understood that public preaching by women involved a fatal breach of their female modesty. Salome's conclusion is in perfect synchronization with the conservative strain that predominated in Ulster Presbyterianism. While this religious culture entertained some expansion of the domestic role of women to include the "motherly" work of the church, it would not allow women to step out of their original sphere entirely. "We hold that it is not in accordance with the institution of Christ that women should preach the Gospel publicly and authoritatively in the assembled congregation. Under the Gospel woman holds a noble position. She is queen of the household, the sunshine of the cottage and the castle, the light of the happy Christian home. Let her be contented with her legitimate influence, and let her not be drawn from her proper sphere by either vanity or ignorance."[93] Church plebecites were not held on such matters, but there is little doubt from the tone of the debate in various Presbyterian organs that this conservative view held sway well into the early decades of the twentieth century, with only a few liberal-minded opponents.

"Should Women Preach?" was not used just as the title of serious articles brimming with biblical exegesis. It was also the name of a humorous and gently mocking tale which described how the arrival of some "lady Pilgrims" and their revival tent in the peaceful Ulster village of "Ballymiddle"[94] set off an exciting controversy. The question of "the right of women to hold forth publicly on the high things of religion"[95] became the talk of the town. It was decided that a public debate would result in a healthy airing of the various views espoused by the townsfolk on what the author, who used the pseudonym "Denarius," archly referred to as "this dark theological problem."[96] Denarius notes that the three debaters who would argue against female preaching "all bearing the Christian name of Sam, were elderly, married and sedate," their three opponents being "single progressive and confident."[97] The townsfolk[98] took sides and provided the debaters with various suggestions, including this hint to "the Sams": "Dinna forget the Apostle Paul."[99] In his "very racy address" the first Sam blames "the weaker vessel" for being "the ruin of mankind from the beginning" and says that if she wants to redeem herself she can do so by "training her children, teaching in the Sabbath school, praying with the sick; but don't let her preach."[100] Sam clearly felt that God shared his own low opinion of women for, as his finale, Sam cited the passage where "The Lord said unto Adam, "Where art thou?" but unto the woman He said, "What is this that thou hast done.""[101] By this period, 1912, blatantly misogynist arguments such as Sam's use of the story of Adam and Eve were never used in serious discussions of this subject. Rather, as we saw in the Methodist Conference debate, those who opposed the expansion of women's role were more effusive in their praise of "noble womanhood" than their adversaries. Sam's "anti-woman" sentiments were inconsistent with the dominant discourse of the cult of True Womanhood and such "old-fashioned" ideas were held up for ridicule in this story.[102]

A comic rebuttal of the first Sam's argument that women were untrustworthy began with a return to the Garden. "We have heard a lot of what Eve did in the Garden of Eden, and what she didn't do. But how does Adam come out of the business? Manly fellow, he shared the apple he hadn't the courage to pluck, and when confronted with the terrible consequences rolled the blame over on his poor wife. (Tremendous effect on the ladies.)"[103] Sam's opponent also makes use of conventional arguments in favour of women's mission. "If woman was the cause of man's downfall, who has the better reason to help in his uplifting? (None.) What agent is there more to his liking? (Hear, hear)."[104] When all six debaters had finished, Denarius states, there was very little left unsaid on the topic, though the "woman party" appeared to have won the debate. The debate had furnished Ballymiddle theologians with enough material, Denarius noted, to keep the discussion of female preaching going for weeks. It appears that Denarius him or herself was in favour of the "woman party," for the comic old Sams were straw men whose outlandish and clearly outdated views on women's nature were easily ridiculed. Yet serious opposition to the admission of women to public leadership roles was not viewed as lightly as the backward views of the old Sams. Because women and their divinely appointed domestic role were so treasured by Ulster evangelical Protestants, it was argued, great caution needed to be exercised lest their mighty work be undermined by injudicious changes to their sphere. Behind much of this concern about changes in gender roles within the church lay the fear that those who advocated change were being influenced by developments in secular society. Could the New Woman possibly be the True Woman of the evangelical Protestant ideal?

THE NEW WOMAN VERSUS
THE TRUE WOMAN

One way in which the New Woman could be tamed and rendered palatable for Ulster evangelicals was if she were redefined somewhat. At the outset of an article ostensibly on the topic of the New Woman, the author asks whether her readers had ever met the New Woman, "that monstrosity evolved in the latter years of the nineteenth century."[105] She assumes her readers would reply in the negative, even though she says they encountered the New Woman every day in all walks of life. Because of the caricatures of the New Woman found in the comic papers and elsewhere, the author observes, it is doubtful that they would be able to recognize a real New Woman if they saw one, for "as the monster of your prejudiced imagination she simply does not exist."[106] The very use of the term "New" is misleading, the author opines, for "her type of woman has existed in all ages." She then goes on to mention the capable women of the Bible and of church history who, without neglecting their domestic role, did a great work in the public sphere. Thus the New Woman has been transformed into the True Woman with only slight modification – the expansion of her sphere of influence, her womanly nature intact. Moreover, concerns about the "mannishness" of the New Woman are brushed aside by praising the virtues of men. While she considers the gross caricature of the cigar-smoking, trouser-wearing New Woman to be beneath mention, she admits that the New Woman does imitate man to a certain extent, but she only imitates his virtues. "She longs to lose her own feminine weaknesses – jealousy, petty spite, and love of gossip in his breadth of mind, and thus, while retaining her own gentleness and gaining his magnanimity, she will, indeed, realise the dream of our great poet – 'A perfect woman nobly planned.'"[107] While this article was an interesting attempt to disguise the New Woman as the True Woman, for traditional Protestants her wanton smashing of the boundaries of the ideology of separate spheres for men and women made the New Woman appear as a real threat to the life of church and state.

A "wise and witty" address by Lord Plunkett on the subject of the True Woman was quoted in *The Christian Advocate*. Lord Plunkett told his audience of girls at the Alexandra School, Dublin, of his doubts about the worth of "advanced women." "I do not like the new woman, I am afraid of the blue woman, and I have a misgiving about the nothing-to-do-woman."[108] The ideal construction of the True Woman was, however, more to his liking. "I will tell you what I do like, and that is the true woman – the woman that is true to her womanly instincts, to her womanly sympathy, to her womanly responsibilities, a woman who feels she has a mission from God to go forth into the world and engage in those ministrations, whether within her own home or among the poor and the sick, the sinful or the wayward – ministrations which women alone can efficiently discharge."[109] "New, blue and nothing-to-do" women, whom Lord Plunkett held up for ridicule, were

considered the antithesis of the Christian True Woman. For most
Protestants, there was no transforming the New Woman into the True
Woman; the former was reviled or ridiculed while the latter was
cherished.

An urgent sense of what might be lost pervaded the evangelical
critique of the New Woman. Women who advocated a broader sphere
for female activity had to avoid any taint of the "mannishness" that
stigmatized the New Woman.

"The Wind in Woman's Wings" was printed as the lead editorial
piece in the 12 April 1895 number of *The Christian Advocate*. Within
this one article, all the *fin de siècle* fears of a conservative people seeing
their way of life rapidly changing in a modernizing Ulster are
expressed. The editor writes that there is an unhealthy preoccupation
with the new and a devaluation of the old. Among these new fashions
"is the conviction that woman has not yet taken her proper place
either in society or in the Church of God."[110] According to the author,
this is patent nonsense, for woman has always had "a special place of
influence and power among God's ordained servants." She needs no
new public platform in order to fulfil her God-given role. Rather, "the
success of woman's work depends upon this, that the angel in her is
developed." And the angel features of the woman minister are
"sympathy, patience, purity."[111] Modern innovations such as the "lady
evangelist" – which he feels are influenced by the secular development
of the New Woman – could well do more harm than good, for "Is it not
possible that those who are foremost in claiming for woman a place in
Christian work side by side with man are unwittingly making her 'a
little lower than the angels?'"[112] The editor places female piety on a
pedestal – the realm of angels – where she must remain or be degraded. He states baldly that "woman cannot work on a level with man. She
must be either above him or his inferior."[113] Lest this be misinterpret-
ed, he hastens to add that woman's "elevation" does not consist in her
greater ability. "It is rather in the gentleness and quietness, the
patience and purity of her spirit that woman is made angel-like."[114]
The likely negative repercussions of changing the boundaries of
woman's divinely ordained sphere meant that her apologists are
actually harming woman. "Let her not try to wrest the Scriptures to the
destruction of her divine endowment of wings ... [Apologists] have
used arguments on her behalf that threaten to rob us of imperishable
treasure. The Spirit's teaching through Paul is in perfect harmony
with the angel ministry of woman – it does not agree with mannish
womanhood."[115] The spectre of the New Woman informed this fear of
"mannish womanhood" that so deeply troubled conservative evangelical Protestants. This was no trifling matter for many evangelicals,

clerical and lay, men and women. They held a shared belief in the sanctity of woman's mission: its significance to the eventual salvation of the world. All of them would agree with the writer of this editorial that "unconsecrated womanhood … is the living danger of the race," and that "the women who are to purify the world must have the mind of God in their wings."[116] Differences of opinion lay only in where "the mind of God" was directing women. Charity Hope, minister's wife, nonmilitant suffragist, and True/New Woman would aver with no less pious fervour than the author of this editorial that "the race" depended on women having "the mind of God in their wings."[117] "Womanly" Ulster Protestant women were, in this period, stretching their "wings" while at the same time remaining sensitive to the concerns of their more traditional co-religionists.

ROMAN CATHOLICS AND THE ROLE OF LAYWOMEN

It is difficult to compare Protestant and Roman Catholic discussions of women's role in the church simply because of the large differences between the sphere of activity of evangelical Protestant laywomen and that of their Roman Catholic counterparts. This issue, as has been shown above, generated considerable interest in the Ulster evangelical press, yet it received little mention in major Roman Catholic publications such as *The Irish Monthly*. There is also the danger of failing to compare like with like. In the early twentieth century, when Roman Catholic writers did begin to consider the matter of women's expanding sphere, they were not usually referring to their role in the church per se. Rather, the discussion centred on the involvement of Roman Catholic laywomen in philanthropic activity, whether connected to the church or not. This debate drew into opposition those who felt Irish Catholic laywomen were not doing enough charitable work and those who felt that it was not their place.

As in the Protestant literature, we hear the refrain that women should be "keepers at home" – this is not surprising, given the discussion in chapter 2 about Catholic adherence to the cult of domesticity – but it was not a very loud cry. It need not have been, for Roman Catholic laywomen did not have a plethora of church activities – Sunday school teaching, Band of Hope meetings, and Missionary sewing societies – to take them away from their homes. "Motherly" work in the Catholic church – educating the young and aiding the poor – was done, overwhelmingly, by orders of nuns. Irish Catholic laywomen, of the middling and upper classes (a very small group in Ulster) – did participate, increasingly, in philanthropic activities in this period. Yet the tone of several articles I found on this subject was that of chastisement. Catholic laywomen were criticized for their selfishness and willingness to leave charitable work almost entirely to the professional religious. Thus the cry of "keepers at home" was directed at those aimless women of fashion who were neglecting their families in favour of amusement or at those New Women who were abandoning their God-given domestic sphere in favour of the "mannish" pursuits of business and politics. Given the skewed nature of my data, then, I proceed all the while aware that when Catholics were discussing the role of women it was not so much in the context of what evangelicals called "church work" or "ministry," but in the area of philanthropy.

Sister Mary Francis Cusack, the Nun of Kenmare, expressed "home first" views that sound similar to those expressed by evangelicals. She called for women to teach, "not in the pulpit or in the professor's chair, but in the household and at the domestic hearth. No woman need want a mission nor occupation, nor interest in life, while she has the care of immortal souls."[118] The problem here, though, was not a concern about balance between a woman's domestic and church activities. Rather, Cusack was arguing against the erosion of domesticity by the rise of the New Woman who sought to participate in the masculine world. Nora Tynan O'Mahoney expressed her fear that "in these degenerate days of militant suffragettism and similar foolishness" a menace lay "in woman herself, and in the gradual distortion of her nature, slowly but surely being brought about by the hysterical shrieking of the suffragette sisterhood."[119] In "seeking for outside worldly power and influence," O'Mahoney maintains that the modern woman "is losing her own greatest and most royal prerogative as undisputed mistress and queen of the home."[120]

The conservative evangelical writers whose ideas we have examined would have agreed with O'Mahoney's sentiments, but the focus of their debate within their churches was over the possibility that infiltration of the churches by secular ideas such as suffragism could destroy women's "angel ministry" *within* the church.

In a passage reminiscent of Charity Hope's critique of "home only" advocates, Charlotte O'Conor Eccles states, "Home is a woman's true and proper sphere. Would that it were secured to all."[121] Yet she does not discuss women's contribution to the departments of the church as Charity Hope did, simply because this was not occurring in the Catholic church.

Married Catholic laywomen of the middle classes were not expected to participate in church activities; indeed, the organizational structure did not exist to the extent to which it was the norm in evangelical circles. I did find one mention of the important nurturing role of single women. "I love old maids," enthused Mrs Frank Pentrill, "Yes, though the world sneers at them, though *Punch* makes endless fun of them, though all mankind pities them, with that pity which is so near akin to contempt."[122] While she admits some old maids are bitter and selfish, "there remains a vast number of unmarried women whose life is one of constant self-sacrifice, and who, having no special duties of their own, take on their gentle shoulders all the troubles of other people."[123] Pentrill gives the impression that these Catholic laywomen were active everywhere: "We all know such women: the priest has no more devoted coadjutor, the doctor no more intelligent nurse, the sick and sorry no kinder friend."[124] Yet their unobtrusive work created no debate about women's role, perhaps because of their marginal existence in Irish society.

These few brief mentions of the role of Catholic laywomen – married women in their homes and single women as assistants to local male worthies – provide only a scant picture of the activities of Catholic laywomen. They were involved in works of Catholic charity, but references to their doing the "motherly" work of the church were few. Sister Cusack does urge women who "are not mothers according to nature" to be mothers "according to grace."[125] As pious Catholic women, they should look out for those who need help. "It was a woman who sought the Infant Jesus, when He appeared to have strayed from His home. Let us learn from her to watch with tenderest care over those who wander from the path of truth, to follow them with our prayers, with our anxieties, with our presence if necessary."[126] While this sort of sentiment was expressed frequently in Protestant literature, it does not seem to have merited much attention in Catholic circles. Again, nuns were doing much of the "motherly" work of the Roman Catholic church.

The value which Catholics and Protestant groups placed on women's domestic mission was very similar, and both groups found the extension of "woman's sphere" to be a somewhat contentious prospect. Protestant concern with these issues came at an earlier point simply because Protestant women took a more active role in their churches earlier than Catholic laywomen did for straightforward organizational and economic reasons.

7 "The Cursed Cup Hath Cast Her Down": Images of Women in Ulster Temperance Literature

Yet, modest grace was once her crown,
And love a very queen confessed her;
The cursed cup hath cast her down,
Dishonoured, vanquished, and possessed her.
"On Seeing a Drunken Woman"[1]
William Maxwell, Belfast, 1894

Ulster temperance literature provides an intriguing avenue of access into the most deeply cherished ideals and the most consuming fears of the pious evangelical laity. The construction of ideal womanhood that was made manifest in this material reveals much about the desires of Protestants for their own communities and their fears of Roman Catholics. Yet, again, we find that Roman Catholics employed the same type of prescriptives in their moulding of the ideal, sober, and pure "true woman" that the Protestants did. It was only in the realm of lay action that the paths of Catholics and Protestants diverged.

Temperance activism in Ulster was primarily the preserve of evangelical Protestants, who were active in a plethora of organizations and institutions. Women were referred to as the "foot soldiers" in the evangelical war against "drink," and indeed they carried out much of the work of the gospel temperance movement. The construction of Christian womanhood in evangelical Protestant temperance literature was patently paradoxical. Domestic ideology and the superior piety of women were used to demonstrate the crucial influence of women in the home as the preservers of a sober nation. Yet in this ideology the various weaknesses of women made them susceptible to the ravages of "drink" and their descent into evil put the family, and by extension all of civilization, at risk.

Interdenominational groups such as the Irish Temperance League were careful to praise the efforts of Catholic temperance work. Very little virulently anti-Catholic sentiment appeared in the pages of their widely circulated journal. Organizations such as the Irish Templars were not so circumspect. They presented a grotesque caricature of the drunken Catholic "Biddy" as the antithesis of godly Protestant woman-hood. Yet the heroines of Catholic temperance tales were not to be outdone in virtue. They were every bit as selfless, holy, and pious as their Protestant counterparts. In this sectarian war of words over the virtue of women, the model of a good woman was the same, be she Protestant or Catholic.

A lively discussion of the proper role or "sphere" of female activity also informed the evangelical Protestant temperance discourse. The example of radical American temperance women gave activists in Ulster an opportunity to examine their own activities, operating principles, and gender values. The result was an affirmation of a conservative gradualism when it came to enlarging "woman's sphere." Temperance activities afforded middle-class Ulster Protestant women an avenue in which they could expand their range of work, yet these women themselves expressed concerns that their work for the temperance cause should do nothing to render them less womanly.

BACKGROUND – THE GOSPEL TEMPERANCE MOVEMENT IN ULSTER

During the gospel temperance movement of the last quarter of the nineteenth century – as distinguished from earlier, more secular anti-drink movements in the United Kingdom – evangelical Protestant piety was wedded to a social reform movement whose goal was the regeneration of the nation. For Irish reformers, this meant that their beloved, downtrodden, disgraced, and drowning "Erin" was to be rescued and returned to her rightful place among the nations through the elimination of the "drink curse." This subject attracted the atten-tion of both Roman Catholic and Protestant temperance reformers throughout the Victorian and Edwardian ages.[2]

The major Irish temperance organizations in the last quarter of the nineteenth century, such as the Irish Temperance League and the Irish Women's Temperance Union, were almost entirely Protestant. Periodicals such as *The Irish Temperance League Journal* contained articles approving of Catholic temperance efforts, yet Catholics did not feel welcome in these organizations that were so clearly based on evangelical Protestant foundations. Catholic laymen and laywomen did not participate in temperance work to the same high degree that Protestants did in this period.[3] The few Catholic laywomen who did participate in temperance activities were primarily wealthy and Dublin-based. The Ulster Protestant temperance movement, on the other hand, was predominantly middle class and employed many women of modest means who could afford the time to work in this area of "gospel" effort. Reformminded Ulster Protestant women found in temperance[4] activities an outlet for their energies and skills.

Women's temperance organizations had an earlier start in Ulster than they did in the rest of the United Kingdom. In 1838 the Belfast Ladies' Temperance Society was formed and in 1862 the Belfast Ladies Temperance Union was organized. These early organizations were described as home-based societies that brought women together for the purpose of prayer and to prepare them for visitation work among the poor. In 1874 the Belfast Ladies Temperance Union was reorganized as the Belfast Women's Temperance Association.[5] Later, in 1884, the Belfast WTA merged with the Irish Women's Temperance Union. The branches from Ulster proceeded to dominate this all-Ireland organization.[6]

An article in *The Irish Temperance League Journal* in February 1881 titled "Woman's Work" described the origins and activities of the Belfast Women's Temperance Union. The article mentions that Belfast committee members must have abstaining homes and be personal abstainers themselves.[7] Thus at the highest organizational level the personal influence of women over their children, servants, husbands, and other members of their households was considered their most significant contribution to the temperance cause.

THE IMAGE OF WOMEN IN ULSTER TEMPERANCE LITERATURE

The portrait of Protestant womanhood in Ulster temperance literature was, fundamentally, a paradoxical one. Women were portrayed as having real moral power in their role as an "angel in the house." Through the strength of their "moral suasion," women could determine the course of the nation, whether it would be "on the side of righteousness" or "fall into ungodliness." Yet women were portrayed as morally and physically weak. Their purity, innocence, and virtue – their chief weapons in the war against "the demon drink" – were fragile creations indeed.

The "silent influence" of women was deemed an awesome source of female power and responsibility, and the pages of Protestant temperance literature overflowed with images of virtuous, self-sacrificing women who through sheer dint of their holy example and gentle admonishments could save those cursed by "drink." Christian women could only have a significant influence for good, if they themselves were morally suited to the task. At the annual meeting of the Belfast Ladies Temperance Union in May 1884, the Reverend J. Waddell had the following to say about female piety. "Women were especially fit to engage in a work like this, because they were possessed of a keen moral perception. They see the right at once and they did not allow their judgement to be warped with regard to consequences. Woman instinctively pronounces in favour of what was right and just and true ..."[8] [At this point he received a Hear, Hear from his mixed audience.] As we have seen in previous chapters, the supposedly heightened moral sensitivity and natural piety of women were part of a transAtlantic evangelical Protestant dialogue on women and Christianity that included Ireland. Male Irish temperance advocates frequently commended their diligent female workers by praising what they believed to be the innate spirituality and pious "feeling" of their female adherents.

The female readers of temperance literature would hardly have been surprised when told that they had an enormous influence over the men and children in their care. Notions of "the hand that rocks the cradle rules the world"[9] and "behind every great man there lies a great woman" had been around for centuries and were still in broad circulation during this period. The notion of children as *tabulae rasae* upon which parental influence could be exerted without impediment was somewhat newer (having recently replaced more Calvinistic views on the morality of the young), but it was potent nonetheless.

In advice to children, the central role of the mother became apparent. During times of trouble chidren were advised to remember her teachings, especially if she had "passed beyond the veil."[10] In a story in the *Youth Temperance Banner* titled "Home and Mother" by Mrs J.E. McConaughy, a young boy makes his way home from a friend's house despite a threatening storm.

But the thought of "home and mother" cheered him on ... but, more than all, the mother-love which watched and waited by the window-pane, would more than make amends for the dreary ride. And so the home was reached, and all his pleasant visions realized. Those two words, "home and mother," were Harry's watchwords all through the perilous road of boyhood and early manhood. They led him safely on through dangers far greater than those which beset him on that stormy night. When lads urged him to join their moonlight excursions, the thought of mother by the mellow lamplight always caused him to give the decided "No." ... O boys! cherish the home-love warm and strong in your hearts, and it will shelter you from a thousand storms of temptation. And oh! if you have a mother on the blessed shore, ponder her teachings well and often. She has left "a light in the window of heaven for you." Do not turn away from that blessed light to stumble and fall upon the dark mountains.[11]

The mother's pious teachings and moral purity make her a figurative "beacon" by whose light those over whom she has influence, children in this example, can make their way through temptation to the safe ground of religious orthodoxy. The "Juvenile Department" pages of temperance periodicals are full of examples of this model of Christian motherhood. Mothers were depicted as a conduit of grace through which sin could be avoided and the sinner could be redeemed.

The following piece of advice, published in *The Puritan*, an American magazine, 40 years previously and subsequently reprinted in the March 1881 issue of *The Irish Temperance League Journal*, was recommended by the editor because he thought that "Hints to Females" contained "excellent thoughts and precepts." The anonymous author notes that "A woman then should promote temperance by example ... But it is on the children that a woman's influence will be most apparent. They are little images of plaster clay, put into her hands to be moulded into vessels of utility or ruin ... In a word, a mother should remember in training her children up to the practice of virtue, she has a double sting in her hand – the body and the mind, and if she is successful, she may be a blessing to future generations."[12] This indicates the enduring nature of this belief in the awesome power of Christian mothers to influence their children "for weal or woe." A mother's influence over her children was held to be second to none and one that would determine not only the future of her own offspring but also that of future generations.

A woman's moral influence over her own husband was a constantly repeated theme in Irish temperance literature. While clearly the temperance advocates, male and female, clerical and lay, all felt that this influence was a significant one, they were always careful to couch it in language that was acceptable to religious orthodoxy concerning the headship of the husband. Just as Christ was the head of his bride the Church, so, according to St Paul, wives were to submit to the headship of their husbands. Despite this obstacle, the construction of female piety that we are examining clearly gave wives the moral authority to redeem, retrieve, and restore errant husbands. Women were not to "usurp" male authority, but rather by moral suasion, restore their menfolk to righteousness. The following excerpts from a temperance poem by the Reverend E.E. Wilmot illustrate how this process was supposed to work. The poem starts with a description of Johnny McCree's ideal marriage, which was going to ruin as Johnny "liked something stronger than tea." According to the third verse

> He'd a good little wife,
> As you saw in your life,

> And sober and tidy was she;
> She both washed and she charred,
> But t'was all labour marred,
> As he liked something stronger than tea.

By the seventh verse Johnny was drinking away his wages and coming home in various stages of inebriation and causing his dear wife a great deal of grief.

> When she'd got him to bed,
> Like a fool off his head,
> She wept, did poor Nancy McCree;
> But the big tears of grief,
> Gave her little relief,
> As he liked something stronger than tea.

In her sorrow Nancy turned to God and lovingly prayed for her poor husband's redemption.

> But like a kind prudent wife,
> She avoided all strife,
> Nor scolded her Johnny McCree;
> When he cursed her and swore,
> She more gently forbore,
> As he took something stronger than tea.[13]

These tactics eventually proved successful and Johnny McCree became an abstainer and temperance advocate. He was now content with a cup of tea. But note how it was stated explicitly that Mrs McCree did not harass or criticize her husband about his behaviour. Instead she used "moral suasion." Women were told by temperance writers that their gentle, self-sacrificing forbearance was essential to their success as agents of redemption.[14] No usurpation of a husband's authority was allowed even though the righteousness of their anti-alcohol campaign afforded them the moral high ground. Gentle persuasion was to be used because it fitted evangelical Protestant gender norms and because it was said to work.

Male temperance authors readily admitted the ubiquitous authority of the women in their lives. Later, some theories explaining their propensity to turn the tables of gender authority upside down in such a fashion will be suggested, but for now let us just examine what construction of female strength they were presenting. In an article in the first issue of *The Irish Temperance League Journal* titled "Words for

Wives," the editor, William Church, had the following advice to give his female readers.

I believe the influence of a wife, to be always, for good or bad, very decided. There is not a woman living, unless she has forfeited all claim to her husband's respect, but is making her mark day by day upon his character. We men are foolishly proud, and do not like to let the women see how they influence us, but we know that, outside of our business, and sometimes even in it, – all our doings are more or less controlled by our wives, and he is a knave who will not honestly own it. Is it a disgrace to a man that he is kept at home, away from bad company, away from doubtful pleasure and foolish expense, through his wife's influence? Some poor, cowardly souls think so, and utter senseless cries against her who, as a guardian angel, stands between these and their victim.[15]

The many volumes of *The Irish Temperance League Journal* produced during this period do not reveal a single voice which contradicted this opinion. It appears to have been universally accepted in evangelical Protestant circles that women did wield a powerful influence over their husbands' lives. Needless to say, this power was not political or physical. Rather it was entirely moral or spiritual. Whether this constitutes what modern feminists would consider *real* power is not at issue here. What is important for our purposes, is that the authors of this construction of Christian womanhood, both male and female, depicted women as having significant moral authority and moral power.

Frequently in temperance fiction (the vast majority of which was written by women), the heroine actually martyred herself to reach an unrepentant man. Heroines in these popular temperance tales were usually the wives, mothers, sisters, or daughters of alcoholic men. Exactly what malady brought about the inevitable decline of the heroine's health the authors seem strangely reluctant to say. The presence of alcohol in the home or the decline into an inebriate state of the central male figure in these stories usually results in the woman's "fading," "sinking," or "wasting" with incredible rapidity. Nonetheless their holy, patient, and virtuous example, especially on their deathbeds, had the effect of shaming the male drunkard into repentance.[16]

In "A Narrow Escape," written by Mrs Bewsher, a popular writer of temperance fiction, the heroine, Martha Newton, makes just such a sacrifice. When Martha discovered that her husband had started to drink, "She tried to undo the mischief that bad company had wrought; [she] made her home as cheerful as possible, for she knew how quickly untidy homes sent men to fill the public-houses."[17] Obviously Martha knew her temperance literature, for a frequently repeated prescription for keeping men from "drink" was the requirement that the household be a bright, clean, cheerful, and welcoming place.[18] As was mentioned previously, one of women's "rights" was to "brighten earthly homes with pleasant smiles and gentle tones." This, however, was not enough for the Newton household. Mr Newton's drinking worsened and Martha was "fast sinking ... [because] of his behaviour to her." The author did not specify whether his behaviour was physically abusive,[19] but such conduct was a common cause of suffering and sometimes death for the spouses of alcoholics in Victorian times. The narrative continues:

But death was coming nearer, nearer every moment to Martha. Yet *she* was not the one to be pitied. The drunkenness of her husband, the cruel usage, the penury, all had led her to look out of herself, and out of the world, for support. Her heavy afflictions had led her to God, to prayer, the weapon of the Christian warrior on the battle-field of life. With her last breath she warned him once again not to give way to this besetting sin drink! 'Better that you should know at once from one who has never deceived you what an awful thing drink is – drink has killed me through you!'"[20]

Fortunately for her husband, these are not Martha's final words. Rather, she told him of God's mercy and saving grace and then went "beyond the veil." Not surprisingly, "Remorseful anguish filled his soul; he saw his vileness; he accused himself of being his wife's murderer.[21] Then Mr Newton begged for God's mercy and vowed never to touch another drop of intoxicating spirits again. Even though Martha died (there was no "narrow escape" for her), her self-sacrifice was, according to this model of Christian womanhood, worth the making. Through a personal relationship with God, Martha transcended her suffering and misery. As Mrs Bewsher instructs us, it was her husband, who if he had died unrepentant faced eternal damnation, whom we should pity. Because of Martha's virtuous example, not to mention the powerful agent of guilt at work here, Mr Newton, providentially, had a "Narrow Escape." The reader was not meant to feel real pity or outrage on Martha's behalf; she had triumphed and fulfilled her role of Christian womanhood to the utmost degree.

Not only adult women but also female children were deemed to have a peculiarly powerful influence over those "caught in the grip of the demon liquor." A short story, titled "What Love Can Do," illustrates this point in typically Victorian melodramatic tones. The author, a temperance worker, begins by saying "This short story has a beautiful moral. One wonders at the fidelity of the dear child, even more than the brutality of the father."[22] She recounts the tale of little Millie, whose father was a drunkard.

I tried to take her home with me; she was a martyr to her faith, she struggled from me, and returned to the now dark and silent cabin. Things went on for weeks and months, but at length Lee [the father] grew less violent, even in his drunken fits, to his self-denying child; and when he awoke from a slumber after a debauch, and found her preparing breakfast for him, and singing a childish song, he turned to her, and with a tone almost tender, said: —

"Millie, what makes you stay with me?"

"Because you are my father, and I love you."

"You love me? ... "Millie, what makes you love me? I am a poor drunkard. Everybody despises me; why don't you?"

"Dear father," said the girl, with swimming eyes, "Mother taught me to love you, and every night she comes from heaven, and stands by my little bed, and says, 'Millie, don't leave your father; he will get away from that rum-fiend some of these days, and how happy you will be.'"

The quiet, persistent love of this child was the redemption of this man.[23]

Thus, in combination, the persistent love of the female child and the love of a Christian mother from beyond the grave had an awesome redemptive power. These are but a few examples of the motif, recurrent in temperance literature, of female piety as a redemptive force.

Not all temperance tales dedicated to the subject of female influence were so tragic in tone. In the same style as the "Johnny McCree" poem, the influence of young women over their suitors is brought to the fore in a sprightly manner in temperance literature with a "lips that touch liquor will never touch mine" theme.[24] In a temperance recitation[25] by Uncle Edward – the author of a children's section in *The Irish Temperance League Journal* – the determined character of one Miss Angelina Parker is portrayed. Angelina is a cheerful, "bonnie maiden" who "makes a very heaven" wherever she goes. Trouble arises when, at seventeen, a nonabstaining swain arrives on the scene.

> But Angelina Parker
> Was quite a steady lass,
> And Lionel, her lover,
> Loved also "just a glass."
>
> So when he told her plainly
> She lived within his heart,
> Sweet Angelina answered,
> "I'm only in a part."
>
> And if you want to have me
> To share with you my life,

And you desire to make me
Your happy little wife,

There's only one condition,
I won't consent without —
You've got to leave those glasses
Of bitter beer and stout.

And if you think I'm asking
A sacrifice too great,
You'd better seek another
Before it is too late.[26]

Angelina's show of strength in laying down this ultimatum to Lionel is not considered unwomanly. Rather, she is taking the moral initiative and ensuring that her marital home will be an abstaining one. Occasionally in temperance literature this tactic does not work; the man goes off and marries someone else and the woman usually remains single. His intemperate life is always hell and in the end either the former lover or his descendants tell the woman that she made the right choice by standing by her temperance principles.[27] Fortunately for Angelina and Lionel, her words have the desired effect on her beau.

Then pressing Angelina
In tender, fond embrace,
He fixed his eyes intently
Upon her blushing face.

"My darling Angelina,
Pray do not have a fear;
I am not going to lose you
For stout and bitter beer.

If all the world were offered,
I wouldn't give you up;
I've made my choice for ever,
I've finished with the cup.[28]

In recitations such as this and in scores of other temperance tales[29] young girls exhibit strength in maintaining their temperance principles. The young men seem almost helpless in the face of such determination. "Moral suasion" in this case involves the young woman using what leverage she has – the desire of the young man to marry her – in order to practically bribe her lover – "If you want to have me / To share with you my life" – into temperate behaviour. This type of behaviour is not described as forward, brazen, or manipulative – all of which would not accord with the cult of true womanhood; rather it is an acceptable expression of female power. The "lips that touch liquor" refrain demonstrates the strength of the naturally pious and pure young woman working to ensure the temperance of her own home, thus safeguarding her children's future and the future of her country.

Women were also seen as uniquely suited for this restorative role because of their good-hearted and affectionate natures. It was thought that Christian women had an enormous capacity for compassion and love.

Oh, woman, whoever you may be, wherever you may be placed, remember your influence is great. One word "fitly spoken" may turn the footsteps of an erring one. By your exemplary life a brother may be saved from ruin. A look may melt a heart of stone ... What would our world be were it not for the great fountain of affection placed in the heart of woman? Its constant ripplings have been flowing on from age to age. Silently, steadily, we see it raising the fallen, guiding the erring, protecting the weak, and its workings shall never cease till the last woman's heart shall have ceased to throb over the last object of pity.[30]

This passionate declaration of women's capacity for compassion was an affirmation of the moral power of women.

So strong was this perception of female moral power, that when clerics and temperance activists felt that women were not doing all that they could to further the anti-alcohol campaign, they held women responsible for its failure. In the following example, the belief in women's power and moral influence is again unequivocally stated, but it was also implied that by not doing all they could women were only impeding the way of temperance. The female author of this piece in *The Irish Templar*, titled "Women's Rights," encouraged her readers by stating, "Yes! women have rights, and rights that belong to themselves in an almost boundless degree. If they do not claim their rights and make the use of them that God intended they should make, the fault lies at their own door ... We want the women of Ireland to see their duty in this matter ... Oh! if we could rouse women to see and exercise their God-given rights at home, not in apathy to say, "boys will be boys you know," but to remember the boys will soon be men, and with us rests the issue what kind of men they will be."[31] The "right" of women to influence their sons meant that they were somehow responsible if their sons were intemperate – theirs was the power to determine the future. Pleas for women to do their part and wield their considerable moral influence for the temperance cause were not always this moderate, however. Editorials heaping scorn on women who did not lend their aid to the temperance crusade through personal abstinence and moral influence fulfilled the dual function of further reinforcing the construction of the strength of female piety, while attempting to regulate and channel that power. The Reverend John Pyper, in an editorial praising the good work of the Belfast Ladies Temperance Union, made the following remarks: "... no human agency has contributed so largely to the sum of domestic happiness, nothing has been so greatly blessed of God to the preservation and restoration of home-comfort; and yet the movement has few, if any, more serious hindrances in its way than the wives and daughters of Ireland. Happily, there are many honourable exceptions, and amongst these our glorious cause has no more devoted and earnest workers than the members of the Belfast Ladies' Temperance Union."[32] With moral power came responsibility, and those who contributed to the construction of female moral authority did not hesitate to castigate women whom they felt were not living up to their model of female piety.

This brings us to the reverse side of this paradoxical model. According to temperance writers, women may have had many strengths, but their weaknesses were thought to be considerable. The purported physical weaknesses of women were inextricably linked with their potential moral failings and susceptibilities. From the same female temperance author who exhorted her sisters to further temperance activism in the above quote came the following warning.

With the drunken woman the case is even worse – the very delicacy of her system, its special sensibility, is of itself enough to make her feel keenly the consequences of her sin ... Man will do much to get drink ... but we have never known a man to do what woman has done. She has parted with everything dear to woman, ... She has done things which for meanness could not be surpassed, and which for vileness no man could equal. And we believe the constitution of the female frame – its very delicacy and sensitiveness – accounts for this. Words ... cannot describe the degradation of a female drunkard, it so shocks every feeling and is so utterly repugnant to every idea of what a woman ought to be.[33]

While intemperance was sinful for men, it was somehow *more* sinful or vile for women. It was a complete negation of all that Christian women were meant to be. It struck at the very essence of evangelical Protestant womanhood. Yet, ominously, women in their weakness were highly susceptible to it. They needed the care and protection of orthodox teaching, Christian medical warnings, and godly legislation. A paper delivered by the Reverend William Caine, a former chaplain at the Manchester County Jail, to a Belfast meeting of the Economic Science and Statistics Section of the British Temperance Association, had this to say about women and alcohol.

Female drunkenness is increasing to a frightful extent – 60 per cent in four years – and their drinking leads to the commission of other crimes. We are told by Plutarch, ... that in the early ages of Rome women were strictly prohibited from tasting intoxicating wine; and other ancient writers tell us that they were punished with death for their crime, just as if they had committed adultery, "because the drinking of intoxicating liquor was regarded as the beginning of adultery." When will English legislators be as wise as Romulus and Numa so far as to prevent females from using these poisonous drinks? ... It appears almost incredible that men professing to be followers of Jesus Christ should allow women, who ought to be models of everything pure and holy and lovely, to sink to such a degraded condition ... Let us imitate old Romulus and Numa and prohibit women from tasting this destructive poison, alcohol, which leads to such fatal results.[34]

This type of "expert" opinion is prominent in the pages of the *Irish Temperance League Journal.* Caine goes on to describe the sex ratios of the prison population in Manchester, and, not surprisingly, they presented a shocking picture of female depravity. But it was depravity of a uniquely sectarian nature. The Protestant inmates charged to Caine's care were, he says, predominantly male. He said he sympathized with the sad plight of his Roman Catholic fellow chaplain, the Reverend Father Nugent, who had the unfortunate task of administering to the spiritual needs of a total of 12,420 inmates, the majority of whom were women. Caine does not point out that the difference between the respective proportions of Protestant and Catholic women was only a matter of 5.4 percent; rather he presents the raw data – 4,742 Catholic women and 1,931 Protestant women – and highlights his finding that, among Roman Catholics, "in fact more females than males were incarcerated."[35] Given his forceful comments concerning the greater depravity of intemperance in women, it is impossible to avoid his unspoken conclusion: Catholics were more depraved then Protestants."[36]

Rarely was any protest made against this depiction of female drunkards as being *more* depraved than their male counterparts. In the September 1877 edition of *The Irish Templar,* an article titled "A Woman's Protest and Impeachment" decried the sexual double standard with regard to alcohol. "We intend to have one standard of morality in the country and that is God's standard. There is no sex in guilt, in crime. It is as bad for a man to get drunk as for a woman. 'Oh! young men,' it is said, 'must sow their wild oats,' but let it be remembered that whatsoever a man's [sic] sows that shall he also reap; ... The law of nature and of God is inexorable, and a public sentiment must be created that shall require conformity thereto on the part of men as well as of women."[37] This was not, however, the consensus on the issue. For most temperance writers, female drunkenness was more morally depraved then male intemperance.[38]

The tragedy of female drunkenness, the ease with which women could fall into intemperance, and the measures necessary to remedy this were all topics of temperance fiction; again, these were most frequently penned by female authors. The realm of "scientific" and medical opinion was reserved, of course, for male temperance advocates. In their prescriptive temperance tales women activists employed the "evidence" of the horrors of female drunkenness (which appeared in temperance literature in a highly repetitive fashion) produced by the male "experts".

In a serialized story by Mrs M.A. Paull, "Our Bill at the Grocer's," with the subtitle "Founded on Fact," the plight of a young husband and father, Anthony, whose wife has become an alcoholic, is described. The wife had deserted her husband and small children and Anthony told his elder brother of his troubles.

"Oh, James! that you should have come to see my home deserted, myself bereaved, my children worse than motherless ... My house didn't look like this when you saw it last ... there never was a better mistress of a poor man's home than she was before she took to the drink, and she never would have gone to the public-house in the beginning; she was above it. It all came of the grocers selling the drink; curses on the wicked law, I say, that ever enable them to do it: it has ruined one good woman, anyway ... she has brought shame not only upon me, but upon the innocent children of our love."[39]

Anthony tells his brother of how he gave his wife money to purchase boots for their handicapped child and how, in an act that was the ultimate betrayal of her womanhood, she bought liquor with it instead. Needless to say it all ended in tears. Anthony continued: "It was nearly midnight when she reeled into the house, a loathsome, drunken woman; instead of the honoured, sober, industrious wife I had loved and cherished ... if ever strong drink made an incarnate fiend out of a gentle, loving woman, it was done then. I could hardly trace in that fiery-eyed, sensual, bold-faced woman the idol of my early manhood, the beloved, the trusted, tender wife of latter days."[40] There was no redemption for Anthony's wife. She had subverted the moral order and betrayed her role as wife and mother. For a woman who stepped outside of the boundaries of this model of female piety, there was little hope.

Drunken mothers were described as fiendish "un-women" who sacrificed their children to their "lust for drink." Again, this is a perversion of the ideal order in which the mother is supposed to sacrifice herself for her children. Children were idealized and romanticized in this high-Victorian period. Thus the destruction of a child's beautiful innocence by a drunken mother was considered a particularly heinous crime. Moreover, as has been mentioned previously, the welfare of society and of "the race" was said to depend upon the proper inculcation of moral principles into the youth of the nation. Drunken mothers, then, were a danger to the very fabric of society. Henry H. Grant of Omagh, wrote the following verse on the subject of the drunken mother and her child.

> I saw a child, a fair young child,
> And its laugh was full of glee;
> Oh, bright was its glance when e'er it smiled,
> And merry its eyes, so sweet and mild,
> When upon its mother's knee;
> But it sucked in death
> At every breath
> On its drunken mother's knee.[41]

Mother's milk, which normally represents life for a child, in this instance brought death. The possibility of the hereditary nature of alcoholism was frequently discussed in temperance literature during this period,[42] and in this poem we see the child inheriting the vice of drunkenness from his mother: "But the smoulder fire / Of a wild desire / Was his by right of birth."[43] Having "sucked in death" rather than life at "its drunken mother's knee," the child has no hope in life. No mention is made of the father in this poem. The mother's influence over the child was deemed the most significant; if she was a drunken "un-woman" her child was doomed. Implications for the broader society were clear; if many women were that most wretched of human specimens, the drunken mother, then society was in grave peril.

Given that temperance workers were concerned not only with prohibition of the sale of intoxicants but also with the reclamation of the "fallen," the gendered nature of the discourse on drink bears further examination. The author of "Womanly Influence" explains that she had "known cases of men who, without seeking God's grace have by force of their own strong will, become sober men again; but very rarely of a woman."[44] The reason for women's supposed inability to fight their way back to sobriety lay in their delicate "natures." "Womanly nature," the author continues, "is more highly strung, and has so much the more need of God's restraining grace to keep them, and to rest on for stability."[45] This theme is brought home time and again in temperance literature; men can have "Narrow Escapes" and come back to the straight and narrow, but it is next to impossible for "fallen women" to be redeemed. In the reports of temperance missionaries who visited jails and distributed temperance literature, in the testimonials of those who ran homes for intemperate women, and, of course, in temperance fiction, the belief that women were nearly impossible to rescue was repeatedly stressed.[46]

In the tragic temperance poem "A Woman's Story" by Rosina H. Sadler, the moral that alcohol reduces women to "un-women" comes across in a poignant yet deeply misogynist way. The wife and mother in the story falls ill with fever and during her recovery is prescribed brandy (Ulster temperance literature devoted scores of articles to castigating those in the medical profession who prescribed alcohol as a medicine) and becomes a hopeless alcoholic. Her infant son dies of neglect and then her husband falls prey to the peculiar "fading" malady that afflicted those living in a household where "drink" was present.

> From the time of the death of our baby,
> My husband had seemed to fade,
> And soon he, like our little child,
> On his bed of death was laid.
> They said of decline he was dying;
> I knew 'twas the work of his wife;
> I knew it was *I* who had killed him,
> For whom I'd have laid down my life.
> I knew that his heart, so good and true,
> Was crushed with its sense of shame
> For the sin and vice of the woman
> To whom he had given his name.[47]

The full spectrum of female behaviour within this construction is thus revealed, from the ideal of the woman who has sacrificed all for those she loves to its perverted mirror image – the woman who has sacrificed the one she loves because of her all-consuming love of alcohol. When using her "moral suasion" and "gentle influence" a woman was the ultimate warrior in the evangelical Protestant crusade against sin. Once she was lost to sin herself – and remember, this could happen very easily because of women's physical and moral weakness – she was the ultimate sinner, bringing down not only herself, but also her husband, her children, her community, and her nation. Woman's influence was a two-edged sword; it could earn her the highest commendation or the most damning indictment.

PROTESTANT IMAGES OF IRISH CATHOLIC WOMEN: THE "BIDDY" MODEL

Lurking in the background of this construction of Protestant womanhood was the sometimes dark and shadowy, sometimes comic, but always distorted presence of Irish Catholic women. In large-circulation periodicals such as *The Irish Temperance League Journal*, which praised Catholic temperance efforts[48] and rarely made blatantly sectarian comments, the presence of the drunken Irish Catholic woman was only found in the reports of "experts," like the Reverend Mr Caine, who used the veil of science to cover any sectarian ugliness. In fiction, especially in *The Irish Templar*, Protestants were not so circumspect.

In a play called "Comparisons," that appeared in *The Irish Templar*, John Bull, a sanctimonious reformer and the "feckless" Paddy Erin meet several times. Paddy's wife, Biddy, is everything the ideal Protestant woman was not. The Erins' home was filthy – John Bull helpfully suggests that "a pailful of white-wash for your walls is far better than a skinful of whisky for your bodies."[49] Paddy replies that his "jewel" Biddy is of the opinion that "Bread may be the staff of loife but whisky's loife itself."[50] Instead of gently advocating moderation, Biddy encourages her family to drink. Unlike Johnny McCree's wife, who refused to chide or scold her husband, Biddy delights in upbraiding the hapless Paddy. She shrewishly scolds him about his manners, ignores his opinions, and generally dominates every scene she is in. Unlike the silent and gentle heroines of evangelical Protestant temperance tales, Biddy never holds her tongue. She leaves the stage as she entered, on a cloud of words and oaths, chasing after a goat who, Biddy says, is like her master Paddy: "There's no taching her manners."[51] Although Biddy was, ostensibly, a comic figure, in her intemperate and domineering personality there was an image of womanhood that Protestants loathed and perhaps feared. In Biddy's bragging about her "darlin" son who might one day "go and obstruct the Parliament – whatever that manes – and get a great name for himself and all the Erins,"[52] we see the concern of "patriotic" Templars about the influence mothers on the "Biddy" model were having over the men of Catholic Ireland.

The "Biddy" model in Protestant temperance fiction created the caricature of an Irish Catholic woman encouraging her husband in all of his worst tendencies while indulging her own base desire for drink. In "How Pat took the Pledge," we see how a woman based on the "Biddy" model had a negative effect on her weak husband. Pat and Bridget Cahill were "well-known characters" in their district who were known to take more than a "wee drop" at times. A temperance orator came to town who had "liberal" views on securing temperance pledges; if he could not get a pledge for total abstinence, he would compromise on milder terms. Pat and Biddy went to hear the temperance speaker and Pat, being greatly affected by the arguments made, went forward to sign the pledge with Biddy trailing behind him. But she did not go to the front to sign the pledge as well; rather, she had an entirely different motive. "'Don't be afther making it too sthrong, Pat,' she whispered loud enough for every one to hear."[53] Resolutely, Pat replied "Don't tempt me, Biddy,"[54] as he continued towards the platform. Biddy continued to harass Pat as he told the temperance man what form his pledge would take. When Pat said that it should read "Pat Cahill will not taste a drop of liquor," Biddy pleaded again "Not too strong, Pat, not too strong."[55] Finally, "wavering a bit" Pat instructed the man to write down that "Pat Cahill will not taste a drop of liquor except at a christening, a wedding, or a wake, and when he meets a friend."[56] The author caustically remarked that "these terms were liberal enough to satisfy Biddy," and thus while Pat boasted of having taken the pledge there was nothing to prevent him from going on drinking sprees without violating its terms. The contrast between Biddy dissuading her husband from taking a real, total abstinence pledge and the "true" women of temperance tales who prayed, suffered, and even died in order that their men might become sober Christians, could not be more stark.

The final example of the "Biddy" model I would like to discuss may be found in a prize-winning temperance tale titled "The Shadow of Shame." This example differs from the earlier two in that it is not written in a comic style, but is presented in the typically melodramatic fashion of most Victorian temperance literature. "The Shadow of Shame" is the story of Silas Harding, a working man who, though born in Scotland, is of Irish descent and who took an Irish wife. Both Silas and his wife, Biddy, are described as being on the road to ruin through drink when Silas goes to a temperance meeting and signs the pledge. Silas induces Biddy to sign as well, but she is too weak to keep her promise. Apparently "Biddy's health often induced her to take the old medicine by medical prescription."[57] Silas, however, was progressing well in his new temperance lifestyle and had become a popular speaker at temperance meetings. He was unaware of the extent of Biddy's drinking. One evening he was speaking in the town marketplace on the subject of the duties of husbands and wives when "a blear-eyed half-drunken woman whom he had formerly admonished cried or screamed out, 'ga awa hame, man, ga awa hame, yere not expected the neet, an' Bridget will get gloriously on the spree, when the bairns are locked up stairs, thin talk aboot men's wives, ha, ha, ha.'"[58] Silas rushed home and found his wife drunk. Biddy tottered, a bottle of whisky almost empty in her hand, fell onto the fire and quickly died. Silas's life was in ruins – he became almost deranged at his wife's death, was charged with manslaughter, and sent to prison – and his promising work for gospel temperance destroyed by Biddy's weakness. While this story does not make a caricature of Biddy, it reinforces the stereotype of Irish Catholic women: "Biddies" as prone to drink. To the minds of Protestant temperance reformers, the "Biddy" types bring down their husbands, their children, and "dear old Ireland"[59] through their intemperance.

Perhaps the creation of the "Biddy" type as the antithesis of Protestant womanhood – as a sort of negative reference point – made conservative evangelical Protestants who were fearful of the supposedly drunken and rebellious Catholic majority, enforce even more rigorously this definition of themselves and their women as diametrically opposed to those whom they feared.

While I did not find any Catholic material which refuted the "Biddy" model – Catholics tended simply to ignore patently ridiculous sectarian bigotry – Catholic nationalist writers did provide their own rationale for the tragic reality of intemperance among "the sons and daughters of Erin" at home and abroad. The Reverend Father Matthew Russell, Catholic nationalist and founder and long-time editor of *The Irish Monthly*, was particularly troubled by the fact that Ireland's "enemies" used the reputation of the Irish for drunkenness as the proverbial stick with which to beat them. Russell argues that one of the best motives for all Irish men and women to be temperate is the fact that "poor Ireland's enemies are fain to hiss / Their spiteful sneers against her children's fame."[60] Russell considered a temperate lifestyle proof of Irish patriotism. "A drunken patriot is a lie and fraud: He loves not Ireland who loves not God."[61] Although *The Irish Monthly* was aimed at a highly literate, middle-class readership, Russell makes an appeal to the Irish peasant – whose noble character was frequently romanticized by Russell and others in the pages of *The Irish Monthly* – to restore Erin's good name.

Dear Irish peasant, brave and pure and true,
Ah! let this scandal rest no more on *you*
Honest, contented with your scanty store,
And Catholic, aye to the very core;
Yet why let Pharisees their eyebrows lift
At your intemperance and lack of thrift?
If by no nation are ye left behind
In generous qualities and gifts of mind,
Why not do justice to your creed and race
By stamping out this vulgar, vile disgrace?[62]

In the play "Comparisons" discussed above, John Bull, dispenser of patronizing advice to the hapless Paddy Erin, was an example of the "Pharisee" model that Russell so resented. Aside from these elements of nationalist tension, though, Catholic temperance prose and poetry contained similar views on women and alcohol and on the role of women in securing the destiny of the nation. As was discussed in chapter 2, Catholics and Protestants constructed ideal gender roles around the locus of the cult of domesticity.

Like the long-suffering women of Protestant temperance fiction, Catholic wives and mothers endured male intemperance. Russell relates the story of one Mary Dempsey, who, unwittingly, when she became Mrs Thomas Houlahan, "linked with a drunkard's life [her] lot."[63] Her husband's choice of "the stupid tankard's foam" over "the true comforts of a loving home" raises the ire of Russell, an ardent votive of the cult of domesticity: "Home, home, sweet home! It maddens one to think / Of happy homes laid desolate by drink."[64] As in the Protestant gospel temperance literature, woman in Catholic writing is by nature paradoxically pure and holy yet also highly susceptible to the perils of drink. Her fall into disgrace is painted by Catholic writers in language no less melodramatic and sentimental than that employed by their Protestant counterparts.

O womanhood, kind, tender-hearted, pure!
Alas, not even *thy* sacred name is sure
'Gainst this malignant spell, this damning taint.
But no, I cannot, will not, dare not paint
That saddest scene on God's poor earth below,
Worst depth of all life's tragedy of woe,
Plague-spot unholy with dire miseries rife —
The miscalled home cursed with a drunken wife.[65]

According to Russell, the ideal home, with a temperate wife and temperate husband "in thousands form a happy state / And make a nation prosperous and great."[66] But a drunken woman made a home an "un-home" or a "miscalled home." A pious and temperate Catholic woman could ameliorate the negative effects of her husband's drinking through her patient prayer and holy example, but when a woman subverted domestic norms and brought evil into the home that she was supposed to nurture and protect, all was lost. This was the worst tragedy, for the family, and by extension, for the state.

THE ROLE OF WOMEN IN TEMPERANCE WORK: THE GREATEST VICTIMS OF DRINK AND THE CHAMPIONS OF TEMPERANCE

In article after article enlisting the support of women for the Ulster Protestant temperance cause, it was stated that women were intemperance's greatest victims. Women were said to suffer the most because of "drink." In "An Appeal for Women's Influence and Aid" the author states,

Ever and anon we read of wife-beating and murder associated with drink; but only a case here and there comes to light. Vast is the number of wives and mothers, daughters and sisters, who have suffered silently, no ear hearing what was said to them, no eye seeing what they had to endure. Oh! the misery that females have endured through Intemperance – the broken hearts, the wasted frames, the down-trodden love, the disappointed hopes, the crushing woe. Oh! woman! if thou could'st but see the thousandth part of what this direful drink has done unto they sisters in our land, ... thou would'st raise thy voice of warning, and employ thy most persuasive power to turn men from it, as from the cup of misery and death.[67]

While this appeal is chiefly to women's much-lauded natural compassion, the following editorial emphasized the more practical concern of self-interest.

Nowhere, however, is the evil more painfully felt than within the domestic circle – "woman's kingdom, her state, her world." Where the female sex exercises its most refined and sacred influences, there the bane of intemperance is most keenly felt; and hence it has been well remarked, that "woman is the greatest relative sufferer from the national vice." If there were no other reason than this why the ladies should throw their influence into the Total Abstinence cause, we cannot help thinking it as an all sufficient one. Self-defence, and the defence of all that is dear, should enlist every woman in the ranks of personal abstinence.[68]

It would be a grave error to interpret these statements simply as manifestations of Protestant self-interest and social control. There can be little doubt that alcoholism caused women and children great suffering. Moreover, while paternalism, class prejudice, and self-interest may have informed the evangelical Protestant temperance movement in Ulster, one should not be too quick to dismiss out-of-hand motives of compassion and earnest Christian love. One has only to read the testimonials of female temperance workers (making allowances for sentimental Victorian language) to see the deep concern that these women felt for those they called the "victims of drink."

As the quotations that have been presented demonstrate, both men – chiefly clergymen but also laymen – and laywomen contributed extensively to this model of evangelical Protestant female piety. Naturally, a major question that arises is, "Why did this alliance of interests occur?" The material cited provides several suggestions. The clergy's obvious enthusiasm in presenting women as naturally more pious and loving than men seems odd at first, but when we realize the importance of women to the strength and growth of evangelical Protestant congregations under adverse, secularizing conditions, this phenomenon seems less peculiar. Women, as the "chief victims of drink," may have needed temperance, but the temperance cause, as its advocates readily admitted, needed women.

The following passage contains a description of one important incident that created dissonance in this otherwise harmonious picture. The work of female anti-alcohol advocates in the United Sates was well publicised in Irish temperance literature and the arrival in Belfast for a series of meetings in 1874 of Mrs Stewart, the leader of the "women's whisky war" in Ohio and her associates was greeted with a great deal of fanfare. Anna Maria Hall, an English temperance advocate, enthused in the *Alliance News* that "The work these heroic women are doing in Ohio, and in other States of America, is, of a surety, woman's work; they are doing it, as women ought to do it always and in every cause, not by usurping to men, but by the weapons that are essentially theirs – by persuasion and prayer. God give them fruit of the seed they are planting."[69] Those who eagerly anticipated the arrival in the British Isles of these American temperance "heroines" frequently battled the impression that what the American women were doing – denouncing male clergy for inaction and holding hymn-singing and prayer sessions adjacent to or inside saloons and bars in order to shut them down – was somehow unwomanly. According to this construction, with its emphasis on gentle suasion and domestic influence, they clearly were outside of evangelical Protestant gender orthodoxy. Yet the American activists and their Irish supporters went to great lengths to convince others, and perhaps to convince themselves, that this was not the case. Every article emphasized that these women were not usurping male authority, that they were not fearsome "Amazons." Why all of this concern? As historian Marilyn Westerkamp pointed out in her study of female puritan prophetesses, dissonance is created when those who by gender definition should not have authority: women become spiritually empowered.[70] But in this case, the American women who heeded "God's call" gained spiritual authority. As we shall see, this was very disturbing for Ulster Protestants, for Amazonian women would be out of place in the construction of female piety as it evolved in Ulster.

A flurry of letters and articles appeared in *The Irish Temperance League Journal* in anticipation of the American women's arrival. The following letter from America is a good indicator of the radical nature of the women's crusade there. "Some call it imprudent, others injudicious; many speak with open contempt ... They would do good, but quietly; close the stores, but orderly; use persuasion, but not prayers. Let your women be 'keepers at home.' They tell us it makes them brazen-faced, takes away their dignity, makes the young bold, gives them a domineering manner and a haughty appearance. The lovers of order tremble, but progression marches onward."[71] When the American women arrived in London, Francis Craig wrote an advance report for temperance activists in Ireland. Note how her admiring description of "Mother" Stewart seeks to conform this radical woman to the evangelical Protestant model of female piety. "Her voice is sweet, and, though not loud, is clear, and some times penetrating ... Ones' [sic] heart goes out to Mother Stewart, standing there pleading for help in her righteous cause ... her eye flashes, her ardent feelings and aspirations heighten the colour in her face; now and then the voice will falter just a little to prove how womanly she is."[72] At the annual soirée of the Irish Temperance League in Belfast in April 1876, Mrs Stewart was the keynote speaker. She had these inspiring words to say.

The time was come when the Master called His handmaidens to take a stand against this giant curse. The gentlemen friends of the Temperance cause had laboured for years against great opposition and discouragement, but the missing link was the women. Now, if the Lord would only put it into the hearts of the women of Ireland to rise up and say this iniquity shall stop, it would be stopped. (Applause.) Although men had had a prejudice against women taking any public part in this movement, still they had acknowledged woman's influence in this direction; ... They had felt that they were helpless; they had seen their dear ones sacrificed; they had seen hearts broken and homes desolated, yet felt powerless, everyone saying, "No; a woman would be out of her place doing anything." But they must learn this lesson – "The servant is not above his master." They had exalted the idea of womanhood to an improper and false standard. The true woman was a true follower of the Master, ready to go and help and relieve suffering anywhere.[73]

This was a frontal assault on the construction of domestic female piety as it developed in Ulster Protestant temperance literature. Mrs Stewart recognized that relegation to the domestic sphere was not "natural" or divinely ordained, but that it was an "idea of womanhood." She attacked what she saw as a "false standard" a century before feminist historians theorised about gender as a social construct.

Yet "Mother" Stewart understood her own role to be an orthodox one; it was the evangelical Protestant status quo that she felt was deficient. Her orthodoxy lay in her being spiritually empowered not by her own strength, but by God's.

It was time that all obstruction was removed out of the way, and let the women come forward and help as they could. It was not for her to advise – that was God's work. When He saw them ready He would put it into the hearts of His handmaidens, ... The Lord sent His handmaidens out in their weakness, but in His strength and power, to shock the Christian world up to a sense of their condition and what they were coming to ... She called upon them, in the name of the souls that were perishing in their island, to rise up in the might that God had given them and fight this iniquity. It was laid upon her sisters to go forth and take a stand that they never had done before.[74]

How did the Ulster evangelical Protestants respond to this challenge to their accepted construction of female piety? This call for women to leave their gradualism and "gentle suasion" and to "rise up in the might of God" went unheeded.

The radical action advocated by the American women was entirely out of keeping with the methods of the Belfast women's temperance groups since their inception. At the first annual meeting of the Belfast Ladies' Temperance Union on 16 January 1863, the chairman, the Reverend Dr Morgan, noted that while he found it gratifying to read in the newspapers of the temperance exploits of celebrated English women such as Mrs Wightman, "he was glad to know that there were ladies in Belfast doing as much, silently it might be, as any ladies in the kingdom."[75] In the same conservative vein, the words of Mrs Margaret Byers, a ubiquitous presence in women's education and reform movements in the province, give us an indication of the resistance to radical, potentially "unwomanly" behaviour in the period after the visit of the American reformers. She had the following comments to make when delivering the 1878 annual report of the Belfast Women's Temperance Association. "This year your committee has to report nothing specially new in the working of the Women's Temperance Association. Its plans and operations have been carried on as heretofore in a quiet, unobtrusive way. Its action has been none the less powerful for good because it has never been characterised by anything that was startling or sensational."[76] This was an unequivocal repudiation of Mrs Stewart's call for women to operate, under Godly influence, outside of the gender orthodoxy for evangelical Protestant women. The American woman's call to "shock" Christians into awareness of the evils of intemperance is rejected by the province's single most influential Protestant woman. Mrs Byers stated that work with female prisoners was popular with the women of the association because they were "deeply touched by the degraded condition of poor women, the victims of intemperance. Cast out by society, disowned frequently by their own kindred, ... to give these unfortunate sisters one more chance of recovering themselves, is a proper outlet for womanly compassion."[77]

Clearly, "proper outlets for womanly compassion" did not include critiquing the failures of the church hierarchy or staging demonstrations masquerading as hymn-sings on the doorsteps of public-houses. That this was the consensus among Ulster lay women is indicated by their taking a gradualist approach to the temperance cause. They continued to use their moral influence within their own homes and among other women. But why? Some indication of Mrs Byers' reasons may be found in the latter part of her report, where she attributes to the daughters of a famous anti-slavery advocate a significant influence over their father's political and social activities. "In the same way," she says "many a statesman, and many an author, many a professional man, and many a man of business, has had his flagging zeal in temperance work stimulated by the gentle approval and tender sympathy of her who, though she may shrink from public work, accomplishes, it may be, more by her personal influence at her own fireside."[78]

Yet when a woman's "own fireside" was threatened by male intemperance, what was she to do? In the "Random Shafts" section of the November 1890 number of *The Irish Temperance League Journal*, the following pithy temperance axiom was quoted.. "The home is woman's sphere – when it is not drink's. When politicians let in this invader, her sphere is wherever she can soonest obtain redress and protection."[79] This sentiment was in keeping with the increasing political temperance agitation carried out by prominent Ulster women like Isabella Tod, yet it was not taken to its full logical conclusion by Ulster temperance advocates. Clearly, there were limits to the sphere in which women could act for temperance and still be considered womanly. Pro-female suffrage sentiments were expressed in the *Irish*

Temperance League Journal, using the standard temperance argument that if women were allowed to vote they would vote for prohibitionist measures because they suffered disproportionately from the ill effects of alcohol.

The most radical sentiments to be heard in the pages of the League's journal were not penned by Ulster writers. The source was usually American, as was the case with "The Helpless Mothers," which was reprinted from the *Women's Suffrage Journal*. In this poem the hellish lot of a woman whose husband and son are drunkards and whose daughter has been "sacrificed to lust" is described. But she is not to blame for her family's lot. As has been mentioned, in many temperance poems and stories women are blamed for the drunkenness of their families; they are accused of failing to make their homes comfortable and cheerful enough to counteract the lure of the pubs. This mother "works as a woman should" and thus she did nothing to force her family out into the unsavoury streets. The injustice of a situation in which a devoted mother does all she can – but to no avail – is highlighted in these verses.

> She breaks her heart for the boy astray,
> Or the girl that is defiled;
> But has not even the right to say: –
> "*They shall not tempt my child.*"

> The streets are filled with the snares that lurk
> In the wayward children's path,
> Yet people say that a woman's work
> Is still by the homely hearth.
> But the stagnant air of the world is stirred
> By the voice despised so long;
> The woman's voice in the land is heard –
> The words of a strange new song.
> We'll know the worth of a purer youth,
> When the women rule with men,
> For love of virtue and peace and truth
> Shall save the world again.[80]

But rising up and fighting the "drink curse" in the public sphere had its dangers. The cult of true womanhood prescribed certain womanly traits that were not commensurate with public struggle. Another American author whose work was published in an Ulster periodical expressed frustration at the limits imposed by woman's domestic sphere.

"Keep to your sphere," said the liquor men,
At home is the woman's place;
Take care of your children, cook, and sew,
And cherish your womanly grace.
These forward women who war on us
Disgrace themselves and their sex,
Plunging in filthy politics
The peace of the land they vex.[81]

What was the point, this poet argued, in raising up children when "a monster lurks in the street" that can destroy them? Even this radical writer uses the language of the cult of domesticity to justify the erosion of the artificial boundary between private and public.

Yes, home is a woman's truest sphere,
Its spoiler her direst foe;
If a viper coil by your sleeping child,
Is the gentlest too mild for a blow!
Because you are womanly, tender, and true,
And your home is your chosen sphere,
Fight, fight, as for life! If you shrink or fail
You may lose all that life holds dear.[82]

While toward the end of the period under study the palpable level of frustration with the male-controlled, gradualist program in Ulster became increasingly evident,[83] no "strange new song" of women's protest was heard in Ulster. Though Ulster temperance activists agreed enough with the sentiments in poems such as these to print them in their periodicals, this was not the path which women's temperance work in Ulster took. While "drink" was assaulting "all that life holds dear," it was thought that a loss of womanly virtue might lead to even more disastrous results.

At the height of the "Women's Whiskey War" in Ohio, a serial temperance tale was published in an Ulster periodical in which the young heroine had these words to say on the subject of women's role in temperance reform. "The controversial arena is entirely contrary to that gentleness a woman should ever try to exemplify, I hold with the poet's[84] beautiful lines:

Man for the field and woman for the hearth;
Man for the sword and for the needle she;
Man with the head and woman with the heart.
Man to command and woman to obey.[85]

By 1914 laywomen in Ulster had a greater leadership role within their temperance organizations, yet their mode of operation had not changed a great deal. "Moral suasion" within the home was still their key role in the fight against alcohol, although they were increasingly involved in supporting the agitation of male temperance reformers[86] for anti-drink legislation.

This powerful alliance between Protestant clergy and Protestant laywomen gave a certain measure of satisfaction to both of its constituent groups. For women, the tangible benefits of this construction might, at first, seem difficult to discern. The manner in which the temperance crusade was implemented in Ulster ensured that women activists only gradually enlarged their sphere of activity, from their own homes, to the homes of other women, to public places where they could assist other women. Yet, if, according to this construction of female piety, Protestant women could exert more influence and exercise more power by conforming to this gender ideology of gentle "moral suasion" within their own "proper sphere" of home and church, and if stepping outside of these norms meant a loss of influence and power, clear reasons existed for women to support the maintenance of the gender status quo.

"She Hath Done What She Could": The Gendered Construction of Female Piety in Ulster Protestant Women's Missionary Literature

Missionary work provided unprecedented areas of activity for Ulster Protestant women who served in the mission fields of India and China and for those who organized and ran the burgeoning women's mission societies at home in Ulster. At the same time, however, traditional constructions of female piety held sway in the literature of the mission societies. Moreover, ideals of true Christian womanhood – of women who labour, love, and pray – and the concomitant cult of domesticity were exported with the gospel message to the women of the East. Women's missionary literature simultaneously reinforced the traditional discourse on woman's "nature" while allowing greater scope for independent action by Ulster women.

My focus in this chapter will not be on Ulster women who went out as foreign missionaries; rather, I intend to examine how missionary literature contributed to the discourse on female piety and how it may have influenced the spiritual life of the "stay-at-homes" who supported "women's work for women" on the foreign mission field. The paradox of "heathen" women, in this context both Irish Catholic and Asian, as "sisters" and as "other" will also be investigated. Thus this chapter will be divided into two main areas. In the first section, I will discuss how the ideal characteristics of "true" Christian women – elevated to their lofty status by Christianity – were contrasted with the degraded nature and status of "heathen" women. This juxtaposition of the character and lives of Protestant Christian and "heathen" women also informed how Ulster Protestants viewed Roman Catholic women. "Heathen" women, while grudgingly admired for their devotion to their faith, were considered a major stumbling block to the gospel because of the tenacity with which they held to their "superstitions." In keeping with the rhetoric of the cult of domesticity, the mother was the key to the salvation of any nation; for she had the greatest influence on the rising generation. This lent great urgency and significance to women's mission work, for it was believed by the leadership of the Protestant church mission boards that only women could reach "heathen" women and convert them to Christianity. The stereotype of Irish Roman Catholic women as "un-women," domineering "Biddy" types was also found in the literature of the Protestant missions to the Roman Catholics in the West of Ireland. In mission literature, Protestant women who "shed the light of the Gospel" in the West had the purity of their lives contrasted with the dark, hard heart of the "superstitious" Irish Catholic mother.

In the second part of this chapter the role played in missionary activity by women at home will be examined. Missionary literature tried to awaken their consciences to their own good fortune and to urge them to exercise their womanly virtues of labour, love, and prayer in aid of their "sisters" who were not so fortunate. Presbyterian, Church of Ireland and Methodist women all had their own women's foreign missionary societies. Irish Presbyterian women had an independent missionary society called "The Female Association for Promoting Christianity among the Women of the East," or, as it was more frequently styled, the Zenana Mission,[1] while Church of Ireland women belonged to the Hibernian Auxiliary of the Church of England Zenana Missionary Society (CEZMS) and Methodist women could support the Women's Auxiliary of the British Wesleyan Methodist Foreign Missionary Society. Regardless of the Protestant denomination, foreign missionary societies that were supported by women, staffed by female missionaries, and whose target group was Asian women were called "Zenana" missions. "Zenana" is a Hindi term for an enclosed area where women of high cast conducted their daily activities in the company of other women. There was some misunderstanding among Protestant women in Ireland about the nature and extent of "Zenanas." Some women's missionary literature for home consumption gave the impression that *all* Eastern women were "imprisoned" in single-sex "Zenanas" and denied all freedom of movement.

Initially, the call for single female Protestant missionaries to go to India stemmed from the inability of male missionaries to enter Zenanas and evangelize amongst these influential, high-caste Indian women. Missionaries' wives assisted somewhat in visiting enclosed native women, but it was thought that this work distracted them from their primary duty of nurturing their children and husbands.[2] The call for single women to do evangelistic, medical, and educational work in established Presbyterian, Anglican, and Methodist missionary stations in India began the Zenana mission phenomenon. Even after the field of Irish Protestant missionary endeavour expanded to China and elsewhere in Asia and Africa, the term "Zenana" was still used to denote women's missionary work.

"TRUE" WOMEN VERSUS "HEATHEN" WOMEN

In Ulster Protestant missionary literature we find, once again, praise for woman's pious "nature." In his article "Woman's Work for Missions," the Reverend A.T. Pierson, a Presbyterian minister, includes all of the major themes of "true womanhood" and the cult of domesticity in the course of arguing in favour of participation by women in missionary endeavours. Woman's very constitution, he asserts, was fitted by God for gospel service. "Woman is pre-eminent above man in her sentimental, emotional and religious nature, and so it is that she holds the very keys of the domestic sanctuary in the opportunity to form youthful character ... She is especially fitted to care for, sympathize with and reach her own sex."[3] Pierson observes that the Protestant churches had ignored woman's special "nature" and talents to their cost, but now, "the time has come when her capacity and sagacity, her intelligence and her consecration, bid fair to constitute her the leader of the modern missionary host."[4] As will be discussed in the second section of this chapter, enthusiastic Ulster Protestant churchwomen were the de facto leaders of their churches' missionary efforts. "Consecrated womanhood" was a powerful force in the considerable missionary work of Ulster Protestantism in this period.

In a paper read to her fellow Irish Presbyterian female medical missionaries at a conference at Newchwang, China, Dr Elizabeth Beatty urged Christian women to seek out the particular gifts which God had made available to women. While her paper was written for her fellow female missionaries, the editor of *Woman's Work*[5] thought that the spiritual advice contained therein would be beneficial to women at home as well, and thus Dr Beatty's paper was printed in the magazine. Among God's gifts that women missionary workers could use was "the Diadem of Beauty." Dr Beatty described this gift in the following manner. "We are to be winsome, and this good gift God is willing to give us, so that we may win souls for our Master by our Christ-like lives. It is wonderful how the Holy Spirit can fill our souls with love and our hands with tenderness, and give us the gentle, loving, sympathetic words that reach the heart ... Let us pray that the '*Beauty* of the Lord

188 Love, Labour, and Prayer

may be upon us.'"[6] This distinctly feminine "winsome" character of female Christian workers was viewed as a key aspect of their success in missionary work.

The authors of Ulster women's missionary literature maintained that there was a unique relationship between women and Christianity. According to this construction of female piety, women were particularly keen to serve in the gospel's cause because they felt deeply their debt of gratitude to a gospel which alone had elevated and conferred upon them their rightful status as true women. "Well may woman be devoted to Christ," opined Pierson, "Christianity was the first great step in her elevation to her true rank and place."[7] This debt of gratitude that women owed Christianity was supposedly reflected in their zeal for missions. "Woman's work for the conversion of the world is a natural result of her conscious indebtedness to her Saviour and his salvation. Woman feels her indebtedness to Christianity for what she is."[8]

A frequent theme in missionary addresses was this elevating effect that the gospel was supposed to have upon women. Women at home were told that the gospel alone made them equal with men. Misogynist elements in Eastern religions were presented as proof of the unique benefits that Christianity brought to women. At the 1889 Annual Meeting of the Presbyterian Women's Missionary Society, an address was given on this subject. The Reverend John Shillidy, a Presbyterian missionary to India, quoted various passages from Confucian, Hindu, and Islamic texts. In all of the passages which Shillidy cited, women were treated with contempt or disrespect. After arguing that the founders of "heathen" religious systems had negative attitudes towards women, Shillidy asks, "And how would you, Christian women, like to be under the regime of Confucius, or Manu, or Mohammed, and have the tender 'Go in peace, thy faith hath saved thee,' or the sympathetic 'Woman, why weepest thou?' of Jesus of Nazareth exchanged for their teachings?"[9] The loving personality of Jesus is directly contrasted here with a portrait of other religious leaders as cold and brutal. As was mentioned in chapter 2, "feminized" Protestantism was a Jesus-centred creed which downplayed the harsher aspects of Christianity. It was not a fire and brimstone message; thus the speaker was able to contrast the loving nature of Christ and the empowerment for women that was available in his elevating gospel with the alleged misogyny of "heathen" religious systems.

What they saw as the spiritual degradation of their "Eastern sisters" was of great concern to Ulster Protestant churchwomen. Part of the emphasis on educating female missions supporters at home in Ulster about the nature of "heathenism" and its deleterious effects on womankind was to awaken the women at home to a sense of their duty towards foreign missions, (more on this in the second section of this chapter) but it also had the effect of reinforcing the satisfaction of Protestant women with their own lot. They were repeatedly told that their spiritual equality with men and their respected position as wives and mothers were all due to the elevating influence that Christianity had on their sex. Pierson argues that while both men and women owe to Christianity their spiritual regeneration, "woman owes even her *social* and *domestic* dignity and liberty to the gospel. Independent of the influence of Christianity, what has she been everywhere and in every age? The slave, the tool, the victim of man."[10] This discussion of the social and spiritual degradation of "heathen" women permeates Ulster women's missionary literature. It provides a foil for the construction of ideal evangelical Protestant womanhood. By contrast with the "thraldom" and "slavery" of "heathen" women, the burdens and self-sacrifice of the "true woman" are diminished. Equality and freedom are the defining elements of Protestant female piety according to this discourse which juxtaposes the "true" woman with the "heathen" woman.

George T. Rea, an Ulster Presbyterian missionary to India, was asked by a home worker for the Zenana Mission about the advantages which Christianity confers on women in "heathen" countries. Rea provided his answer to this question in an article in *Woman's Work*. First and foremost, Rea asserts, Christianity brings to the women of India their rightful place in society and hope of eternal salvation. He presents a portrait of Hindu society in which women are little better than the slaves of men: uneducated, downtrodden, and degraded. What effect was Christianity supposed to have? "Christianity lays the axe to the root of all this male tyranny and belief in the natural degradation of woman. It asserts that her position is on the same level with that of man, and keeps her there."[11] In the realm of female education, the Ulster missionaries certainly effected great changes and when Hindu families converted to Christianity the status of the women within the family did change.

However, the difference between the domestic status of Hindu and Ulster Presbyterian women may not have been as great as the missionaries thought. At the beginning of the period under study – the 1860s – there were Ulster Presbyterians who argued that a Christian woman's sphere should be exclusively within the home (see chapter 6). Yet, in 1893, Rea castigates Hindu society for confining the upper-caste woman to the Zenanas where "she is qualified only for domestic duties, and this is her sole sphere of life."[12] How different is this, really, from the very recent past in Ulster? Despite the relative newness of woman's expanded sphere in Ulster, this new freedom of Protestant women is presented as an intrinsic part of Christianity's timeless attraction for women.

My purpose here is not to test the claims the missionaries made concerning the elevating effect of Christianity on women; that is beyond the scope of this inquiry. Rather, it is important for our purposes here to understand how this use of contrast reinforced for Ulster Protestant churchwomen their belief in the blessings that their own religion bestowed upon them. This message was not only aimed at adult women; children were also exposed to the belief that the gospel elevated women. In *Daybreak*[13] the story was told of a woman of the far East who upon hearing the gospel message from female missionaries could not believe that she could be saved. The narrator observes that "is it not strange that she should lay such strong emphasis upon the last word: – 'Is it for *me*?'"[14] Her anxiety is not the result of a particularly wicked life, states the narrator; rather "It is *just because she is a woman* that she despairs. If only she were a man, she might have hope. She is dethroned, enslaved, degraded. All her life long she has been treated with contempt."[15] In case the young readers could not, on their own, see the contrast between the life of this Eastern woman and the lives of Protestant women in Ulster, the narrator makes the comparison for them. "Not thus are our mothers and sisters taught. They are respected and beloved. But they live in a Christian land. Did they live in China or India, neither tongue nor pen could tell their awful degradation. It is because she is despised, rejected, trampled on, that this poor woman asks her pathetic question: – 'Is it for *me*?'"[16] This often heard refrain of the spiritual and secular benefits which Christianity conferred upon them could have reinforced the adherence of Ulster Protestant women to the gendered prescriptions of their religious culture. Their belief that they were "respected and beloved" members of their own communities might have had the effect of affirming and deepening the commitment of these women to the ideals and activities of their churches.

While the authors of missionary literature criticized Eastern societies for causing their women to "languish" in Zenanas and seraglios, devoid of all self-esteem and desire for self-improvement,[17] the resulting passivity of women was not necessarily perceived as a negative thing. Rather, some missionaries saw the "lowly" condition of Eastern women as a boon in winning them to Christ. In a diary kept during her first several years as a missionary to India with the Presbyterian Women's Association for Foreign Missions, Lizzie Macauley of Clough, Co. Down, noted what she saw as the characteristics of the average Hindu woman. According to Macauley, the typical Hindu woman was "gentle and docile and there is a childlike simplicity and humility about her which is very winning and attractive, she is also very affectionate."[18] That Macauley finds the gentleness and docility of Hindu women a very attractive aspect of their personalities says far more about the religious culture in which Lizzie Macauley was raised than it does about Indian women. Macauley enthuses further. "Centuries of subordination have developed in the Hindu woman to a wonderful degree, the qualities of patience, longsuffering and forbearance."[19] The unmurmuring resignation of Hindu women in the face of suffering was, in Macauley's eyes, heroic.[20] Though she regarded them as "heathen," for Lizzie Macauley, the self-sacrificing nature of these Hindu women's lives made them potential candidates for "True Woman" status. Macauley detected nothing of the stridency of the Western "New Woman" about these women of the East; instead their humility and self-effacing manner allowed them, despite their "heathen" condition, to approximate her ideal woman.

Macauley's diary indicates that she struggled to yield her own will to what she felt was her call to be a missionary. On the first day of 1902 she wrote her motto for the new year in her diary; she chose the words "Not I but Christ."[21] Below this motto she wrote out a brief prayer in which she asked Jesus Christ to make her "pliable" in his hands. She ended her prayer with this request: "Lord Jesus grant that from now I may die unto self and live unto thee."[22] To a woman like Macauley, who grappled with her own willfulness and who sought complete submission to the will of God, what she saw as the humility and self-abnegation of Indian woman would be compelling indeed.

The admiration of missionaries like Macauley for "heathen" women was limited to their perceived patient, obedient, and childlike "natures." Because of their devotion to their own creeds, however, Eastern women were regarded as being major stumbling blocks to the dissemination of the gospel message. The great emphasis placed by Ulster Protestant missionary activists on the task of converting the "mothers of the East" to Christianity demonstrates the significance of the cult of domesticity to missionary discourse.

Clearly, the rhetoric of the cult of domesticity informed the call for women's missions. As mentioned above, the seclusion of some Eastern women within their homes made it clear from the earliest time of Irish missions in India that women alone could minister to women. Missionaries' wives were, like ministers' wives at home, responsible for the welfare of their families first, leaving them little time for conversion work among Indian women. Thus the call for single women to form a missionary force as educators and teachers – opening a door for missionaries into the lives of Indian women – came about. Yet this was not the sole justification for a special mission to Indian women. The language of the cult of domesticity was used to argue in favour of the particular significance, and indeed urgency, of converting the women of the East. The Reverend A.T. Pierson uses the following familiar argument in the course of asserting the importance of missionary efforts aimed at "heathen" women. "The mother shapes the character and influence of the child, the child determines the future man and woman; and so in the hands of mothers God puts the character of the whole generation."[23] As we saw in our discussion of domestic ideology in chapter 2, this type of thinking pervaded the literature on women's nature and influence.

In his history of the Irish Presbyterian mission in Gujarat, India, the Reverend Robert J. Jeffrey of Portadown, Co. Down, describes what he refers to as "the subordinate and depressed place" held by women in that society. Despite this lowly status, Jeffrey asserts, the Gujarati Hindu woman exercises a powerful influence over her own family. In many important concerns "as a wife and mother, she is the controlling spirit: her will is the rule of the household."[24] How women who were portrayed by the missionaries as being so utterly disrespected by their male family members and by their society in general could wield so much influence in their own households is not explained. Leaving inconsistencies in logic aside, what can be seen at work here is the rhetoric of the Western cult of domesticity being applied to a foreign culture. Where the "true woman" in the Western home was to use her influence to ensure the moral uprightness of her family, the "heathen" woman tenaciously holds onto her "heathen errors." Jeffrey continues, "She is usually, if not indeed always, ignorant, and bitterly conservative on the basis of prejudice ... her opposition to religious change is by far intenser than that of the men of the family, strong though that may be."[25] This state of affairs is perplexing to Jeffrey. "She is at once a domestic slave and a domestic autocrat."[26] His solution to this problem is the conversion of this Janus-faced creature, for "were she only educated [in Christian principles and Western culture] her slavery would vanish, her autocracy abide, and she would become the chief regenerating force in her country."[27]

A similar perspective was taken by missionary workers on the subject of Chinese women. At the 1914 Methodist Annual Conference, a meeting of the Women's Auxiliary of the Wesleyan Methodist Missionary Society was held in Donegall Square Church, Belfast. One of the missionary speakers referred to the important medical work being done among the women of China. The reason given for the urgency of this work was the backward and intransigent nature of Chinese women. "The most determined opposition offered in China to

Christianity is that of the non-educated, instinctively conservative Chinese woman. Therefore we must have women missionaries."[28] Paradoxically, the missionaries saw the power and influence within their own homes of these supposedly degraded and enslaved women as a major impediment to mission work. Their interpretation of "heathen" domestic life was informed by their own understanding of domestic ideology. "The needs of China's daughters constitute a missionary call. The call is all the more urgent when we remember that in China, as in every other country woman wields an influence that is incalculable. She may be dethroned, but still the sceptre of influence is hers."[29]

The rhetoric of the cult of domesticity was universalized at this discursive level. Female missionaries used this line of reasoning to promote the necessity of their own work. At the 17 March 1911 meeting of the Fisherwick (Presbyterian) Women's Working Association[30] a lecture on Chinese missions was given. The speaker told of the urgent need for more Christian teachers to instruct the girls at the mission schools. Without these teachers the country would be lost to "heathenism," for "the hope of China is to have Christian Mothers."[31] For the denominational mission boards with which women's missionary societies were affiliated, hearty support for women's missionary activities made sense, given their understanding of the pivotal role of mothers in all cultures. The Reverend Robert Boyd, the Organising Secretary of the General Assembly of the Presbyterian Church in Ireland, wrote in his book on his church's mission in Manchuria of the strategic importance of women's missionary work among women. "To evangelize China," Boyd states, "the children must be taught, and before they can be properly taught, their mothers must be led to Jesus Christ. From the point of view of strategy and policy there is nothing more important than the Zenana Mission."[32] The very "nature" of women and their perceived transcultural domestic destiny provided justification for missions and identified native women as both the most significant barrier to missions, but, once converted, the most important agents of the new religious culture.

The pages of *Woman's Work, Daybreak, India's Women* and *China's Daughters*, and other denominational publications that contained articles on women's missionary efforts were replete with descriptions, illustrations, and photographs that contrasted the darkness – both figuratively, in a spiritual sense, and literally – of "heathen" life with the light of the gospel and Western culture. A report on Zenana Day at the Lucknow, India, Exhibition is typical of this trend in the literature. The reporter's description of the native Christian women is most illuminating. "To one interested in the souls of the people the latter class was the most striking. The plain white dress, the neatly arranged *chaddar*, the absence of tinkling bangles, ... no excess of jewellery, the bright, intelligent faces, the clean white teeth, with no *pan*-stained lips – these all spoke of change of habit, customs, and heart."[33]

Before conversion, "heathen" women were viewed, as has been noted above, as a barrier to the gospel. Metaphors involving darkness and evil were used to link the physical and spiritual degradation of "heathen" women. Christian women were described using metaphors of light and goodness. In her history of the medical missionary work of the Church of England Zenana Mission (the Hibernian Auxiliary of this organization also supported this work), Irene Barnes's description of the unique opportunities which medical work afforded female missionaries also reveals a great deal about how white women viewed themselves and their "heathen" sisters. The woman physician, Barnes states, can walk directly into "... the most inaccessible strong-hold of heathenism – the home – taking the Gospel with her. Called to the inmost recesses of harem and zenana to take pity on mother or child, the woman Missionary doctor comes as the first streak of God's pure sunlight which permeates those polluted prisons; as the lowly yet true herald of that Sun of Righteousness risen with healing in His wings."[34] This tendency of Protestant writers to contrast their own freedom, equality, and cleansed status with the slavery, degradation, and physical and spiritual squalor of "heathen" women may have led to some self-righteousness. However, the dominant tone of the material written by women missionaries and missions activists at home was one of agonizing concern, involving labour, love, and prayer and no little sacrifice in order to accomplish what they felt called of God to do in "rescuing" their sisters in "heathen" lands.

Ulster Protestants were by no means unique in their view of the women of the East. American and English Protestant women's missionary societies[35] also used the language of "true womanhood" and the cult of domesticity in their efforts to promote their work and to render recognizable to them the social relations of the foreign countries they entered. Light and dark metaphors were universally used in foreign missionary material.[36] What was unique about the way Ulster missionary activists used these concepts was the way they used similar language in their literature on "home missions": Protestant missions to Irish Catholics.

"IRISH HEATHENS," "BIDDY" AND THE PROTESTANT MISSIONS

To those Protestants who were committed to home mission efforts among the Roman Catholics of Ireland, the Irish Catholic population were "absolute heathen in all save the name."[37] The "heathen" state of the majority of the population of Ireland was, according to these Protestant missions activists, the chief cause of the country's social and economic ills.[38] Just as in foreign-missions literature, the "heathen" were portrayed as dark, ignorant, and enslaved. "Fellow-Christians," one such writer appealed to his Protestant readers, "these poor, misguided souls are to be found, not in the interior of Africa, but at our own doors."[39] Irish Catholic women were described by Protestant missions activists in similar terms to those used in Protestant writings about the "heathen" women of India and China. In the area of "superstition" they were considered as ignorant and thus dangerous to their children and society, as "heathen" women. The supposed stubbornness and conservative instincts of Irish Roman Catholic women were considered a barrier to gospel conversion, just as "heathen" women were considered a major stumbling block. Like the "heathen" women of foreign missionary literature, Irish Catholic women provided a contrast: the darkness of their "ignorance" heightened, metaphorically, the light brought by Protestant female missionaries.

Yet, I found few direct comparisons made by Irish Protestants of the foreign "heathen" with the "home" heathen. In her *Glimpses of an Indian Dawn*, Miss E.M.C. Jellett tells her young readers that the Indians are surprisingly like Irish country folk. She praises both groups for being friendly and pleasant spoken, but she says both "country" Irish and Indians "are often very lazy and leisurely ... Possibly they [the Indians] think, as an old man in County Cork once said – 'Sure if the wrong way will do as well what's the use of bothering about the right way?' But I hope we are learning better ways here, so perhaps they will too."[40] "We," of course, does not refer to Jellett's own Dublin, middle-class Church of Ireland milieu, but rather to the predominantly Catholic "country people" of Ireland. In *Glimpses of an Indian Dawn* Jellett also describes a Hindu *Mela* festival where pilgrims travel from all over the country to visit sacred hot springs "which are looked upon by the Hindus somewhat as 'holy wells' are at home"[41] by Roman Catholics. The similarities Jellett describes between this "heathen" practice and the folk religion of Irish Catholics positions Irish Catholics closer to the Indian "heathen" on a scale of religious devotion than it does to "Christian" Protestants. What was seen as the indolence and the superstition of Irish Roman Catholics made them clearly fit the label of "heathen" according to Protestant missionaries.

Like "heathen" women, Irish Catholic women were sometimes viewed as the chief victims of the "errors" of their religious cultures and also as the obstinate defenders of their creed. As in Irish Protestant temperance literature, "Biddy," as she was created in Protestant "home" missions literature, was to be pitied for the harshness of her life and intemperance of her men. At the same time, however, she was frequently held to be at fault for allowing intemperance to occur. She was accused of failing to keep up the high standards of the cult of domesticity – e.g., an unkempt home drove Irish men to the drink – or actively encouraging male drunkenness by being intemperate herself. A similar view of Irish Catholic women as both innocent victims and unrepentant "heathen" was presented in home mission literature.

An article in *Daybreak* about the burning of a witch in 1895 illustrates this view of Roman Catholic women as helpless victims of their erroneous folk religion. The author tells of how "the poor woman, Bridget Cleary, was burned to death owing to the woefully gross superstitious opinions of her husband and relatives who fancied she had become a witch."[42] Were all of Ireland to be converted to the Gospel of Christ, the author reasons, then Ireland would no longer "be behind other nations in all that is godly and Christian."[43] Cleary's death is described as a "terrible revelation of the power of superstition in Ireland."[44] Just as only the Protestant missionaries' gospel could free Indian and Chinese women from the degrading customs of their respective religions, so too, it was thought by missions activists, that only the gospel could dispel the dangerous superstitions of Catholic Ireland.

Of course it was Irish Catholic women themselves who were seen by their would-be-rescuers as the chief hindrance to the "Gospel regeneration" of Ireland. In the 1896 Annual Report of the Scripture Readers' Society for Ireland, the readers' reports tell of the pride and sinfulness of certain Catholic women, who, from what the readers referred to as "fear of the priest," refused to allow the reading of scripture and distribution of tracts among young people.[45] The picture of a drunken woman appeared alongside an article about colportage work done by the Presbyterian Church's Irish Mission.[46] The article began, "Our picture gives a view of an open-air meeting in Queen's Co., and of a drunken woman, who was disturbing the meeting, being removed by a policeman.[47] The rest of the crowd was described as "eager to hear the precious words of life and love" spoken by the colporteurs; a drunken woman – an "unwoman" in Ulster Protestant discourse – tried to disrupt the work of evangelization.

Even when Protestants did not depict Irish Catholic women as being drunken or obstreperous, they still considered them dangerous to the well-being of Irish families and of Ireland as a whole because of their tenacious adherence to the "superstitions" of folk religion. Another article in *Daybreak* includes a photograph of a Catholic woman dipping her child into a holy well. The author, the Reverend Thomas Lyle, explains that the child was "dipped in the water of 'a holy well' in order to make it grow up strong and vigorous ... the water is believed to possess miraculous or magical virtues."[48] The photograph clearly indicates to the children reading *Daybreak* that it was women who carried out this "superstitious and unscriptural practice" in the "country districts" of Ireland. A clear message for the readers of *Daybreak* was that these Roman Catholic women were holding Ireland back through their "superstition," for, according to Lyle, "A country whose inhabitants do not enjoy a true knowledge of God cannot prosper like other countries where the Gospel light shines clearly."[49] Presbyterian children, who were enjoined to be true Irish patriots and love their beleaguered land,[50] were told that Ireland was kept "in the dark" by the "superstition" of Irish Catholic women.

The stark contrast that Protestant missionaries drew between their own female representatives and "ignorant" Irish Catholic women may be clearly found in the serial story, "The Church in the Glen." Through descriptions of the religious practice and personality of an Irish mother, through metaphors of light and dark, and also through the story's illustrations, a portrait emerges in which the "heathen" Irish mother is an un-woman when compared to the ideal "true woman" Protestant missionaries.

"The Church in the Glen" is, according to its author, M. McDonagh, a story "taken from real life" set in the West of Ireland. The story centres on the life of a certain Widow McShane and her young son, Johnny. Before his death Shane McShane, Johnny's father, had been contacted by female Protestant missionaries and had taken an interest in the gospel message. With great difficulty he read the Bible the missionaries gave to him, but his wife constantly harassed him and tried to stop him from associating with the "black Protestants." With his dying breath Shane told his son that he was going where "a blessed company praise the Saviour always" and that Johnny was "to come too, *agra machree,* but mind ye come through the DOOR."[51] Despite his mother's protests throughout the story, Johnny seeks out the missionaries to learn more about the gospel story that made his father so happy and that promised him the hope of joining his father again.

But it is with the women of the story that we are most concerned here. The portrait drawn of Widow McShane was of a woman who let her pride and bigotry alienate her from her family. McDonagh describes her in the first chapter of the story as possessing "a very devotional turn of mind, and a strong will, that seldom listened to another person's view on any subject connected with religion."[52] She took great pride in her devotion to her faith (e.g., walking four miles through hail and snow to attend mass faithfully) and great satisfaction in the high esteem in which her neighbours held her as a result of her piety. McDonagh frequently takes the opportunity throughout the story to attack Catholic practices, such as paying for masses for the dead. The author makes Widow McShane staunchly defend paying her last few pence to the priests while her son Johnny quietly questions the fairness of it all. Johnny is attracted to the singing and Bible reading services of the missionaries at the Church in the Glen and, thus, despite his mother's threats and his fear of her violent temper, he goes to see the Protestant missionaries. The gentleness and "nobility" of Mary Archer, the missionary who takes a special interest in Johnny when he comes to the church, are contrasted with the hardness of his own mother. At one point, Mary Archer tells her sister, Mrs Lee, who was also a mission worker, that Johnny's mother, was "a desperate character – quite blinded by error and superstition. She helped, by her taunting, to shorten old Shane's life."[53] Shane had told Mary Archer how his wife had actually flung the Bible that she had given him into the fire, but that he had recovered it before it was much injured.[54] The author clearly draws a portrait of a wife and mother whose behaviour, because of her pride and religious "bigotry," fell far short of the ideal of the cult of domesticity. Here we do not see the loving, supportive, prayerful wife and mother nurturing her family with "Gospel truth"; instead the Widow McShane's religious devotion is described as being equal parts pride and ignorance and her methods for dealing with her husband and son are harsh and uncompromising.

In the fourth chapter, "More Light," Johnny found his father's partially burnt Bible and began to read from it while his mother was out at a wake. The preternaturally wise child, guided by what the author calls "the sure Guide" (the Holy Spirit) begins to understand the gospel message that had made his father so peaceful. As the child was dressing to go to bed, "his eye fell with a sorrowful look upon a small square piece of dirty cloth that had hung around his neck since he could remember his mother's face. 'It's no use in this world,'"[55] the boy said. Yet, the author notes, the scapular, which the enlightened child could tell was useless, was important to Widow McShane. After returning home from the wake, Johnny's mother held a rushlight over her son to see that he was all right. When she saw the scapular resting on his head she was greatly pleased, for she took this to be a good omen. The Widow McShane is described as clinging to "superstition," little knowing the trust Johnny "had in the everlasting arms of his reconciled heavenly Father."[56] The child was receptive to "Gospel truth" while the Irish mother, like her "heathen" Indian and Chinese counterparts, was an impediment.

When the Widow McShane discovered that Johnny had been visiting the missionaries and reading his father's Bible, she turned him out of doors, despite the bitterly cold weather. Mary Archer found the boy at his father's grave and she and her widowed sister took the lad into their home. The "noble" – both by birth and, more importantly the author notes, spiritually – Mary Archer is all that Johnny's own mother is not. When Johnny first met the missionary he expressed surprise at her beauty and gentleness and blurted out, "but yer like a bright angel that wasn't dirty at all wid the smut of this world – sure you're not what they call a black Protestant at all."[57] Johnny was taken into the Protestant missionaries' household where he was looked after by Mary Archer's maid, "an elderly Christian woman, who followed the example of her mistress in serving the Lord Jesus in humility and truth."[58] All the Christian [read: Protestant] women of the household were "true" women in their labour, love, and prayer. McDonagh makes it clear that there was none of the haughty self-righteousness or hollow spiritual pride of the Widow McShane in this Protestant household.

The author takes the opportunity, while describing the Widow McShane's cold and lonely vigil waiting for her son's return, to criticize another element of an Irish Catholic mother's devotional practice. McDonagh tells how the Widow McShane was distracted by worry "as she counted her beads over the dying embers, thinking more of a cold little dead face turned up to the stars, than of her "Hail Mary."[59] The emphasis here is on what Protestants considered to be the empty ritualism of Catholic practices, such as saying the Rosary. McDonagh questions whether Johnny's mother actually prayed for her boy whom she thought was out alone in the cold. "I fear there is little of the spirit of prayer where there is counting of beads for the sake of much repetition."[60] The author states that there was little comfort for the Widow McShane in her beads, but for the "Christian" mother there was true comfort in prayer: "But well for the Christian mother who ... can lift up hands in prayer to Him who follows His children with love and care ... Christian mother, pray on! thy children need thy prayers."[61] Protestant missionaries did not recognize a Catholic mother's telling of her Rosary beads as true prayer. Without the gospel, they felt she was, like her "heathen" counterparts in Asia, a victim of "superstition" and a barrier to the spread of the Protestant message of salvation.

The cabin where the Widow McShane lived and the condition in which it was kept were used, metaphorically, to represent the sinful and ignorant condition of this "un-Christian" woman. Though she calls the missionaries "Black Protestants" and the Bible the "black book," it is Widow McShane and her world that are depicted as dark. When Mary Archer wrote to her cousin Jane asking her to take

Johnny in, she presented his situation in the following manner. "His mother turned him out of doors, and you know if I keep him here she will find him out, and either take him back to her cabin and darken the little light, or follow him daily with taunts and threatenings."[62] According to the Protestant missionaries, an "un-Christian" Irish Catholic mother could, through her negative influence, "darken the little light" of a converted child. She could force the return of her child to her own dark superstition and ignorance. Mary Archer tells Jane that she is seeking a Christian home for Johnny that is clean and "white." She flatters Jane by telling her, "your heart is white."[63] Cousin Jane does take him in and she describes how the first night in her home she saw him kneeling by his bed to say his prayers, "reminding me of angels in white robes, and of a land where poverty casts no dark shadows on happy souls."[64]

While the Widow McShane was characterized throughout the story as proud and hard-hearted, she was not beyond redemption. On Christmas Eve, Mary Archer went to visit the lonely and broken widow. The "noble" figure of Mary Archer enters the widow's gloomy cabin – symbolically opening "the door" – and brings with her the light — a metaphor for "Gospel truth." The Widow McShane offers no resistance to the "black Protestant;" instead, she is grateful, meek, and repentant. "An' ye have my Johnny safe, an' ye came to comfort me wid them blessed words – a wicked creature that I am."[65] Mary Archer spent the evening telling the Widow McShane the gospel story. The narrator reports that "that Christmas eve had worked a change in poor Widow McShane's creed, life, and temper. She had been humbled by suffering, till her proud self-sufficient heart listened to the Saviour's voice, 'Come unto Me.'"[66]

"The Church in the Glen" reveals how the authors of Home Missions stories used characterization and metaphor to contrast the "heathenish" superstition, pride, and spiritual darkness of Irish Roman Catholic women with the gospel faith, gentleness, humility, and radiating pious glow of Protestant female missionaries. Unrepentant "un-women" threatened the well-being of their families – and of Ireland itself – bringing physical or spiritual death. The representation of "heathen" women in foreign and home Protestant missions literature as the Other magnified the purity and goodness of the ideal Protestant woman who laboured, loved, and prayed.

WORKERS AT HOME: USING "THE RIGHT TO LABOUR, LOVE AND PRAY"

Protestant women at home in Ulster who participated in missionary societies received significant messages about themselves and their role within the evangelistic work of their churches. Increasingly during the period under study women's missionary societies increased in size and influence within their own denominations. In her work on Canadian Presbyterian women's missionary work in India, Ruth Compton Brouwer observed that these Canadian women, "In seeking to liberate their 'heathen sisters,'... had made considerable progress in enlarging their own sphere."[67] A similar process occurred in Ulster's Presbyterian, Methodist, and Church of Ireland congregations. Women's missionary societies gradually experienced more independence, and important matters such as collecting money for missions and publishing missionary literature were increasingly the sole responsibility of women. Female missionaries on the foreign field in every denomination sent out by every national group had more power – spiritual and temporal – than they would have had in congregations at home. Thus in missions literature one does not find the sort of controversies over women's role and place that were present in general denomination publications (see chapter 6). What is evident in the literature, however, is the development of the ideal of the true woman who "labours, loves and prays" adapted – seamlessly, it might be added – to missions work.

In her article, "Stay at Homes," Mrs Huston of Randalstown reminds the readers of *Woman's Work* that there is a great deal that they can do for missions even though they are not able to go out to the mission field. She urges her readers who "feel their hearts so deeply touched with loving pity that they long to go forth ..." but who are unable to do so to "take heart," for "the Lord can make a missionary out of you just *where you are.*"[68] "Stay-at-homes" can be missionaries, according to Mrs Huston, by being obedient to God's will in their own sphere. "'Kept for the Master's use,' she informs her readers, "exactly in the circumstances and in the position where He has placed you He can use you."[69] The ideal "stay-at-home" laboured, loved, and prayed for missions and through her patient self-sacrifice and noble efforts was a true missionary without leaving her circle of home, church, and community.

LABOUR
Rise up, ye women that are at ease, (Isaiah 32:9)

Dear Sisters – We live in solemn times. We cannot in these days afford to get into a corner of our own, and be content to live at ease – idle, listless, and careless of our surroundings. God has set us in *this world*, in this *Presbyterian Church*, to be something for Him, to do something for Him ... May I ask you in love, as I would ask myself – Are you each serving the Lord Christ?[70]

With these words Mrs Williamson opened the 1897 conference on Zenana Mission work at Fisherwick Presbyterian Church, Belfast. In her address, she exhorted the members of her church's Zenana Missions auxiliaries to search their hearts to see if they were doing their utmost for the mission cause. "Does it not stir our hearts," she asked her audience, "as we read His loving words – 'She hath done what she could.' Are we each doing what we can? As we to-day gather thus about work let the breathing of each heart be, 'Lord, what wilt thou have me to do?'"[71] Clearly, these missions activists who devoted much of their time and effort to missionary support work were concerned that they were not doing enough. "Marjory," one of the members of the "King's Daughters in Council," expressed the concern that Ulster Methodist women were not doing enough for the missions cause. "I feel strongly," she wrote in a letter to the column's editor, Charity Hope, "that the King's Daughters must not be 'at ease in Zion'."[72]

The King's Daughters sponsored their own female Methodist missionary in India – they referred to her as OOM, Our Own Missionary – and took a keen interest in every aspect of her work.[73] Ulster Protestant churchwomen were involved in myriad activities in support of missions work. In an open letter urging the members of her church's Zenana Mission auxiliaries to redouble their efforts for missions, "M.C.B." gives an indication of the range of missionary work performed by "stay-at-homes." "So whether your way of helping be by going, by self-denying giving, by organizing, collecting by boxes, by gaining subscribers and readers for *Woman's Work*, by directing or joining in a meeting for sewing or for learning about missions, by prayer for missions, see that Jesus may be able to say of you as He said of the loving woman of old – 'SHE HATH DONE WHAT SHE COULD'"[74]

One aspect of these labours that was frequently stressed was that of self-denial. Doing without to add a few more pence to the missions box, making do without the latest fashions, or allocating scanty extra family resources to support Zenana work were all frequent themes in the literature written by female Zenana workers.[75] By putting aside money for missions in their own homes and teaching their children to do likewise, mothers, the author of an article on the subject of giving to missions wrote, could foster self-denial in themselves and in their children. "Our boxes being insignias of membership in a "Do-without" Society, we shall grow more close-fisted to self, more open-handed to self's Saviour, more ready to hear the still voice say, 'You can "do without" this; the heathen cannot "do without" Christ.'"[76] The author also promises that the example of the mother giving to missions will train female children and show them the spiritual rewards of self-denial. "The tender heart of your child grows big with the thought that

Jesus knows of her gift. Such joy is so ennobling, that it pours contempt on all the enjoyment sucked out of all the candies of creation."[77] Giving to missions, then, was thought to have an ennobling effect on both mother and young daughter "stay-at-homes."

The deep sense of satisfaction that these women felt with their labours is impossible to gauge, yet one can get an impression of the pride they took in their accomplishments from the pages of their publications. At the annual Presbyterian Zenana Conference in 1892, Mrs Margaret Byers, Ulster's pioneer for women's higher education and an active Zenana missions supporter, gave an address in which she remarked that she was glad to have lived to see the day when the women of her church were rising to meet the challenges of Zenana missions. People at home, Byers stated, now "realise the power and importance of women's work on behalf of women."[78] And, as the delegates at the conference had heard from the various speakers that day, the women's work was being richly blessed of God – money was flowing in and missionaries were being sent out to do God's work.[79] While humility was an important feature in the "true" Christian woman and while throughout missions literature emphasis was placed on being a humble "instrument of the Master," Zenana support workers took evident delight in the success of their efforts. In "Holding the Lamp," an analogy was drawn between a faithful Chinese servant who held a lamp through a long operation performed by a Zenana medical missionary and those who "held the lamp" for missions by working for its support at home, especially those who popularized the cause of women's missions by operating *Woman's Work*. In the following excerpt from "Holding the Lamp," one can see the pride the author felt in the success of this aspect of women's work for women. "We think this magazine has achieved a unique distinction; for, without a single paragraph on 'the fashions,' or one patent medicine advertisement, a paper edited by a woman, contributed to by women, and subscribed to by women, has reached a circulation of 12,000 copies, and is now more than paying its way."[80] *Woman's Work* was something that its supporters took seriously, and this particular supporter was proud of the serious tone and manner in which this important work was being carried out by women.

Those Ulster Protestant churchwomen who had sufficient time and means to support Zenana missionary activities and who felt it their duty to do so were certainly not at ease. Missions literature constantly sent out the call for more workers and disappointment was expressed with those who could not or would not find the time to help.[81] Yet, for the most part, Zenana missions workers expressed satisfaction with their labour as "stay-at-home" missionaries.

LOVE

A central goal of women's missionary literature was to make the reader feel a sense of duty, obligation, kinship, and even love towards her "dark sisters" who were suffering without the "light of the Gospel" in the East. Throughout, the language of "sisterhood" is used. As in temperance literature, the authors sought to create an emotional tie between their readers and those women whom they sought to help through their work. Her kind and loving "nature" was a key characteristic of the "true" Christian woman. Her sympathetic soul responded instantly and unhesitatingly to those in need. Her own family came first in her attentions, but, during this period international temperance groups such as the World Women's Christian Temperance Union and the Zenana missions of the various Protestant denominations sought to evoke some of the tenderness that the ideal woman instinctively felt towards her own sisters at home and direct it towards her "fallen" or "heathen" sisters beyond the borders of her domestic sphere.

Contrast, as was mentioned above, was used to reinforce the difference between "true" Christian women and "heathen" women. But contrast between the freedom and wealth of Western woman and the slavery and poverty of Eastern women was used to evoke pity and a feeling of benevolent sisterliness on the part of the former towards the latter. The many[82] stories on Eastern practices such as female infanticide, widow burning, and foot-binding horrified workers at home. A sense of outrage at the treatment of the women of the East can be detected in the letters, stories, poems, and reports published in women's missionary magazines. Though Ulster Protestant churchwomen knew little of the actual lives of the Indian and Chinese women to whom they sent missionaries, they made ethnocentric assumptions about what the women of the East wanted and needed.

"The Chinese want to be like us,"[83] recorded the secretary of the Fisherwick Women's Working Association in the minute-book on the occasion of a lecture about Chinese missions. Perhaps this belief that their "dark sisters" wanted to be like them, whether true or mistaken, fostered a greater sense of kinship between the "stay-at-home" workers and those they sought to help through their work. It certainly reaffirmed their own belief in the significance of missions support work. Knitting socks, organizing bazaars, and collecting shillings and pence were not just time-consuming, trivial labour. They felt their work had a broader significance. "We are co-partners with Him in the greatest work in the world,"[84] noted the recording secretary. Leaving aside entirely the thorny question of cultural imperialism, for the women at home missions work was a rewarding experience, in part, because through it they felt they could make a significant impact on a global scale. Though their understanding of their "heathen" sisters may have been seriously flawed, their vision of the women of the East evoked from them much concern and sisterly love.

"There is so much work at home that interests me, I really cannot pay much attention to foreign fields. To tell you the truth, I am not interested in missions, they are too far off."[85] So said the narrator of "The Voices of the Women" one stormy evening to the patient Zenana worker who had come to her door collecting for foreign missions. She tells her readers that she tried to think of more pleasant matters as she settled down in her chair by a cosy grate, but the "disagreeable facts" told her by the collector intruded on her thoughts. Later, as she drifts off to sleep the steady dripping of the eaves turns into the sound of many approaching feet. The narrator tells how legions of women of the East were brought before her by a stern and majestic woman who raised her up on a high platform from which she could see the women approach. The Indian and Chinese woman told of the horror of their lives and mocked her hypocrisy. One of them scorns her by saying, "Degraded, ignorant, despised at home, she too despises us and calls herself a follower of the meek and lowly Nazarene! He cares for us and commands His children to bring us good tidings, but this child of His grudges a single half-hour to hear of our needs; she even refuses us her prayers, because she is 'not interested' in missions."[86] After they had told their tale and accused her of hard-heartedness the Eastern women disappeared, leaving the narrator alone with the stern-faced woman. In tears, the narrator asked her companion who she was and the reply came: "I am Conscience, ... I have brought truth to your door; shall it knock in vain?"[87] "Conscience" explained to the narrator that she viewed the women from a platform because she is "above the sisters whom you have seen, but the platform that raises you is the Rock, Christ Jesus. Will you be content to stand there alone, or have you at last interest to spare for the nations low in the dust at the feet of Allah and Brahma?"[88] "Conscience" left the narrator on her knees begging God's forgiveness and with a fresh determination to do all in her power to help her "dark" sisters. In this tale, which clearly owes a great deal to Dickens, we find an example of the way women's missionary literature reminded "stay-at-homes" of their Christian duty towards the women of the East. The descriptions of the Eastern women in this tale stress their beauty and their convincing pathos when they tell of the horror of their daily lives. A mixture of guilt and sisterly love melts the hard heart of the narrator and moves her to action.

Zenana missions literature also aroused feelings of sisterly love and duty by reminding "stay-at-homes" that it was only through the unique agency of "women's work for women" that their sisters in the East could be saved. It was their special responsibility and privilege to help "raise" the women of the East. The logo of the Hibernian Auxiliary of the CEZMS shows a shamrock garland intertwining and holding together three different scenes – one Indian, one Chinese and one Irish. Women's missionary writings sought to create an emotional bond between women at home and women on the mission field.

In one of her columns, Charity Hope tried to encourage and cheer her members who might be feeling weary and unloved by reminding them of the joy and hope for the future that was a part of their faith. At the same time, she links the spiritual journey – she calls it the search for "the blue sky beyond" – of the King's Daughters and the spiritual condition of Eastern women. "We have been lately praying and think-ing a good deal about our poor dark sisters in heathen lands and our duty towards them. Do we ever, I wonder, think of them with regard to their hopes for the larger life beyond this."[89] Charity Hope makes a connection here between the comfort that their Christian faith brings the King's Daughters and the spiritual needs of their "heathen" sisters. Empathy is created by associating the King's Daughters' own spiritual needs with what were seen as the aspirations of their "dark" sisters. "Shall we not put forth more earnest effort to send some ray of light into their darkened lives, by which they may have hope of future light?"[90] By reminding Methodist women of the importance in their own lives of their Christian faith – how it gives them hope and sustains them through trials – Charity Hope has made the mission cause seem very close to home and significant. Could Methodist women imagine life without the hope that their faith brings? Yet millions of their "dark" sisters live without such hope that "would make the present lot easier to bear."[91] In such a fashion, feelings of sisterly compassion and missionary zeal were evoked. Charity Hope also notes that, as a bonus, "as we thus try to send the light to others, whether near to us or distant from us, our own sky will become more blue."[92] Emotional sisterly bonds are thus forged when the spiritual needs and aspirations of Eastern women were presented as being the same as those of the women at home.

According to women's missionary literature, the happiness both in this world and in the next of the women of India and China depended on the efforts of the women at home for missions. The Reverend John Shillidy, an Ulster Presbyterian missionary to India, urged women at home to support the Zenana mission, because the "restoration" of the East, he believed, depended first, on the "restoration" of Eastern women to their God-given rights. "But that restoration," Shillidy noted, "can only be achieved through the Gospel of Jesus, and the blessed message of that Gospel can only as a rule reach through you, their Christian sisters."[93] In their letters and addresses to the "stay-at-homes," missionaries constantly tried to reinforce feelings of sisterliness in the women of their home congregations towards the women of India and China.[94]

One of the urgent needs of the Zenana missions was for female missionaries. "Stay-at-home" mothers were urged to practise self-denial and resignation to God's will by not holding their children back if they felt called to go to the mission field. The voices of their "dark" sisters were calling. Protestant mothers were told that, in love they they must resign themselves to the sacrifice of rarely seeing their child or even losing their child on the missions fields of India and China where the mortality rate for female missionaries was very high. In "An Appeal to Mothers" by "A Mother," the author asks mothers to search their souls and prayerfully ask, "How is it with me? Am I keeping back my children?"[95] If the answer is "yes" then, she tells them, "you are hindering a great blessing to your children, your dark sisters, and yourself."[96]

All of this labour and loving sacrifice for foreign missions could be quite tiring. The Zenana support workers realized this and tried to pick up the flagging spirits of their auxiliaries by praising their efforts and tweaking their consciences when they were falling short of the required commitment. "Only for those weary in well doing" is a brief dialogue in which the dramatis personae are Mrs Ireland, her Daughter Zenana, and Miss Eastlove. Daughter Zenana remains silent while her mother complains of all the time and trouble that her daughter causes her. Miss Eastlove rises to Daughter Zenana's defence, telling her mother that Zenana is "such an interesting child, with her wistful dark eyes and quaint foreign name. I wonder that you can find her anything but a delight."[97] When Mrs Ireland complains further of all the demands that Zenana makes upon her, Miss Eastlove tells her that she is being too hard. She accuses her of treating Zenana like a stepdaughter instead of as one of her own children. Mrs Ireland relents and acknowledges that she can well afford to support Zenana more wholeheartedly. She resolves to become a better mother to her distant daughter.[98] By characterizing the Zenana mission as the daughter of the women at home, this little sketch tries to evoke feelings of motherly responsibility and love on the part of its readers towards Zenana work. Making sacrifices for family members was a central part of the ideology of domesticity; by tapping into this rhetoric missionary activists could involve "stay-at-homes" in mission work. The women of the East were not just faceless "heathens" to the readers of this literature. Glowing stories of the transformed lives of native Christian women and the desperate need of the "unsaved" helped the women at home to take a keen interest in their spiritual "sisters" and "daughters" in Asia.

PRAYER
"She that tarrieth at home divideth the spoil." (Psalm 68:12)

The emphasis placed by missionaries and missions activists on the importance of the prayers of the "stay-at-homes" cannot be overestimated. Prayer for missions permeated every aspect of missionary work at home. Every type of meeting opened and closed with prayers for missions, special groups were devoted solely to praying for the success of missionary efforts, and women were repeatedly encouraged to remember female missionaries and the Eastern women they worked among in their personal prayers at home. In the women's missionary writings of these Ulster Protestants it is clear that, theologically, they felt that prayer was crucial to the success of Zenana work.

An article appearing in *Woman's Work* titled "At Home" used Psalm 68: 11 and 12 as its text. The author proposes that those who "publish the tidings" (Psalm 68:11) – the missionaries – will share the spoil, or reward, with "she that tarrieth at home" – the "stay-at-home" workers. "But how can we stay-at-homes share the spoil when we never see our Indian sisters?"[99] the author asks. The key to this shared endeavour, she purports, is prayer. She quotes from a speech made in London by a missionary to Mongolia in which he says that those who pray for missions at home contribute as much to the conversion of the "heathen" as missionaries on the field. He says that the missionaries are the agents of the people at home and that their success is directly proportional to the earnestness of the prayers of the people at home. The words of this missionary, the author tells her *Woman's Work* readers, "should ring in our ears and send us to our knees. Don't you see what a tremendous responsibility and wondrous privilege rests on us who tarry at home?"[100] By praying earnestly for missions, women at home could vicariously share in the foreign missions work.

The ideal woman who lived a life of labour, love, and prayer was also the ideal "stay-at-home" missions worker. Her loving self-sacrifice on behalf of her "dark" sisters in the East made her a model "stay-at-home" missionary. And there was nothing in this model of female piety that would appear unseemly to a Catholic woman of the same class; as was discussed in chapter 2 on domestic ideology, Catholics had the same approval for the ideal woman who laboured, loved, and prayed. During this period, though, Catholic foreign missions efforts in which the laity made a large contribution had not yet "taken off." This happened later, in the twentieth century, and Catholic laywomen were important contributors to this movement.

9 Conclusion

By weaving the religiosity of middle-class Ulster women into the historiographical literature, a contribution has been made to the broader tapestry of women in Ireland. As David Fitzpatrick cautioned us in an insightful review article in *Irish Historical Studies*, much of the recent historical writing on the subject of women in Ireland focuses on several themes. "Catholicism, poverty, wage labour and political struggle are emphasised, almost to the exclusion of Protestantism, prosperity, family life and social integration."[1] In adding the colourful strands of discourse gleaned from the pages of Ulster religious literature, I hope to have helped to redress this imbalance.

Poems, stories, sermons, and "improving" articles flooded from the religious presses of Ulster during the period 1850–1914 in an unprecedented stream. The views of the various authors of this religious literature clashed on many points, ranging from theology to politics. Controversies raged within denominational groups and vituperative attacks were launched across sectarian lines at the supposed transgressors of one's own religious liberties. This rich and varied literature teemed with moralizing, pathos, bigotry, humour, hyperbole, anxiety, righteousness, and ardent spiritual striving – in short, the broad spectrum of thoughts and emotions that result when such touchstones as religion, family, and community are addressed.

Consensus – not of the perfectly neat variety, but rather of the rougher, more ragged at the edges sort – may be detected in Ulster religious literature when it came to one crucial matter: the ideal

Christian laywoman. Her virtuous life was described by didactic writers in very similar terms regardless of affiliation. Her primarily domestic role was deemed crucial to the life of the family, community, and nation by Protestant Ulster Unionists and by Catholic Irish Nationalists. The centrality of this construction of idealized female piety and the consensus on its shape and significance reveal an important similarity between Protestant and Catholic bourgeois religious cultures as they developed in Ireland in the late nineteenth and early twentieth centuries.

Both Protestants and Catholics saw women's religious faith and its role in preserving and transferring to the next generation the religious values of their respective belief systems as a crucial element in their very survival. Conservatism in matters concerning gender construction and understanding of gendered roles was a feature of the popular religious literature of Catholics and Protestants. Each for their own particular reasons sought to prevent change in the realm of the family.

As a religious and political culture, Ulster Protestantism was feeling threatened by the growing influence of Catholic Nationalism and by the Home Rule campaigns, and thus their traditionalism is readily understandable. They saw themselves as a people under siege.

As a group, Ulster Catholics were not at the forefront of Irish Catholic Nationalism. Yet from the centre of this movement, Dublin, material was distributed to Ulster. Also, influential Irish Catholic writers such as Father Matthew Russell, Rose Kavanagh, and "Magdalen Rock" were from the "Black North."[2] Writers who contributed to popular Irish Catholic periodicals such as *The Irish Monthly* and *The Catholic Bulletin and Book Review* had a distinctly bourgeois point of view that romanticized peasant life and the Gaelic past. Ideologically, these "genteel" middle-class writers had much in common with their Protestant counterparts. The differences in activities and emphasis can be accounted for by the position of the Catholic community on an economic modernisation curve; they lagged behind the Protestants in this regard.

Contemporary observers were obsessed with the differences between Protestants and Catholics. Their ability to see only difference was the result of a distorting parallax. They were too close to the situation to view it accurately. That their view of difference was, in many respects and particularly with regard to women, demonstrably inaccurate makes it especially deserving of historical investigation.

Questions of agency confront any researcher who delves into the realm of women's spirituality. While agency remains at the core of feminist theoretical approaches, it is that element of human existence which is least tangible. What power did these women have over their own religious lives? Did they unthinkingly conform to pious prescriptions, or did they derive their own personal meanings from the rites of their churches and the daily rounds of lives as Christian women?

The religious periodical literature that provides the documentary base for this study allows us to look at the religious beliefs that they held and the way they viewed their gendered experience of their faith but "through a glass darkly." At certain points the glass is clearer than it is at others. When "the-Reverend" huffed and opined on the sacred realm of women, did women perhaps roll their eyes in exasperation or did they nod appreciatively, recognizing themselves in his words and considering the power that was theirs as Queens of the parlour, temperance crusaders, and Sabbath-school leaders? When earnest women (one can think of no other word to describe them) such as Charity Hope anxiously pleaded with her sisters to take seriously their "women's mission" did her readers think her a sanctimonious bore or a spiritual delight? That her column ran for more than thirty years and that she received regular correspondence from her "King's Daughters in Council" – is this enough to prove that Charity Hope's views were representative ones that she shared with a community of women? These women-to-women columns – one narrow strip of print in the back pages of denominational magazines – in these do we see "real" women"? Or did they just keep up pious appearances, even when solely in each other's company? Was it just prescriptive and pedagogic or was there an element of dialogue, of receptivity?

I am inclined to think that, while didactic, this literature was not primarily pedagogic. Even those pieces characterized by a lecturing tone were part of a periodical that was engaged in a dialogue with its readers. The degree of interaction, particularly in columns and journals written by women for women on the subject of female piety was quite high. The consumers of this literature supported these views with their participation through buying, reading, and responding. A continuum existed, then, between the written word and the lived experience. Accurate or not, for middle-class Ulster churchwomen this literature was reality.

Some of the women to whom you have been introduced in this study lived lives of quiet, tenacious piety, while others boldly sought to change the status quo within their churches and challenged the limits of their own faith in themselves and in their God. In private and in public and on every intersecting plane in between, Ulster women's experience of their faith was as individual and as varied as the women themselves. Yet the particular limits, and strengths, of the data examined herein have allowed us to look at these women not as individuals standing before us as they truly were, but as the women, their pens, and, later, typewriting machines, told us they hoped to be. The spiritual aspirations and striving of these women are contained in the articles, poems, and stories that they published in denominational journals, magazines, and newspapers. We have also seen, through these data, what the men of these religious cultures thought their women should be and whom they thought they were. The views of ministers and laymen about such matters as the sanctity of home and the domestic mission of women reveal a great deal about the fears and desires of the community as a whole, and about what it valued and what it disparaged.

In their religious writings, the men and women of Victorian and Edwardian Ulster reveal a tragic misunderstanding, fear, and, occasionally, a hatred of those members of the Christian faith who belonged to a different communion. The incongruity of reading a vitriolic, bigoted barb alongside a message of Christian love and hope is truly jarring. Protestants and Catholics saw each other as being fundamentally different. To be sure, significant differences existed. They followed different rites, prayed different prayers and belonged to different social groups. It is not surprising that they focused on differences between themselves and their opposite numbers. Indeed, it would be surprising if they had not. For we have been dealing with a binary system here: Protestant and Catholic. Of course there are gradients within Protestantism, but this does not alter the binary nature of belief systems in Ulster. However, this overwhelming awareness of difference subsumed some fundamental similarities. In examining the ways in which Ulster Protestants and Catholics constructed the ideal Christian laywoman, it is the similarities that are the most striking. When it comes to a matter of an understanding of female piety – what it entails and how it should be nurtured and protected – consequential differences between the different denominational groups were not significant. They wanted the same thing. Both Catholics and Protestants wanted a Christian woman who would lovingly and tenderly create a home environment in which children and men (they are often linked in this discourse) could be guided and renewed. The female influence was to be a holy one which would protect their families and strengthen their communities. Women were expected to be willing to make any sacrifice to ensure the continuation of their faith within their homes and nation.

Notes

1 Ruether and Keller, *Women and Religion in America*, xx.

2 For a penetrating analysis of this trend in scholarship, see Palmer, *Descent into Discourse*, passim. Kaplan's *Motherhood and Representation* is typical of this trend in its use of the "linguistic turn" in literary criticism. Her habit of putting the words "history" and "historical" in quotation marks indicates the degree to which language has been reified at the expense of material reality. Yet her analysis of the construction of the Mother is at times highly perceptive.

3 Most of the work that has been done on this phenomenon has used evangelical Protestant sources. Irish Catholics borrowed material from and participated in a flow of information with North Americans as well as with Continental Catholicism. These "streams" did not often meet (temperance literature is one exception) yet they had similar things to say about women.

4 The tendency of nineteenth and early twentieth century writers to use the singular, woman, when the prescriptive message was actually targeted at women, plural, leads naturally into discussions of representations and archetypes. Clearly, an Ideal Woman was being constructed.

5 The notion that "separate spheres" defined the lives of historical women has come under attack in several recent works of scholarship. That "separate spheres" was a recurring leitmotif in gender constructions is not being questioned; rather doubt is being cast of the actual effect of this on women's lives. It appears that public/private is emerging in the historiography as a false dichotomy.

6 Daly, *Beyond God the Father*, passim.

7 Coon, Haldane, Sommer, eds., *That Gentle Strength*, 4.

8 Of course essentialism is not the only strand in the multifaceted feminist discourse, yet it does seem to be, at present, the most vocal. Cultural critic Edna Longley offers refreshing insights on the "nationalism vs. feminism" dilemma in her LIP pamphlet *From Cathleen to Anorexia*. She suggests that both Unionism and Nationalism are patriarchal strait-jackets, but that the Republican "hijacking" of feminism has prevented unionist women any participation in Northern feminism. She argues for examining common ground between Ulster women without employing reductionist determinisms.

9 Fox-Genovese, *Within the Plantation Household*, 42.

10 Ibid.

11 A major exception to this is the temperance literature which was inter-denominational, though overwhelmingly evangelical Protestant.

12 Adams, *The Printed Word and the Common Man, Popular Culture in Ulster 1700–1900*, 161–2.

13 For all of their talk of the power and influence that women wielded with-in their own "circle," clearly, by any qualitative measurement, men had real institutional power in this society.

14 These women were loyal to their respective male elites.

15 Akenson, *Small Differences, Irish Catholics and Irish Protestants, 1815–1922*, 12.

16 Ibid., 24.

17 Hepburn uses the census manuscript material for 1901 and 1911 (the only years available to historians) and the published census material for the entire 1871–1922 period. He took a large random sample of Belfast households (5,461) and linked the information from the original indi-vidual census forms to housing valuation records.

18 While I am aware that prior to the disestablishment of the Church of Ireland in 1871 the term "Protestant" referred only to Anglicans, in this study I use "Protestant" to cover all non-Catholic Christians.

19 Hepburn, "Work, Class and Religion in Belfast, 1871–1911," 49–50.

20 Ibid., Table I.

21 Ibid., 42–3.

22 Ibid., 43.

23 There was an odd tendency in the "humour" columns of Protestant periodicals to include patronising jokes about the seemingly biologically based inability of women to operate that most complex of time-saving devices, the pencil sharpener.

24 As Hepburn's article demonstrates, Church of Ireland Belfastians were also disproportionately among the working class. This is a phenomenon that did not apply to Anglicans in the rest of the province, which was mostly rural or small-town in character.

25 Influential works in this field include Ryan's *Cradle of the Middle Class* and Blumin's *The Emergence of the Middle Class.*

26 Connolly,"Religion and History," 79-80.

27 Larkin, "The Devotional Revolution in Ireland," 639.

28 Dairmuid Ó Laoghaire refers to this "modern" tendency as a counter-Reformation spirituality. "It was to have its base in the towns and, as its vehicle, the printed prayer-book in English". Ó Laoghaire, "Irish Spirituality in Modern Times," 137. I would add that Catholic periodicals were also powerful conveyors of modern Catholic practice and ethics.

29 Larkin, "The Devotional Revolution," 639.

30 Ibid., 639.

31 Ibid., 644. Larkin also states that this new, modern Catholicism provided the Irish with a "substitute symbolic language" to replace their dying Irish language and folk culture (649).

32 Clear, *Nuns in Nineteenth-Century Ireland*, 143.

33 Ibid., 149.

34 Ibid., 143, 157.

35 In this literature "Irish" was equated with "Catholic" in no uncertain terms. Despite the anomalous presence of a few Protestant Irish patriots, Protestants were not deemed to be Irish at all.

36 Bebbington, *Evangelicalism in Modern Britain*, 271.

37 Hempton, "Evangelicalism in English and Irish Society, 1780-1840," 171.

38 Ibid.

39 Rawlyk, *The Canada Fire*, xv. Rawlyk agrees with Bebbington in his definition of the characteristics of evangelicalism.

40 Ibid. Bebbington's *Evangelicalism in Modern Britain* examines this matter of evangelical Calvinists. He concludes that "what Evangelicals agreed on seemed of infinitely greater importance than their disagreements" (17).

41 Hempton and Hill, *Evangelical Protestantism in Ulster, 1740–1890*, 161.

42 Ibid., 189.

43 Ibid., 146.

44 Holmes, "Lifting the Curtain on Popular Religion," 67.

45 Ibid., 68.

46 In this study, "Ulster" refers to the historical nine county province of Ulster: Fermanagh, Antrim, Tyrone, Londonderry, Armagh, Down, Donegal, Cavan, and Monaghan, not the current six-county province of Northern Ireland.

47 See Daly, *The Great Famine in Ireland*, 118. She contends that many economic and demographic trends (e.g., agricultural diversification and lower birth rates) in the post-famine decades were continuations of pre-famine trends. See also Kennedy, "The Rural Economy, 1820–1914," 49–50 for a discussion of the Ulster context.

48 Clarkson, "Population Change and Urbanisation, 1821–1911," 137-57. In this article Clarkson describes three major demographic trends in

Ulster in the period 1841–1911: 1) Population declined from 2.4 million to 1.6 million; 2) Ulster's share of the total population of Ireland went from 29 to 36 percent; 3) The proportion of Ulster's population living in towns grew to 40 percent from less than 10 percent.

49 Ibid., 138.

50 This table begins with 1861 because, regrettably, there was no Irish religious census in 1851.

51 Between 1841 and 1911 the rate of urban growth in Ulster was faster than in any other province in Ireland. Ibid., 138.

52 Hepburn, "Work, Class and Religion in Belfast, 1871–1911," 33.

53 Clarkson, "Population Change," 139–40, 153.

CHAPTER TWO

1 Although they might perfunctorily acknowledge that the other group was a part of the historical Christian tradition, Protestants would not allow that Catholics possessed the "true faith," and vice versa.

2 I did find Catholic material in Protestant archives, but it was the type of Catholic devotional literature (usually Marian) that would only demonstrate to Protestants what they already knew: that Catholics were not "true" Christians.

3 See Barbara Welter's generative study, "The Cult of True Womanhood, 1820–1860" in *Dimity Convictions*. The American literature on this topic is voluminous. Key works include Rothman, *Woman's Proper Place*, Harris, *Beyond Her Sphere*, Cott, *The Bonds of Womanhood*, Ryan, *Cradle of the Middle Class*, Halttunen, *Confidence Men and Painted Women*. The cult of true womanhood, as characterized by Welter, held that such women were to be "pious, pure, domestic and submissive." Historian Jo-Anne Preston asserts that this new (late eighteenth, early nineteenth century America) social ideal "relegated women to a separate sphere where they, because of their supposed biologically-determined qualities were to uphold moral values." Preston, "Female Aspiration and Male Ideology," 172.

4 Hempton and Hill, *Evangelical Protestantism in Ulster*, 1740–1890, 129.

5 Elisabeth Schüssler Fiorenza has suggested that in a patriarchal religious culture male and female authors do not necessarily present a different point of view. She states, "Women as well as men are socialized into the same androcentric mind-set and culture. Only if one would claim a clearly definable innate feminine quality of cognition could one establish "feminine" as essentially different from "masculine" authorship. Yet such an attempt would only perpetuate the prejudices and sexual asymmetry created by the androcentric cultural mind-set ... the conjecture of female authorship does not in and by itself suggest a feminist perspective of the author." Fiorenza, *In Memory of Her*, 61.

6 See chapter 5 for a discussion of changing ideas about women's sphere for Ulster evangelical Protestants.

7 "The Rights of Woman," *The Irish Presbyterian* 3, no. 25 (January 1855): 15. Another version of this poem appeared in *The Witness*, no. 14 (April 3, 1874): 6. One of several interesting additional verses reads as follows:

> The right to show a spirit meek,
> When angry words a quarrel seek;
> The right to wear a modest dress,
> When fashions bold around may press.

Appropriate female dress, especially in church, generated a great deal of discussion in denominational periodicals. It was not seen as a frivolous concern but rather as an important part of the discourse on female modesty.

8 Quoted in Ada Whitla's "Women's Rights," *The Christian Advocate* (31 August 1900): 415.

9 Ibid. Although the idea of women's spiritual and domestic "rights" was taken seriously in popular religious literature, the denominational publications followed the lead of secular magazines in ridiculing the demand for women's political rights. This "Scrap from Punch" was published in *The Banner of Ulster* no. 1,729 (28 March 1857). "The Rights of Woman. – The following may be adduced as just a few of the privileged rights of woman – to wit: – A gentleman's right arm ... always the right side of an argument."

10 "Woman's Rights," *The Irish Presbyterian* 5, no. 7 (July 1857): 185.

11 Ibid., 186.

12 T. DeWitt Talmage, "Woman's Rights," *The Witness*, no. 122 (5 May 1876): 3.

13 Ibid. Emphasis in original.

14 DeBerg, *Ungodly Women*, 24–35.

15 Cusack, *Woman's Work in Modern Society*, 195.

16 F.C. Kolbe, "Women's Best Vote," *The Irish Monthly* 40, no. 12 (December 1912): 656.

17 Ibid. See also A Member of the Order of Mercy, *Leaves from the Annals of the Sisters of Mercy*, 15–16.

18 Welter, "The Cult of True Womanhood," 21.

19 Desiree declares: "I have always yielded my mother a kind of hero-worship, a very unmodern attitude of mind. There are two accepted ways of treating mothers now-a-days. If they are of the old school, they are treated as negligible quantities and tolerated scornfully; if they are of the up-to-date species ... they are either considered casually as "not a bad sort of pal," or distrusted as a rival who grabs partners in the ball-room. My mother did not come under either of these categories. She belonged to the company of valiant women whose children rise up and call them

blessed." This final accolade which Desiree bestows upon her mother is one which both Catholics and Protestants used with great frequency to designate true Christian women. Mary Butler, "A Medieval Modern," *The Catholic Bulletin and Book Review* 4, no. 3 (March 1914): 188.

20 Ibid., (May 1914): 274.

21 Mrs H.W. Beecher, "What is a True Home?" *The Irish Presbyterian* n.s., 1, no. 6 (June 1895): 115.

22 M.D.A., "Womanliness," *The Christian Advocate* (24 November 1905): 555.

23 Ibid.

24 Ibid.

25 Ibid.

26 Ibid.

27 The contributors were asked to use pseudonyms when submitting letters or articles. Unusual names such as Maidenhair and Sunbeam were among those used by regular contributors.

28 Joan [pseud.], "The Ministry of Woman," *The Christian Advocate* (5 June 1914): 266. For a discussion of woman as the "highest ornament of nature" see Dr Blair, "Woman," *The Irish Presbyterian*, n.s., 16, no. 2 (February 1910): 45.

29 The poem "Woman" by Elizabeth Barrett Browning was quoted in this inaccurate and unattributed form in J. Kennedy Elliott, "Florence Nightingale, The Soldier's Friend," *The Monthly Messenger* (February 1882): 19. I also found the same poem misquoted in Bryson, *The Three Marys of the Four Gospels*, 24. In *The Christian Advocate* (1 April 1910): 154 the poem is attributed to Browning and accurately quoted.

30 Elliott, "Florence Nightingale," 19.

31 D. Mitchell, "Woman," *The Banner of Ulster* no. 1,242 (18 February 1854): 3. See also "Woman," *The Banner of Ulster* no. 1,305 (15 July 1854): 3.

32 "Woman," quoted in *The Irish Presbyterian*, n.s., 1, no. 3 (March 1895): 55. See also F.Y.P., "What is Woman?" *The Irish Presbyterian*, n.s., 6, no. 6 (June 1900): 299. The only passage I found that mentioned the moral superiority of men did so in a decidedly mocking manner. In an item in the "Woman's Sphere" column the author begins her brief vignette by stating, "The feeling of superiority in the sterner sex is in born" and then describes an exchange between mother and son in which the child asks his mother if she thinks she will go to heaven. " 'Yes, dear, if I'm good,' said the little mother cautiously, wondering what would come next. 'Then please be good, for papa and I would be so lonesome without you.' " "Man's Superiority," *The Irish Presbyterian*, n.s., 3, no. 1 (January 1897): 12.

33 The term patriarchal is used, with some imprecision, to denote a family system in which the father or husband dominates other family members. Stearns, *Be a Man*, 26. The orthodox theology of the "headship" of the

Christian father was still present in Ulster religious literature, yet it existed alongside this championing of female moral superiority.

34 See Welter, "The Feminization of American Religion: 1800–1860," 137–57; and Douglas, *The Feminization of American Culture.*

35 See Filene, *Him/Her/Self,* and Stearns, *Be a Man.*

36 Welter, "The Feminization of American Religion: 1800–1860," passim.

37 Douglas, *The Feminization of American Culture,* passim.

38 For examples of this tendency in Ulster Methodism see Charity Hope, "King's Daughters in Council. The Friendship of Jesus," *The Christian Advocate* (30 November 1993): 568, and "The Gentleness of God," *The Christian Advocate* (5 June 1914): 275.

39 See Clarkson, "Population Change and Urbanisation, 1821–1911," 137–57.

40 Harris, *Beyond Her Sphere,* 33.

41 David Gregg, "The Power of a Good Woman," *The Irish Presbyterian,* n.s., 3, no. 9 (September 1897): 148.

42 Ibid.

43 Ibid.

44 It should be pointed out that this notion of women as "the neck" was entirely unscriptural. The "headship" of the husband had the sanction of scripture; anything that undermined this was clearly unorthodox. Granted, the pivotal role of a woman as the neck to a man's head was presented half-jokingly, yet Spurgeon's statement that women have always been controlling men in this fashion indicates that the author was trying to describe what he took to be the actual state of relations between women and men. This was not a case of women being castigated as shrews; rather women were presented as naturally doing what men were incapable of. Men were being criticized here and made to look foolish.

45 "Woman's Trust," *The Christian Advocate* (2 November 1888): 540.

46 Ibid.

47 Maude Lutton, "At the Foot of the Hills," *The Christian Advocate* (28 July 1911): 359. There is no mention made of the father, nor of the woman's being a widow; the adult male presence is simply absent.

48 Ibid. Emphasis in original.

49 "The Worth of a True Wife," *The Irish Presbyterian* 6, no. 1 (January 1858): 12–13.

50 Selected, "The Nature of Women," *The Witness* 4, no. 168 (23 March 1877): 7.

51 "The New Woman," *The Irish Presbyterian,* n.s., vol. 2, no. 7 (July 1896): 111.

52 Ibid.

53 "Dorthea's Friend," *The Irish Monthly* 27, no. 309 (March 1899): 126.

54 Nora Hanrahan, "A Valiant Woman," *The Catholic Bulletin and Book Review* 1, (July 1911): 331–2.

55 Cusack, *Woman's Work*, 130.

56 Ibid. It should be noted that Cusack was a controversial figure who had many skirmishes with Church authorities. Nonetheless, her many publications on topics ranging from Irish Church history to the education of women were very popular.

57 Ibid. Cusack is particularly harsh in describing the actions of the priesthood. She states that women "entered sisterhoods, and remained in them, while men preached celibacy and practised matrimony. It was women who went through all kinds of home persecution, in following the directions they learned from men – who fasted, who confessed, who attended daily service, at a time when such things were a stigma and a reproach." Ibid, 130-1. This criticism of the priesthood was very rare. Other writers subtly remonstrated with Catholic men for being irreligious, but few attacked the priesthood; priests were lovingly written of by female Catholic writers as allies, true fathers, their own *Soggarths* (fathers). See Mrs Frank Pentrill, "Every-day Thoughts," *The Irish Monthly* 13, no. 132 (August 1885): 412–3.

58 Ibid., 129–30.

59 Charlotte O'Conor Eccles, "A Plea for the Modern Woman," *The Irish Monthly* 32, no. 372 (May 1904): 329–30. Emphasis in original.

60 Ibid., 330–1.

61 Ibid., 331.

62 See Theodore L. Cuyler, "Mothers in Israel," *The Christian Advocate* (2 August 1895): 362. He contended that the moral condition of the home depends "on the mother as the sovereign of the home. There is her throne; there her sway; there she can make or mar the destiny of the immortal soul beyond anyone this side of the throne of God."

63 John G. Whittier, "Granted Wishes," *The Irish Presbyterian*, n.s., 3, no. 1 (January 1897): 12.

64 Ibid.

65 Ibid.

66 Ibid.

67 See also Ada Whitla, "The Busybody (no. 2), *The Christian Advocate* (21 September 1900): 450; Maude Lutton, "God-Restrained," *The Christian Advocate* (24 February 1905): 86; Bryson, *The Three Marys of the Four Gospels*, 10.

68 Madeline Vinton Dahlgren, "When is a Woman at her Best?" *The Irish Presbyterian*, n.s., 3, no. 2 (February 1897): 29.

69 Helen D. Tainter, "Some Practical Hints on the Education of Children," *The Irish Monthly* 10, no. 104 (January 1882): 48. Emphasis in original.

70 Nora Tynan O'Mahoney, "The Mother," *The Irish Monthly* 41, no. 485 (October 1913): 531.

71 Jessie Tulloch, "In a Mud Cabin," *The Irish Monthly* 16, no. 180 (June 1888): 365.

72 Ibid.

73 Ibid.

74 Ibid.

75 John Hamilton, "A Jewel Unknown," *The Irish Monthly* 21, no. 361 (August 1903): 449. For an excellent example of a dutiful Catholic daughter and sister see Hanrahan, "A Valiant Woman."

76 In her article "The Minstry of Women," Joan purports that "it matters not whether women have children of their own or not, they all possess the mother heart" (266). While it is a mother's love that is singled out for praise in the religious literature, all women were called upon to be faithful and loving influences within their home circle. See Charity Hope, "King's Daughters in Council. The Ministry of Woman." *The Christian Advocate* (5 June 1914): 266.

77 "A Mother's Love," *The Irish Presbyterian* 6, no. 11 (October 1858): 269. See also "The Law of Thy Mother," *The Monthly Messenger* (July 1868): 109-10.

78 Ibid., 270.

79 Ibid. I did find one poem where a mother's love was simultaneously lauded and criticized. In "On the Death of a beloved Mother" the author, a Presbyterian minister from Letterkenny, Co. Donegal, says that his mother's sole fault was a "too deep maternal love" which prevented her from giving all to God. She refused, initially, to trust God's will in all things because her love for her children was too great. Eventually she gave "Her dearest all to His command, who says 'all things are mine.'/Hard was the lesson to a soul filled with such mother's love;" *The Monthly Messenger* (2 March 1868): 47.

80 "As One Whom His Mother Comforteth," *The Irish Presbyterian*, n.s., 2, no. 11 (October 1896): 152. This story was in the "For the Heavy Laden" column. Emphasis in original.

81 R.M., "A Mother's Reverie," *The Irish Monthly* 1, no. 9 (September 1873): 144. See also, Janet Ellis, "The Mother's Prayer," *The Irish Monthly* 9, no. 91 (January 1881): 22-3; The Present Writer, "On Mothers," *The Irish Monthly* 8, no. 83 (1880): 278; "Help the Poor Orphan, an appeal made in Chapel of Nazareth House, Belfast," *The Irish Monthly* 29, no. 334 (April 1901): 174-5; and O'Mahoney, 530-1.

82 O'Mahoney, "The Mother," 530.

83 "The Influence of the Wife," *The Christian Advocate* (10 August 1906): 383. One cannot help but wonder if Methodist wives and mothers hooted with derision when they read that their lives were similar to those

of medieval anchoresses. In "The Prayerless Mother," *The Irish Presbyterian* 3, no. 12 (December 1855): 324, busy women were chided for failing to keep up their spiritual duties and urged to pray more faithfully for "No time is lost that is spent at the foot of the Cross."

84 In early numbers of *The Irish Presbyterian* (1850s–1860s) many references were made to family devotions which featured the father in the leading part.

85 "Help the Poor Orphan," 174–5.

86 Sometimes Princeton is named; sometimes the school is unnamed.

87 "Praying Mothers," *The Monthly Messenger* (April, 1868): 61. Emphasis in original. See also "The Godly Mother," *The Irish Presbyterian* 2, no. 17 (May 1854): 129–30.

88 William J. Hart, "Influence of Christian Mothers," *The Christian Advocate* (19 May 1911): 240iii. See also "Mother, Do You Pray With Your Son?" *The Irish Presbyterian* 1, no. 8 (August 1853): 212-13; "The Happy Mother," *The Irish Presbyterian* 1, no. 10 (October 1853): 277; "A Mother's Prayer," *The Irish Presbyterian* 3, no. 33 (September 1855): 237; "My Mother's Prayers," *The Monthly Messenger* (October 1879): 157.

89 Charity Hope, "My Open Letter-box," *The Christian Advocate* (16 November 1906): 542.

90 In the next chapter I will discuss the use made by Protestant writers of Mary as a model of female piety.

91 Magdalen Rock [pseud.], "The Prayers of Mothers," *The Irish Monthly* 38, no. 449 (October 1910): 550. In his *Rose Kavanagh and her Verses*, Father Matthew Russell refers to her as an "Ulster poet, who is known to the reading world only as "Magdalen Rock" (8). On this theme see also, Janet Ellis, "The Mother's Prayer," *The Irish Monthly* 9, no. 91 (January 1881): 22–3.

92 Michael Earls, "To an Irish Mother," *The Irish Monthly* 38, no. 439 (January 1910): 20. See also "A Mother's Reverie" and M.R., "Amen Corner XIV. – On the 'Hail Mary,'" *The Irish Monthly* 37, no. 427 (January 1909): 38.

93 See Tainter, "Some Practical Hints," 49–50.

94 Richard H. Steele, "A Mother's Prayer-Meeting," *The Christian Advocate* (2 September 1898): 415. See also Mrs E.S. Kennedy, "A Thought for Mothers," *The Christian Advocate* (4 March 1892): 120iii; Eileen, "A Woman's Causerie," *The Christian Advocate* (11 March 1891): 119; Miss Nixon, "Prayer," *The Christian Advocate* (24 July 1896): 359; Islay Burns, "A Mother's Influence," *The Irish Presbyterian* 2, no. 14 (February 1854): 47–8.

95 "A Model for Mothers," *The Irish Presbyterian* 4, no. 47 (November 1856): 293.

96 See "A Mother's Influence," *The Irish Presbyterian* 2, no. 16 (April 1854): 99–100, and "The Godly Mother," *The Christian Advocate* (3 August 1900): 375.

97 Charity Hope, "A Note of Warning," The Christian Advocate (20 April 1901): 196. See also, Bryson, The Three Marys of the Four Gospels, 108–11; M.S.L., "The Mother's Responsibility," The Irish Presbyterian, n.s., 1, no. 1 (January 1895): 7-8.

98 Burnside, *The Sexton's Daughter*, 23. See also "The Son Unguided, His Mother's Shame," *Primitive Wesleyan Methodist Magazine* (March/April 1850): 138-42.

99 Ada Whitla, "Prayer Makes Our Lives More Beautiful," *The Christian Advocate* (12 October 1900): 495.

100 Ada Whitla, "A Bag with Holes," *The Christian Advocate* (September 28, 1900): 463. According to Whitla, the woman who fails to exert a Christian influence and practice the domestic virtues deserves whatever she gets. If she is "a slipshod slattern" Whitla sympathizes with the woman's husband "I don't wonder or blame him that he gets drunk and beats her. She richly deserves it. She is a bag full of holes." It should be noted that the tone of Whitla's remarks is harsher than that taken by most authors on the subject of drunken husbands and abused wives. As will be discussed in the chapter on temperance, though, women who failed to meet the Christian ideal of womanly virtue were blamed for their ordeal.

101 Corish, "Women and Religious Practice," 212. For a similar description of the influence of Irish women in a North American setting see Clarke, *Piety and Nationalism*, 77.

102 M.A. Curtis, "Mothers and their Work," *The Irish Monthly* 33, no. 386 (September 1905): 436. See also Moi-Meme, "The Family Circle," *The Catholic Bulletin and Book Review* 1 (July 1911): 322.

103 "On Mothers," *The Irish Monthly* 8 (1880): 280. See also Cusack, 33.

104 Ibid.

105 Mrs Frank Pentrill, "Everyday Thoughts," *The Irish Monthly* 10, no. 111 (August 1882): 526.

106 Ibid.

107 Ibid., 528.

108 Cusack, *Woman's Work*, 36.

109 Ibid., 50-1.

110 S. Andrews, "Home," *The Monthly Messenger* (September 1880): 133-4. Emphasis in original.

111 See Akenson, *God's Peoples*, 119, passim. Akenson observes that within the Ulster-Scots community each person played a role in "protecting the polity against the Canaanites, that is, the Catholics" (120).

112 Andrews, "Home," 134.

113 "Decay of Home Life," *The Christian Advocate* (31 July 1914): iii.

114 Ibid.

115 Bryson, *The Three Marys*, 112.

116 Atkinson, *Mary Aikenhead*, 60–1.

117 Morgan, *Rome and the Gospel*, 105–6.

118 Ibid., 108–9.

119 D. Kelly, "The Nun," *Primitive Wesleyan Methodist Magazine* (November/December 1852): 28–9.

120 Ibid., 29.

121 Along with the standard attack on nunneries as "clerical seraglios" Bryson puts forward the theory that "Rome" actually drove wealthy young nuns into early graves in order to make more money from dowries. Bryson, 80–90.

122 Ibid., 81. Emphasis in original.

123 Ibid., ix.

124 Ibid. See also "The Virtuous Woman," *The Evangelical Witness and Presbyterian Review* 3, no. 3 (March 1864): 57–9. The passage in the book of Proverbs, chapter 31, praising "the virtuous woman" is described as being "decided against Romanism. Its 'virtuous woman,' whose price is above rubies, is not a lady abbess ... nor a recluse of any kind whatever, but a good, true wife ... Romanism has no place here. See this type of womanly worth among the common duties of daily life" (57).

125 Roman Catholic public worship was condemned for "the sensuous manner in which it is conducted ... lust is seized on to captivate the attention ... The design is merely to astonish, to charm, or to excite, not to edify. Mere animal gratification takes the place of instruction." Ibid., 123–4.

126 Morgan, *Rome and the Gospel*, 111.

127 See chapter 4, footnotes 125, 126.

128 Brockman, *Letter to the Women of England Against the Confessional*, 2. In this pamphlet, speeches from the Irish tour of the famous anti-Catholic firebrand, Alonzo Kelly, are cited.

129 Ibid. There is also an important sexual subtext here. It was thought that if women confessed to priests things they "would blush to name ... even to a loving mother" it would taint their "purity" and "innate modesty" (3).

130 Brockman's pamphlet had several scripture verses as epigraphs, one of which was printed as follows: "*Of this sort are they which* CREEP *into houses, and lead captive* SILLY *women laden with sins.*" – " Tim. III. 6. Emphasis in original.

131 As has been mentioned, the Catholics did not just praise the role of the self-sacrificing mother within the household. Single sisters, aunts, and

nieces who gave their all in service to their families were also praised as "valiant women." See Hanrahan, passim.

132 Atkinson, *Mary Aikenhead*, 67. See also, Tynan, "A Nun." At the convent schools, Catholic girls who were "to be corporally or spiritually the mothers of souls were prepared for their vocation" (66).

133 O'Mahoney, "The Mother," 532.

134 See Atkinson, *Mary Aikenhead*, 67 and "Help the Poor Orphan," 171.

135 *Bean A'Tighe* [pseud.], "For Mothers and Daughters," *The Catholic Bulletin and Book Review* 4 (January 1914): 66.

136 Butler, "A Medieval Modern," 684.

137 Matthew Russell, "On the Literary Studies of Ladies," *The Irish Monthly* 4, (1876): 486.

138 "On Mothers," 282.

139 Ibid.

140 See "Political Jesuitism," *The Irish Presbyterian* 2, no. 16 (April 1854): 99.

141 Atkinson, *Mary Aikenhead*, 60.

142 Lady Herbert of Lea, "The Workhouse Children: A True Tale," *The Irish Monthly* 3 (1875): 119.

143 Ibid.

144 Matthew Russell, "St. Bridgid's Orphans," *The Irish Monthly* 4 (1876): 456.

145 Ibid. See also "Help the Poor Orphan," 173.

146 Molly Malone [pseud.], "A Crying Evil," *The Catholic Bulletin and Book Review* 1 (April 1911): 217–8; "Miscellaneous," *The Catholic Bulletin and Book Review* 1 (April 1911): 200 (referring to children's picture books, the author of "Miscellaneous" notes that "often under the pretty petal of the English rose, the proselytising thorn lies hidden"); and Butler, (March 1914): 189 and (June 1914): 416.

147 See "A Word to Young Ladies," *The Irish Presbyterian* 5, no. 50 (February 1857): 43.

148 Malone, "A Crying Evil," 218.

149 Again, actual Protestant religious practice is not being criticized here; it is the impiety and irreligion of the dominant English Protestant culture which is being warned against. A visitor to Desiree's home comments, "One of the many reasons why this house is so delightful is that it forms a Franco-Irish oasis in the midst of the West-British desert in which we live." Butler, "A Medieval Modern," 416. The warmth and spirituality of the Irish (with continental influences – Desiree's mother is French and her deceased father was Irish) are contrasted with the moral aridity of British Protestant culture.

150 Butler, "A Medieval Modern," 683.

CHAPTER THREE

1 "Mariology" denotes Marian doctrine and practises, while "Mariolatry" is a derogatory term used by those who saw the Marian cult as actually usurping the rightful worship of God.

2 The term Immaculate Conception refers to the miraculous conception of the Virgin Mary by St Anne. This meant that the Roman Catholic Church regarded Mary as the only fully human person free of the stain of original sin. This idea is sometimes confusing for Protestants, who think that "immaculate conception" refers to Mary's conception by the Holy Spirit of Jesus Christ.

3 Warner, "Alone of All Her Sex," 236.

4 O'Dwyer, *Mary: A History of Devotion in Ireland*, 264–5.

5 Ibid., 267.

6 Matthew Russell, "Maria Sine Labe Concepta," *The Irish Monthly* 9, no. 91 (January 1881): 49. Emphasis in original. Clear evangelical overtones can be detected here.

7 Mary's many titles, taken from litanies invoked in her name, include the following: Mother of God, Virgin most powerful, Mirror of Justice, Seat of Wisdom, Cause of our joy, Spiritual Vessel, Mystical Rose, Tower of David, Tower of Ivory, Ark of the Covenant, Gate of Heaven, Morning Star and Refuge of sinners. *Month of Mary*, passim.

8 Della Madonna, "Child of Mary," *The Catholic Guardian* (1853): 295.

9 Russell, "To the Most Pure Heart of Mary" in *The Harp of Jesus*, 73.

10 Ibid.

11 The author discusses Mary's role in human salvation, in contrast to Eve's role in human damnation.

12 T.E.B., "The Two Mothers: A Contrast," *The Irish Monthly* 21, no. 235 (January 1893): 32. This Marian interpretation of John 3:16 "For God so loved the world, that he gave his only begotten Son," which draws a close parallel between God's and Mary's actions in giving Christ up for the salvation of humans, is just the type of Marian sentiment that prompted Ulster Protestant anti-Catholic diatribes.

13 "The Immaculate Conception," *The Irish Rosary*, (December 1914): 421. See also "The Two Mothers," passim.

14 Morgan, *Rome and the Gospel*, 125.

15 Ibid., 126.

16 Bryson, *The Three Marys of the Four Gospels*, 56.

17 Ibid., 55.

18 John G. Whittier, "The True Wife," *The Christian Advocate* (14 July 1887): 327.

19 Frances Mary Maitland, "A Little Scotch Catholic," *The Irish Monthly* 16, no. 181 (July 1888): 396.

20 "The Month of Mary," *Tales of the Festivals*, 4.

21 Emily P.H. Hickey, "To Our Mother of Grace," *The Irish Monthly* 30, no. 349 (July 1902): 386.

22 Emily P.H. Hickey, "Ad Matrem, Sanctam Ecclesiam," *The Irish Monthly* 30, no. 343 (January 1902): 70. See also, Della Madonna, "The Penitent to the Blessed Virgin," *The Catholic Guardian* (1853): 102–3; Alice Esmonde, "Reveries," *The Irish Monthly* 8, no. 86 (1880): 433–4; Sister Mary Agnes, "To Mary Immaculate," *The Irish Monthly* 11, no. 126 (December 1883): 659–60; Katherine Tynan, "My Lady: A Portrait," *The Irish Monthly* 12, no. 137 (November 1884): 583–4.

23 Alice Gill, "A Mother's Lament," *The Irish Monthly* 40, no. 485 (November 1913): 602.

24 Magdalen Rock, "Consolation for Mourning Mothers," *The Irish Monthly* 30, no 350 (August 1902): 452.

25 Magdalen Rock, "Mary," *The Irish Monthly* 39, no. 455 (May 1911): 245.

26 Tynan, *Miracle Plays*, 38. Emphasis in original.

27 For example, in the Flight into Egypt scene, Mary's motherly compassion causes her to heal Leah's son, Dimas, of his leprosy. Tynan, *Miracle Plays*, 81. This play is based on apocryphal stories of Mary's power.

28 See also Alice Esmonde, "Mother and Child," The Irish Monthly 27, no. 314 (August 1899): 410-11.

29 See Greeley, The Mary Myth and Boff, The Maternal Face of God.

30 Ethel Clifford, quoted in The Irish Monthly 35, no. 405 (March 1907): 170-1.

31 See Warner, passim.

32 Benko, *The Virgin Goddess*, 221.

33 Tynan, *A Nun*, 94.

34 The Confraternity of the Child of Mary was a devotional organization that promoted Marian piety, chastity, and prayer. Margaret MacCurtain describes how the guidebook of the society – "the Child of Mary manual" – had a profound impact on the lives of convent-educated women. MacCurtain states that "the initiation into, and practice of the Sodality, usually referred to as the E. de M. (*Enfant de Marie*), or the "Blue Ribbon" signified a mid-adolescent rite of passage ... Admittance to the ranks of the Sodality conveyed an aura of dignity and conferred status, even privilege, on a class educated into middle-class virtue." MacCurtain, "Fullness of Life," 233.

35 Ibid., 120.

36 "The Virgin Mother," *The Catholic Guardian* (1853): 647.

37 Ibid.

38 Ibid.

39 In her poem "Mother and Child" Alice Esmonde sentimentally describes

the domestic life of the Holy Family. Mary is depicted as a gentle and loving mother, gathering the infant Jesus into her arms after the child had tired himself out in play. In this idealized portrayal of motherhood the author writes about how Mary must have felt "when first He tried / To lisp your name and call you 'Mother, Mother!' / your God and Saviour, yet your little child." *The Irish Monthly* 27, no. 314 (August 1899): 410–1.

40 Tynan, *Miracle Plays*, 21.

41 Ibid.

42 Eleanor C. Donnelly, "Her Darling Virtue," *The Irish Monthly* 22, no. 256 (October 1894): 554. Emphasis in original.

43 Ibid.

44 T.W. Allies, "The Forming of the Mother," *The Irish Monthly* 22, no. 256 (October 1894): 522.

45 Attie O'Brien, "A Rosary of Sonnets," *The Irish Monthly* 8 (1880): 88.

46 Tynan, *Miracle Plays*, 24.

47 O'Brien, "A Rosary of Sonnets," 219.

48 Warner, *Alone of All Her Sex*, 190.

49 It is important to recall that Protestants had far less material to work with than Catholics did when discussing the Virgin Mary. Catholic writers could use the large body of apocryphal legends concerning Mary and the various teachings of the Church while Protestants were restricted to the scant biblical record.

50 Mursell, *Mary, the Mother of Jesus*, 37. Referring to the declaration (in 1854) of Mary's immaculate conception and sinlessness by the Roman Catholic Church, the Reverend Mr. Mursell flatly states that "It is because of such extravagances that so little is said of Mary in our pulpits" (39).

51 Ibid.

52 Ibid., 37–8. Mursell charitably suggests that "Romanists" initially set off on the misguided course of Mariolatry through "a species of religious gallantry." Protestants, then, "must beware of suffering a kind of chivalry to exaggerate the meed of obeisance we pay to this holy woman."

53 Ibid., 38.

54 Perhaps the fact that Bryson was writing shortly after Pius IX's promulgation of the doctrine of the Immaculate Conception of Mary accounts for some of the heated vituperation in this passage.

55 While Bryson discusses the lives of Mary of Bethany and Mary of Magdala in some detail (with only the occasional sidebar on the evils of "nunism" and the like) he does not make full prescriptive use of the available biblical information about Mary of Nazareth. In the Introduction he states his intention to explore in his exposition "the maternal and female influences ... found in the delineation of the Scriptural characters" and

present "the features of the Marys, as seen in the mirror of the Divine Word" (ix-x), yet he chooses to ignore information about Mary that was used by other Protestant authors. This would lead one to believe that Bryson's actual purpose in writing *The Three Marys* was not so much to edify Protestant women as it was to rail against "Mariolatry."

56 Bryson, *The Three Marys*, 56–7.
57 Mursell, *Mary, the Mother of Jesus*, 44.
58 T.A. Gurney, "The Incarnation and Womanhood," *India's Women* 15, no. 104 (February 1895): 51. Emphasis in original. *India's Women* was distributed among Church of Ireland women and it contained reports of the activities of the Hibernian Auxiliary of the Church of England Zenana Mission Society (CEZMS). In 1896 it became *India's Women and China's Daughters* with the expansion of the CEZMS's work into China.
59 Ibid.
60 Ibid., 52.
61 J.E. Sampson, "The Women Workers of the Bible. Chapter VII. – Mary," *India's Women* 2 (May 1882): 133.
62 Ibid., 133. Emphasis in original.
63 Ibid., 134. Emphasis in original. The author's use of "we" here is somewhat misleading. Clearly, he is referring to his female readers and not to himself.
64 Ibid., 133.
65 Ibid.
66 Ibid.
67 Mursell, *Mary, the Mother of Jesus*, 44.
68 Ibid. Emphasis in original.
69 Ibid.
70 Ibid.
71 Ibid. Emphasis in original.
72 Ibid., 46–7.
73 See Miss Cusack "formerly the Nun of Kenmare," "Christmas in a Convent," *The Christian Advocate* (6 December 1892): 617; "Mariolatry," *The Christian Advocate* (19 June 1896): 297; "Worship of Mary," *The Christian Advocate* (8 October 1897): 493; "Mariolatry," *The Christian Advocate* (24 August 1900): 401; H.S., "Worship of the Virgin," *The Irish Presbyterian* 3, no. 2 (March/April 1855): 97–99.
74 Mursell, *Mary, the Mother of Jesus*, 38.
75 Warner, *Along of All Her Sex*, xxii, and "The Mother of God," *Daybreak* 50 (May 1912): 58.
76 "The Immaculate Conception," 419.
77 Russell, "Our Lady's Magnificat," in *Madonna*, 15–16. See also in the same volume "Enfant de Marie," 21–2.
78 Morgan, *Rome and the Gospel*, 125.

CHAPTER FOUR

1 In a forty-year run of the Roman Catholic journal *The Irish Monthly* I found only two references to women of the Old Testament: one small poem about Rebecca and one long piece in the first person about Judith.
2 Unless otherwise noted, all references are from the King James Version of the Bible.
3 Tynan, *The Middle Years*, 9.
4 Her very name became synonymous with female sexual sin, as the tendency to call inmates of homes for "fallen women" "Magdalenes" attests.
5 M.B., "The Two Marys," The Irish Monthly 25, no. 286 (April, 1897): 199. This poem is slightly unusual in that it refers to Mary Magdalen as "stained" by sin after her redemption. Usually, post-conversion, it is only her penitence and faithfulness that are described; she is not usually described as "stained" at this point. The purpose of "The Two Marys" was evidently to contrast the two women, thus the abberation from convention.
6 Warner, *Alone of All Her Sex*, 235.
7 Ibid., 225.
8 Who was Mary Magdalen? According to her Catholic cult she was the wanton woman who was forgiven by Christ "because she loved much," the contemplative who listened to Christ's teaching and wiped his feet with her hair, and the woman who was first to see the resurrected Christ. A close examination of the Gospels does not reveal a clear identity for Mary Magdalen, but it does indicate that these elements of the Catholic Magdalen were three different women.

    Before examining how Protestant and Catholic didactic literature used Mary of Magdala's life, the outline of her story needs to be explained. The unnamed woman in the seventh chapter of Luke who came to Simon the pharisee's house and washed Jesus' feet with her tears, dried them with her hair, anointed his feet with costly ointment and whose sins were forgiven "because she loved much" (Luke 7:47) has been understood in the Roman Catholic tradition to be Mary of Magdala. Marina Warner notes that it has always been assumed that the woman's sins were of a carnal nature, despite the lack of any concrete reason for this in the text. Simon the pharisee was horrified that Jesus would allow a sinful woman to defile him by her touch (thus allowing for a nice segue into the parable of the debtor), yet it was never assumed that her sin was that of murder, say, or theft; rather the assumption was always made that her sin was of a sexual nature. Warner points out that even Christ's explanation, "for she loved much" – the verb *agapo* in the Greek has no erotic connotation – which clearly refers to her kind gesture towards Christ, has

been misread as a reference to her sexual sins (226). Given that the
woman is unnamed, this connection with Mary Magdalen would seem
strange were it not for other references in the gospels that brought
Catholics to link "the sinner" with the Magdalen. Mark and Matthew tell
a similar story of an unnamed woman anointing Jesus, but many details
are different.   In their version of events, the scene takes place at a later
period in Christ's ministry in the town of Bethany, at the house of Simon
the leper. The woman is not called a sinner, she anoints Jesus' head, not
his feet, and Christ defends the woman against his disciples' criticism of
the waste of the costly ointment by saying that she has anointed his body
in preparation for his burial (Matthew 26:6–13; Mark 14:3–8).

When Mary Magdalen appears by name, it is in an entirely different
context.   In the Synoptic gospels, Mary Magdalen is described by name
as a woman from whom Christ cast out seven devils and who became his
diligent follower. In these gospels she is shown participating in Jesus'
ministry, appearing at his crucifixion, and meeting him after the resurrection. The conflation of Mary of Magdala with the "sinner" of Luke
and the other women who anointed Christ occurred because of the
passage in Mark that describes Mary Magdalen going with some women
to Christ's grave to anoint him. Jesus' prophetic words she "did it for my
burial" seem to prefigure Mary Magdalen's bringing unguents to Christ's
tomb.   Thus the exorcised Mary of Magdala becomes "the sinner" who
anointed Christ's feet and was forgiven. Warner also points out that the
passages concerning Mary of Magdala's demonic possession have been
virtually eliminated from her Catholic cult (227).

The Gospel of John further complicates this "muddle of Marys." John
has Mary of Bethany, the sister of Lazarus and Martha, anointing Jesus'
feet and wiping them with her hair, despite the disapproval of a disciple,
in this case, Judas. Jesus defends the woman's actions by saying "against
the day of my burying hath she kept this" (John 12:7). It is in this gospel
that we find the dramatic and poignant story of Mary of Magdala's vigil
at the empty tomb.   Mistaking Christ for the gardener, she begs him to
tell her where they have taken her Lord's body. When Jesus calls her by
name, she replies "*Rabboni*" (Master) (John 20:16). Thus, Mary of
Bethany too becomes conflated into the same person as Mary of
Magdala.

9 The Greek Church, following Origen's exegesis, has always distinguished
   three different women, each with her own feast day. Ibid., 228.

10 See C.H. Crookshank, "Jesus Appears to Mary," *The Christian Advocate*
   (April 5, 1904): 166.

11 The following editorial note accompanies the poem: "These lines follow
   at first a legend narrated by Gerbert and then the sacred text."

12 Attie O'Brien, "Magdalen," *The Irish Monthly* 6 (1878): 385. Curiously,

despite the fact that Mary Magdalen was a Syrian woman, her hair, which wiped Christ's feet, was always described as "golden" or "of streaming gold" or some such phrase. See Wilfrid Meynell, "A Magdalen," and Anon. "Nec Virgo Nec Martyr," *The Irish Monthly* 7, no. 73, 380, 382, M.L., "Magdalene," *The Irish Templar* 5, no. 11 (January 1882): 174.

13 Ibid., 385.

14 Ibid., 385.

15 Ibid., 386.

16 Ibid., 387. In O'Brien's poem it is not only women, but also chaste men who are discomfited at the Magdalen's presence. When she looks around the room for Jesus, "and John's angelic face first meets her view,/The blushes rise upon his pure, young cheek,/Beneath the curious boldness of her gaze."

17 Ibid., 387.

18 Meynell, "A Magdalen," 380.

19 Ibid.

20 "The Magdalens of High Park," *The Irish Rosary* 1, no. 4 (July 1897): 178.

21 Ibid., 179. See also "The Magdalen," *The Catholic Guardian* (1853): 699–700.

22 M.L., "Magdalene," *The Irish Templar* 5, no. 11 (January 1882): 175.

23 Ibid.

24 Ibid. These are Christ's words in Mark 14:8 to the woman, assumed to be Mary of Bethany because of this passage's similarities to the one in John where Mary of Bethany is referred to by name, who anointed Christ's feet with ointment and wiped them with her hair. See "Mrs Brandon: Memorial Service," *The Christian Advocate* (9 December 1892): 626 and George Alley, "Mary's Memorial: A Coronation Year's Tribute to Christ," *The Christian Advocate* (26 May 1911): 242.

25 See A.C. Murphy, "She Loved Much," *The Monthly Messenger* (2 August 1869): 120.

26 "The Magdalenes of High Park," 178.

27 "The Magdalenes of High Park," 178, and M.L., 175.

28 Alice Esmonde, "Magdalen's Tears," *The Irish Monthly* 7, no. 73 (1879): 379.

29 Lord Houghton, "The Madeleine at Paris," *The Irish Monthly* 7, no. 73: 382. See also M.R, "The Sister of Lazarus," *The Irish Monthly* 7, no. 73: 380; Esmonde, "I Will Take Him Away," *The Irish Monthly* 7, no. 73: 381; Russell, "Communion Day," in Emmanuel, 20.

30 Marina Warner mentions that Mary Magdalen is one of the few female saints in the liturgy who is not entitled "virgin." Warner, 234. This is clearly the case in "Nec Virgo Nec Martyr" where she is described as having "a throne apart." Yet the epigraph of "Magdalen Sonnets" goes

as follows: 'There of pure virgins none / Is fairer seen, / Save One [the Virgin Mary], / Than Mary Magdalene.' She is second only to the Virgin Mary, as she is in "Nec Virgo Nec Martyr," but in this epigraph she is included among the virgins.

31 "Nec Virgo Nec Martyr," 382.

32 In Attie O'Brien's sonnet "Mary! Rabboni!" the weeping Mary Magdalen "utters passionate wild cries – / Her Love is gone!" when she discovers Christ's tomb empty. According to O'Brien's biographer, "a steady war was waged" between O'Brien and Father Matthew Russell "on the subject of the amount of love-making permissible in the stories she furnished to his Magazine ... Father Russell always seems to have had his own special public before his eyes, into which Boarding Schools largely entered, and to have wished to reduce the romantic element to the smallest possible compass." O'Connell, *Glimpses of a Hidden Life*, 148. O'Brien's flare for the passionate was not confined to her short stories, it imbued her poetry as well.

33 See also Edward Harding, "Sundry Sonnets. No. IV. Mary Magdalen," *The Irish Monthly* 9, no. 95 (May 1881): 235.

34 He is the son of Samuel Taylor Coleridge.

35 Hartley Coleridge, "She Hath Loved Much," *The Irish Monthly* 7, no. 73: 381. In *The Witness*, Coleridge's sonnet is called "Mary" and there are several differences in punctuation (for example, exclamation marks are used after "much" and "tears").

36 "Magdalene," *The Evangelical Witness and Presbyterian Review* 1, no. 8 (August 1863): 203.

37 Ibid.

38 Ibid.

39 Warner, 227.

40 "Magdalene," 204.

41 Ibid.

42 Ibid.

43 Ibid.

44 R. Butler, "The Woman of Sychar," *The Christian Advocate* (17 August 1900): 392.

45 J.E. Sampson, "The Women Workers of the Bible. III. – The Woman of Samaria," *India's Women* 1, no. 4 (July–August, 1881): 201.

46 Sampson, 200–1. Emphasis in original. He also assumes that she brought her message to the men, not to the women because the women would have shunned her.

47 Ibid., 201.

48 Attie O'Brien, "Stone the Woman – Let the Man Go Free," *The Irish Monthly* 7, no. 72 (1879): 291–2.

49 Ibid., 292.

50 Ibid.

51 Ibid.

52 Ibid., 293. Evangelical writers took exception to the creative licence exercised in this type of passage. Changing the words of scripture, even if the meaning was the same, was considered a "vain" and dangerous enterprise, not that avowed biblical literalists did not allow their biblical imaginations to run away with them also. See note 103.

53 Ibid.

54 Ibid.

55 Ibid.

56 Of course, this scene is entirely a creation of the author's imagination. Nowhere in scripture is the "man who took her in adultery" ever mentioned.

57 Ibid., 295. This same passage with slightly different punctuation appears in "Stone the Woman," *The Irish Presbyterian*, n.s., 9, no. 8 (August 1903): 127.

58 Ibid.

59 Ibid. Emphasis in original. In *The Irish Presbyterian*'s version, the word "then" was not italicized.

60 See also Whitla, *Thoughts from Sinai*, 13 and 35-7. Lady Ada Whitla, a prominent Belfast Methodist, staunch conservative, and no "New Woman" also took on the sexual double standard. Her own poetic effort on this theme goes as follows:

> The woman repented and turned from sin,
> But no door opened to let her in.
> The preacher prayed that she might be forgiven;
> But told her to look for mercy – in Heaven.
> For this is the law of the earth, we know:
> That the woman is stoned, while the man may go!

One wonders whether Whitla had read Attie O'Brien's poem on this same subject.

61 Warner, *Alone of All Her Sex*, 235.

62 One must keep in mind, of course, that Roman Catholics considered Martha's sister to be Mary of Magdala.

63 Aikenhead, *Letters of Mary Aikenhead*, vi. See also O'Connell, *Glimpses of a Hidden Life*, passim. In her dedication of the book to the Children of Mary, the author states that these "gladsome young maidens ... can learn from this story of a woman's life, how the spirit of Mary can animate the works of Martha, and how suffering does not of necessity mean sadness, since 'Patient endurance is God-like.'"

64 Notable pro-Martha writers were Lady Ada Whitla and Margaret Byers, who were heavily involved in women's organizations in Ulster Protestant churches.

65 "The Nephalists; or, the Parish Difficulty and its Remedy," *The Church of England and Ireland Temperance Magazine* (July 1863): 113. Emphasis in original.

66 White equates Martha's excessive concern with her domestic duties to what he sees as Christians' obsession with material things: "We forget how few things are really needful. How few dishes. How few courses. How few dainties. How few enjoyments. How few possessions." Dr Alex. Whyte, "Martha," *The Christian Advocate* (27 May 1898): 251. See also J.E. Sampson, "The Women Workers of the Bible. IX. – Martha and Mary," *India's Women* 2, no. 11 (September–October, 1882): 246-8.

67 Whitla, *The Sisters, A.D. 33. You Sisters, A.D. 1902*, 8.

68 Ibid., 9.

69 Ibid., 9-10.

70 Ibid., 9.

71 Ibid., 12.

72 Ibid., 19.

73 Ibid., 25.

74 At the beginning of her description of the first meeting of Jesus and Martha, Whitla primly pronounces that "I do not want to be fanciful." But her imagination does play an important part in her interpretation of the lives of these two sisters.

75 In *The Sisters*, Whitla says that Martha's only fault lay in "cumbering" herself with excessive work. "Martha's desire was to do too much, and Mary's fault, it seems to us, was indifference to the bodily needs of their unexpected guests," (10). But Christ never faulted Mary at all!

76 In a later article in *The Christian Advocate*, Whitla veers further away from biblical literalism when she lavishes superlative praise on "the Martha in any house." For "She who serves best is the greatest in the home," according to Whitla. No mention is made of Mary's "better part" here. "Notes from an Address by Lady Whitla," *The Christian Advocate* (9 December 1910): 580.

77 Several columns of the "King's Daughters in Council" by Charity Hope in the Methodist *Christian Advocate* were devoted to this subject. She tells her readers of "the limitless possibilities for good of a consecrated tea table" and that "even 'drudgery' may be made 'divine'" for "'She who sweeps a room as for the Lord makes it and the action fine.'" See 21 December 1900, 615; 2 December 1910, 568; 27 January 1911, 38.

78 Whitla, *The Sisters*, 9. While Sampson cautioned his female readers against getting too caught up in domestic affairs as Martha had, he is careful to state that: "I will not undervalue the service of Martha. It was love, it was love for Jesus that prompted it." J.E. Sampson, "The Women Workers of the Bible. IX – Martha and Mary," *India's Women* 2, no. 11 (September–October 1882): 246.

79 The author explained that "by the 'better part' we usually understand the contemplative life as distinguished from the active one. Magdalen, seated at the feet of Jesus in the house at Bethany, is the highest type of it." "St Mary Magdalen," *The Irish Rosary* 1, no. 4 (July 1897): 159.

80 Ibid., 160.

81 Warner, *Alone of All Her Sex*, 228-9.

82 Sampson, "Women Workers of the Bible. IX.," 247.

83 Bryson, *The Three Marys of the Four Gospels*, 10. Emphasis in original. The use of the phrase "She hath done what she could" was very popular in Ulster Protestant literature for women. For example, the epigram in the popular Presbyterian women's missionary magazine *Woman's Work* was "She hath done what she could." See also M.B. 'She hath done what she could,' *India's Women* 2, no. 11 (September-October 1882): 245 and J.E. Sampson, The Women Workers of the Bible. XI. – Martha and Mary – Continued," *India's Women* 3, no. 14 (March-April, 1883): 72.

84 Ibid., 21. See also Whitla, 19, where she says that both Mary and Martha "are remembered for what they did."

85 "Lost Names," *The Christian Advocate* (27 February 1885): 105.

86 "Ibid.

87 She was sometimes referred to by her Aramaic name of Tabitha, but the Greek name Dorcas was more commonly used.

88 "Dorcas Raised to Life," *The Christian Advocate* (30 September 1892): 493. Emphasis in original.

89 Ibid.

90 Ibid.

91 J.E. Sampson, "The Women Workers of the Bible. VIII. – Tabitha," *India's Women* 2, no. 10 (July-August 1882): 202.

92 Ibid., 203. Emphasis in original.

93 J.E. Sampson, "The Women Workers of the Bible. I. – Lydia," *India's Women* 1, no. 1 (January–February 1881): 36. In this series of articles Sampson alternates between lavishly praising "women's work" and subtly denigrating it.

94 J.E. Sampson, "The Women Workers of the Bible. II. – Lydia – (continued)," *India's Women* 1, no. 3 (May–June 1881): 128. Emphasis in original.

95 Ibid., 129.

96 Ibid., 130.

97 "Lydia – (continued)," 131.

98 See also the reprint of a sermon preached at Fisherwick Place Presbyterian Church on this subject. H.M. Williamson, "A Faithful Woman," *The Witness* (19 January 1877): 3.

99 J.E. Sampson, "The Women Workers of the Bible. VI. – Phœbe," *India's Women* 2, no. 7 (January-February 1882): 4. Of course, to succour means

to give aid or assistance; it does not necessarily mean "womanly" nursing of the ill or the preparation of food, as Sampson assumes it does in the case of this Deaconess of the church at Cenchrea.

100 J.E. Sampson, "The Women Workers of the Bible. XIV. – The Roman Workers," *India's Women* 3, no. 18 (November-December 1883): 295.

101 Ibid.

102 Ibid. Emphasis in original.

103 Ibid., 296. Despite his penchant for taking great liberties with his biblical texts, Sampson says: "I protest most earnestly against those vain imaginings;" (books in which the words or thoughts of biblical characters are fictionalized) "It is no good sign that such books should be so popular" he complains. And, again, while praising "women's work," he belittles it.

104 The dedicatory page goes as follows: "This Sermon is affectionately dedicated to the Mothers of the Flock, by their sincere Friend and Pastor R.J.A."

105 R.J. Arnold, *Lois and Eunice. A Sermon for the Times* (Belfast: Moat Bros. n.d.), 2. Emphasis in original.

106 Ibid., 6. Emphasis in original.

107 Ibid., 9. In this document as well we see the problem encountered by biblical literalists when dealing with the women of scripture. The entire biblical record of Lois and Eunice's lives is as follows: Paul says that he is filled with joy when he remembers "the unfeigned faith that is in thee, which dwelt first in thy grandmother Lois, and thy mother Eunice; and I am persuaded that in thee also" (I Timothy 1:5). In his sermon, Arnold, due to scarcity of material, had to take various sidetracks on subjects ranging from the shortage of young men entering "the ministry" to the problem of excessively showy female dress. He exhorts women to follow Lois and Eunice's example, but there is not a lot to go on here.

108 Ibid.

109 Ibid. Note how echoes of the "women's rights" poems – "the right to labour, love, and pray" – may be heard here.

110 Of the various female saints who appeared in the pages of Roman Catholic popular literature, after the Virgin Mary and Mary Magdalen, Monica was the most popular.

111 See "The Immaculate Conception of Joseph!" *The Christian Advocate* (30 September 1898): 471, and "A Strange Saint. Blood Sweating Johanna," *The Christian Advocate* (17 April 1914): 186iii.

112 F.C. Kolbe, "St. Monica among the Philosophers," *The Irish Monthly* 30, no. 350 (September 1902): 519.

113 "Monica. Some Chapters in Her Life," *The Irish Presbyterian*, n.s., 8, no. 2 (February 1902): 601.

114 Ibid.

115 Ibid.

116 He dedicated his *Madonna: Verses on Our Lady and the Saints* to his mother who "taught me to love Our Mother who is in heaven" and included a quotation from Augustine's *Confessions* in which the saint asked God to remember his mother Monica.

117 Russell, *Madonna*, 74. Emphasis in original. See also A.W., "St Monica," *The Irish Monthly* 35, no. 407 (May 1907): 249–50, and Matthew Russell, "On the Literary Studies of Ladies. An Afternoon Lecture," *The Irish Monthly* 4, (1876): 490–1.

118 Ibid.

119 See S.E. "The Antithesis of the New Woman," *The Irish Presbyterian* 1, no. 4 (April 1895): 71; "Mrs John Neil," *The Christian Advocate* (5 August 1892): 408iii, and Charity Hope, "King's Daughters in Council – Kitchen Work," *The Christian Advocate* (2 December 1910): 568.

120 Joseph Beaumont, "Female Excellence," *Primitive Wesleyan Methodist Magazine* 18 (November/December 1852): 439. Emphasis in original.

121 For a discussion of the debate concerning Protestant women's gradually expanding sphere see chapter 6.

122 "Hebrew Women," *The Witness* 3, no. 109 (28 January 1876): 7. Selected from *New Quarterly Magazine*. The author also takes an opportunity to criticize Roman Catholicism in his paean to domesticity. He argues that the ancient Hebrews placed a high value on domesticity and that "Monkish celibacy, with its train of attendant evils ... never had any place in the ethics of Judaism."

123 Ibid. The author also observes that among Hebrew women (the life of Hanna is used as an example) one can see "that spirit of romance which we sometimes imagine to be only the fruit of modern life and sentiment." Of course, it is his sentimental view that colours biblical scenes with the delicate tint of romance.

124 "The Virtuous Woman," *The Evangelical Witness and Presbyterian Review* 3, no. 3 (1 March 1864): 57. Clearly, though, the "virtuous woman" or women modelled on her type were praised in Catholic literature.

125 Ibid.

126 Ibid.

127 Ibid.

128 L.A.M. Priestley (pseudonym for Mrs George McCracken), "Ruth," *The Irish Presbyterian*, n.s., 8, no. 12 (December 1902): 735.

129 Ibid.

130 Priestley, 735. See also The Bishop of Derry, "Ruth and Boaz," *The Christian Advocate* (8 March 1888): 110; C.H. Crookshank, "Ruth's Choice," *The Christian Advocate* (11 October 1895): 490; C. H. Crookshank, "Ruth and Naomi," *The Christian Advocate* (5 December 1902):

594; R.P., "Ruth and Orpah," *The Monthly Messenger*, n.s., 1, no. 10 (October 1857): 145–8; W. Young, "Readings on the Book of Ruth," *The Monthly Messenger*, n.s., 8, no. 10 (October 1863): 173-7. The only Catholic reference I found to Ruth was in Mrs Morgan O'Connell's biography of the Irish poet Attie O'Brien.

131 She was the Queen of the Persian Empire who when asked by her drunken husband, Ahasuerus, to appear before his male friends refused for: "the sacredness of womanhood more than outweighed the allurements of the palace." Lyncaeus, "Some Bible Heroines," *The Irish Presbyterian*, n.s., 1, no. 5 (May 1898): 66. Vashti's husband chose Esther to be queen in her place (Esther, chapters 1 and 2). See also Dr Talmage, "The Banished Queen," *The Witness* 3, no. 118 (7 April 1876): 5.

132 Lyncaeus does remark, however, that "the touching story of Jephthah's daughter is, no doubt, familiar to you" (Ibid., 67). He or she assumes that his Ulster Presbyterian readers are acquainted with the story.

133 Ibid.

134 Ibid.

135 Ibid.

136 Ibid.

137 Ibid.

138 Mrs James Martin, "The Cry of the Women in the Present Crisis," *The Christian Advocate* (7 May 1886): 217.

139 Talmage, "The Banished Queen," 5.

140 A Lady, "Deborah," *The Christian Advocate* (14 February 1896): 698. This paper was written for the Killarney Methodist Bible class.

141 Ibid.

142 Ibid.

143 Joseph Farrell, "Judith. A Study," *The Irish Monthly* 4 (1876): 314.

144 Ibid., 315.

145 Douay Rheims version of the Holy Bible, Judith 13:10.

146 Farrell, 315.

147 Ibid., 317.

148 Ibid.

149 A similar interpretation of a woman "unsexed" by a violent deed may be found in the Rev. J.E. Sampson's, "The Women Workers of the Bible. XII. – Jael, The Wife of Heber," *India's Women* 3, no. 16 (July–August, 1883): 180–2.

CHAPTER FIVE

1 Fahey, "Nuns in the Catholic church in Ireland in the nineteenth century," 7, 10. See also Taylor, *Irish Homes and Irish Hearts*, 4.

2 Ibid., 20.

3 Ibid.

4 Quoted in Fahey, "Nuns in the Catholic church in Ireland," 21.

5 Ibid., 23.

6 Ibid.

7 Taylor, *Irish Homes and Irish Hearts*, 13.

8 Tynan, *A Nun*, 2–3.

9 Connell, "Illegitimacy Before the Famine," passim.

10 Ibid., 3.

11 Cusack, *Woman's Work in Modern Society*, 140.

12 Ibid., 131–2.

13 Ibid., 134.

14 Ibid., 158.

15 See P.J.C., "The Convent Girl's Burial," *The Catholic Guardian* (1853):
    267; Sister Mary Stanislaus, "A Convent Elegy," *The Irish Monthly* 7
    (1880): 501-3; "A Little Convent Girl," "The Convent Garden," *The Irish
    Monthly* 3, no. 353 (November 1902): 650-1; and L.M. "To Mercedes On
    the Day of her First Communion," *The Irish Monthly* 33, no. 387 (September 1905): 523.

16 Matthew Russell, "The Little Flower Strewers," *The Irish Monthly* 7, no. 74
    (1879): 421. Emphasis in original. In a note accompanying the poem,
    which borrowed its title "from one of the prettiest stories ever written –
    'The Little Flower Seekers,'" Father Russell notes that his inspiration for
    writing the verses was his witnessing the girls "kissing each handful of the
    flowers with which they strewed the corridors of the Convent of Mercy,
    Baggot-street, Dublin, during the Procession of *Quarant 'Ore*, June 24
    1879."

17 Ibid. Emphasis in original.

18 Ibid. Emphasis in original.

19 L.M., 523.

20 A.L., "Spared! A Mother's 'Deo Gratias,'" *The Irish Monthly* 28, no. 323
    (May 1900): 237–40.

21 Ibid., 301–2.

22 Sister Delores, "May and Mary's Children," *The Catholic Bulletin and Book
    Review* 1, no. 5 (May 1911): 239.

23 Ibid., 241–2.

24 See Tynan, *A Nun*, 171–2.

25 Sister Delores, "May and Mary's Children," 242.

26 Ibid., 240.

27 Ibid., 240–1.

28 Tales of the Festivals (Dublin: The Catholic Truth Society, 1901), 4.

29 Ibid., 11.

30 Ibid., 15.

31   Keenan, *The Catholic Church in Nineteenth-Century Ireland*, 34.

32   In the dedication of *Madonna*, Father Russell writes, "I earnestly commend 'Madonna' to the care of Her after whom I have dared to name it,
as well as to the kind favour of the numberless sodalities of her children
– *Enfants de Marie* – those especially in whose pious exercises it is my
privilege to take part."

33   See also, Melbournenesis, "An Australian Child of Mary," *The Irish
Monthly* 5 (1877): 685–7.

34   In a note, Father Russell quotes the correspondence between mother
and daughter: "*Je me leve a six heures, et, aussitot habillee, je vais allumer la
lampe devant l'autel de la Sainte Vierge.*" He does not provide an English
translation.

35   Russell, *Madonna*, 19. Emphasis in original.

36   In twentieth-century convents, being a blue-ribboned Child of Mary was
an honour that was earned by convent school girls by their demonstrat-
ing exemplary behaviour and remarkable piety. The honour could be
taken away for bad behaviour. I would hesitate to argue from negative
evidence, but I found no mention of this use of the withdrawal of Child
of Mary status as punishment in my research. In Father Russell's *Madonna*, one poem, "The Madonna of the Schoolroom," shows how elements
of the Marian cult were used to control the girls' behaviour. Every verse
of the poem ends with "'Tis Mary looking on!" or some variation (25–8).

37   This poem was published in *The Irish Monthly* 8 (1880): 58 with the title
"E. DE M." and the note that "these initials are appended to their
signature by many *Enfants de Marie*.

38   Ibid., 22.

39   Ibid.

40   Ibid. Emphasis in original.

41   See Tynan, *A Nun*, 119–20.

42   Charlotte, O'Conor Eccles, "The Girls of To-day and Their Education,"
The Irish Monthly 15, no. 290 (August 1897): 421–3. She notes that at
least seven out of ten girls "are destined to be wives and mothers, to live
in the world."

43   Ibid., 422.

44   Ibid., 424.

45   Ibid. She does not single out nuns in this matter, but no doubt they
would have been particularly reticent on matters of marital relations. In
Katherine Tynan's memoirs (Katherine Tynan, *Twenty-five Years: Reminiscences*. London: John Murray, 1913) she recalls how as a schoolgirl at the
Sienna Convent Drogheda in the 1870s the nuns avoided the subject of
relations between men and women. As the girls sewed a nun would read
aloud to them, usually from spiritual books, but occasionally from novels.
"When the nun came to a passage of love-making – there were several in

the *Heir of Redcliffe* – she would turn very red, and laugh, or she would say with contempt that what followed was great nonsense. The result was the same, for the love-making passages were huddled away out of sight to our extreme disgust and disappointment." (47) "The heavenliness of the convent atmosphere" (50), was, for Tynan, its greatest recommendation. Yet even such an ardent supporter of convent education as Katherine Tynan saw the drawbacks of the inability of nuns to prepare their students to live in a world that included men: "The nuns added a counsel which was surely mediaeval. It was that we should not look male creatures in the face when we encountered them" (59).

46 Ibid. Eccles also considers sensible talks for senior girls on matters of marriage and motherhood necessary as "an antidote to the poison of silly novels and silly sentimentalism."

47 Nora Hanrahan, "A Valiant Women," *The Catholic Bulletin and Book Review* 1, no. 7 (July 1911): 331. In her biography of Mother Xaveria, Katherine Tynan mentions that her subject's mother had wanted to be a nun as well but "God meant her not for a nun, but for a mother of nuns. Her four daughters all entered religion; so her obedience seems to have been fully blest" (67).

48 Ibid., 332.

49 Ibid., (August 1911), 394.

50 Ibid., 394–5.

51 Hanrahan, "A Valiant Woman" (October 1911): 493. For Catholic ideals of Christian service, see also Bryan O'Hara, "Kathleen O'Mara's Petition." In this story the heroine saves the life of one her father's workers, Con, who had a problem with drink. Kathleen helped Con materially, but she also prayed for his reform and future happiness with her maid, Bridget. Her prayers were answered. "Our Lady had blessed the prayers of that white-souled Irish girl ... Good reader, within the circle of your acquaintances there may be "Cons" and "Bridgets," and you, like Kathleen O'Mara, may have the means to help them, even a little. If so, try to interest yourself in them and endeavour particularly to keep them at home in their own land; it is the land that suits them best and it never need them more than it does at present." *The Catholic Bulletin and Book Review* 4, no. 6 (June 1914): 414.

52 Hanrahan, "A Valiant Woman" (September 1911): 449. For Catholic women there could be two vocations: nun or wife and mother. Anne's mother is criticized in this story for rebelling against God's will that she should be a wife and mother rather than a nun.

53 Ibid., 449.

54 Hanrahan, "A Valiant Woman" (October 1911): 492. This echoes Proverbs 31:27.

55 Ibid.

56 Hanrahan, "A Valiant Woman" (December 1911): 615. In the Roman Catholic Douay Bible, the woman of Proverbs, chapter thirty-one is described as "valiant;" the King James Version uses the term "virtuous" (Proverbs 31:10).

57 The Lodge, Fortwilliam Park, Belfast. Ladies' School. (Belfast: n.p. 1915).

58 Ibid.

59 Ibid.

60 Breathnach, "Charting New Waters," 55.

61 Ibid., 3.

62 On the legislative front, girls were included in the Intermediate Act of 1878 which brought about public examinations for second-level students and in 1879 the new University Bill for Ireland which set up the Royal University of Ireland as a nondenominational examining body, allowed for the admission of women to degrees. Breathnach, 57-58.

63 Tod, *Advanced Education for Girls of the Upper and Middle Class*, 4.

64 Ibid.

65 Ibid., 4–5.

66 A pseudonym used by Mrs William L. Coade, a Belfast Methodist minister's wife.

67 For example, see Charity Hope, "Girls in Council." *The Christian Advocate* (16 December 1898): 601; 17 February 1899: 74, and 5 October 1900: 484iii.

68 Quoted in Charity Hope, "King's Daughters in Council," *The Christian Advocate* (9 November 1900): 541.

69 Among other matters, pride – of intellect, spirituality and physical beauty – and lack of moral stamina were also seriously discussed in these columns. See *The Christian Advocate* (10 March 1899): 117 and 11 May 1900: 224.

70 Charity Hope, "King's Daughters in Council: A Disciplined Heart," *The Christian Advocate* (18 April 1902): 183. See also "The New Woman," *The Irish Presbyterian*, n.s., 2, no. 7 (July 1896), 110-11.

71 Ibid.

72 Charity Hope, "Girls in Council," *The Christian Advocate* (3 March 1899): 108iii.

73 Charity Hope, "Girls in Council," *The Christian Advocate* (31 March 1899): 155.

74 Sometimes "her girls" wrote asking Charity Hope about serious spiritual issues (e.g., "How can I know that I am saved?") or moral questions (e.g., "Is it right for a Christian girl to go to dances?"), but frequently they wrote just to tell Charity Hope about some trial at home or school that they had overcome, to share a favourite scripture verse or poem, or to express their hopes and ambitions.

75 Ibid.

76 Ibid.

77 Charity Hope, "King's Daughters in Council: Saved to be a blessing," *The Christian Advocate* (1 March 1901): 98.

78 See *The Christian Advocate* (28 July 1899): 369; 18 October 1901: 509; and 24 March 1911: 143.

79 Charity Hope, "Girls in Council," *The Christian Advocate* (18 August 1899): 412.

80 Although this story was published in *The Irish Presbyterian*, I include it here because it succinctly expresses the ideals of a "girl-worker" that were discussed in the "Girls in Council" columns. Most stories in the evangelical Protestant literature impressed upon their readers this idea of service. For example, see Clare Carrington, "Nora's Commission," *The Christian Advocate* (11 December 1900): 1.

81 "The Service of Margaret," *The Irish Presbyterian*, n.s., 17, no. 9 (September 1911): 136.

82 I have tried to follow the usage of this term adopted by the various Protestant denominations. The Presbyterians always used the term "Sabbath school" while the Methodists and the Church of Ireland used both "Sabbath school" and "Sunday school." The latter usage became more popular at the turn of the century.

83 Quoted in Charity Hope, "Girls in Council," *The Christian Advocate* (22 September 1899): 473.

84 Ibid.

85 See "Where Are the Men?" *The Christian Advocate* (3 August 1906): 371.

86 Samuel Hutchinson, "New Methods in the Sunday School," *The Irish Church Quarterly* 5, no. 17 (January 1912): 60. Throughout this article Hutchinson always refers to the teacher as "she." In advocating a new "know the child" method of teaching he says: "The teacher must know the capacity of the children of her class, must know the sort of ideas that are in their minds, if she wants, by what she tells them, to touch their hearts, their minds, and their character" (61). One gets the impression from the literature that the majority of teachers were female, while most superintendents were male.

87 Charity Hope, "King's Daughters in Council: Sunday-school teaching," *The Christian Advocate* (10 March 1911): 119.

88 Ibid. On the matter of the age of Sunday school teachers, Hutchinson stated that "Girls of fourteen years have been known to do good work, but perhaps fifteen is the best limit to aim at." (62)

89 This woman also contributed many poems and short stories to *The Christian Advocate*.

90 Miss Nixon, " 'Feed My Lambs.' An address to Sunday-school teachers," *The Christian Advocate* (6 March 1896): 111.

91 There was some heated discussion on this issue in the "Correspon-dence" section of the April 1914 numbers of *The Christian Advocate*.

92 Charity Hope, "Sunday-school teaching," 119.

93 Miss Higginson, "The Infant Class," in the Presbytery of Ards Sabbath School Union, *Report of Sabbath School Conference held in Newtownards on 28th and 29th August, 1911* (Reproduced from "Newtownards Chroni-cle" of September 2nd and 9th, 1911), 14.

94 Ibid.

95 Ibid.

96 Charity Hope, "Sunday-school teaching," 119.

97 Ibid.

98 Ibid.

99 H. Ball, "In Memoriam. Miss Curry, Belfast." *The Christian Advocate* (7 April 1899): 163.

100 Ibid.

101 Ibid. See also "A Sabbath School Teacher Called Home. A Little Tribute by one who knew her well," *Daybreak* 48, no. 10 (October 1910): 137-8. Touching tributes were also made to young female Sunday school scholars. For example, see J.T., "The Happy Death-Bed of a Sunday-school Scholar," *The Christian Advocate* (25 September1891): 468 and Maggie Magill, "She Did What She Could," *Daybreak* 36, no. 6 (June 1898): 67-8.

102 Maud Lutton, "The Little White Teacher," *The Christian Advocate* (11 December 1900): 28.

103 Ibid.

104 Ibid.

105 "Ellen Dalton; or, the Sunday School," *Irish Sunday School Teacher's Magazine* (June–July 1853): 182. The girls attending the Sunday school were primarily farmers' and labourers' daughters.

106 In an article in *Daybreak*, a girl complains, "Dress, dress, dress! Always lecturing us girls about dress!" The author replies, "Yes, dear girls, you have many things written and said to you on this subject, and perhaps if you could see with older eyes how greatly this much-discussed matter of dress can add to or detract from your fresh, girlish sweetness, you would listen patiently – even read eagerly – just one more little 'lecture.'" "Dress," *Daybreak* 16, no. 9 (September 1888): 105. The letters of Charity Hope's young correspondents indicate that "dress" was something that they themselves were very concerned about. They wondered what degree of frippery was becoming in a godly woman. They believed that excessive or immodest dress could detract from their Christian witness. See the "Girls in Council" columns in the 20 January 1899, (33) and 25 February 1899, (93) numbers of *The Christian Advocate*.

107 In religious fiction, both Roman Catholic and Protestant, disaster always accompanied mixed marriage.

108 M.C., "Lillie's Lapse," *The Irish Monthly* 35, no. 403 (January 1907): 42.

109 Ibid., 43.

110 Ibid.

111 Ibid.

112 "On Novel Reading," *The Primitive Wesley Methodist Magazine* 18 (July and August 1852): 263.

113 Tynan, *Twenty-five Years*, 59.

114 Nora Tynan O'Mahony, "The Popular Novel," *The Catholic Bulletin and Book Review* 1, no. 1 (January 1911): 44.

115 Molly Malone (pseud.), "A Crying Evil," *The Catholic Bulletin and Book Review* 1, no. 4 (April 1911): 217.

116 Ibid., 218.

117 Ibid. The author also notes that "still further does it behove the Catholic parent and employer to support works which bear the stamp of Catholicity."

118 Mary A. Coleman, "Domestic Libraries and Other Things," *The Catholic Bulletin and Book Review* 1, no. 4 (April 1911): 200. The religious segregation in Irish reading habits was noted by Katherine Tynan in the second volume of her autobiography: " … in Ireland, if you are a Protestant you read one class of books, and if you are a Catholic you read another; and if you want to depart from this course your Protestant or Catholic bookseller sees that you are kept in it." Tynan, *The Middle Years*, 192.

119 Charity Hope, "Girls in Council. A Plea for Character," *The Christian Advocate* (23 February 1900): 96.

120 Quoted in ibid.

121 Charity Hope, "Girls in Council. What Shall We Read – continued," *The Christian Advocate* (9 February 1900): 63.

122 See Tynan, *Twenty-five years*, 14.

123 Matthew Russell, "On the Literary Studies of Ladies," *The Irish Monthly* 4 (1876): 554.

124 Ibid.

125 Charity Hope, "Girls in Council," *The Christian Advocate* (March 2, 1900): 104.

126 See George Brown, "A Loyal Witness," *The Christian Advocate* (May 13, 1891): 239 and Miss Cusack, the "Nun of Kenmare" (this article was written after her conversion to Protestantism), "Christmas in a Convent," *The Christian Advocate* (December 6, 1892): 617.

127 Quoted in Charity Hope, "Girls in Council. Protestant Girls and Convent Schools," *The Christian Advocate* (16 March 1900): 125.

128 Ibid. Elsewhere, Charity Hope expresses vehemently anti-Catholic senti-
     ments, so this praise of the nuns' holy lives is quite surprising. Given
     the increasing sectarian tension in the province, it is astounding that a
     Protestant writer would praise convent education so highly. This clearly
     reflected the concern felt by conservative Christians at the increasingly
     academic nature of Protestant middle-class girls' education. The so-
     called preoccupation with " 'ics and 'ologies" would, it was feared, turn
     young women away from the pursuit of holiness.

CHAPTER SIX

1 Hempton, "Evangelicalism in English and Irish Society, 1780–1840,"
   156.
2 See chapter one.
3 Queue (pseud.), "Women in the Church," *The Irish Presbyterian*, n.s., 18,
   no. 11 (November 1912): 161. See also William Gorman, "Woman's
   Work in the Church," reprinted in *The Christian Advocate* (27 November
   1891): 566. This American Methodist minister asserts that while the
   position of woman "rose with the Reformation; Methodism has been the
   Zerubbabel of her liberty." The author is referring to Zerubbabel the
   hero of Nehemiah, chapter five, who led many Israelites out of captivity
   from Babylon.
4 Ibid.
5 Mrs Clarke, "Woman's Work in the Church," *The Irish Presbyterian*, n.s., 4,
   no. 12 (December 1900): 381–2. Emphasis in original.
6 Charity Hope, "King's Daughters in Council. Sisterliness," *The Christian
   Advocate* (20 October 1911): 503.
7 "Woman's Sphere," reprinted in *The Witness* 3, no. 144 (6 October
   1876): 3. See also Gorman; 566; George R. Osborn, "The Work of
   Women in the Church," *The Wesleyan Methodist Magazine*, 6th ser., 5
   (January 1881): 31.
8 Charity Hope, "King's Daughters in Council," *The Christian Advocate*
   (1 July 1910): 312.
9 Gorman, "Woman's Work in the Church," 566.
10 A., reply to "Women's Work in the Church, by J.E.H.," *The Christian
    Advocate* (17 August 1888): 401. See also, Charity Hope, "King's Daugh-
    ters in Council. The Ministry of Women," *The Christian Advocate* (12 June
    1914): 280.
11 Mrs E.M. Bewley, "Noble Women," *The Christian Advocate* (22 January
    1886): 40.
12 Ibid. See also "The Throne of Woman," *The Christian Advocate* (30
    January 1885): 59 in which the importance to church and state of
    woman's domestic "mission" is emphasized.

13 Ibid. Emphasis in original.

14 Ibid.

15 Ibid. A similar version of this poem, titled "Noble Women," was published in the 27 November 1885 number of *The Christian Advocate*, 588. The author was given as E.M.B. of Blackrock.

16 George R. Wedgwood, "Piety at Home," *The Christian Advocate* (30 September 1898): 462. Mrs Jellyby was a notorious busybody – her own home went to ruin while she devised schemes for the conversion of the natives of Borriobola-gha – in Dickens' *Bleak House*. See Brouwer, *New Women for God*, 21.

17 Ibid. See also, A., "Letter in Response to 'Women's Work in the Church,'" *The Christian Advocate* (17 August 1888): 401.

18 Ibid. See also, Mrs G.W. Crossland, "Mother," *The Christian Advocate* (19 June 1914): 297.

19 Charity Hope, "King's Daughters in Council. A Devoted Life," *The Christian Advocate* (11 October 1901): 491.

20 Ibid.

21 Ibid.

22 Ibid.

23 Ibid.

24 The writings of Margaret E. Sangster, a popular American campaigner for such causes as temperance and moral purity, were frequently reprinted in Ulster evangelical periodicals.

25 Margaret E. Sangster, "In Error," *The Christian Advocate* (12 August 1892): 411.

26 H. Acheson, "Entertaining Angels," *The Irish Presbyterian*, n.s., 1, no. 2 (February 1895): 30.

27 For a full discussion of Mary and her sister Martha as role-models for female piety, see chapter 4.

28 Acheson, "Entertaining Angels," 30.

29 John N. Spence, "The Late Mrs R. Crawford Johnson. A Tribute," *The Christian Advocate* (21 July 1911): 340.

30 Charity Hope, "King's Daughters in Council. Keepers at Home," *The Christian Advocate* (3 April 1914): 160.

31 Charity Hope clearly outlines the class dimension of this particular problem: "We have been dealing with the problem of middle-class women, because it is only on the lips of middle-class men one hears the silly reiteration about 'keepers at home.' Women of the upper-class have made a fine art of the business of not staying at home. They travel ... and rush from one entertainment to another, with a little philanthropic effort thrown in ." Charity Hope also describes the lot of working-class women and widowed or deserted wives who were "forced into factories and sweat-shops and other uncongenial occupations by our modern

civilisation. What here avails the glib advice of men to 'stay at home and darn the socks?' It would add gross insult to injury." Actually, middle-class women sometimes used the "keepers at home" refrain to try and convince working-class women they would be better off staying at home and being better managers on their husbands' wages. See Martin's *Keepers at Home*, passim. Also, when Charity Hope referred to the "keepers at home" slogan as "silly" she was borrowing trouble, for the often-used phrase was a quotation from Titus 2:5.

32 She adds that even if this was possible it would be "somewhat stultifying to a woman whom God had endowed with rich gifts for human service to be obliged to spend her strength and time scrubbing floors and cooking dinners." Ibid. It is interesting to note that she sees men as the primary proponents of an exclusively domestic sphere for women; as I have shown in chapter 2, women were enthusiastic supporters of the cult of domesticity. Perhaps at this late date (1914) only a few very conservative men and some women, judging by the response to her column, still held to the total confinement of women to the domestic realm. In another 1914 column, it is mentioned that in the British Isles there were two million more women than men, thus "there are many that could be spared" for work outside of the home. (12 June 1914): 280.

33 Ibid.

34 "Women," *The Witness* 1, no 16 (17 April 1874): 5.

35 All the while she was careful not to offend the sensibilities of her critics. "I believe if we could discuss our differences over a cup of tea we should discover heaps of affinities," Charity Hope assured one of her critics. *The Christian Advocate* (24 April 1914): 196.

36 Ibid.

37 Ibid.

38 "A Minister's Wife," *The Witness* 1, no. 39 (25 September 1874): 3.

39 Ibid.

40 Ibid.

41 Ibid.

42 Ivor MacIvor, "A Day's Visiting," *The Irish Presbyterian*, n.s., 1, no. 5 (May 1895): 87.

43 Funds for the education of ministers' daughters were important causes in Methodist and Presbyterian circles during this period. I found many references to the phenomenon of ministers' wives commonly being ministers' daughters as well.

44 While a minister's wife would ordinarily have a servant to assist her with her household duties, many clerical families appear to have been on the edge of middle-class respectability in their means. In an article entitled "Sustentation," the anonymous author says that most Irish Presbyterian ministers were "respectable paupers" and calls being a minister a worse

fate than being a sweated labourer! *The Irish Presbyterian*, n.s., 19, no. 7 (July 1913): 122.

45 Mrs J.S. McNair, "Parson's or Church's Wife?" *The Witness* 3, no. 146 (29 October 1876): 7.

46 In a humorous article, the process of selecting a minister is described. The members of the committee had decided against the candidate in question, but one member ventured to ask, "'couldn't we call his wife?' If it could have been done, it would have been done, straight out of hand; not a soul knew a defect in her ... *She* was the altogether eligible, *he* was (in part) the detrimental." Zeta. (pseud.), "The Minister's Wife," *The Irish Presbyterian*, n.s., 8, no. 12 (December 1902): 734.

47 One of Them, "A Plea for Ministers' Wives," *The Irish Presbyterian*, n.s., 1, no. 5 (May 1895): 85. See also Evan Roberts, "The Brae-church Minister," *The Irish Presbyterian*, n.s., 6, no. 11 (November 1900): 374-6. "One of Them" adds that, in her opinion, the "ideal life" is that of the country charge where, she thinks, the minister's wife is eagerly welcomed and cared for by the "simple folks" who are the secret strength of "our old Presbyterian Church." I would have been interested in a reply by the wife of a country minister to this ideal view of her life, but, alas, none was forthcoming in pages of *The Irish Presbyterian*.

48 Ibid.

49 Ibid. See also A Pastor's Wife, "Ministers' Wives," *The Christian Advocate* (24 July 1885): 367 and (12 October 1888): 503.

50 Given that this story was published in *The Christian Advocate* when Charity Hope was writing her "King's Daughters in Council" column and contributing other stories and articles, I assume that "C. Hope" is another pen-name for Mrs William L. Coade, a Belfast minister's wife.

51 This is not surprising, for *The Christian Advocate*; the wife in this case is a lapsed Protestant and her intemperate husband is a Roman Catholic.

52 C. Hope, "The Minister's Missing Wife," *The Christian Advocate*, (13 December 1899): 23.

53 Ibid.

54 The only person with whom she was not gentle and loving was the drunken Roman Catholic husband. She was "stern and commanding" with him. One wonders if this would have been acceptable if the man had been a member of her husband's Methodist congregation.

55 J.C. Johnston, "In Memoriam. Isabella Moffat Thompson," *The Irish Presbyterian*, n.s., 10, no. 6 (June 1904): 83.

56 Ibid.

57 Ibid.

58 See Zeta, "The Minister's Wife," 734.

59 J.C. Johnston, "In Memoriam. Isabella Moffat Thompson, concluded," *The Irish Presbyterian*, n.s., 10, no. 7 (July 1904): 104–5.

60 Johnston, "In Memoriam" (June 1904) 81.

61 For a rebuke of women who criticized ministers' wives and a call for women to support and work with their minister's wife, see the "Woman's Sphere" column by An Old Maid, "The Minister's Wife" *The Irish Presbyterian*, n.s., 1, no. 12 (December 1896): 188.

62 "Making Our Lives Beautiful," reprinted in *The Christian Advocate* (2 August 1901): 375.

63 Quoted in Charity Hope, "King's Daughters in Council. The Ministry of Women," *The Christian Advocate* (12 June 1914): 280.

64 Also, as I mentioned above in the case of Charity Hope's critics, women were frequently staunch defenders of the gender status quo.

65 At the annual Conference members passed legislation that applied to the Methodist circuits in Ireland. I have chosen to follow Irish Methodist usage and refer to this gathering, simply, as they did with the word "Conference."

66 "Women and the Methodist Conference," *The Christian Advocate* (8 February 1895): 67.

67 Ibid.

68 "Women as Conference Representatives," *The Daily Christian Advocate* (21 June 1910): 5. During Conference the Irish Methodist weekly paper was published daily.

69 Ibid.

70 Ibid.

71 Ibid., 6. This comment, it was noted, received a "Hear, hear" from the assembly.

72 Ibid.

73 Ibid.

74 Ibid., 5.

75 Ibid., 6.

76 Ibid.

77 Ibid.

78 Edward Smith, "Woman's Place in Modern Evangelism," *The Christian Advocate* (25 June 1888): 312iii.

79 This was a women's column in *The Advocate*, chiefly concerned with social and domestic matters, which preceded Charity Hope's columns.

80 Eileen, "A Women's Causerie," *The Christian Advocate* (5 March 1897): 120iii.

81 Eileen, "A Women's Causerie," *The Christian Advocate* (28 August 1896): 409. Outside of the women's columns, I found no mention of the Ulster visits of female preachers in *The Christian Advocate*.

82 Ibid.

83 "Should Women Preach?" *The Irish Presbyterian*, n.s., 3, no. 12 (December

1897): 187. Reprinted from a short-lived women's missionary magazine called *Women's Signal.*

84 After establishing that some women in the Old Testament prophesied, to determine the meaning of prophesying, the author quotes I Corinthians 14:3: "He that prophesieth speaketh unto men edification, and comfort, and consolation." Thus prophesying and preaching become conflated for the sake of the author's argument.

85 The conventional evangelical interpretation of women's role in the early church was that of "helpmeet," not preacher or leader. For a discussion of this interpretation of the biblical record, see chapter 2.

86 These included Paul's salutations to female church workers such as Tryphena, Tryphosa, Persis, and Phebe, but the author also took a different approach by citing Galatians 3:28: '*There* is neither Jew nor Greek, *there* is neither bond nor free, *there* is neither *male nor female*, for ye are all *one in Christ Jesus.*' Emphasis in original article. The King James Version of the Bible does not use italics in this verse.

87 Ibid.

88 "Should Women Preach?" reprinted in *The Irish Presbyterian*, n.s., 4, no. 1 (January 1898): 7 and *The Irish Presbyterian*, n.s., 4, no. 2 (February 1898): 26.

89 It was a more conservative, smaller-circulation Presbyterian monthly than *The Irish Presbyterian*. About half of its content was concerned with the instrumental music controversy raging in Ulster Presbyterianism at this time.

90 Though the pseudonym is feminine it is doubtful that the author of the article was a women, for all of the named contributors to the magazine were men, mostly clergymen, and the rest of the pseudonyms were masculine. The magazine itself was not geared to a general or family readership as *The Irish Presbyterian* was; rather it considered dry theological subjects at considerable length with little humour or colour.

91 Salome (pseud.), "Is It in Accordance with the Teaching of the New Testament that Women Should Preach the Gospel Publicly?" *The Christian Banner* 11 (1883): 18.

92 Ibid.

93 Ibid. See Smith, "Woman's Place in Modern Evangelism" for a similar view in a Methodist source.

94 In naming this sleepy fictional town "Ballymiddle" the author pokes fun at the proliferation of small Ulster towns that begin with the prefix "Bally."

95 Denarius (pseud.), "Should Women Preach?" *The Irish Presbyterian*, n.s., 18, no. 4 (April 1912): 57.

96 Ibid.

97 Ibid.

98 Denarius mocks the ill-guided literalism of an enthusiastic, but dim, local biblical scholar who upon reading that "when Peter's wife's mother was healed she rose and *ministered*," (Luke 4:38–39) thought he had found 'a clincher' for the affirmative side. Of course, "ministered" does not mean "preached."

99 They were referring to the Pauline prescriptions (I Corinthians 14:34–5) against women speaking in church.

100 Ibid.

101 Ibid., 58.

102 Denarius pokes fun at Sam's outdated Presbyterianism when he notes that Sam called Abraham the patriarch "a guid auld Covenanter."

103 Ibid. Parenthetical comment in original.

104 Ibid.

105 "Woman's Sphere. The New Woman," *The Irish Presbyterian*, n.s., 2, no. 7 (July 1896): 110. No author's name or pseudonym is given, but because the majority of those who wrote for the "Woman's Sphere" column were women, I assume that the writer was a woman.

106 Ibid.

107 Ibid.

108 Lord Plunkett, "The True Woman," quoted in *The Christian Advocate* (18 December 1896): 609. See also "The Advanced Woman," *The Irish Presbyterian*, n.s., 1, no. 1 (January 1895): 8.

109 Ibid. "Blue" here is a derogatory reference to "blue-stockings" – intellectual women.

110 Ibid., 175.

111 Ibid., 176. "Minister" here does not mean "preacher," rather it means, literally, someone who ministers.

112 Ibid.

113 Ibid.

114 Ibid. He also notes that, "as her Master's exaltation was the direct fruit and issue of His subordination so must her's be." His language here is similar to that used in the feminized American theology that I mentioned in the second chapter. Women are seen as more Christ-like than men because women share with Christ a common subordination.

115 Ibid.

116 Ibid.

117 See Charity Hope, "King's Daughters in Council," (1 February 1994): 56.

118 Cusack, *Woman's Work in Modern Society*, 158. This book was not aimed solely at a Catholic audience; it makes specific references to concerns about secularism and scepticism within the Church of England. That might explain her reference to women who wanted to teach from the "pulpit."

119 Nora Tynan O'Mahoney, "The Mother," *The Irish Monthly* 41, no. 485 (October 1913): 529.
120 Ibid.
121 Charlotte O'Conor Eccles, "A Plea for the Modern Woman. II," *The Irish Monthly* 32, no. 382 (June 1904): 321.
122 Mrs Frank Pentrill, "Every-Day Thoughts. No. IX – Old Maids," *The Irish Monthly* 13, no. 146 (August 1885): 412.
123 Ibid.
124 Ibid.
125 Cusack, 159.
126 Ibid.

CHAPTER SEVEN

1 The poem "On Seeing a Woman Drunk" was published in the August 1894 issue of the *The Irish Temperance League Journal* and in the June 1907 edition of *Everybody's Monthly*. The primary material for this chapter is largely taken from a sixty-year run of the Irish Temperance League's publications found in the Northern Ireland Public Records Office. The *Irish Temperance League Journal* was published from 1863–1903 and *Everybody's Monthly* existed from 1906–40.
2 For a comprehensive treatment of the activities of Irish temperance reform organizations, see Malcolm's *'Ireland Sober, Ireland Free'*.
3 Visiting the poor and dispensing temperance and "hygiene" advice was something done by laywomen in Protestant areas, but in Catholic areas this was left chiefly to the official representatives of the Church. According to historian Caitriona Clear "the ubiquity of nuns as Catholic social workers did not leave much room for the initiative of the laity." Clear, *Nuns in Nineteenth-Century Ireland*, 162.
4 While the term "temperance" was frequently used, for all intents and purposes, gospel temperance workers followed a total abstinence or tee-total program.
5 BWTA was used as an acronym for both the British Women's Temperance Association and the Belfast organization. Some confusion resulted. For the sake of clarity I will use BWTA for the national group and Belfast WTA for the Ulster organization. The Belfast WTA became affiliated with the BWTA in 1877. Of the 192 branches claimed by the BWTA in 1882, more than 39 belonged to the Belfast WTA. Lillian Lewis Shiman, "'Changes are Dangerous,'" 205.
6 "Will you help us?" The Story of the Belfast Women's Temperance Association and Christian Worker's Union. (pamphlet, 1935), 2, 3, 13.
7 "Woman's Work," *The Irish Temperance League Journal* 9, no. 2 (February 1881): 20.

8 "Ladies Temperance Union Annual Report," *The Irish Temperance League Journal* 22, no. 5 (May 1884): 59.

9 See "Woman's Works," *The Witness* 2, no. 124 (19 May 1875): 7.

10 See "The Dead Mother's Letter," *The Monthly Messenger* 23, no. 7 (July 1879): 107-10.

11 J.E. McConaughy, "Home and Mother," reprinted in *The Irish Temperance League Journal* 9, no. 6 (April 1871): 54.

12 "Hints to Females," *The Irish Temperance League Journal* 9, no. 3 (March 1881) : 36.

13 E.E. Wilmot, "Johnny McCree," *The Irish Temperance League Journal* 10, no. 1 (January 1872): 11.

14 See Lizzie C. Reid, "The Green Dragon of Wierdale," *The Irish Presbyterian* 16, no. 3 (March 1910): 56. In this story a wife tries to convince her publican husband to give up the trade, but "she had weakened her influence over her husband by nagging ... and died without accomplishing a reform."

15 "Words for Wives," *The Irish Temperance League Journal* 1, no. 1 (February 1863): 15.

16 See M.C., "Tom Jones: A Sketch," *The Irish Presbyterian* 17, no 10 (October 1911): 152–1 and A.L.W., "The Drunkard's Home," reprinted in *The Church of Ireland Temperance Visitor* 3, no. 8 (August, 1880): 81. In both of these stories, the wife does not actually die. The shock of almost losing their wives through their irresponsible drinking is enough to make these men repent of their ways.

17 Mrs Bewsher, "A Narrow Escape," *The Irish Temperance League Journal* 16, no. 7 (July 1878): 84.

18 This responsibility of women to keep their men from the drink by being expert housekeepers was considered a given in temperance literature. One interesting voice of protest may be heard in a satirical article titled "A Gauntlet for the Men," found in the *Church of Ireland Temperance Visitor* 6, no. 11 (October 1884): 156. The author, Fanny Fern, ridicules men for their weaknesses and touts the superior character of the supposedly "weaker sex." She skewers "poor" cowardly men who because they do not find life exactly to their liking become drunkards: "'Took to drinking because he was unhappy!' Bless-his-big-Spartan-soul! How I admire him!" Not so for a woman. When fate gives her a bad, improvident husband she "works all the harder, to be sure, to make up his deficiencies."

19 Isabella Shaw of Belfast, a temperance and women's rights activist, wrote a poem "on a true story" for *The Irish Templar* 6, no. 1 (March 1882): 13, that is typical of "true to life" temperance poetry which takes abuse and blood as central motifs.

> And instead of a kindly greeting
> She is struck a cowardly blow,

>And she reels and falls insensible,
>Then the life-red blood begins to flow.
>And gush in a crimson tide,
>Till the baby resting on her breast
>Is almost choked in its mother's blood,
>As close to her heart it's press'd.
>Then shun the sparkling wine cup,
>Look not when it is red;
>Touch not the gambler's dice box,
>You see to what it led.
>last verse ...
>Changing man into a demon,
>Killing a loving wife,
>Spreading death and desolation,
>Causing tears, and blood, and strife.

20 Bewsher, "A Narrow Escape," 84. Emphasis in original.

21 Ibid. A very similar tale, "A Priceless Jewel," *The Irish Templar* 3, no. 10 (December 1879) 153–4, tells of a wife who accuses her drunken husband of killing her: "'Look my husband what you have done' ... she made a last dying effort to save him from his tyrannic foe." But this one has a different twist. The wife is not an innocent victim. As she tells her daughter Nell, "'but I am justly punished ... On our marriage day ... [I] handed him the wine to toast our future health, and – my God, it has come to this.'"

22 "What Love Can Do," *The Irish Temperance League Journal* 12, no. 1 (January 1874): 14.

23 "The Baby in the Brown Cottage," *The Irish Templar* 5, no. 1 (March 1881): 9-12; "Lily of Hurstdale," *The Monthly Messenger* 20, no. 8 (August 1876): 124-6; Mrs Ellen Ross, "Marty's Christmas Present," *The Monthly Messenger* 20, no. 12 (December 1876): 183–5; and Louisa C. Keegan, "Annie Miller," *The Monthly Messenger* 24, no. 6 (June 1880): 88-92 all contain the same elements of a drunken father and self-sacrificing female children. In the three *Monthly Messenger* stories the young daughters all die and their remorseful fathers swear to give up the drink. In "Lily of Hurstdale" the following passage foreshadows the heroine's eventual death. "Father, if my dying would make you never touch drink again, I would gladly die for it" (125). Her death was the cause of her father's redemption. In the deathbed scene she persuaded him, for her sake and his own, to give up alcohol. As with Martha Newton, Lily was described as having "not suffered in vain." Her sacrifice brought about her father's salvation.

24 This was a very popular element in American women's temperance work in the late nineteenth and early twentieth centuries. Girls in many states,

particularly in the Midwest, signed pledges to refuse the attentions of any young man who would not sign a temperance pledge. "Maggie's Resolve," written by Nancy Nelson is set in a farming community in County Down. This story contains the "lips that touch liquor will never touch mine" message within a rural Ulster setting. Maggie's resolve, of course, ensures she finds a strong, sober and upstanding mate, one who is susceptible to her good influence. Nancy Nelson, "Maggie's Resolve," *Everybody's Monthly* 3, no. 3 (November 1909): 62-3.

25 The metre of works such as "Johnny McCree," and "Miss Angelina Parker" also indicates that they were meant to be read aloud at temperance gatherings.

26 Uncle Edward, "Miss Angelina Parker," *The Irish Temperance League Journal* 34, no. 6 (June 1896): 91, also reprinted in *The Christian Advocate* (14 August 1896): 395.

27 See M.A. Fulton, "Bootlaces," *Everybody's Monthly* 3, no. 2 (October 1908): 35 and M.A. Fulton, "Her Lonely Christmas," *Everybody's Monthly* 7, no. 5 (January 1913): 108.

28 Uncle Edward, 91.

29 See, for example, T., "Laura's Vow," *The Christian Advocate* (5 February 1892): 62 and Nelson, 62–3.

30 *The Irish Temperance League Journal* 1, no. 2 (February 1863): 15.

31 M.L., "Woman's Rights," *The Irish Templar* 4, no. 12 (February 1881): 183.

32 John Pyper, "Belfast Ladies' Temperance Union," *The Irish Temperance League Journal* 14, no. 3 (March 1876): 37.

33 "An Appeal for Woman's Influence and Aid," *The Irish Temperance League Journal* 12, no. 10 (October 1874): 153–4. See also "Total Abstinence. From a Woman's Point of View," *The Christian Advocate* (7 May 1897): 219, in which a woman's drunkenness was described as having "utterly obliterated the Divine image which was stamped upon her."

34 "The British Association," *The Irish Temperance League Journal* 12, no. 10 (October 1874): 158. For a discussion of the increase in female drunkenness, see "A National Shame. Drunken Women," reprinted in *The Church of Ireland Temperance Visitor* 24, no. 11 (November 1892): 166 and J.N. Spence, "By Night on the City Streets," *The Christian Advocate* (6 February 1914): 65.

35 Ibid.

36 "Report of a paper given by William Caine," *The Irish Temperance League Journal* 12, no. 10 (October 1874): 159-60.

37 Annie, "A Woman's Protest and Impeachment," *The Irish Templar* 1, no. 7 (September 1877): 128.

38 See Henry Osborne, "To Lads and Lasses," *The Irish Temperance League Journal* 1, no. 1 (February 1863): 32. "Now, if there be one thing more

awful than a drunken man, it is – what think ye? It is, *a drunken woman.* O, lasses! Ye expect to be wives and mothers, and to have houses of your own. Let me kindly tell you the best thing to begin housekeeping with. It is A STRICT HABIT OF TEMPERANCE." Emphasis in original.

39 Mrs M.A. Paull, "Our Bill at the Grocers," *The Irish Temperance League Journal* 12, no. 10 (October 1874): 162. A pledge to boycott grocers who sold intoxicants was part of the IWTU's campaign. See "A Women's Causerie," *The Christian Advocate* (18 September 1896): 445, 9 October 1896: 481, and "Do women tipple secretly?" reprinted in *The Church of Ireland Temperance Visitor* 15, no. 10 (October 1893): 155.

40 Ibid.

41 Henry H. Grant, "Suckled on Gin," *The Irish Temperance League Journal* 29, no. 7 (July 1891): 97.

42 See "How Female Drunkenness Affects the Children," *The Christian Advocate* (2 February 1900): 50.

43 Ibid. See also Maude Lutton, "Teddy's Mother," *The Christian Advocate* (12 July 1901): 330.

44 "Womanly Influence," *The Irish Temperance League Journal* 19, no. 12 (March 1881): 29.

45 Ibid.

46 "Total Abstinence," 219 and Whitla, *Thoughts from Sinai*, 13, 35.

47 Rosina H. Sadler, "A Woman's Story," *The Irish Temperance League Journal* 20, no 6 (June 1882): 73. Emphasis in original. See also "Little Lucy," reprinted in *The Monthly Messenger* 23, no.1 (January 1879): 10–12.

48 Eliza Lamb, "Temperance Tour in the South of Ireland," *The Irish Temperance League Journal* 29, no. 12 (December 1892): 185. Lamb, an English temperance speaker, was delighted by the positive response that she received from Roman Catholic women in the South. Lamb states that "The women were so demonstrative in their appreciation of my remarks that my gravity was nearly upset by the many benedictions that greeted my ear: – 'The Holy Mother presarve ye!' 'The blessin' of all the saints be on ye!' &c., &c." Visits from foreign temperance organizers such as Lamb were often the occasion for information concerning temperance activities among southern Catholics. When the honourary secretary of the World's Women's Christian Temperance Union toured throughout Ireland, it was reported in the Methodist periodical *The Christian Advocate* that "it is most cheering to learn that a goodly number of Roman Catholic ladies have enlisted under the banner of the W.W.C.T. Union as the outcome of Miss Slack's visit to Ireland, and are now working earnestly to spread the total abstinence cause in dear old Ireland." "Methodist Women's Total Abstinence Union," (May 1896): 216.

49 H.T. Basford, "Comparisons," *The Irish Templar* 5, no. 5 (July 1881): 70.

50 Ibid, 71.

51 H.T. Basford, "Comparisons. Dialogue, No. II," *The Irish Templar* 5, no. 7 (September 1881): 102.

52 Ibid.

53 "How Pat Took the Pledge," *The Church of Ireland Temperance Visitor* 16, no. 7 (July 1894): 104.

54 Ibid.

55 Ibid.

56 Ibid.

57 T. Lightfoot, "The Shadow of Shame," *The Irish Templar* 6, no. 6 (August 1882): 87.

58 Ibid.

59 W.G.L., "To Erin," *The Irish Templar* 3, no. 5, (July 1879): 71. The last verse reads as follows:

> 'Tis the Drink! 'tis the Drink that is blighting my country!
> It rolls o'er the land like a fierce surging tide!
> Blighting homes once so bright, crushing hearts once so happy,
> Drowning brave men and women on every side!
> Oh! Irishmen, haste to the rescue of Erin!
> We have truth on our side; we have help from above!
> Let us drive the Drink traffic from Erin forever,
> And bright days shall dawn on the land that we love.

60 Matthew Russell, "The Amethyst. A Temperance Lecture," *The Irish Monthly* 22, no. 252 (June 1894): 281–2. While Russell argues for temperance throughout this long poem, he says that the "noisy, self-parading sin" of intemperance is the only slur that can fall upon the name of the otherwise blameless Irish. He goes on to call Ireland's enemies "smug hyocrites" who hide within their hearts "far deeper, deadlier guile – / Worse sins than this, though more respectable, Surer, though more decorous, roads to hell" (282). See also John Hannon, "By the Waters of Babylon," *The Irish Monthly* 27, no. 315 (September 1899): 464-5. In this piece, the author bemoans the lost innocence of "Erin's daughters" who have become "girl-bacchantes" in their forced exile in London, "Babylon by the Thames."

61 Ibid., 282.

62 Ibid. Emphasis in original.

63 Ibid., 286.

64 Ibid. See also "That Brutal Vice," *The Irish Monthly* 30, no. 352 (October 1902): 581–3 and Katherine Tynan, "Erin Aroon: A Temperance Song," *The Irish Monthly* 37, no. 428 (February 1909): 111.

65 Ibid., 287–8. Emphasis in original.

66 Ibid., 286.

67 "An Appeal for Woman's Influence and Aid," *The Irish Temperance League Journal* 12, no. 10 (October 1874): 153.

68 John Pyper, "Belfast Ladies' Temperance Union," *The Irish Temperance League Journal* 14, no. 3 (March 1876): 37.

69 "Address to the Women of America," *The Irish Temperance League Journal* 5, no. 6 (June 1874): 95.

70 Westerkamp, "Puritan patriarchy and the problem of revelation," 573.

71 "Temperance Work in Ohio," *The Irish Temperance League Journal* 12, no. 10 (September 1874): 126-7.

72 "Mrs Stewart's Visit," *The Irish Temperance League Journal* 12, no. 4 (April 1874): 66.

73 "Report of the Annual Conference," *The Irish Temperance League Journal* 12, no. 5 (May 1874): 73.

74 Ibid.

75 "Annual Meeting of the Ladies' Temperance Union," *The Irish Temperance League Journal* 1, no.1 (February 1863): 17.

76 "Annual Report of the BWTA," *The Irish Temperance League Journal* 16, no. 6 (June 1878): 78.

77 Ibid.

78 Ibid. See also "Woman's Work," *The Irish Temperance League Journal* 31, no. 3 (March 1893): 41.

79 "Random Shafts," *The Irish Temperance League Journal* 28, no. 11 (November 1890): 241.

80 Henry Lawson, "The Helpless Mothers," reprinted in *The Irish Temperance League Journal* 30, no. 2 (February 1892), p.17. Emphasis in original.

81 Ada E. Ferris, "Woman's Sphere," reprinted in *The Christian Advocate* (11 June 1897): 281. This poem was published in the "A Women's Causerie" column. Eileen, the editor of the column, and Charity Hope both published pieces that were more radical in nature than the general content of *The Christian Advocate*.

82 Ibid.

83 See "What's a Poor Woman to Do?" *Everybody's Monthly* 8, no. 9 (May 1914): 197.

84 The "poet" is Alfred, Lord Tennyson.

85 "An Irish Lady," "Westerly: A Temperance Tale, chapter IX," *The Monthly Messenger* 21 (September 1877): 137.

86 Ulster suffragists like Isabella Tod tried to unite the cause of suffrage and temperance. See "Report of the Irish Temperance League's Annual Meeting," *The Irish Temperance League Journal* 23, no. 2 (February 1885): 39.

CHAPTER EIGHT

1 Mrs Park, "Our Silver Jubilee. Then and Now," *Woman's Work*, n.s., no. 29 (January 1899): 97.

2 Jeffrey, *The Indian Mission of the Irish Presbyterian Church*, 217-8.

3 A.T. Pierson, "Woman's Work for Missions," *Woman's Work* no. 12 (October 1888): 4.

4 Ibid.

5 The full name of this quarterly magazine was *Woman's Work, In connexion with the Foreign Mission of the Presbyterian Church in Ireland, for promoting Christianity among the Women of the East.* The magazine was commonly referred to among Presbyterian churchwomen as "The Pink Paper" because it had a pink cover.

6 Elizabeth Beatty, "Some Helps to Holy Living," *Woman's Work*, n.s., no. 68 (October 1908): 199. Emphasis in original.

7 Pierson, "Woman's Work for Missions," 7.

8 Ibid.

9 "Report of the Annual Meeting," Woman's Work, no. 15 (July 1889): 4–5. See also, Pierson, "Woman's Work for Missions," 7 and A.F., "Our Missions," *The Irish Presbyterian*, n.s., 13, no. 3 (March 1907): 43.

10 Pierson, "Woman's Work for Missions," 7. Emphasis in orignal.

11 George T. Rea, "Some Secular Benefits which Christianity Brings to Women," *Woman's Work*, n.s., no. 8 (October 1893): 186-7.

12 Ibid., 186.

13 *Daybreak: The Children's Missionary Magazine of the Presbyterian Church in Ireland.* Most of the articles in this periodical were written by women in Ulster and women missionaries in India and China.

14 A.O.S., "'Is it for Me?'" *Daybreak* 45 (June 1907): 61. Emphasis in original.

15 Ibid. Emphasis in original.

16 Ibid. Emphasis in original. See also "Zenana Missions (Irish Presbyterian Church) The Story of a Year (1887)," (Belfast: John A. Murphy, 1888): 23 (Irish Presbyterian Historical Society Pamphlet 1148) and Mrs Scott (a missionary's wife in Rajkot, India) "How we conduct Women's Meetings," *Woman's Work*, n.s., no. 17 (January 1896): 114-5.

17 See Rea, 187.

18 Lizzie Macauley's diary, undated entry from 1903. Irish Presbyterian Historical Society.

19 Ibid.

20 Ibid. Elsewhere in an undated entry in her diary, Macauley relates an anecdote of an exchange that took place when a missionary friend of hers was addressing a women's Zenana meeting at home in Ulster. The missionary told her audience that an Indian wife nevers sits down to eat her meal until after her husband and son have finished. The missionary heard one woman at the meeting whisper to another "wee wadna pit up wi' that here." Macauley made no further note about this story, but it is interesting that the whispering woman's words were put in Ulster country dialect.

21 Ibid,. (1 January 1902): 1.

22 Ibid.

23 Pierson, 5.

24 Jeffrey, *The Indian Mission*, 113.

25 Ibid.

26 Ibid., 114.

27 Ibid.

28 "The Women's Auxiliary," *The Christian Advocate* (10 July 1914): 334.

29 Boyd, *Manchuria and Our Mission There*, 79.

30 "Working" in this context meant needlework. The women of this upper-middle class congregation on the Malone Road in Belfast worked on items that they sold at their annual Sale of Work. The money raised at these sales went to support women's missionary endeavours. Addresses on such subjects as missions, temperance, and colportage were given at the association's meetings.

31 Fisherwick Women's Working Association, Minutes, 17 March 1911. [PRO D1812]

32 Boyd, *Manchuria and Our Mission There*, 79.

33 "Zenana Day at the Lucknow Exhibition," *The Christian Advocate* (5 March 1886): 119.

34 Barnes, *Between Life and Death*, 9.

35 American and English literature was frequently reprinted in Ulster missionary publications, especially during the early years when American and English organizations provided models for fledgling Irish Protestant foreign missionary groups.

36 Callaway, *Gender, Culture and Empire*, passim.

37 W.L. Berkeley, *The Church's Duty: A Sermon bearing on the Claims of the Irish Mission* [of the General Assembly of the Presbyterian Church in Ireland] (Belfast: n.p. 1885), 5. See also, Lowry Edmonds Berkeley, *Evangelization in Ireland* (Belfast: The "Witness" Steam Printing Works, 1880), 11.

38 Ibid., 5–6.

39 Ibid., 7.

40 Jellett, *Glimpses of an Indian Dawn*, 7.

41 Ibid., 56.

42 T.L., "The House of the Tragic Burning, Clonmel," *Daybreak* 33, no. 5 (May 1895): 62.

43 Ibid., 63.

44 Ibid.

45 *Seventy-fifth Annual Report of the Scripture Readers' Society for Ireland* (Dublin: n.p. 1896): 38, 48.

46 Irish colporteurs were itinerant Protestant evangelists who sold, or sometimes gave away, Bibles and religious literature among the Catholic population in the South and West of Ireland.

47 "Irish Mission. Report of the Children's Colporteurs, 1907," *Daybreak* 46, no. 2 (February 1908): 17.

48 Thomas Lyle, "What Young Ireland Is Doing for Ireland," *Daybreak* 50, no. 2 (February 1912): 21. See also "A Holy Well," *Daybreak* 47, no. 1 (January 1909): 6-8.

49 Ibid.

50 Ibid.

51 M. McDonagh, "The Church in the Glen," *The Church of Ireland Parochial Magazine*, no. 12 (April 1872): 255. Emphasis in original.

52 Ibid., no. 11 (March 1872): 234.

53 Ibid., no. 16 (August 1872): 73.

54 Ibid.

55 Ibid., no. 14 (June 1872): 33.

56 Ibid.

57 Ibid., no. 12 (April 1872): 256.

58 Ibid., no. 17 (September 1872): 90.

59 Ibid., 91.

60 Ibid.

61 Ibid.

62 Ibid., no. 17 (September 1872): 93.

63 Ibid.

64 Ibid., 94. Poverty in this story refers to both physical and spiritual poverty.

65 Ibid., no. 19 (November 1872): 131.

66 Ibid.

67 Brouwer, *New Women for God*, 52.

68 Mrs Huston, "Stay at Homes," *Woman's Work*, n.s., no. 2 (April 1892): 27. Emphasis in original.

69 Ibid.

70 "Women's Conference on Zenana Mission Work," *Woman's Work*, n.s., no. 23 (July 1897): 242.

71 Ibid.

72 Charity Hope, "King's Daughters in Council. 'Our Own Missionary' Scheme Discussed," *The Christian Advocate* (8 February 1901): 68.

73 The council sponsored several OOMS over the years, printing in full in the column all of their letters from the mission field.

74 M.C.B., "A Message to All Zenana Mission Helpers," *Woman's Work*, n.s., no. 16 (October 1895): 96. Emphasis in original. See also "Report of the Annual Meeting," *Woman's Work*, n.s., no. 55 (July 1905): 145-8, for a typical description of the activities of the auxiliaries.

75 See Charity Hope, "King's Daughters in Council. The Simple Life," *The Christian Advocate* (19 May 1905): 237.

76 E.F., "A Plea for Boxes," *Woman's Work*, n.s., no. 4 (October 1892): 91.

77 Ibid.

78 "Zenana Conference," *Woman's Work*, n.s., no. 1 January 1892): 2.

79 Ibid.

80 Miss McCallum, "Holding the Lamp," *Woman's Work*, n.s., no. 52 (October 1904): 92.

81 For a scathing indictment of a hypocritical young woman who allowed her work for missions to slide after her marriage, see Maud Lutton, "Passed On," *The Christian Advocate* (13 April 1906): 180iii.

82 Practically every issue of *Woman's Work* and *India's Women and China's Daughters* contained stories of this type, usually taken from missionaries' letters.

83 Fisherwick Women's Working Association, Minutes, 17 March 1911. [PRO D1812]

84 Ibid.

85 "The Voices of the Women," *Woman's Work*, no. 24 (October 1891): 19.

86 Ibid., 20.

87 Ibid., 21-2.

88 Ibid., 22.

89 Charity Hope, "King's Daughters in Council. There's Blue Sky Beyond," *The Christian Advocate* (19 April 1901): 188.

90 Ibid.

91 Ibid.

92 Ibid.

93 "Report of the Annual Meeting," *Woman's Work*, no. 15 (July 1889): 5.

94 See A.P. "Pray for Us," *Woman's Work*, n.s., no. 11 (July 1894): 219 and "Letter from Miss Nicholson," *Woman's Work*, no. 17 (January 1890): 9.

95 "A Mother," "An Appeal to Mothers," *Woman's Work*, no. 20 (October 1890): 7.

96 Ibid. See also "One of the Daughters," "A Plea," *Woman's Work*, n.s., no. 6 (April 1893): 123, and "Lines Addressed by Miss Alevina Mackay to her Mother," *Woman's Work*, n.s., no. 32 (October 1899): 170.

97 "Only for Those Weary in Well-doing," *Woman's Work*, no. 64 (October 1907): 74.

98 Ibid.

99 A.H., "At Home," *Woman's Work*, n.s., no. 10 (April 1894): 217.

100 Ibid. See also S.T.F., "For a Mission Work Party," *Woman's Work*, n.s., no. 58 (April 1906): 237; Huston, 28; "Hibernian Auxiliary," *India's Women and China's Daughters* (February 1900): 43; and Charity Hope, "King's Daughters in Council," *The Christian Advocate* (9 September 1910): 430.

CONCLUSION

1 Fitzpatrick, "Review Article," 269.
2 Ulster in general was sometimes referred to as "the Black North" by Irish Catholics. See An Irish Soggarth [pseud.], "In the Black North a Hundred Years Ago," *The Irish Monthly* 30, no. 347 (May 1902): 272–85.

Bibliographic Essay

The history of Irish women is just beginning to be told. In a historiography obsessed with battles and wars, leaders and losers, women's history has, until very recently, received short shrift. Even with the coming to fruition of much new research in Irish women's history, the subject of women and religion in Ireland has remained relatively unexplored. This *terra incognita* is attracting attention for quite compelling reasons. In an article appraising the current state of writing on the history of Irish women, Maria Luddy states, "It is almost impossible to examine nineteenth-century Irish women without first of all acknowledging the important role religion played in their lives" (Luddy, "An Agenda for Women's History," 20). Yet Irish women's history, particularly in its infancy, has focused primarily on political issues such as suffrage and on the lives of "great" women like Anna Parnell and Countess Markiewicz. This is perfectly understandable given the feminist agenda of most of those who write in the field. In a 1991 review article, David Fitzpatrick observes that "the struggle to eliminate legal and political discrimination against women continues to preoccupy many feminist historians" (Fitzpatrick, "Women, gender and the writing of Irish history," 269). The subject of women and religion in Ireland is one which is only beginning to attract, in earnest, the interest of Irish scholars. The pieces considered in this review of the literature on women and religion in Ireland vary greatly in their scope and in their focus. Some are organizational studies while others examine piety and religious practice. Thus this small, but vibrant, literature is not readily discussed as "a literature," yet what follows is an attempt to assess some of its central features.

The few works that have been written on this subject have fallen, broadly, into the same historiographic trends that may be seen in the writing of Western women's history. Because of the centrality of the concept of the "cult of domesticity" to the present work, I use American research in this field as an example of major trends in Western women's history. In the 1970s, groundbreaking studies by major historians of women, such as Barbara Welter, emphasized the oppression of women by a patriarchal society. For these early feminist scholars the hallmark of the cult of domesticity was patriarchal oppression. Welter saw the antebellum bourgeois American woman as a "bird in a gilded cage"; confined to a limited sphere by the ethos of the "cult of domesticity." Later writers such as Nancy Cott shifted the emphasis of American women's history away from the earlier "damage" or "victim" model. These historians saw the cult of domesticity containing the potential for women to create bonds of sisterhood in their separate "women's sphere" that would become the foundation for female consciousness and the nascent feminist movement. These new social historians also saw the designation of women as the moral guardians of the nation as being potentially empowering, for women's sense of "holy mission" eventually brought about their participation in evangelical religion and the formation of female-dominated reform societies and educational institutions. Thus writers in this "empowerment" school saw women as active agents in forging their own destiny.

Margaret MacCurtain and Donncha Ó Corráin's 1978 collection, *Women in Irish Society: The Historical Dimension*, was a generative work in Irish history. One of the essays in this collection addressed an aspect of the subject of Irish women and religion. In an essay titled "Women and the Church since the Famine," Professor J.J. Lee skilfully considers the changes that occurred in women's status after the famine, how their economic worth fell with fewer employment opportunities, and how a rigid marriage market and the materialism of the strong farmer class encouraged emigration and low marriage rates in Ireland. The Irish clergy, Lee asserts, failed to see the connection between high emigration, which they deplored, and the dissemination of the materialistic values of the "respectable" farming class through their own institutions. According to Lee, Protestant and Catholic clergy (who were drawn, overwhelmingly, from the tenant farmer class) had their strong class biases reinforced at Trinity and Maynooth. "It is one of the ironies of the intellectual history of modern Ireland that at a period when Catholic propagandists lovingly portrayed everybody as out-of-step except our Paddy, and when they were prone to denounce England as decadent, they imbibed unconsciously, as their Protestant brothers did more consciously, the prudish values of Victorian middle-class morality, with simultaneously idealised and repressed women" (Lee, "Women and the Church since the Famine," 40). Lee does not provide any evidence of this "repression." In the "Notes and Further Reading" section at the end of the article Lee does not include any material written by women. The two contemporary accounts that he recommends to readers looking for information on this subject were written by Catholic priests. What is this assumption of "repression" based on, then? Lee seems to be relying rather heavily on the conventional wisdom circa 1978 concerning women and the churches. In women's history circles at that time the repressive nature of bourgeois Christianity was a given.

Lee's treatment of the diffusion of Victorian "prudery" throughout Catholic Ireland is particularly revealing. He links the disappearance of Gaelic culture with an increase in "prudery" and the repression of women. Furthermore, he equates evangelicism – he notes that it was not only the Protestants of Trinity College who "succumbed to evangelicism" but that their Catholic counterparts at Maynooth "succumbed" as well – with middle-class morality and "prudery." I would not venture to argue that the cultural trends outlined by Lee in this article did not occur as he describes. Yet his barely concealed contempt for the "prudery" of evangelicism and all that he assumes it entailed causes one to wonder if his summary rejection of the values of evangelicals, both Catholic and Protestant, at this early stage in the writing of women's history in Ireland, thwarted potential research in this area. Lee decries the fact that "the physical realism of the Irish love poems as late as the eighteenth century ... was notably absent from the sentimental slush that passed as love songs in English in post-Famine Ireland" ("Women and the Church since the Famine," 40). Clearly, the culture of an anglicised late Victorian Ireland is one for which he has little use. No doubt moral "prudery" was very common in late Victorian and Edwardian Ireland, but did it alone define the understanding of Christian womanhood that was being worked out by Protestants and Catholics, men and women? Their voices are not heard in this admittedly brief, exploratory article. Nonetheless, their creed is effectively dismissed as being patently repressive – a tool used against women.

Clearly, Lee's essay fits into the "damage" school that dominated women's history in the 1970s. The victimization of women by patriarchal religious, political, and economic systems was the focus of the research done in this period, almost to the exclusion of other lines of inquiry.

Since Lee's seminal 1978 article was published, important work has been done on the subject of women and religion in Ireland. The only published monograph entirely devoted to this topic, however, is

Caitríona Clear's *Nuns in Nineteenth-Century Ireland*. In Clear's work we can see a shift away from the "damage" school of early women's history to the "empowerment" model which comes to dominate the writing of women's history in the 1980s. Clear accomplishes this without invalidating the pioneering work done in early writing on women and patriarchy. According to Clear, "Nuns were, without doubt, an institutional embodiment of the caring, self-sacrificing and essentially subordinate woman, and their existence played a strong part in perpetuating this image. To categorise them as just that – empty vessels into which pliable wax was poured, pet puppets of patriarchy – is to dismiss as valueless the `invisible' caring and maintenance work which they performed, and which women traditionally carry out. It is to disown most of our female ancestors and the majority of our contemporaries." (Clear, *Nuns in Nineteenth-Century Ireland*, 166). In her assessment of the actions of the Irish nuns she studied, Clear comes to the conclusion that they were not merely passive victims of fate. These women brought to life by Clear's research made choices, employed survival strategies, and made their way in life as best they knew how.

While the subject of Clear's work is women religious, it does provide us with several important insights into the lives of lay Catholic women and the influence that the phenomenal expansion of convents in nineteenth-century Ireland had on the Catholic laity. According to Clear, nuns spread "the culture of the middles classes" and an "increasingly formalised, ultramontane, and canonical (as opposed to customary) Catholicism" among the Catholic poor and among Catholic women of all classes (Ibid., 157). Clear points out the lack of coordinated social action amongst Catholic lay women and blames this trend, in part on the high degree to which nuns controlled Catholic philanthropic work and to the weaknesses of the Catholic social action movement. "The profusion of socially active communities of women religious," Clear observes, "played its part in delaying the development of a Catholicism which was progressively socially conscious" (Ibid., 150, 160). Clear seems concerned by the lack of "gender identity" among nuns – she says the nature of their work caused nuns to form an identity that was primarily religious – and speculates that this lack of gender identity on the part of Irish nuns retarded the development of active, coordinated groups of Irish lay women. While Clear is obviously concerned by the lack of "female consciousness" amongst Irish nuns (in much feminist historical writing the author hopes to discover a hidden feminist agenda in the lives of his or her subjects), Clear asserts the validity of investigating the lives of these traditional, non-feminist women. By way of support, Clear quotes Anna Davin, who noted that "the study of struggle should look for where women *did* struggle, instead of

denouncing them for their absence from male-dominated organisations" (165).

In her recent article in *Irish Historical Studies*, Maria Luddy echoes
Clear's conclusions regarding the interrelationship between the roles
of nuns and those of lay Catholic women. "The overpowering importance of convents to the religious life of Catholic females may," Luddy
posits, "have had a detrimental effect on the involvement of lay
Catholic women in social life" ("An Agenda for Women's History in
Ireland, 1500–1900," 24). Lay Catholic women were "conspicuous by
their absence" from the sphere of philanthropic activity which so
concerned their Protestant counterparts. Luddy also notes that the few
philanthropic initiatives made by lay Catholic women were almost all
"eventually given over to the care of nuns" (Ibid., 24). Luddy continues, however, adding that while this dominance of women religious in
Catholic social action may have had significant implications for the
tardy development of a "social consciousness among lay women, it also
had deeper implications for their political awakening" (Ibid., 24).
Luddy's article, like Clear's monograph, exhibits a concern with the
political and social implications of the relationship between nuns and
lay women. This focus on the political ramifications for women of any
historical development, movement, or phenomenon has been a recurring leitmotif in Irish women's history. It does, however, distract
somewhat from the primary question of women and religion.

Historians of religion Margaret MacCurtain and Patrick Corish have
both published brief essays on the subject of Catholic lay women.
MacCurtain's 1990 essay, "Fullness of Life: Defining Female Spirituality in Twentieth-Century Ireland" is really two brief portraits of two very
different Irish Catholic laywomen; noted Blasket Island story-teller Peig
Sayers and Edel Quin, missionary of the Legion of Mary in Africa. The
lives of Sayers and Quin reflect, MacCurtain avers, "two paradigms of
religious culture in twentieth-century Ireland." (MacCurtain "Fullness
of Life," 261). Sayers's spiritual life was rooted in the rural, Gaelic
culture that survived from pre-Famine times, while Quin's Catholicism
was derived from the post-Famine Catholic devotional revolution that
was clearly middle-class and English-speaking. While MacCurtain's
essay provides a fascinating look at the lives of these two women, aside
from a brief overview in the opening pages of the essay of the changes
occurring in Catholic religious practice towards the end of the
nineteenth century, it does not provide much information on "defining
women's spirituality" beyond the confines of its two subjects. I would be
wary of using the lives of these two women as spiritual archetypes; the
one representing traditional Gaelic Catholic spirituality and the other
a model for understanding "modern" Irish Catholicism. That is

perhaps asking too much of the subjects of this article. Nonetheless, it is interesting to note that the focus here is exclusively religious. No political motives or nascent feminist consciousness are attributed to Quin or Sayers.

Corish's 1991 article, published in a collection about Irish women in the early modern period, begins with thoughtful musings on the intangible nature of religious experience and on the significance to Irish Catholic life of "domestic religion." Corish states that he finds it puzzling that while the lives of Irish nuns have received some scholarly attention, Catholic mothers have been virtually ignored. Given the position of awesome influence often attributed to the Irish Catholic mother, Corish notes, this is indeed odd. When discussing eighteenth century "house masses" Corish also states that he finds it strange that "we have been slow to draw what might seem to be the obvious inference, that a `domestic' religion must be a religion very much influenced by women and especially by wives." (Corish, "Women and Religious Practice," 214) In the early modern period, Catholic religious practice was centred on the home – due, chiefly, to the constraints placed on public Catholic worship by the Penal Laws – to an extent unparalleled elsewhere. Corish states that it was only in the nineteenth century that "the `rites of passage' associated with birth, marriage and death left the home for the church." (Ibid., 213). Both Corish and MacCurtain emphasize the positive or "empowering" aspects of the Catholic faith in the lives of women. And both of these essays differ from overtly feminist writing on women and religion by focusing solely on matters of Catholic religious experience.

But what of Protestant laywomen? In their book *Evangelical Protestantism in Ulster Society 1740–1890*, David Hempton and Myrtle Hill have made an outstanding contribution to the topic of women and religion in Ireland. "Born to serve: women and evangelical religion" is the title of a chapter in which they thoughtfully explore such questions as what attracted women to evangelical Protestantism and how did the role of women within Ulster evangelical sects change over time. According to Hempton and Hill, achievements (including preaching and leading meetings) made by women in the eighteenth century during the early stages of the evangelical revival were not sustained into the nineteenth, when males regained full control of these denominations. Powerful roles for women, such as preaching, within these churches, may "be seen as exceptional and transitional rather than officially sanctioned and accepted." (Hempton and Hill, *Evangelical Protestantism in Ulster Society*, 134) In the nineteenth century, however, many opportunities for women had opened up in church-sanctioned philanthropic activities (Ibid., 130).

Like Clear and Luddy, Hempton and Hill ponder the implications of lay women's religious activities for their later social and political achievements. In writing of lay Catholic women, Clear and Luddy deplore the lack of opportunities for Catholic women who were not nuns to develop organizational skills and a sense of gender identity. The situation was considerably different for middle-class Protestant Ulster women. Hempton and Hill view female "church work" as an incubator for women's political and social development. "The network of voluntary societies and organizations which clustered around the religious denominations," Hempton and Hill posit, provided evangelical Protestant Ulster women with the opportunity to engage in social and administrative work (Ibid., 138). They go so far as to assert that "there is much evidence to support the suggestion that evangelical religion was more important than feminism in enlarging women's sphere during the nineteenth century." (Ibid., 129). This enlarging of "women's sphere" through denominationally sanctioned channels of "service" for others did not threaten cherished views of the "naturally" submissive place of women. Rather, Hempton and Hill portray women working within the context of these ascribed gender norms, confident of their ability to influence, for good, those with whom they came in daily contact.

This brings us to another important point about Hempton and Hill's work on Ulster evangelical Protestant women. Unlike the majority of feminist writers who have focused on the differences between men and women and on the creation of a unique "female consciousness," Hempton and Hill hasten to remind us that "although accepted notions of what constituted `natural' female behaviour helped to perpetuate ideal stereotypes, the characteristics upon which they were built, including zealous expressions of piety, excessive spirituality and emotional responses to evangelical sermons, were common both to women and men in this period. In addition, women are no more a cohesive social entity than men and a shared gender does not in itself produce a common experience" (Ibid., 131). In Hempton and Hill's work, the experiences of evangelical Protestant women are located in the context of their communities, churches, and families where affinities of class, creed, and clan were interwoven with the bonds that they may have forged as women with other women.

David Fitzpatrick, in a 1991 review essay, observed that the omissions in the works he was reviewing "express prevalent ideology as well as personal choice. Catholicism, poverty, wage labour and political struggle are emphasised, almost to the exclusion of Protestantism, prosperity, family life and social integration." (Fitzpatrick, "Review Article: Women, gender and the Writing of Irish History," 269) I think that, with the exception of Hempton and Hill's work and that found in a collection of essays published in late 1994 by the Institute for Irish Studies, Fitzpatrick's comment holds true for most of what has been written in Irish women's history in general and in the history of women and religion in Ireland in particular. This is most unfortunate, for, to quote Fitzpatrick again, "the more subtle struggles and accommodations between men and women of other backgrounds, and foregrounds, also requires analysis (Ibid., 270). By examining the creation of ideals of Christian womanhood in Catholic and Protestant literature, it has been my goal to engage with the "subtle struggles and accommodations" that are part of the rich tapestry of human experience.

Bibliography

PRIMARY SOURCES

ASSOCIATION AND PERSONAL DOCUMENTS

Northern Ireland Public Record Office, Belfast (NIPRO)
  Minute Book of the Fisherwick Working Women's Association 1892–1914

Irish Presbyterian Historical Society
  Diary of Lizzie Macauley, missionary to India

NEWSPAPERS AND PERIODICALS

The Banner of Ulster (1851–66)
The Banner of Truth (1851–56)
The Bible Temperance Educator (1882)
The Catholic Bulletin and Book Review (for the first two issues it was called *The Catholic Book Bulletin*) (1911–14)
The Christian Advocate (1885–1914)
The Church of Ireland Magazine (1878)
The Church of Ireland Parochial Magazine (1871–75)
The Church of Ireland Temperance Visitor (1879–86 and 1891–94)
Daybreak: The Children's Missionary Magazine of the Presbyterian Church in Ireland (1873–1914)
Erin's Hope: Irish Church Missions Juvenile Magazine
The Evangelical Witness and Presbyterian Review (1862–71)
Everybody's Monthly (1904–14)

India's Women and China's Daughters (monthly magazine of the Church of
   England Zenana Mission Society) (1880–1901)
The Irish Church Quarterly (1908–1914)
The Irish Monthly Magazine (1873–1914)
The Irish Presbyterian (1853–58 and 1895–1914)
The Irish Presbyterian Sabbath School Teacher (1869)
Irish Temperance League Journal (1863–1903)
The Monthly Messenger (1857–82)
The Presbyterian Churchman (1878–81)
Presbyterian Review (1863–71)
The Primitive Wesleyan Methodist Magazine (1855–56)
Victoria College Magazine (1897–1905)
The Witness (1874, 1876–90, 1892, 1907–13)
Woman's Work (1892–1914)

BOOKS AND PAMPHLETS

Aikenhead, Mary. *Letters of Mary Aikenhead.* Ed. P.M. MacSweeney. Dublin:
   M.H. Gill and Son 1914
A Member of the Order of Mercy. *Leaves from the Annals of the Sisters of Mercy,*
   Vol. I. Ireland. New York: The Catholic Publication Society Co. 1888
Arnold, R.J. *Lois and Eunice.* n.p. 1880
Atkinson, S. *Mary Aikenhead: Her Life, Her Work, and Her Friends. Giving an
   History of the Foundation of the Congregation of the Irish Sisters of Charity.* Dublin:
   M.H. Gill and Son 1879
Baillie, John. *The Revival: or, what I saw in Ireland; with thoughts suggested by the
   same. The result of two personal visits.* London: James Nisbit and Co. 1859
Band of Hope Centenary 1847–1947, Souvenir Handbook. Belfast: Irish Temper-
   ance League 1947
Barnes, Irene H. *Between Life and Death: the Story of the C.E.Z.M.S. Medical Missions
   in India, China, and Ceylon.* London: Church of England Zenana Missionary
   Society 1901
Berkeley, Lowry Edmonds. *Evangelization in Ireland.* Belfast: The "Witness"
   Steam Printing Works 1880
Berkeley, W.L. *The Church's Duty: A Sermon Bearing on the Claims of the Irish
   Mission* [of the General Assembly of the Presbyterian Church in Ireland].
   Belfast: n.p. 1885
Bowman, John A. *Old Gems in a New Setting: a Layman's Researches in Divine
   Truth.* Belfast: Marcus Ward n.d.
Boyd, Robert. *Manchuria and Our Mission There.* Belfast: Wm. Strain & Sons
   1908
A Brief Memorial of Jane Hill. Londonderry: Sentinel Office 1858
Brockman, H.J. *Letter to the Women of England Against the Confessional.* London:
   Protestant Evangelical Mission n.d.

Brooke, Richard Sinclair. *Recollections of the Irish Church.* London: Macmillan and Co. 1877

Brown, Andrew. *Early Faded Flowers: An Inquiry into the State of Such as Die in Infancy.* Belfast: Shepherd and Aitchison 1856

Bryson, John. *The Three Marys of the Four Gospels.* Belfast: Shepherd and Aitchison 1856

Burnside, S.D. *Sexton's Daughter.* Belfast: Alex S. Mayne 1859

Correspondence between the Reverend Wm. MacIlwaine, Incumbent of St. George's Church, Belfast, and the Right Reverend Dr Dorrian, with introductory remarks and notes. Reprinted from the "Belfast News-Letter." Belfast: Printed at the "News-Letter" Office 1865

Crookshank, C.H. *Memorable Women of Irish Methodism in the Last Century.* London: Wesleyan-Methodist Bookroom 1882

Cusack, Mary Francis. *Woman's Work in Modern Society.* London: Longmans, Green, and Co. 1874

The Dairyman's Daughter: A Narrative from Real Life. Dublin: Jones n.d. Reprinted from The Christian Guardian

Dease, Alice. *Good Women of Erin.* London: R. & T. Washbourne 1905

Guthrie, Dr Thomas. *An Address by the Late Dr Guthrie, to the Mothers of England, on one of the Gravest Questions of Modern Times.* Edinburgh: n.p. 1870

Harkness, I.N. *Temperance Papers.* Belfast: A.S. Mayne 1868

Higginson, Miss. "The Infant Class." In the Presbytery of Ards Sabbath School Union, *Report of Sabbath School Conference held in Newtownards on 28th and 29th August, 1911.* Reproduced from "Newtownards Chronicle" of September 2nd and 9th, 1911. n.p.: 1911

Houston, Robert. *Sketches from My Notebook: A Record of Facts, Illustrative of Methodism and Ministerial Life in Ireland.* London: Wesleyan Conference Office n.d.

Jellett, Miss E.M.C. *Glimpses of an Indian Dawn, A Sketch for Children of the Work of the Dublin University Mission in Chota Nagpur.* Dublin: Sealy, Bryers & Walker 1912

Kind Words for the Kitchen: or, Pleasing One's Self. Second edition. London: Jarrold & Sons n.d.

Martin, Mrs James. *Keepers at Home: A Word to my Working Sisters.* Belfast: C. Aitchison 1868

McCarthy, Micheal J.F. *Priests and People in Ireland.* Dublin: Hoggis, Figgis & Co. 1902

McKenna, L. *An Irish Catholic Women's League.* Dublin: The "Irish Messenger" Office 1917

MacSorley, Catherine Mary. *Ireland and Her Church: A Simple History for Children.* Dublin: Association for Promoting Christian Knowledge n.d.

Memorials of Mrs Mary Smith, and her sister Miss Smith, Late of Donaghadee. Londonderry: Sentinel Office 1858

Morgan, James. *Rome and the Gospel.* Belfast: W. McComb 1854

Month of Mary; or, meditations for each day of the Month of May, calculated to inspire devotion to the Most Holy Mother of God: revised by a Catholic Priest. Third edition. Dublin: James Duffy 1864

Mursell, Arthur. *Mary, The Mother of Jesus.* n.p., n.d.

Nolan, John. *The Rector and Purgatory: A Study on the Eschatology of the Trinity.* Belfast: The Catholic Book Co. 1911

O'Brien, Mrs William. *Unseen Friends.* London: Longmans 1912

O'Connell, Mrs Morgan John. *Glimpses of a Hidden Life: Memories of Attie O'Brien.* Dublin: M.H. Gill and Son 1887

Patterson, R.J. *Catch-My-Pal: A Story of Good Samaritanship.* London: Hodder and Stoughton 1912

Rules for the Associations of Men and Women in Honour of the Sacred Heart of Jesus. Dublin: Dollard Ltd. 1883

Russell, Matthew. *Emannuel A Book of Eucharistic Verses.* Dublin: M.H. Gill and Son 1885

− *Erin, Verses Irish and Catholic.* Dublin: M.H. Gill and Son 1881

− *The Harp of Jesus.* Dublin: M.H. Gill and Son 1890

− *Madonna: Verses on Our Lady and the Saints.* Dublin: M.H. Gill and Son 1880

− *Rose Kavanagh and Her Verses.* Dublin: M.H Gill and Son 1909

− *The Three Sisters of Lord Russell of Killowen and their Convent Life.* London: Longmans 1912

Seventy-fifth Annual Report of the Scripture Readers' Society for Ireland. Dublin: n.p. 1896

Sheehan, P.A. *Mary, the Mother of God.* Dublin: Catholic Truth Society 1901

Smith, George Hill. *The Best Safeguards for a Young Man.* Dublin: John Robertson 1860

Smithson, Annie M.P. *The Walk of a Queen.* Cork: the Mercier Press n.d.

Tales of the Festivals. Dublin: Catholic Truth Society 1901

Taylor, Jeremy. *The Rule and Exercise of Holy Living.* London: James Parker and Co. n.d. [the author was Lord Bishop of Down, Connor and Dromore]

Taylor, Fanny. *Irish Homes and Irish Hearts.* London: Longmans, Green, and Co. 1867

Tod, Isabella M.S. *Advanced Education for Girls of the Upper and Middle Classes.* London: W.W. Head 1867

Tynan, Katharine. *A Nun: Her Friends and Her Order: Being a Sketch of the Life of Mother Mary Xaveria Fallon Sometime Superior-General of the Institute of the Blessed Virgin in Ireland and its Dependencies.* London: Kegan Paul, Trench, Trubner & Co 1891

− *Father Matthew.* London: Macdonald and Evans 1908

− *The Middle Years.* London: Constable 1916

− *Twenty-five Years: Reminiscences.* London: John Murray 1913

Whitla, Ada. *Remember Lot's Wife.* Belfast: Wm. Strain and Sons 1903

– *The Sisters, A.D. 33. You Sisters, A.D. 1902.* Belfast: Wm. Strain & Sons 1902
– *Thoughts from Sinai.* Belfast: Wm. Strain and Son 1904
Will you help us? The Story of the Belfast Women's Temperance Association and Christian Worker's Union. n.p. 1933

SECONDARY SOURCES

Adams, J.R.R. *The Printed Word and the Common Man: Popular Culture in Ulster, 1700–1900.* Belfast: Institute for Irish Studies 1987

Akenson, D.H. *Small Differences. Irish Catholics and Irish Protestants, 1815–1922: An International Perspective.* Kingston and Montreal: McGill-Queen's University Press 1988

Angerman, Arina et al., eds. *Current Issues in Women's History.* London: Routledge 1989

Armstrong, Karen. *The Gospel According to Woman: Christianity's Creation of the Sex War in the West.* London: Pan 1987

Barkley, John. "'The Christian Irishman' and Its Predecessors." *The Christian Irishman* (December 1982): 16–20

Bebbington, David W. *Evangelicalism in Modern Britain: A History from the 1730s to the 1980s.* London: Unwin and Hyman 1989

Benko, Stephen. *The Virgin Goddess: Studies in the Pagan and Christian Roots of Mariology.* New York: E.J. Brill 1993

Bergamasco, Lucia. "Female Education and Spiritual Life: The Case of Ministers' Daughters." In *Current Issues in Women's History,* edited by Arina Angerman et al., 39–60. London: Routledge 1989

Blumin, Stuart M. *The Emergence of the Middle Class: Social Experience in the American City, 1760–1900.* Cambridge: Cambridge University Press 1989

Boff, Leonardo. *The Maternal Face of God: The Feminine and Its Religious Expressions.* San Francisco: Harper and Row 1987

Bourke, Joanna. "'The Best of All Home Rulers': The Economic Power of Women in Ireland, 1880–1914." *Irish Economic and Social History* 18 (1991): 34–47

Brady, Anna. *Women in Ireland, an Annotated Bibliography.* Westport, CN: Greenwood Press 1988

Breathnach, Eibhlín. "Charting New Waters: Women's Experience in Higher Education, 1879–1908." In *Girls Don't Do Honours: Irish Women in Education in the 19th and 20th Centuries,* edited by Mary Cullen, 55–78. Dublin: Women's Education Bureau 1987

Brookes, Barbara. "Women and Reproduction c.1860–1919." In *Labour and Love: Women's Experience of Home and Family, 1850–1940,* edited by Jane Lewis, 149–74. Oxford: Basil Blackwell 1986

Brouwer, Ruth Compton. *New Women for God: Canadian Presbyterian Women and India Missions, 1876–1914.* Toronto: University of Toronto Press 1990

Burman, Sandra, ed. *Fit Work for Women.* London: Croom Helm 1979

Caherty, Therese. *More Missing Pieces: her story of Irish women.* Dublin: Attic 1985

Callaway, Helen. *Gender, Culture and Empire.* New York: Macmillan Press 1987

Carmichael, Kay. "Protestantism and Gender." In *Sermons and Battle Hymns: Protestant Popular Culture in Modern Scotland,* edited by Graham Walker and Tom Gallagher, 213–30. Edinburgh: Edinburgh University Press 1990

Cassidy, James F. *The Old Irish Love of the Blessed Virgin Mary Queen of Ireland.* Dublin: M.H. Gill and Son 1933

Clarke, Brian P. *Piety and Nationalism: Lay Voluntary Associations and the Creation of an Irish-Catholic Community in Toronto, 1850–1895.* Montreal and Kingston: McGill-Queen's University Press 1993

Clarkson, L.A. "Population Change and Urbanisation, 1821–1911." In *An Economic History of Ulster, 1820–1939,* edited by Líam Kennedy and Philip Ollerenshaw, 137–57. Manchester: Manchester University Press 1985

Clear, Caitríona. *Nuns in Nineteenth-Century Ireland.* Dublin: Gill and Macmillan 1987

Cominos, Peter T. "Innocent Femina Sensuales in Unconscious Conflict." In *Suffer and Be Still: Women in the Victorian Age,* edited by Martha Vicinus, 155–77. Indiana: University of Indiana Press 1972

Concannon, Mrs Thomas. *Daughters of Banba.* Dublin: n.p. 1922

Condren, Mary. *The Serpent and the Goddess: Women, Religion and Power in Celtic Ireland.* New York: Harper and Row 1989

Connell, Kenneth Hugh. *Irish Peasant Society: Four Historical Essays.* Oxford: Clarendon Press 1968

Connolly, S.J. "Religion and History." *Irish Economic and Social History* 10 (1983): 79–80

Coon, Lynda L., Katherine J. Haldane, and Elisabeth W. Sommer, eds. *That Gentle Strength: Historical Perspectives on Women in Christianity.* Charlottesville: University Press of Virginia 1990

Corish, Patrick J. "Women and Religious Practice." In *Women in Early Modern Ireland,* edited by Mary O'Dowd and Mararet MacCurtain, 212–20. Dublin: Wolfhound Press 1991

Cott, Nancy F. *The Bonds of Womanhood: "Women's Sphere" in New England, 1780–1835.* New Haven: Yale University Press 1977

Cullen, Mary, ed. *Girls Don't Do Honours: Irish Women in Education in the Nineteenth and Twentieth Centuries.* Dublin: Women's Education Bureau 1987

Curtain, Chris et al., eds. *Gender in Irish Society.* Galway: Galway University Press 1987

Daly, Mary. *Beyond God the Father.* Boston: Beacon Press 1973

Daly, Mary E. *The Great Famine in Ireland.* Dundalk: Dundalgan Press for the Dublin Historical Association 1986

Daly, Miriam. "Women in Ulster." In *Irish Women: Image and Achievement,* edited by Eiléan Ní Chuilleanáin, 51–60. Dublin: Arlen House, The Women's Press 1985

DeBerg, Betty A. *Ungodly Women: Gender and the First Wave of American Fundamentalism.* Minneapolis: Fortress Press 1990

Dolan, J.P. *Catholic Revivalism: The American Experience, 1830–1900.* Notre Dame: University of Notre Dame Press 1978

Douglas, Anne. *The Feminization of American Culture.* New York: Avon Books 1977

Doyle, C.M. *Women in Ancient and Modern Ireland.* Dublin: Kenny Press 1917

Epstein, Barbara Leslie. *The Politics of Domesticity: Women, Evangelism, and Temperance in Nineteenth-Century America.* Middletown, CN: Wesleyan University Press 1981

Fahey, Tony. "Nuns in the Catholic Church in Ireland in the Nineteenth Century." In *Girls Don't Do Honours: Irish Women in Education in the 19th and 20th centuries,* edited by Mary Cullen, 7–30. Dublin: Women's Education Bureau 1987

Fiorenza, Elisabeth Schüssler. *In Memory of Her: A Feminist Theological Reconstruction of Christian Origins.* London: SCM Press 1983

Fiorenza, Elisabeth Schüssler and Mary Collins, eds. *Women: Invisible in Church and Theology.* Edinburgh: Concilium 1985

Fitzpatrick, David. "The Modernisation of the Irish Female." In *Rural Ireland, 1600–1900: Modernisation and Change,* edited by Patrick O'Flanagan, Paul Ferguson, and Kevin Whelan, 162–80. Cork: Cork University Press 1987

– "Review Article: Women, Gender and the Writing of Irish history." *Irish Historical Studies* 27, no. 107 (May 1991): 267–73

Fox-Genovese, Elizabeth. *Within the Plantation Household: Black and White Women of the Old South.* Chapel Hill: University of North Carolina Press 1988

Garcia, Jo, and Sara Maitland. *Walking on the Water: Women Talking about Spirituality.* London: Virago 1983

Gorham, Deborah. "The Ideology of Feminity in Reading for Girls, 1850–1914." In *Lessons for Life: The Schooling of Girls and Women, 1850–1950,* edited by Felicity Hunt, 39–50. Oxford: Basil Blackwell 1987

Greeley, Andrew M. *The Mary Myth: On the Femininity of God.* New York: The Seabury Press 1977

Hall, Catherine. "The Early Formation of Victorian Domestic Ideology." In *Fit Work for Women,* edited by Sandra Burman, 15–32. London: Croom Helm 1979

Halttunen, Karen. *Confidence Men and Painted Women: A Study of Middle-class Culture in America, 1830–1870.* New Haven: Yale University Press 1982

Hardesty, Nancy A. *Your Daughters Shall Prophesy: Revivalism and Feminism in the Age of Finney.* New York: Carlson 1991

Harris, Barbara J. *Beyond Her Sphere: Women and the Professions in American History.* Westport, CN: Greenwood Press 1978

Hempton, David. "Evangelicalism in English and Irish Society, 1780–1840," in *Evangelicalism: Comparative Studies of Popular Protestantism in North America, The British Isles, and Beyond, 1700–1990*, edited by Mark A. Noll, David W. Bebbington, and George A. Rawlyk, 156–76. New York: Oxford University Press 1994

Hempton, David, and Myrtle Hill. *Evangelical Protestantism in Ulster Society 1740–1890*. London: Routledge 1992

– "Women and Protestant Minorities in Eighteenth-Century Ireland." In *Women in Early Modern Ireland*, edited by Mary O'Dowd and Mararet MacCurtain, 197–211. Dublin: Wolfhound Press 1991

Hepburn, A.C. "Work, Class and Religion in Belfast, 1871–1911." *Irish Economic and Social History* 10 (1983): 33–50

Holmes, Janice. "Lifting the Curtain on Popular Religion: Women, Laity, and Language in the Ulster Revival of 1859." Master's thesis, Queen's University, Kingston 1991

Hunt, Felicity, ed. *Lessons for Life: The Schooling of Girls and Women, 1850–1950*. Oxford: Basil Blackwell 1987

Inglis, Tom. *Moral Monopoly: The Catholic Church in Modern Irish Society*. Dublin: Gill and Macmillan 1987

Keenan, Desmond. *The Catholic Church in Nineteenth Century Ireland: A Sociological Study*. Dublin: Gill and Macmillan 1983

Kennedy, Líam. "The Rural Economy, 1820–1914." In *An Economic History of Ulster, 1820–1939*, edited by Líam Kennedy and Philip Ollerenshaw, 1–61. Manchester: Manchester University Press 1985

Kerr, Donal. "The Early Nineteenth Century: Patterns of Change." In *Irish Spirituality*, edited by Michael Maher, 135–44. Dublin: Veritas Publications 1981

Larkin, Emmet. "The Devotional Revolution in Ireland." *American Historical Review* 80 (1972): 625–52

Lee, J.J. "Women and the Church since the Famine." In *Women in Irish Society: The Historical Dimension*, edited by Margaret MacCurtain and Donncha Ó Corráin, 37–45. Dublin: Arlen House, The Women's Press 1978

Lewis, Donald M. "'Lights in Dark Places': Women Evangelists in Early Victorian Britain, 1838–1857." In *Women in the Church*, edited by W.J. Sheils and Diane Wood, 415–27. Oxford: Basil Blackwell 1990

Lewis, Jane, ed. *Labour and Love: Women's Experience of Home and Family, 1850–1940*. Oxford: Basil Blackwell 1986

Longley, Edna. *From Cathleen to Anorexia: The Breakdown of Irelands*. Dublin: Attic Press 1990

Luddy, Maria. "An Agenda for Women's History in Ireland, 1500–1900. Part II: 1800–1900." *Irish Historical Studies* 28, no. 109 (May 1992): 19–37

– "Prostitution and Rescue Work in Nineteenth Century Ireland." In *Women Surviving: Studies in Irish Women's History in the 19th and 20th centuries*, edited by Maria Luddy and Cliona Murphy, 51–84. Dublin: Poolbeg Press 1990

- "Women and Charitable Organisations in Nineteenth-Century Ireland." *Women's Studies International Forum* 11, no. 4 (1988): 301–5

- *Women and Philanthropy in Nineteenth-Century Ireland.* Cambridge: Cambridge University Press 1995

Maitland, Sara. *Map of the New Country: Women and Christianity.* London: Routledge and Kegan Paul 1983

MacCurtain, Margaret. "Fullness of Life: Defining Female Spirituality in Twentieth Century Ireland." In *Women Surviving: Studies in Irish Women's History in the 19th and 20th Centuries,* edited by Maria Luddy and Cliona Murphy, 233–63. Dublin: Poolbeg Press 1990

- "Towards an Appraisal of the Religious Image of Women." *Crane Bag* 4 (1980): 26–30

- "Women: Part of the Laity?" In *Pobal: The Laity in Ireland,* edited by Seán MacRéamoinn, 54–64. Dublin: The Columba Press 1986

MacCurtain, Margaret, and Donncha Ó Corráin, eds. *Women in Irish Society: The Historical Dimension.* Dublin: Arlen House, The Women's Press 1978

McCormick, Rita W. *Your Daughters Shall Prophesy.* Belfast: n.p. 1979

McLeod, Hugh. *Class and Religion in the Late Victorian City.* Hamden, CN: Archon Books 1974

Maher, Michael, ed. *Irish Spirituality.* Dublin: Veritas Publications 1981

Malmgreen, Gail, ed. *Religion in the Lives of English Women, 1760–1930.* London: Croom Helm 1986

Messenger, Betty. *Picking up the Linen Threads.* Austin: University of Texas Press 1978

Murphy, Cliona. *The Women's Suffrage Movement and Irish Society in the Early Twentieth Century.* New York: Harvester Wheatsheaf 1989

Ní Chuilleanáin, Eiléan, ed. *Irish Women Image and Achievement: Women in Irish Culture from Earliest Times.* Dublin: Arlen House, The Women's Press 1985

O'Dowd, Mary, and Mararet MacCurtain, eds. *Women in Early Modern Ireland.* Dublin: Wolfhound Press 1991

O'Dwyer, Peter. *Mary: A History of Devotion in Ireland.* Dublin: Four Courts Press 1988

O Faolin, Julia and Laura Martines, eds. *Not in God's Image.* London: Maurice Temple Smith, Ltd. 1973

Ó Gráda, Cormac. "Did Ulster Catholics Always Have Larger Families?" *Irish Economic and Social History* 12 (1985): 79–88

Ó Laoghaire, Dairmuid. "Irish Spirituality in Modern Times." In *Irish Spirituality,* edited by Michael Maher, 47–56 Dublin: Veritas 1981

Owens, Rosemary Cullen. *Smashing Times: A History of the Irish Women's Suffrage Movement, 1889–1992.* Dublin: Attic Press 1984

Palmer, Bryan D. *Descent into Discourse: The Reification of Language and the Writing of Social History.* Philadelphia: Temple University Press 1990

Porterfield, Amanda. *Female Piety in Puritan New England: The Emergence of Religious Humanism.* New York: Oxford University Press 1992

Preston, Jo-Anne. "Female Aspiration and Male Ideology: School Teaching in Nineteenth Century New England." In *Current Issues in Women's History,* edited by Arina Angerman et al., 171–82. London: Routledge 1989

Prochaska, Francis. *Women and Philanthropy in Nineteenth Century England.* Oxford: Clarendon Press 1980

Rawlyk, George. *The Canada Fire: Radical Evangelicalism in British North America, 1775–1872.* Montreal and Kingston: McGill-Queen's University Press 1994

Rothman, Sheila M. *Woman's Proper Place: A History of Changing Ideals and Practises, 1870 to the Present.* New York: Basic Books 1978

Ruether, Rosemary Radford, and Rosemary Skinner Keller. *Women and Religion in America.* Vol. 2, *The Nineteenth Century.* San Francisco: Harper and Row 1983

Ryan, Mary P. *Cradle of the Middle Class: the Family in Oneida County, New York, 1790–1865.* Cambridge: Cambridge University Press 1981

Schneiders, Sandra Marie. *Women and the Word, the Gender of God in the New Testament and the Spirituality of Women.* New York: Paulist Press 1986

Shiman, Lillian Lewis. "'Changes Are Dangerous': Women and Temperance in Victorian England." In *Religion in the Lives of English Women, 1760–1930,* edited by Gail Malmgreen, 193–215. London: Croom Helm 1986

Smart, Carol, ed. *Regulating Womanhood: Historical Essays on Marriage, Motherhood and Sexuality.* London: Routledge 1992

Taggart, Norman. *The Irish in World Methodism.* London: Epworth 1986

Turner, Barry. *Equality for Some: The Story of Girls' Education.* London: Ward Lock Educational 1974

Valenze, Deborah M. *Prophetic Sons and Daughters: Female Preaching and Popular Religion in Industrial England.* Princeton: Princeton University Press 1985

Vicinus, Martha, ed. *Suffer and Be Still: Women in the Victorian Age.* Indiana: University of Indiana Press 1972

Ware, Vron. *Beyond the Pale: White Women, Racism and History.* London: Verso 1992

Warner, Marina. *Alone of All Her Sex: The Myth and Cult of the Virgin Mary.* London: Picador Books 1976

Welter, Barbara. "The Cult of True Womanhood, 1820–1860." In *Dimity Convictions: The American Woman in the Nineteenth Century,* edited by Barbara Welter, 21–41. Athens, Ohio: Ohio University Press 1976

Westerkamp, Marilyn J. "Puritan Patriarchy and the Problem of Revelation." *Journal of Interdisciplinary History* 23, no. 3 (Winter 1993): 571–95

Index